HX44 ARA

From Neo-Marxism to Democratic Theory

From Neo-Marxism to Democratic Theory

Essays on the Critical Theory of Soviet-Type Societies

— Andrew Arato —

M.E. Sharpe

Armonk, New York
London, England

Library of Congress Cataloging-in-Publication Data

Arato, Andrew.
From neo-Marxism to Democratic theory:
essays on the critical theory of Soviet-type societies /
by Andrew Arato.
p.   cm.
Includes bibliographical references and index.
ISBN 0-87332-882-5 (cloth)
1. Socialism.
2. Civil society.
3. Frankfurt school of sociology.
4. Marxian sociology.
5. Europe, Eastern—Politics and government—1945–.
6. Soviet Union—Politics and government—1945–
I. Title.
HX44.A72   1992
320.5'312—dc20
91-21128
CIP

Printed in the United States of America

The paper used in this publication meets the minimum requirements of
American National Standard for Information Sciences—
Permanence of Paper for Printed Library Materials,
ANSI Z39.48–1984.

MV   10   9   8   7   6   5   4   3   2   1

To My Mother, Alice Arato

and

To the Memory of My Father, Louis Arato

1901–1977

CONTENTS

Preface

The following essays of the last ten years are well marked by the time they were written. The first six were to be parts of a project formulated in terms of two questions: Is a critical theory of Soviet-type societies possible? Is such a theory capable of staying within the Marxian tradition in any meaningful sense? I originally intended to give a truly "dialectical" answer to these questions: yes to the first, but only on the condition of a no to the second. This answer was, however, paradoxical to the extent that critical theory from Horkheimer to Habermas always maintained its adherence in some—always changing—sense to the Marxian tradition. I hoped to resolve the paradox by emphasizing an early claim of Max Horkheimer (derived from the young György Lukács) that Marxian critical theory alone was capable of undertaking and withstanding an uncompromising process of self-criticism. The premise, now ironical, that one could remain a Marxist without being a Marxist was indeed my most important debt to Lukács in the 1960s and as late as the early 1980s. I wished to test this premise, by myself undertaking a reconstruction and critique of the best that critical Marxism produced on the topic of Soviet society. While the relevant analyses of classical Marxism have been often analyzed and criticized, most recently and most brilliantly by György Márkus,[1] no similar effort was ever carried out in a comprehensive way for the much more interesting efforts of the "neo" and "post" Marxists: Friedrich Pollock, Herbert Marcuse, Cornelius Castoriadis, Rudolf Bahro, Ivan Szelényi, Mihály Vajda, "Marc Rakovski," Jadwiga Staniszkis, and Márkus himself, for example.

The presence of both Western and Eastern names on this perhaps too partial list indicates a more serious intention behind my project. In the early 1980s, for a never-to-be-published preface I wrote the following: "The question concerning the possibility of a critical theory of Soviet-type societies arises from two traditions, one West, the other East. Both the theory of the Frankfurt School and neo-Marxist social critique in East Europe appear today to be in crisis. Neither has now a living relation to social movements; individual theorists seem to have to choose between isolation and breaking with their theoretical tradition. . . . And yet, these two threatened traditions represent some of the very rare efforts in

recent social theory to undertake critical analyses of *all* contemporary formations. For this reason, at a time when democratic movements East and West seem
to find more to divide than to unite them, critical social theory represents the best
intellectual hopes for bridge building. The crisis of theory assumes a practical
meaning in this context; its reconstruction becomes a political as well as intellectual task."

I intended to contribute to such reconstruction, and to such dialogue, not so
much systematically (although in my essay on Jürgen Habermas I tried this) as
by producing immanent critiques of representative versions of critical theories
West and East, each time asking questions and building relations that would be
possible only from a point of view that maintained the need to criticize both
capitalist and state socialist formations. Given the Frankfurt School's own characteristic avoidance of the whole problem of the Soviet Union, I chose not to
restrict myself to the few exceptions, such as Marcuse's relevant work. Rather, I
wanted to also consider authors affected by critical theory (Szelényi), ones belonging to parallel traditions (Castoriadis, Budapest School), and one author
specifically applauded by Marcuse (Bahro). Since I also wanted to include the
critical theorist who has influenced me the most, namely Habermas, despite his
own rather rare pronouncements on the subject, I attempted in this case to syn-
thesize a few of his remarks, and to begin to develop a theory around his own
methodological conceptions. Beyond the chapters represented here, I also
planned essays on Lukács's generation and the October Revolution, on Jean-Paul
Sartre, on revisionism and the philosophy of Praxis, and who remembers what
else besides.

This project could not be completed not merely because of its internal difficulties, but because of the historical changes that affected its basic assumptions.
The last six essays of the present book indicate that as the decade of the eighties
progressed I came to believe that the cornerstone of a critical theory of modern
society should be a democratic theory built around the concept of civil society,
rather than any, even the most, "self-critical" Marxism. Hence the title of the
book. I came to fully accept Jean Cohen's argument[2] that the built-in limitation
of all Marxian theory was the identification of *civil* and *bourgeois* society, and
the resulting establishment of *class* rather than *civil society* as the vantage point
of the critique of modern society. Increasingly, it seemed implausible that the
project of a self-critique of Marxism *à la* Lukács could eliminate from the theory
all dogmatic substantive assumptions; not only the myth of the proletariat and
the methodological centrality of class but also the philosophical idea of the
subject of history on which I until then always relied. With this idea in doubt, the
hidden premise of my original project was greatly weakened. I gradually realized
that there was no longer any reason to privilege approaches derived from the
Marxian tradition, or to try to build something new out of the self-critique of a
tradition fatally flawed.

I never would have come to these conclusions, of course, if I did not already think I had the chance to develop an alternative conception. Indeed, at a time when I still took the idea of theory building through a self-critique of critical theory quite seriously, under the impact of the Polish events and writings, and my conversations with my friend Mihály Vajda,[3] I began to analyze what was taking place in Poland around the concept of civil society.[4] I continued to use this theoretical framework for my analyses of the problems of democratization in East Europe from the Polish martial law to the "revolutions" of 1989 and beyond. Equally important, I came to the conclusion together with Jean Cohen that, given the testimony of new social movements and initiatives, the idea of the reconstruction *and* democratization of civil society could become the foundation of a critical theory of all modern societies, including the West.[5] Thus the possibility of a potentially fruitful dialogue between social critics East and West could be oriented to the normative framework of a shared democratic theory, rather than the (for us) unacceptable normative and analytical assumptions of even the best version of Marxism. The latter in any case failed, after the 1960s, to provide any such framework of communication, despite such efforts as the Dubrovnik seminars in which we participated.

The two parts of this book thus seem to belong to different theoretical frameworks, even if the time sequence of their writing cannot be so neatly untangled. In any case they are related in important ways. Many of the essays on the critical theorists, especially the last two, were strongly influenced by my change of paradigms. This led to an occasional shift from immanent critique to a more transcendent one, using civil society as its "external" vantage point. More importantly, the radicalism of the version of the concept of civil society used in the second part of the book is due directly to aims inherited from critical theory: to criticize authoritarian formations without canonizing forms of domination and injustice that can do without political authoritarianism. As the essay "Revolution, Civil Society, and Democracy" indicates, I use the concept of civil society for a *critical* theory of the "transition from state socialism."

To be sure, using the concept of civil society means a radical break with the Frankfurt argument that contemporary liberal democracies too are totalitarian, and hence are to be somehow put on the same normative level as the authoritarian state. This argument, taken deadly seriously only by Marcuse, was often rejected within even the older Frankfurt tradition, and has been definitively laid to rest by Habermas. And yet, as the attentive reader will notice, versions of this idea return in some of the essays of part I, not only where I criticize it as in the case of the essays on Marcuse and Castoriadis, but also where I am insufficiently critical toward a methodological parallel between market- and state-based systems of societal steering, as in my essay on Habermas. In this sense I want to insist on the paradigm shift between the two parts of the book, affecting not only the choice of objects of study but also the point of view of the author.

But I also insist on the two parts belonging together, both because of their continuity and because of their difference. I stress the continuity to indicate the need for critical social theory in relation to the great changes that have occurred and are still occurring in the East. All the ideologies of transition available today in East and West seem to tell us, happily or with resignation, that the choice for the new democracies is to imitate the West, or return to disrupted developmental trends of their own past, or both. The valid residue from the tradition of critical theory, preserved by all the theorists analyzed in part I indicates the need to criticize all existing formations and the link of emancipation to the creation of new institutions rather than to mere "imitation" or "restoration." But I stress also the difference, because I believe that East European democratic oppositions, often coming from critical Marxism, were right to focus their attention on civil society rather than class or revolutionary agency as the touchstone of their campaign against the old regimes, and to therefore break with all Marxisms. I maintain this point, even when in the face of new actual and potential economic hardship, and the perceived underrepresentation of the working class in newly elected parliaments, many analysts once again turn to class as the vantage point of social criticism. This mistake would be a serious one under fully established capitalist democracies, where social movements have no (or no longer have) intrinsic connection to class-based social stratification. It is all the more serious in countries where the socioeconomic (as against the transformed political) structure of state socialist old regimes is still in most respects intact. It is important in this context to recall the apologetic and conservative implications of some Marxist theories with respect to state socialism (in this book, Marcuse, Bahro) or at best their theoretical inability to uncover the dynamic possibilities of this social formation. This book represents a warning against repeating old mistakes, as well as an appeal to East Europeans seeking to criticize new and old forms of injustice to use with great caution categories inherited from the Marxian tradition, especially class. It is a plea that they should emphasize instead their own theoretical (re)discovery, the concept of civil society; one that has critical implications with respect to all attempts to establish elite democracy and bourgeois society.

* * *

There are many debts I would like to acknowledge to institutions and individuals both. The Alexander von Humboldt Stiftung of the Federal Republic of Germany might be surprised to see this book as the result of their support in 1980–81. Nevertheless, it was this support and the kind hospitality of the Max Planck Institut für Sozialwissenschaften in Starnberg under Jürgen Habermas that allowed me to draw up a plan for the project and in fact complete at least two of the essays. I very much benefited from discussions with members of the Max Planck Institut, as I did later during presentations of different chapters at the Dubrovnik IUC Seminar on Philosophy and Social Science, the Institute of Sociology of the Hungarian Academy of Sciences, the Kellogg Institute of Notre

Dame University, the École des hautes études in Paris, the Center for European Studies at Harvard University, the Harriman Institute of Columbia University, and the Staff Seminar of the Department of Sociology of the Graduate Faculty, New School for Social Research. I owe a word of thanks to many colleagues at all these institutions, which, unfortunately, I cannot express by naming them all. And while many editors of journals and anthologies have been helpful and encouraging, I have special reasons to mention the sponsors of the earliest essays when the topic was hardly fashionable, John Thompson and David Held, editors of *Habermas: Critical Debates*, and Paul Piccone. Indeed, without my association with the latter and the journal *Telos* from 1971 to 1986, many of the essays here would never have been written. I am indeed sorry still that our ways have parted on the road from neo-Marxism to democratic theory.

No one has been more important for my intellectual development than Jean Cohen. It is fair to say, that while she was never quite as convinced of the strategy of the self-critique of critical theory as I was, most of the essays here, and especially the ones using the paradigm of civil society are results of our joint attempts to develop a common social theory. I have received a good deal of support, helpful criticism, and advice from my friends of the onetime Budapest School: Mihály Vajda, György Márkus, Maria Márkus, Agnes Heller, Ferenc Fehér, György Bence, and János Kis. I have learned a lot even when I disagreed with some of them. I benefited more than I can express here from the joint seminars at the Graduate Faculty that I held with Bence and Jeffrey Goldfarb on social movements in Eastern Europe, and Kis and José Casanova on problems of democracy and dictatorship. More recently, I learned a great deal from discussions with older Hungarian friends like Miklós Haraszti, András Kovács, Sándor Radnóti, Julia Kardos, and Gáspár Miklós Tamás; and from newer ones, especially László Bruszt, Erzsébet Szalai, Elemér Hankiss, Béla Pokol, Ferenc Köszeg, Sándor Szilagyi, Maria Kovacs, Andras Sajó, Julia Szalai, Ferenc Miszlivetz, András Bozóki, Tamás Fellegi, and Miklós Sükösd. Discussions with Claus Offe, Alfred Stepan, Philippe Schmitter, Adam Przeworski, Alessandro Pizzorno, Jeffrey Weintraub, Zbigniew Pelczyński, Ulrich Rödel, Sigrid Meuschel, Dick Howard, Wolff Schäfer, Seyla Benhabib, David Ost, Judith Sedaitis, and most recently, Ulrich Preuss have been especially helpful in working out particular aspects of my conception. I have learned a lot as well from the students at my many seminars and lecture courses dealing with the concept of civil society, and with Eastern Europe. I owe a great deal of thanks to the Open Society Foundation, to the Budapest Soros Foundation, but especially to the Graduate Faculty, its president Jonathan Fanton, and its then dean Ira Katznelson for being able to invite many guest lecturers and instructors from Eastern Europe, among them, aside from several already mentioned, János Kornai, Tamás Bauer, Karoly Attila Soós, Pavel Campeanu, Natalya Baranova, and Aleksandr Smolar. I hope to utilize much that I have learned from all of them even more in a forthcoming book, *Civil Society and Revolution in the Transition in Eastern Europe* (M.E. Sharpe).

I have been fortunate to receive advice and information from several of the people on whose work I have written. Aside from Habermas, György Márkus, Heller, and Fehér, who have been major influences on my work, I was very fortunate to have had the chance to have many conversations with György Konrád and Ivan Szelényi, and to be able to interview at length (unfortunately only in 1987) Jacek Kuroń and Adam Michnik. Last, but definitely not least, Cornelius Castoriadis has been especially generous with his time when discussing with me not only his own intellectual development, but also all conceivable aspects of my overall problem area. His influence has been an important one for my conception as it is visible in more than the one essay dedicated to his work.

I learned much from several debates, two-sided ones with E.P. Thompson and Victor Zaslavsky, and a one-sided one with John Keane. I appreciate the spirit in which the former two handled our disagreements. I wonder what they would think of them now.[6] Finally, I owe a big word of thanks to my editor at M.E. Sharpe, Patricia Kolb. It was due to her encouragement of my work in general that I decided that this project could after all be worthy of publication.

Notes

1. In the first chapter of Fehér, Heller and Márkus, *Dictatorship over Needs* (New York: St. Martin's Press, 1983).

2. *Class and Civil Society: The Limits of Marxian Critical Theory* (Amherst: University of Massachusetts Press, 1982).

3. For a product of these conversations see our joint essay on R. Bahro, "The Limits of the Leninist Opposition," in *New German Critique*, no. 19 (Winter 1980).

4. See chapters 8 and 9 in this volume.

5. Of our several joint articles, see "Social Movements, Civil Society and the Problem of Sovereignty," in *Praxis International*, vol. 4, no. 3 (October 1984), followed by a debate with E.P. Thompson in subsequent issues. See also the result of our ten-year collaboration: *Civil Society and Political Theory* (Cambridge: MIT Press, 1992). For a short (if polemical) statement distinguishing our use of the category of civil society from some others see: A. Arato, "Civil Society, History and Socialism: Reply to John Keane," *Praxis International*, vol. 9, nos. 1/2 (April and July 1989).

6. The debate with Zaslavsky is in *Telos*, nos. 62, 63, and 65.

Part I

Western Marxism and Soviet-Type Societies

1

Authoritarian Socialism and the Frankfurt School

History continues. Not only on the mountains of Kurdistan and in the cities of Russia, but every day and in every country of the Western world we confront the ravages of instrumental and strategic reason gone wild. Who can believe now that we can plan, manage, control through the use of instrumental reason alone the effects and the side-effects of "rational" planning, management, and control? How long do we have to take (or rather, undo) the steps necessary to keep our fully enlightened planet livable? At the same time, do we have the intellectual and moral resources to resist the omnipresent forms of counterenlightenment?

These questions, raised by the critical theory of the Frankfurt School fifty years ago, especially by Max Horkheimer and Theodor W. Adorno in *The Dialectic of Enlightenment*,[1] have not fallen victim to the growing obsolescence of the Marxist tradition. Today, when all of the various Marxisms and neo-Marxisms have lost their credibility one way or another because of the disaster of revolutionary socialism,[2] the radical theses of *The Dialectic of Enlightenment* seem unaffected even by the cataclysmic events of 1989. The same would be hardly true of the works of the Frankfurt School in the 1930s, representing "only" a sophisticated variety of the type of Hegelian-Marxism introduced by György Lukács. But around 1940, in my view in important part under the impact of their final and definitive rejection of the Soviet model, the critical theory of Horkheimer and Adorno was radicalized: The earlier desideratum of the intensification of the instrumental control of nature was now seen as a global tendency leading, if unchecked, to new forms of oppression and to destructive mythology. Instead of providing the solution to the anarchy of the market, the idea of scientific planning championed by all socialisms was now understood as the fulfill-

Written in 1983–84, with the exception of the short introduction produced for this volume. Parts of the original manuscript were presented at a conference of the A. von Humboldt Stiftung in Ludwigshafen in 1984 and published among the conference papers: A. Honneth et al., eds., *Kritische Theorie und die Folgen* (Berlin: deGruyter, 1985).

ment of the destructive possibilities of capitalist rationality.[3] Finally, the commanding heights of the modern state were seen as the locus of a new form of domination, rather than supposedly neutral and transitional instruments of emancipation.

The three critiques, the critique of the domination of nature, of scientism including the fetish of planning, and finally of the state, are the reasons for the philosophical and political strength of the impulse of the Frankfurt School in our present situation. The first critique points to the ecological terrain where human solidarity will be tested through the twenty-first century. The apparently victorious Western capitalist economies of our time have on the whole shifted their destructiveness (primarily though not exclusively) into their natural environment. The second two critiques block the way toward dead-end socialist and statist solutions, which have managed to exacerbate all problems of modern society, including the ecological one. Speaking politically, after the collapse of state socialism, the critiques of the state and of global planning provide the entry tickets into critical discussions to come. The tradition founded by Adorno and Horkheimer does not have to apologize for having apologized for a new destructive form of domination created in the twentieth century.

And yet, this same tradition is not in position today to provide even the main elements of the *theory* we need to carry out its own critical intentions. Amazingly enough, the moment of philosophical breakthrough, namely 1940 or 1941, was the last time that the narrow circle around Adorno and Horkheimer produced social theoretical analyses of global social formations, capitalism and state socialism. By the time *The Dialectic of Enlightenment* (1944–45) was written, the analysis moved to the level of a negative philosophy of history, where it was to stay except for some forays into micrology and culture criticism. By omission rather than by commission Adorno and Horkheimer were to fall into the trap of all of the neo-Marxisms of their time: They never produced (even or especially when living in the Western part of a country whose Eastern part was Sovietized) a single important, critical work dealing with what I call (in part following their earlier terminology) authoritarian state socialism, a formation that, as we all should have known for forty years or more, has accounted for a good part of the horror of our century.[4] Not even the experience of Hungary in 1956 (that motivated some of the best efforts of Cornelius Castoriadis, Claude Lefort and Hannah Arendt) was to affect the strategy of "critical silence."[5]

Here my interest is not primarily in the reasons, political and biographical, that led to impasse. A terrible, and understandably unforgiving, hatred for the German Right, which would supposedly benefit from an unavoidably uncompromising critique of the East, was undoubtedly a major factor. I am more interested in trying to make the apparent silence speak after all. Thus, I wish to focus on the relationship of the central philosophical impulse of the Frankfurt School and the more or less peripheral critical models for the study of Soviet society that can be arguably treated as its complements. These are: (a) models based on hints of the main figures but *before* the philosophical shift of 1940, (b) a significant model produced *during* this shift mainly by Friedrich Pollock, (c) a version of immanent critique worked out by Herbert Marcuse, who was an adherent of the thesis of *The Dialectic of Enlightenment*, and (d) a model that can be generated from some elements of the work of Habermas, the most important student of Adorno and Horkheimer.[6]

<h1 style="text-align:center">I</h1>

In the long history of the Frankfurt School amazingly enough only two major books and two significant essays were actually dedicated to the study of the Soviet Union. This is an astonishing fact given the School's almost permanent interest in authoritarianism and authoritarian social formations. Indeed, the first book, Pollock's 1929 *Habilitationsschrift*,[7] actually predated the term *critical theory* as well as any coordinated intellectual work that was to go under this term. It was almost thirty years later that the second book, Marcuse's *Soviet Marxism*,[8] was published.

But the story is more surprising still. The first major intellectual effort of the group around Horkheimer was the production of the *Zeitschrift für Sozialforschung* (1932–41), one of the best social scientific and theoretical journals of our century; one with genuinely global intentions.[9] Astonishingly enough, not only did this journal in its nine years of existence publish only three insignificant articles, all by a relative outsider (Rudolf Schlesinger), on any topic directly concerning the Soviet Union, but direct references to Russia, the Soviet Union, or the Bolsheviks were extremely rare. Indeed, in 1941 when the two major articles dealing (at least in part) with the Soviet Union were published, one of them, Horkheimer's "Autoritärer Staat," was printed only in a more or less private *Gedächtnisschrift* (for Walter Benjamin), while the other, Pollock's "State Capitalism," published in the *Zeitschrift*, implausibly maintained that it had nothing to do with the Soviet Union. Thus, the questionable purity of the journal was preserved to the end.

Nevertheless, as Helmut Dubiel has carefully shown, their relation to the Soviet Union represented a "central background element for the political theoretical self-understanding of the circle."[10] How are we to explain the paradox? The deep interest in Soviet developments by Marxist theorists who participated in many debates with members of the KPD and the SPD needs in fact little demonstration. More importantly even, in the context of the Great Depression when the possibility of a transition to a planned economy became a major recurring topic of the journal, the experience of economic planning in the Soviet Union remained for many of the participants in the discussion, especially Pollock, a crucial if hidden reference point. Why were the relevant issues not clearly articulated?

Let us leave aside all the very real issues such as the desire not to take a stand in the destructive conflicts of Social Democrats and Communists, the desire not to attack the Communists as political victims of Nazism, as well as caution in French and American exile. Why should all the different political causes and contexts always, even in 1940–41 when Stalin and Hitler were de facto allies, lead to one outcome, namely the suppression of the topic? I believe that at all times a fundamental theoretical ambivalence was also at work; a suspicion that not only politics but Marxist theory itself was at stake. This was to be later confirmed by Horkheimer and Pollock, as we will see.

To be sure, the political attitude to the Soviet Union itself was initially ambivalent. In my view, only in 1937 was an attitude generally or diffusely favorable to the Soviet Union abandoned.[11] Admittedly, Pollock already in his *Habilitationsschrift* expressed a carefully worded but certainly unorthodox doubt concerning the possibility of socialism in one highly underdeveloped country.[12] Nevertheless, he showed no particular sympathy[13] to the Left and Right critics of the First Five-Year Plan (which he knew at that time only in a version that did not yet contain the drastically elevated targets of forced industrialization.)[14] And while he did not think that the Soviet government could dare to abolish private peasant agriculture, it is not possible to deduce from this that he had therefore had to oppose the policy a year later when it was nevertheless initiated.[15] Clearly enough, he too identified a genuine socialist agrarian policy with the abolition of all market-oriented production.[16] The most one could say about the critical dimension of his overall attitude was that he did not think that the road to socialism of this "transitional" society could be accelerated. There was no conception here of the entirely negative consequences of such an effort if undertaken. Of course, in 1929, with the exception of some surviving Mensheviks and the Right opposition, not many people could anticipate the results of the Stalinist "revolution from above." But this is not the issue here. In a 1932 reference,[17] Pollock seems to characterize Soviet planning ("from which the theory and practice of a planned economy has much to learn")[18] in a generally positive way, even if according to him the historically backward conditions of Russia do not allow a clear demonstration of the economic superiority of this system over private capitalism. Thus Pollock's "ambivalence" does not go as far as a negative attitude to Soviet politics, and involved only a juxtaposition of the government's policies with Russia's backwardness, which may limit their success.

Horkheimer's own position on the eve of his assuming the leadership of the Institute and the *Zeitschrift* was even more supportive toward the Soviet Union.[19] Although he admits some uncertainty concerning the actual developments and points to the universal misery of the population, he expresses deep contempt for all those who do not realize, in the context of the injustice of the imperialist world, the continued, painful attempt in Russia to overcome this injustice. Three years later, to be sure, he must have had Russia in mind when he spoke of an enlightened, revolutionary despotism whose hardness and injustice may be explained only if the general level of the ruled masses is taken into account.[20] But the historical character of this despotism, "its progressive or reactionary signifi-cance," he argued, could be decided only on the basis of whether it represented the general interest or a particular one. All the assumptions of Leninist and Lukácsian substitutionism are built into this idea. The language as well as the conception also very much resemble Gramsci's contemporary thoughts on "total-itarianism"[21] (Horkheimer was not in jail, but in exile.) Nevertheless, that he indeed judged (on the basis of the representation of a general interest?) revolu-tionary despotism "progressive" is clear enough from another Aesopean refer-ence of the same year when he spoke of "the great experiences . . . that mankind currently made with attempts at economic planning."[22] The interest involved was not only general but apparently universal.

To be fair, it is unlikely that Horkheimer had any real notion of the extent of the horrors perpetrated by Stalin's regime in this period. The same linking of authoritarianism and progress appears in a much stronger form as late as the great 1936 essay "Authority and Family." After rejecting the "indiscriminate condemnation of authoritarian regimes without regard for the underlying eco-nomic structure," Horkheimer proceeds to define, on the abstract theoretical level, the hierarchical position of expert and manager vis-à-vis labor, the authori-tarian dimension of planning (as long plans have their link to class interest), and the "disciplined obedience of men who strive to bring this state of affairs to pass" as progressive forms of authority in history.[23] Since the first statement clearly defends the Soviet Union against an odious comparison with Nazi Ger-many, we have every reason to surmise that the authoritarian elements of the "underlying economic structure" in the former were defined as progressive in the sense of the stated abstract considerations derived from the Marxist tradition.

Because the evaluation of Soviet developments by critical theory was on the whole positive through 1936, there is no need to adopt Dubiel's explanation for the rarely broken silence of the *Zeitschrift*, according to which the Soviet Union could not be openly attacked because it represented the foremost antagonist of Fascism. This explanation, far more relevant to the positions of critical theory 1937–39, needs to be deemphasized in favor of another; one that would explain why *both* the negative and positive dimensions of the circle's ambivalent posi-tion were kept hidden. I believe that Dubiel is closer to the truth when he points out the fact that while Horkheimer and his closest associates were in the early 1930s closer to the spirit of the KPD than to the SPD of that period, he felt nevertheless, especially in uncertain exile, the need to distinguish themselves from both.[24] An open if critical defense of the Soviet Union could not have sufficiently distinguished the group from the Communists in the eyes of the audience of the journal, with the exception of KPD members themselves who demanded nothing less than total orthodoxy. Only this ambiguous political posi-tion explains Horkheimer's intellectual tactics.

Those kindred spirits whose politics were different had no need to censor themselves. For a left Social Democrat like Otto Kirchheimer, a future collaborator of the Institute and the *Zeitschrift*, it was far easier to openly attack Soviet authoritarianism. In an important 1933 article in his party's theoretical journal, *Die Gesellschaft*,[25] Kirchheimer argued that the implicit tendencies of the Bolshevik organizational model led to the identification of the party with bureaucratic administration, destroying thereby both intraparty democracy, and earlier democratic links to the population. For a centralized and centralizing party this loss of contact with their popular base could only mean Jacobinism and terror.

Kirchheimer's comparison of Leninism and Jacobinism, so much more worthwhile and precise than the Trotskyist attempts to link terror to "Thermidor" or "Bonapartism," was all the more interesting because Horkheimer himself produced in 1938 a major critique of Jacobinism, its structure and its historical analogies.[26] But, unlike Kirchheimer, who by this time joined the Institute now in New York, he did not mention Leninism, in spite of many really striking analogies on both organizational and social psychological levels that would have been far more convincing than the comparisons of Robespierre and Saint-Just to Cola di Rienzo and Savonarola. Notably, Kirchheimer, after having joined the Institute wrote nothing more on the Soviet Union. Nevertheless there is some evidence in the writings of Marcuse and Horkheimer that from 1937 (after some spectacular purges of Communist leaders and intellectuals in the Soviet Union) a position closer to Kirchheimer's earlier one was being adopted by the core members of the Institute now in New York. But this time, really because of the supposed needs of the battle against Fascism, the shift of critical theory's attitude to the Soviet Union in a negative direction was masked in a similar way as was the more positive attitude earlier.[27]

When laboriously extracted from some of the essays of Marcuse and Horkheimer in the late thirties, the position of critical theory is characterized by a new type of ambivalence.[28] On the one hand there was now an intention for the first time to subject Soviet society to immanent criticism. According to Marcuse "criticism is also directed at the avoidance of its full economic and political demands in some places where it is invoked."[29] This indeed Aesopean language calls for an ideology critique of Marxism where it is used as a doctrine of legitimation. Both Horkheimer and Marcuse moreover now stressed that the planned regulation of the work process, the abolition of private property, and the increase of the forces of production "under new forms of cooperative labor" do not amount to socialism unless the realization of the interest of the masses in "freedom and happiness" (Marcuse) and the development of essential moments of "real democracy and association" (Horkheimer) complement these developments. Accordingly, the basic thesis of the Frankfurt School regarding the Soviet Union involved three points:

1. Planning, socialized property, expansion of production are only negative preconditions of socialism. These are already present in the Soviet Union.

2. Since the Soviet Union does not yet embody the positive preconditions already cited, it is not yet socialist.

3. As long as the formation of a particular ruling class interest and great social inequality can be avoided, the Soviet Union remains a transitional society on the road to socialism.[30]

While no relevant text from the period indicates that a new ruling class has emerged in the Soviet Union, as in the case of Trotsky, this criterion, derived squarely from the Marxian philosophy of history indicated a threshold for still considering the Soviet Union to be a "progressive" society. Of course, the problem with this way of analyzing the matter was that the "totalitarian" horror of Soviet society, recognized both by Trotsky and the Frankfurt School, was to be considered to be merely epiphenomenal next to supposedly deeper processes and structures. The possibility that this very totalitarianism could continually decompose class relations, that it could constitute a type of societal domination in which political power rather than socioeconomic class was the foundation of inequality, and that the result could be a new industrial social formation that was neither capitalist nor, in the sense of the Marxian classics, socialist, was methodologically closed to these authors. Thus, their critique of the Soviet Union could not imply a complete break with earlier apologetics.

To be sure, there was a way within the new perspective to develop an uncompromising critique of the Soviet Union; one had to document or claim to be able to document the existence of a new socioeconomic ruling class, based on a new form of "private" property. This was the way of dissident Trotskyists like B. Rizzi, Max Schachtman, and James Burnham, and later dissident Stalinists like Milovan Djilas, all of whom postulated a new bureaucratic ruling class for the Soviet Union. In all these cases, a somewhat questionable sociology served the purpose of abandoning all forms of apologetics. For some of these theorists, it was now possible to anticipate the later totalitarianism thesis, and to maintain that Nazi Germany and the Soviet Union represented the same social formation—yet another piece of normatively justifiable but empirically suspect sociology. It seems that only one essay of the Frankfurt School, Horkheimer's "Die Juden und Europa" of 1939, intended to adopt a perspective such as this, in effect identifying Fascism and Bolshevism.[31] For still unexplained reasons, however, the published version omitted all references to the Soviet Union.[32] A year later, elements of a totalitarianism thesis appeared in several Frankfurt School essays, but now on foundations that involved not only a political but also a methodological break with all earlier writings of the group.

II

The full-scale political reorientation of Horkheimer with regard to Soviet society occurred after the Ribbentrop–Molotov pact and the participation of Stalin in

Hitler's war on Poland, but before the German invasion of the Soviet Union. Does this provide support for a thesis that earlier the topic was avoided only for political reasons, and never theoretical disinterest? In fact, even in the brief period in which the overriding political consideration for self-censorship did not apply, namely the desire not to attack the most determined foe of Hitler, this self-censorship was only partially abandoned. This was the case in spite of the fact that the critique was now relentless and uncompromising. When it came to publication, Horkheimer's 1940 essay, "Autoritärer Staat," was not included in the *Zeitschrift* but was distributed only to the Institute's inner circle in a 1942 memorial volume for Walter Benjamin. This essay discussed Soviet Union under the names of "state socialism" and "integral statism," and described it as a more consistent version of the authoritarian state than Nazi Germany itself. It should be noted that during the 1930s the term "authoritarian state" was reserved by members of the Institute for the fascist dictatorships. Rather obviously, Horkheimer's essay was deeply linked to another, Pollock's 1941 "State Capitalism," published in the American successor of the *Zeitschrift*, *Studies in Philosophy and Social Criticism*.[33] The economic model built by this later essay, on which Horkheimer especially relied,[34] had to do much more with Soviet realities in spite of the author's weak and inconsistent disclaimer than with the capitalist economies of Nazi Germany or New Deal America. Together the two essays provided the first real theory of Soviet society coming from Horkheimer's circle. The two approaches, Horkheimer's ideological-critical and historical tracing of the genesis and meaning of the authoritarian state, and Pollock's abstract, ideal typic model of economic functioning and limits, were thoroughly complementary. Both theorists realized that their approaches represented the end of important assumptions of classical Marxian theory. Horkheimer noted that historical materialism could foretell only the end of the liberal capitalist social formation, but it was deeply wrong about what will succeed it.[35] Instead of socialism, the authoritarian state represented a new and unanticipated modern historical formation, whose reality and potential long-term stability could only be obscured by an orthodox adherence to the schemas of historical materialism. Even worse, the orthodox schemas, allowing no industrial formation outside of capitalism other than socialism or a transition toward it, had to inevitably provide an ideology of legitimation for any new, unanticipated form of industrial domination, such as the Soviet Union. Similarly, if less radically, Pollock argued that despite the name, state capitalism meant the end of capitalism in Marx's sense, and with it the suspension of the laws of economics, and the obsolescence of the Marxian political economy. Contrary to what his critics charged,[36] Pollock did not thereby imply that such a society was stable, without crisis tendencies, or the possibility of transformation, but only that its dynamism is to be sought first and foremost not on the level of a differentiated economy but that of the political system. Just at a time that Horkheimer announced the replacement of historical materialism by the critique of the authoritarian state (linked to the beginning of a new critique of instrumental reason,)[37] Pollock turned from the critique of political economy in the same direction.

There were, however, also differences between the two arguments. Pollock believed that state capitalism could exist in two variants, the authoritarian version and a democratic one (the admittedly less complete New Deal version) which in his view critical theory had no choice but to support. Horkheimer however wished to support only a hypothetically possible council democratic movement; for him as such "state capitalism was the authoritarian state of the present."[38] This difference did not have to affect the evaluation of the Soviet Union. Nevertheless, only Horkheimer was to forthrightly declare that "integral statism or state socialism is the most consistent form of the authoritarian state which has freed itself from any dependence on private capital."[39] This position was consistent with the logic if not the letter of Pollock's argument, since he too considered private ownership to be an entirely residual category under state capitalism, again despite the name. In this case, however, Horkheimer was again more consistent in considering Nazi Germany a mixed form[40] because here state controlled surplus value was still being distributed as profit among the older class of the owners of the means of production. Indeed he was to go so far as to claim that the Soviet system represented "the secret vision of those industrial powers which were going sick on their parliamentarism and could no longer live without fascism."[41] Even if this conception, like Pollock's, tended to conflate several different types of socioeconomic orders in a manner anticipating elements of both later totalitarianism and convergence theories, Horkheimer at least was quite certain that the realization of the completed model of the authoritarian state would be strongly and perhaps successfully resisted under all mixed forms, that is, the state interventionist capitalist societies. Thus, whatever Pollock himself may have thought about his conception of state capitalism, it is quite obvious that for Horkheimer it represented first and foremost a theory of Soviet society.

As I have already said, Pollock himself was rather inconclusive on this subject. The Soviet Union is mentioned only in two contradictory footnotes. To understand these, we should first note that for him (as for Trotsky and the dissident Trotskyists) a new social system to be defined as such required not only a new set of structural, systemic rules but also a new ruling class. Under "state capitalism" this new ruling class, defined primarily by its relation to the state structure and possession of power rather than property, would be an amalgamation of the key bureaucracies of business, state, and party allied with remaining vested interests.[42] In this context one of the footnotes relevant to the Soviet Union goes on to argue that this particular determination of the new class holds true only for Germany and Italy. According to Pollock,

> The situation is different in the Soviet Republic where the old vested interests have been wiped out. Since in Russia property in the means of production has changed hands completely from the private owners to the state . . . it is

somewhat doubtful whether or not our model of state capitalism fits the Soviet Union in its present phase.[43]

A remarkable argument indeed. The doubtful premise that a new set of structural, systemic rules are for some reason insufficient to define a new social formation would have a semblance of validity only if an old ruling class survived in this capacity under the new rules. But in the Soviet Union precisely the opposite is said to be the case, and rightly. By this argument, it corresponds to the entirely new social formation that state capitalism is said to be more than those societies that have incorporated the old ruling class in the new. Moreover, the stress on a new, political rather than economic system of class formation is better suited to describe a society where fused party and state elites rule, than one which has incorporated in the structure of rule groups of economic origins whose social function remains economic. Finally, it is doubtful that all other elements of Pollock's statist model required for their operation the mixed class structure characteristic in his view of Italy and Germany. As Horkheimer believed, there were better reasons to suspect the opposite with regard to the establishment of the model (if not the assessment of its economic success and potential), namely its greater compatibility with a class structure that owes little to the private capitalist system of production. This suspicion is confirmed by Pollock's second footnote on the subject. According to him, "the nearest approach to the state capitalist system of distribution has been made in Soviet Russia."[44] All this confirmed Franz Neumann's criticism directly contesting the applicability of Pollock's model to Nazi Germany and seeming to imply that the model described Soviet society far better.[45]

Of course, both Pollock and Horkheimer, introducing their model in the context of the Institute's discussion of National Socialism, disagreed with Neumann on this score.[46] Thus while the latter squarely belonged to the Marxist tradition that considered fascism as a particular stage of capitalism, the main line of Frankfurt analysis anticipated the totalitarianism theses and focused on the structural similarities not only of economies but of forms of the state. In a peculiar manner, however, they fused the two styles of analysis, as the term "state capitalism" indicates. Accordingly, the synthetic version of this position (held strictly only by Horkheimer) implied that there were two roads to state capitalism = integral statism = state socialism, the culmination of the monopolistic and authoritarian trends of capitalism (Nazi Germany) and the statist-bureaucratic transformation of a postcapitalist society (Soviet Union). Each road implied different survivals, and different degrees of model consistency. The model was furthermore considered a very real possibility in all advanced capitalist countries, to be avoided only by a democratic version of state capitalism (Pollock) or a social revolution and council democracy (Horkheimer).

Only Pollock ever worked out the model in detail. According to him state capitalism signified an entirely new historical epoch, "the transition from a predominantly economic to an essentially political era."[47] Nowhere was this more true than in the Soviet Union, as Horkheimer at least realized. The new system involved a new set of rules, superficially economic but on a deeper level politically determined. In the first version of his argument Pollock insisted on the replacement under state capitalism of the market by a system of centralized planning directing production, consumption, saving, and investment. In a later version (perhaps because dealing exclusively with Nazi Germany) Pollock abandoned the stress on planning and shifted to a notion of centralized steering or command as a sufficient characteristic to define the new formation.[48] In either case the stress is on a system of conscious decisions, ultimately political in nature, that selects the ends and means of the process of production in advance. The planning or command center is also the price setting center; the system fundamentally involves administratively set rather than market prices. According to Pollock (as well as Horkheimer) such a system, extending the principles of scientific management and industrial rationalization, represents the generalization of the structure of the modern firm to society as a whole, an actualization of a well known goal of all statist socialisms.

Under state capitalism, production of commodities was replaced by production for use, again as several classics of socialism demanded. Every facet of production was rigorously controlled. Neither oversaving nor overinvestment, key sources of large-scale disruption under capitalism, were possible here. Errors could be traced down by planning boards and their consequences spread out to the economy as a whole, making them negligible. Distribution problems too, could be solved equally easily, supposedly. There was no need to look for buyers *post festum*; both public and private wants are definable in advance along with the allocated means of satisfying them. Perhaps not being entirely confident of this last diagnosis, Pollock added the possibility of a subsidiary market for consumer goods, involving some free movement of prices, as a possible corrective of planning errors regarding individual needs. He thus anticipated along with a rigid, centralized model of a command system some of its later forms of crisis management.

It is not difficult today (1983), in light of later Soviet and East European experience, to point out how deeply Pollock underestimated the production and distribution problems of centralized command systems. The reasons for his error are interesting nevertheless. While he has obviously given up half of the orthodox Marxian dogma of planning, concerning its necessary connection to a free and "nonantagonistic" society, he has clearly not given up the other half, namely the ability of centralized, global plans to eliminate all aspects of the "anarchy of production." Equally important was the circumstance, that while he derived his theoretical model first and foremost from the Soviet Union that he has been studying since 1928, his impressions concerning the economic performance of such a model came from elsewhere. Aware of the impoverished condition of Soviet society, he chalked up the relevant phenomena probably to underdevelopment. On the other hand, highly impressed by the success of the "incomplete version" of state capitalism in Nazi Germany to solve the problem of economic recovery, and full employment, after the failure of market economy to do so, he tended to attribute this success entirely to the instruments of the command economy. Instead of noticing a new type of experimentation with central steering functions in context of a capitalist economy, he wrongly assumed that the total realization of the primacy of the political would be even more goal-rational from the economic point of view. It was in such contexts that Pollock's protototalitarianism thesis led to confusion, and served him badly.

Of course, Pollock was aware of criticisms of planned economies on the bases of anticipated problems with information, the calculation of costs, with motivation, and with technical development. While he had a surprisingly (even for his time) unlimited confidence in the ability of planning techniques to deal with the first three of these, he believed that armament production could replace economic competition as the motor of technical progress. Thus his conclusion: State capitalism has no immanent *economic* limits; those interested in its dynamic possibilities must look elsewhere.[49]

In itself, the long-term solution of economic problems hardly implied the good society for Pollock. He was clear about the human cost of the totalitarian version of state capitalism: terror, manipulation, the atomization of groups and individuals, the loss of rights already attained under capitalism, and the increasing danger of war. State capitalism, however stable economically, was a thoroughly antagonistic social formation. Hence it was theoretically necessary and normatively obligatory for the critical theorist to investigate its possible limits. Indeed, Pollock was one of the first to make such an attempt regarding the new social formation, and he did in fact manage to work out some initial elements of a political crisis theory.

According to Pollock, the state structure of authoritarian state capitalism is the framework of the constitution of a new political, bureaucratic ruling class. This class is, however, not absolutely unified; crucial differences and conflicts stem from "different positions within the administration, different programs for maintaining or extending power, or the struggle for the monopoly of control."[50] The result may be bad compromise or continuous struggle. While the "class interest in maintaining the new status quo" tends to unite this class against the outside, and antagonisms are generally contained "before they can turn into a menace for the system,"[51] the differences and conflicts do enter into the structure of the plan. Under such conditions Pollock notices that, in striking contradiction to his optimistic assumptions concerning global central plans, "no general plan for the optimum use and development of the given productive forces can be drafted."[52] Equally important, counterpressure from below will further inhibit the freedom of action of the planners. The planning board will become "an arena of struggle among social forces." This perception made Pollock further revise his notion of planning in a way that seems to vitiate his overall analysis: "planning in an antagonistic society is only in the technical sense the same tool as used by a society in which harmony of interests has been established."[53] Unfortunately not only does his analysis of the economics of existing planned societies omit this qualification, he also does not really explore the social and political consequences of "planning" in an antagonistic society. Even the distinction between "plan" and "command" was not analytically established.

Having asserted the unity of political and economic spheres under state capitalism, Pollock's composite picture of political tensions and economic stability is conceptually unconvincing. Being highly impressed by the ability of such a system to potentially deal with the economic problems characteristic of competitive capitalism, he did not fully realize that the price would be political-economic problems ("rationality deficits") specific to the new formation. Even less did he see that this outcome must affect economic functioning itself, in a negative way. Thus we are ultimately left with the impression that political conflicts and tensions, however dramatic, could remain bottled up in the political sphere.

Nevertheless, Pollock did give us one chain of argumentation concerning crisis phenomena ultimately rooted in the antagonistic structure of the new society and the resistance of those below that could actually threaten the overall stability of state capitalist systems. As a peacetime economy such a system would tend to lose its one specific motivation for technological innovation, namely military competition. One might, according to Pollock, try to replace this by motivations tied to a rising standard of living. But he was convinced that under totalitarian state capitalism a dramatic increase in the standard of living, implying "more leisure time, more professional skill, more opportunity for critical thinking," could threaten the spiritual dependence of the masses. The ruling group might therefore decide to maintain a low living standard (illustrating the political limits to productivity in such a system) and to avoid "technological standstill" by maintaining "an armament race and the excitement over the threat of foreign aggression."[54] The step from this conception to Marcuse's later welfare–warfare state, applied to both superpowers was only a small one.

It was controversial in the 1940s, and it remains so in the 1980s, whether the argument that totalitarian state capitalism "cannot endure as a peace economy" applies to the Soviet Union. The fact that Pollock wrote about the Soviet Union without fully admitting it (even to himself) is a confirmation of the relevance of the argument, worked out without ideological blinkers. Interestingly enough both he and Horkheimer, before Orwell, foretold of "friendly-hostile" blocks menacing one another and participating in a seemingly limitless arms race only apparently aiming at domination (Horkheimer)[55] or an impossible world state capitalism (Pollock).[56] While Pollock most directly had National Socialism in mind when he postulated the necessarily militarized nature of state capitalism, there was no reason not to apply the conception to the Soviet Union unless, of course, one considered this society nonantagonistic or democratic or both. On this point at least there is no reason to think that Pollock did not share

Horkheimer's position formulated in "Autoritärer Staat." Accordingly, the absolutism of the Soviet bureaucracy, even if it originated in a warlike environment produced by others, presupposed for its survival the reproduction and extension of this very environment. Only in the case of the democratic version of state capitalism did Pollock (if not Horkheimer) concede the possibility that it was essentially and not only historically reactive to the challenge of the other version. On the other hand, totalitarian state capitalism, apparently stabilizable at home, expresses its internal antagonism in the form of the arms race and the threat of war.

It was not without justification that critics like Neumann charged that, whatever its intentions, the theory of state capitalism ultimately postulated a stabilizable social order whose antagonisms could be suppressed or contained. It is another matter that in Neumann's case the criticism presupposed something like the classical Marxian theory of crisis and conflict as the only valid model of explanation, a model that Pollock and Horkheimer rightly rejected after 1940.[57] They each attempted to take two different, rather voluntaristic roads out of the dilemma. Horkheimer turned back to the Marxian theory of revolution (but without its crisis theoretical underpinnings) and postulated a council communist response to the authoritarian state that peculiarly he considered relevant to Soviet conditions in particular. The fundamental contradiction of "integral statism" according to him was "the limitation of productivity due to the existence of bureaucracies." But he did not forget his earlier critique of historical materialism, and again postulated that yet new forms of domination could be the outcome of this contradiction. Without a crisis theory, however, little linked the general hypothesis to social reality. Horkheimer definitively rejected the idea that one could expect "economic and juridical measures" from above "to democratize the system of control."[58]

Only the will of the ruled, only the reemergence of the tradition of workers' councils can abolish bureaucratic domination.[59] Because, however, the new form of rule under Soviet conditions legitimates itself by an ideology that contains the idea of workers' self-government and by a tradition that goes back to 1871 and 1905, the contradictions of the system are extremely vulnerable to immanent criticism. "The difference between concept and reality . . . is the foundation of the possibility of revolutionary praxis."[60] It was this idea linking theory and praxis to which Herbert Marcuse's critique of the Soviet state in the 1950s would go back to, in spite of his own different, initially reformist diagnosis. Horkheimer himself, however, not having explored the internal, self-induced limits of "integral statism" beyond a statement of its supposedly fundamental contradiction, left his idea of immanent critique and his hope of revolution from below in a strangely disconnected relation.

Pollock's difficulty was a different one. Unlike Horkheimer, or for that matter any other Frankfurt theorist, he did try to explore the self-induced limits of state capitalism. But only half emancipated from the classical Marxian dogma concerning centralized planning, he was able to trace these limits only to the international arena. Less willing than Horkheimer to postulate the possibility of some unified revolutionary will from below, he could not offer any hope within the framework of the Marxian tradition. Because of the logic of his argument, he too had to rely on actors, indeed global ones. Accordingly, if the limits of totalitarian state capitalism lay in the international arena, then only the determined action by the state capitalist democracies could actually lead to the abolition of the totalitarian system.

But which type of action? Armed competition, we might reason with him, would reinforce the logic of totalitarian state capitalism, and indeed supply its missing impetus for technological innovation. Disarmament on the part of the democratic powers would, however, lead to their defeat. Only the actual military diplomatic defeat of totalitarianism by democracy can therefore serve the desired purpose. "A democratic state capitalism, while safe from within, is menaced by totalitarian aggression and must arm to the teeth and be ready to fight until all totalitarian states have been transformed into democracies."[61] And, of course, not surprisingly, in the case of Nazi Germany Pollock stood exactly by this conclusion, during the beginning of the war, although he certainly would have done so before. But what about the Soviet case? The logic of the argument, if not that of Pollock's political inclination, pointed to the same conclusion. And in the brief period between the outbreak of the war and the attack on the Soviet Union there was a danger that Pollock would indeed be forced to draw it.

The second event and before, then, the natural caution regarding the discussion of the Soviet Union inherited from the critical theory of the 1930s saved him from the logic of his own position. After 1941 the Soviet Union had to be defended, if the greater evil Fascism was to be defeated. Even if on a high level of abstraction the two totalitarianisms were identified, the Frankfurt School's experience and critical analysis of Fascism left room for no hesitation on this score. In terms of Pollock's own argument, the fact that the Soviet Union became an ally of the state capitalist democracies fully settled the issue. But neither approach could shield him from the logic of his position, which implied that the alliance between the two forms of state capitalism could be nothing more than strategic and temporary, and with the defeat of their common enemy military political competition of the erstwhile allies was inevitable because of the social character of totalitarian state capitalism.

It was because of this consequence of his theory that Pollock, and I believe his closest collaborators, chose silence rather than the continuation of critical analysis after 1941. Even after the end of the war and during postwar East European developments, which rather confirmed the original analysis, this "critical silence" was maintained, in my view very mistakenly. Critical theorists may have differed on the question whether or not the victorious Western democracies could still be legitimately represented as the subjects of a process of emancipation from totalitarian rule, this time of the Soviet variety. What they certainly agreed on was the lack of any plausible means to accomplish this end. Once again, paradoxically, both the disarmament of the democracies and a new arms race could only serve the consolidation of totalitarian state capitalism. And certainly yet another devastating global war, right after the previous one, could not be advocated even for an instant. For these reasons, I believe, neither Pollock nor Horkheimer ever returned to the analysis of Soviet society. It was simply too distasteful to contemplate the indefinite survival of such a society, the impotent critique of which could only strengthen the most conservative and warlike (indeed authoritarian) segments of Western societies without being able to contribute to anyone's liberation.[62]

I do not believe, however, that, unlike Marcuse who in some respects was to preserve or return to the attitude of critical theory of the late 1930s with respect to the Soviet Union, Horkheimer (and Adorno) ever turned away from the political consequences of the rupture in the history of critical theory tied up with the events of 1939–41. Choosing silence concerning politics, especially after the final defeat of Fascism, they went on to develop on the abstract philosophical level the theoretical insights made at the time of their break with their earlier position, concerning the devastating consequences of an unfettered instrumental reason. And while we may be justly critical of their "critical silence" regarding Soviet society, we should at least emphasize that the central figures of the Frankfurt School after 1940, Horkheimer and Adorno, were never again to hold dogmas regarding centralized planning and state ownership that could lead to new forms of apologetics for authoritarian state socialism.

Notes

1. Original edition: *Dialektik der Aufklärung* 1947; English translation by J. Cumming (New York: Herder and Herder, 1972).
2. And paradoxically also because of the success of the only project Social Democracy ever had, the Keynesian welfare state, which led to its defensive, "conservative" turn.
3. For this thesis I am relying especially on two essays of Horkheimer from this period: "Autoritärer Staat," translated as "Authoritarian State," in Arato and Gebhardt, eds., *The Essential Frankfurt School Reader* (New York: Urizen Press, 1978), and "End of Reason," 1941, in *Studies in Philosophy and Social Science*, vol. IX. The latter essay is the first to introduce themes from the later *Dialectic of Enlightenment*, like the critique of the domination of nature and the thesis of the decline of the individual. The former essay provides the political context for Horkheimer's increasingly dark vision of our civilization. The link between the two essays is the uncompromising critique of central planning that is linked to the reduction of reason to instrumental, i.e., means-ends rationality alone. This line of reasoning was new in 1940, and represented an important break with Horkheimer's earlier conception.
4. The one exception I know of was a review by Adorno of the situation of music in the Soviet sphere of occupation in East Germany: "Die gegängelte Musik" [1948], in *Dissonanzen*, 4th ed. (Göttingen: Vandenhoeck and Ruprecht, 1969). Continuing a line of thought begun by Horkheimer in 1940, the essay repeatedly emphasizes parallels, and in Germany actual continuity, between National Socialist and Stalinist control and utilization

of culture. Adorno also begins to develop, through the Soviet cultural example, his doctrine of the transformation of ideology from false consciousness to the transparent yet omnipotent power of the factual. The essay concludes with the notable line linked to both versions of authoritarian rule in Germany: "Das Volk ist Opium fürs Volk." Would that Marcuse had reviewed this brief essay before writing *Soviet Marxism*.

5. It is reputed that Marcuse, unlike Adorno, Horkheimer, and Löwenthal, was opposed to the revolution and supported Soviet intervention.

6. The first two of these will be presented in this chapter; the other two will be the topics of chapters 2 and 3.

7. *Die planwirtschaftlichen Versuche in der Sowjetunion* (1929) (reprinted: Frankfurt/M: Verlag Neue Kritik, 1971).

8. New York: Columbia University Press, 1958.

9. On the history of the journal see: M. Jay, *The Dialectical Imagination* (Boston: Little Brown, 1971), still the best and most interesting treatment, as well as Alfred Schmidt, "Die *Zeitschrift für Sozialforschung*: Geschichte und Gegenwärtige Bedeutung," reprinted in the nine-volume reedition of the *Zeitschrift für Sozialforschung* (Munich: Kösel-Verlag, 1970).

10. *Wissenschaftsorganisation und politische Erfahrung. Studien zur frühen Kritischen Theorie* (Frankfurt/M: Suhrkamp Verlag, 1978), pp. 29–31, 57–60, and 91–94. I have also explored some of the relevant issues in my introduction to part I of *The Essential Frankfurt School Reader*, pp. 17–20.

11. In this context I believe the texts do not support Dubiel's interpretation according to which the critical dimension with respect the Soviet Union predominated in all periods of the school. Of course, even in the period 1932–36 the ambivalence, indeed the silence of critical theory distinguished it from all Communist and fellow traveler apologetics. But the lack of apologetics should not be confused with a critical attitude: One could be on the whole favorable with some reservations that dampened the enthusiasm so evident elsewhere. It is another issue that from the Communist point of view such a stand was already close to betrayal. We need not adopt their perspective in any case.

12. *Die planwirtschaftlichen Versuche in der Sowjetunion*, p. 366.

13. Ibid., p. 364.

14. As against Dubiel's opinion (*Wissenschaftsorganisation* 30), Pollock could not yet and in fact did not criticize (on the cited page, p. 366) the policy of forced industrialization.

15. Cf. Dubiel, *Wissenschaftsorganisation*, p. 31.

16. *Die planwirtschaftlichen Versuche*, p. 374, note 12.

17. "Die gegenwärtige Lage des Kapitalismus und die Aussichten einer planwirtschaftlichen Neuordnung," *Zeitschrift*, vol. I (1932), p. 27.

18. Cf. Dubiel's opposite interpretation that directly reverses the quoted sentence! (*Wissenschaftsorganisation*, p. 30).

19. Here I rely on Dubiel (p. 29), who, unfortunately, does not give the source of the passage from 1931 whose "skeptical solidarity" with the Soviet Union he maintains.

20. As he later told Dubiel (op. cit., p. 30); see "Rationalismusstreit in der gegenwärtigen Philosophie," *Zeitschrift*, vol. III (1934), p. 36.

21. See the section on Gramsci in chapter 3 of Arato and Cohen, *Civil Society and Political Theory* (Cambridge, Mass.: MIT Press, 1992).

22. *Zeitschrift*, vol. III (1934), p. 228.

23. In Horkheimer, *Critical Theory* (New York: Herder and Herder, 1972), pp. 90; 96–97.

24. *Wissenschaftsorganisation*, pp. 31–32.

25. "Marxismus, Diktatur und Organisationsformen der Proletariat," now in *Politics,*

Law and Social Change (New York: Columbia University Press, 1969) as "Marxism, Dictatorship and Organization of the Proletariat."

26. "Egoismus and Freiheitsbewegung," in *Zeitschrift*, vol. V (1936).

27. See Dubiel, *Wissenschaftsorganisation*, pp. 58–59. I generally accept his interpretation for the period 1937–39, an interpretation based also on reading some of the relevant correspondence. In one letter Pollock went so far as to call Stalin "a gangster."

28. See *Zeitschrift*, pp. 637–38, 629, both cited by Dubiel (p. 60).

29. "Philosophie und kritische Theorie," *Zeitschrift*, vol. VI (1937), p. 637; the reference to the Soviet Union is lost in the English translation. Cf. *Negations. Essays in Critical Theory* (Boston: Beacon Press, 1968), p. 142.

30. "Traditionelle und kritische Theorie," *Zeitschrift*, vol. 6 (1937), p. 630.

31. In *Studies in Philosophy and Social Science* (the English-language continuation of the *Zeitschrift*), vol. VIII (1939).

32. Dubiel, *Wissenschaftsorganisation*, p. 59: a letter of July 20, a few days before the pact, refers to an even further "weakening" (*gemildert*) of the passages referring to Russia. The end of the essay says it was finished in early September; war broke out on September 9.

33. Vol. 9 (1941).

34. See Jay, *Dialectical Imagination*, in particular the chapter on "The Institute's Analysis of National Socialism."

35. "Authoritarian State," p. 95.

36. F. Neumann, *Behemoth: The Structure and Practice of National Socialism, 1933–1944* (New York: Oxford University Press, 1944), pp. 224–26.

37. See "End of Reason."

38. "Authoritarian State," p. 96.

39. Ibid., p. 101.

40. Ibid., p. 102.

41. Ibid., p. 99.

42. "State Capitalism," in *Studies*, vol. IX (1941), pp. 221–22; also see, "Is National Socialism a New Order?" in *Studies*, vol. IX (1941), pp. 441–43.

43. "State Capitalism," p. 221, note 1.

44. Ibid., p. 211, note 1.

45. See *Behemoth*, p. 223, where Neumann reproduces the application of a model such as Pollock's to Russia by Hilferding, contesting only its applicability to Germany.

46. For the discussion see Jay, "The Institute's Analysis of National Socialism."

47. "State Capitalism," p. 207.

48. See "Is National Socialism a New Order?"

49. In the one area where Pollock almost stumbles on such a limit, the question of the supply of raw materials, he assigns this factor to the contingencies of geography, plausibly enough for Germany but completely implausibly in the case of the Soviet Union; see "State Capitalism," pp. 217–18. While he even mentions the possibility that such a system may be more wasteful than a market economy, he does not discover (and actually denies) a systematic link between these problems, one actually based on the "resource constrained" character of "state capitalist" systems.

50. Ibid., p. 218.

51. Ibid., p. 222.

52. Ibid., p. 218.

53. Ibid., p. 219.

54. Ibid., p. 220.

55. "Authoritarian State," p. 110.

56. "State Capitalism," pp. 220–21.

57. *Behemoth*, pp. 224–28.

58. "Authoritarian State," p. 102.
59. Ibid., p. 104.
60. Ibid., p. 109.
61. "State Capitalism," pp. 220–21.
62. Even Herbert Marcuse was ready to publish a work on the Soviet Union only after both the defeat of McCarthyism and the launching of the policy of peaceful coexistence. On this see chapter 2 in this volume.

2

Between Apology and Critique: Marcuse's *Soviet Marxism*

In the period immediately after the death of Stalin, Herbert Marcuse produced a book that is one of the two or three most sophisticated works by a Marxist in the West dealing with the structure and dynamics of Soviet society.[1] It is obviously the only full-length work within the nearly fifty-year history of critical theory that deals with the new social formation.

I can only attempt to surmise the reasons for publishing it in 1958. It is my belief that the Frankfurt theorists avoided a confrontation with the horrors of Stalinism, except in the period between the Hitler-Stalin pact and the invasion of the Soviet Union, in order not to strengthen first the fascist and later the cold war opponents of the Soviet Union. For several reasons Marcuse no longer faced quite the same difficulty in the mid-fifties. For one thing, with the death of Stalin, the Soviet Union apparently stood on the threshold of a reform period. If one took the possibility of reform very seriously, as did Marcuse, one could write about this society in far less negative terms than even minimum standards of honesty would have required in the decade before. Second, with the McCarthy period in the West having drawn to a close, with the opening up of the so-called peaceful coexistence, and with the end of the absolute polarization of the political scene, a critical work on the Soviet Union no longer had to play into the hands of the political right. On the contrary, one may have hoped that a work combining negative and positive projections on Soviet development might help precisely the partisans of a possible "third road", who might need an original and balanced perspective on the two major camps. Third, with Marxism and socialism having been entirely identified with the Soviet Union in the cold war period, there was now a need to distinguish them from Soviet Marxism and Soviet society if an independent socialist politics were to be possible at all. What, apparently, could be a better way to achieve this than to apply the concepts and

---

Written in 1984, with the exception of the last few pages, added to complete the essay for its first publication in this volume.

the norms of historical materialism to the realities and claims of the Soviet Union? Fourth, and this motivation is evident only in the later segments of the work,[2] given Marcuse's developing view on the "one dimensionality" of all industrial societies, Soviet society obviously provided a context in which what he took to be the "totalitarian" implications of contemporary forms of domination involving the decline of the individual, of culture and language, and even of ideology itself, could be studied in its most advanced form. The role that National Socialism played for the prewar synthesis of critical theory, culminating in *The Dialectic of Enlightenment*, was apparently played by the Soviet Union (though only in the cognitive, and never the moral-normative sense) in the works of Marcuse that led up to *One-Dimensional Man.*

Interestingly, after *One-Dimensional Man* (where the theories of *Soviet Marxism* reappear in slightly altered form), Marcuse did not again concern himself with Soviet society until his very last essay, on Rudolf Bahro, written in 1979.[3] In spite of the book *Soviet Marxism*, Soviet society never came to represent a twin concern for critical theory along with late capitalism. It is equally interesting that Marcuse, at least from the thirties to *Soviet Marxism*, and again in his Bahro essay, seemed to fundamentally maintain the one and the same position— one quite different from the violently critical views of Horkheimer in 1940, whose relevant positions were repeatedly altered—with respect to the identity and developmental possibilities of Soviet society.

Nevertheless, *Soviet Marxism* is a unique work, not only in the career of Marcuse, but also in critical theory.[4] It is not just the school's only large-scale work dedicated to the study of the Soviet Union, but most certainly its only extended attempt to bring the now-famous method of immanent critique to bear on the topic.[5] Indeed, as the most extensive single work in immanent criticism, *Soviet Marxism* demonstrates not only the strengths but even more the limitations of the approach. Marcuse's ability to examine Soviet society by its own standards, his success in avoiding an external evaluation of its dynamics that remains estranged from the actual social process, has been noticed by most of his reviewers. Not until twenty years after his work was written was it also noticed that a pure immanent critique, by presupposing the same normative parameters as the society criticized, cannot intend a radically different society.[6] Indeed, among those opposed to an existing society, the method can address only those who accept its fundamental if suppressed values. Equally serious, however, is another objection: that immanent critique seeks not only a communicative or hermeneutic relationship to social actors, but insists also on a social scientific description of objectified processes of a social system, which presupposes that the theories and doctrines criticized represent an adequate and exhaustive description of the functioning of a society. While the notion of completeness is based on Hegelian illusions that are hardly tenable (e.g., that a single philosophy can be the exhaustive self-consciousness of an epoch), the notion of social scientific adequacy itself cannot be applied to all symbol systems merely because they

are the apparently "ruling ideas" of an epoch or a social formation. In the case of
Soviet Marxism in particular, it is only with the utmost difficulty that one can
derive any reasonable representations of Soviet reality from it. While even in this
case immanent critique may be justified as long as one seeks to explore the
hypothesis that the body of ideas itself represents a dynamic element in social
reality, the method can certainly not, even in principle, provide what the critique
of political economy, at least arguably, yielded for Marx: a simultaneous analysis
of reproductive logic and developmental tendencies, *and* the reconstruction of
the objective possibility of the self-constitution of critical and revolutionary subjectivity.[7]

Marcuse, who had ultimately few illusions about the objective value of Soviet
Marxist social science, was implicitly conscious of the limitation this represented
for his general method. Thus he in fact utilized immanent critique next to two
other general components of Marxian theory: an evolutionist philosophy of history, and class analysis. The turn to these dimensions, which in fact was the basis
of his analysis of the identity of the system, its stages of development and its
social structure, did not seem to violate the requirement of immanence, because
Soviet Marxism too presupposes them. But unlike the case of an analysis of
capitalist development, where Soviet Marxism used Marxian concepts to understand, on some level at least, its political, economic, and military rival, when it
came to Soviet society, the same concepts were used to occlude social reality.
Hence Marcuse had to return to the original meaning of Marx's concepts, and
develop them in reference to Soviet society wholly at variance with the Soviet
Marxist utilization of some of them. Immanent critique proper was restricted to
the area where it was in any case most applicable: the critique of the ideology
and the "spirit" of Soviet society.

Marcuse's use of classical Marxian concepts allows us to evaluate not only
Soviet Marxism, the object of analysis, but also the instruments themselves
brought to bear on this object. Indeed, it will turn out in his work too, as Marcuse
himself implies in at least two contexts, that the "schematic" application of
"traditional Marxism" (presumably as against critical theory!) has apologetic
consequences for the "critique" of Soviet society.[8]

Philosophy of History

The question of the identity of a social formation is extremely important if we
are to be able to evaluate the meaning of its continuity and limits, both on an
analytical level and on that of the consciousness of its members, individuals, and
groups. Marcuse does not raise the issue independently, but operates within the
terms established by critical Marxist discourse concerning the Soviet Union,
which was restricted to the question: Is Soviet society capitalist, socialist, or a
transitional mix between the two? Characteristically, Marcuse does not even hint
at two other alternatives posited within the relevant debate: that the Soviet Union

might represent a (perhaps partially modernized) version of a particular type of traditional society—Oriental despotism—or an entirely new type of social formation *sui generis*—(modern) bureaucratic collectivism. These omissions prove what is evident in any case, namely, that he does not work with the exclusive alternative of capitalism/socialism because of the influence of the relevant Marxist discussions, but because the terms of the classical Marxian philosophy of history do not permit a third alternative for a modern, industrial society.[9]

It would be futile to seek a clear resolution in Marcuse of the question already posed, namely, whether the Soviet Union is capitalist, socialist, or "transitional."[10] In this regard it is impossible to connect him to any one dogmatic tradition of interpretation. He genuinely wrestles with the historical connection of the new system to capitalism, and its presumed anticipation of either elements of, or developmental tendencies toward, socialism. Paradoxically, while it is his seriousness in the first context that leads to some results that turn out to be constitutive for his original if problematic work on late industrial society, his superficiality in the second indicates his hidden connection to Marxian dogmatics.

Marcuse is quite emphatic: The Soviet Union *does not* represent merely a new version of capitalism. Nevertheless, in his analysis the interconnections among the two systems are striking. In the unfolding of world history, the development of the Soviet Union represents a parallel sequence to capitalist industrialization, performing the same "function."[11] Accordingly, the *spirit* of the two systems is remarkably similar. While the underlying socioeconomic structures of the two do not converge, there is an apparent convergence of their political and cultural superstructures in the direction of a welfare state that *Soviet Marxism* describes as mass democratic, and *One-Dimensional Man* denounces as "totalitarian." The repressive structure, finally, of the two world systems is symbiotic: The military danger they represent for one another is a constant justification for internal military and police controls. Nevertheless, the peaceful economic competition of the two can lead, at least in the case of the Soviet Union, to liberalization and even experimentation with elements of a non-repressive civilization.

According to Marcuse, the Soviet Union has implemented industrial civilization "through basically different institutions, which are designed to make for a different development."[12] To be sure, this formulation from 1961 was a response to criticism, and was in turn weakened in the theme of "totalitarian convergence" sharpened by *One-Dimensional Man*. Yet even the original text of *Soviet Marxism* sought to grasp both the affinity and the essential difference of *two modes of industrialization*.[13] It is evident that classical Marxian criteria, such as the absence of private property in the means of production and the existence of central planning in the Soviet Union, are the elements constitutive of the difference to Marcuse, while he indicates that the affinity is defined by the all-embracing character of technological processes under industrial civilization.[14] Nevertheless, even if under different and new institutions, the Soviet union created a version of industrial civilization. This is what Marcuse repeatedly indicates as the "success" of the Stalinist epoch.[15] This point, of course, runs into a crucial if obvious objection. Marcuse would have to explain the enormous differences between the two modes of industrialization, which have often enough earned the Soviet Union the adjective "totalitarian,"[16] without confirming the argument of "liberals" like Ludwig von Mises and Friedrich Hayek that these are due precisely to the combination of state ownership and central planning, which Marcuse considers "positive" characteristics of the new society. And indeed, we are supplied with one additional if tortuous and ambiguous line of argumentation. To begin with, Marcuse rejects the label totalitarian.[17] Then he proceeds to use it in various contexts with one constant: totalitarian policies and phenomena are due to the Soviet Union having telescoped stages of industrial development. "The Soviet Union is a latecomer . . . joining and running ruthlessly ahead of a general trend in late industrial society. The skipped stages are those of enlightened absolutism and liberalism."[18]

What is supposedly not skipped however is the ascetic, puritanical, repressive spirit of capitalist industrialization first analyzed by Max Weber, but given a far more negative evaluation here. In terms of the work ethic, family-based morality, and stress on delayed gratification, the Soviet system has resembled, and above all continues to resemble, early stages of capitalist development. But from whence come the phenomena of the totalitarian penetration of all of social life by the party-state? Here Marcuse fatefully oscillates between two contradictory explanations. On the one hand, the need to telescope, to accelerate the stages of industrialization, requires total control in the context of a backward country competing on all levels with the Western capitalist countries economically advanced enough to afford the luxuries of constitutionalization and political democracy. On the other hand, the Soviet Union, having telescoped several stages of development, runs ahead of its rivals, and is merely the first system to realize the common totalitarian implications of late industrial civilization.

The first explanation, most favored by Marxists, culminates in the claim that the economic success of the totalitarian stage prepares the ground for liberalization, for a moment when, in the context of a post-Stalinist welfare state, a liberalized Soviet Union will also be able to afford democratic and constitutional "luxuries." This, in spite of some contradictions, is ultimately the theory of *Soviet Marxism*. The second explanation however is more classical for critical theory, and was anticipated by Horkheimer's *Authoritarian State*. It involves a sweeping condemnation of the social world of the mass democratic capitalist countries, and points out that under conditions of late industrial society, the decline of the individual, the penetration of privacy, the manipulation of public opinion, the end of genuine culture, and even ideological transcendence, are established "either by terror, by the standardizing trends of 'mass culture' or by a combination of both."[19] This is the theory of *One-Dimensional Man*, equally insensitive ultimately to the tragedy of actual totalitarianism and the actual forms of existence of modern civil society.

While the first explanation reveals a characteristically deterministic bias that justifies an evil past (still obviously applicable in many societies!) in the name of a rather dramatically posited better future, the second, far more pessimistic about the future of Soviet society, validates this pessimism by applying the adjective "totalitarian" to all industrial societies, irrespective of the presence or absence of elements of cultural, political, religious, social, and economic independence.[20]

Given the fact that he indeed joins the notions of convergence and totalitarianism, Marcuse's protestations that he is not a "convergence theorist" may sound hollow. There is indeed a double convergence implied by his overall analysis: After the success of "totalitarian" (Meaning One) industrialization, the Soviet Union is evolving toward a liberalized welfare state of the Western type. Contemporary capitalist societies are in turn in the process of realizing "totalitarian" (Meaning Two) controls of social and cultural life. After initially declining the use of "totalitarian" because of its illegitimate bringing together of regimes as different as National Socialism and Soviet Marxism, he gives us two "totalitarian" welfare (or better, welfare–warfare) states with *different* institutional arrangements of their economic base. But will this difference still be relevant? Here we reach one of the key theses of *Soviet Marxism*. The difference will indeed become relevant if the cold war confrontation of the two systems can be replaced by "peaceful coexistence." In other words, Soviet society is both judged to be politically the more progressive on a world historical scale, in the context of peaceful coexistence, and in fact it is argued that its foreign policy will be—for structural reasons—the basis of a transition to a peaceful international order.

While Marcuse does not analyze the place of the military in the social system, and has little to say on the imperial structure of the whole,[21] the maintenance of two great, antagonistic military world blocs has constitutive significance for his analysis. While he too repeats the false and apologetic thesis that the totalitarian and terrorist aspects of the Stalinist period are due to Western encirclement and military pressure,[22] he does not look at the contemporary world constellation in a one-sided manner. The aggressive policies, the military threats, the armament programs of each, help to maintain the repressive structures and policies of the other.[23] However, given the Khrushchevist aim of "catching up and overtaking capitalism," to which Marcuse refers with approval about half a dozen times, he thinks it is up to the less developed Soviet Union to initiate peaceful coexistence by abandoning its own aggressive posture, in order to be able to shift dramatically from military production to production of consumer goods, from guns to butter.[24]

Here we have a possible interpretation of the internal and external policies of the reform period, certainly till 1956, and perhaps until Khrushchev's fall. But from our retrospective, the obvious question emerges: Will not this repressive society, like all others, tend to perpetuate the conditions for its own reproduction, including the international ones? On what basis will it promote new ones that would endanger its own *raison d'être*? Why does Marcuse expect fundamentally

different policies from the Soviet Union than from the leading capitalist countries? The only possible candidate for an explanation, that the Soviet version of
industrialism is fundamentally weaker than its competitor and is doomed to
remain so, cannot even arise for Marcuse.[25]

In Marcuse's case the concept of a more peaceful foreign policy by the Soviet
Union is based on illusions about its social system. According to him, on the
level of the philosophy of history, the difference between the two great world
systems is indicated by the Soviet Union's relationship to socialism. Marcuse
denies that the Soviet Union is socialist,[26] but this denial is something less than
categorical. The Soviet Union is "not yet" socialist. In one of these formulations,
Marcuse even speaks of "the socialist base of production" as the "decisive difference" between Soviet and advanced capitalist society, although five lines later he
indicates that there are "class distinctions at the very base of the system."[27] In yet
another place we hear of "the principles of a socialist economy made into an
instrument of domination."[28] In all these contexts, Marcuse has nothing more
mysterious in mind than "total nationalization," which makes for "an essentially
different developmental tendency beyond the present framework." It is in this
context that Marcuse comes very close to the Trotskyist theory of the transitional
society (except for his almost opposite evaluation of the path that Soviet foreign
policy should take in the world). His conception is this: the Soviet Union has a
socialist base as yet in a totally regressive form, one, however, that inhibits (as
we will see) not so much classlike antagonism as the rigidification of class
relations. Genuine socialist transformation could accordingly leave intact the
material base, "the nationalized productive process," although it would have to
involve the disappearance of "the State, the Party, the Plan, etc. as independent
powers superimposed on the individuals."[29] According to *One-Dimensional
Man*, such a change presupposes a political revolution, presumably from below,
although he also hints that the change could be ushered in by the administration
that would disappear as a result.[30] In this context *Soviet Marxism*, which does not
include "the Plan" in its list of alien powers, is less ambiguous, and clearly raises
the possibility of "*political* change, i.e., transfer of control from above to below
while retaining the same social base (nationalization)."[31] In the manner of Marx
(1843), neither work considers political revolution or political change to be the
final step to human liberation. Social change (*Soviet Marxism*), the most radical
and complete revolution in history (*One-Dimensional Man*), would still be
needed to liberate the new powers of technology. According to Marcuse, this
possibility is based on "coexistence," which would transfer competition from the
military into the economic area, and which would force the Soviet Union into a
policy of accelerated and extensive automation. The fact that no smooth transfer-
ence of control from above to below follows from such a necessity may have
forced Marcuse to shift his stress from political reform to political revolution
(from below or above!) in the period intervening between his two works.

While the link is not made, we can assume that in this confrontation the chances of revolution from below in the Soviet Union are no more favored by international military tensions than those of reform from above. We are, however, left with the claim that the social nature of the Soviet Union is more likely to promote the reduction of these tensions than that of the late capitalist powers. Marcuse's stress in this context does not seem to be on the transitional or protosocialist (Bahro) nature of the Soviet Union. Rather, everything according to him depends on the policy to "catch up and overtake," which is to lead not only to liberalization but also to initiatives toward the reduction of international tension, in spite of the fact that both liberalization and peaceful coexistence in themselves at least would not create all the preconditions for decisive political change *within* the Soviet Union. Let us note that in this argument, we are asked to believe that the Soviet Union has a realistic chance to "catch up and overtake the West." If not, the continuation of military competition, made possible by continued diversion of resources to the benefit of armaments would be a more plausible strategy of international competition than the concentration on economic and social development within the framework of the existing system, which can at best earn a second-rate status for the Soviet Union. In other words, Marcuse believes that the Soviet system of military-industrial organization is neither an intrinsic part of the existing system, nor even a compensation for its unavoidable failures, but a merely extrinsic feature imposed on the Soviet Union by geopolitical constraints. To the extent then that these constraints can be modified, the Soviet Union would have every interest and take no risks in seeking to modify them by reducing military preparedness and the relevant forms of competition with the West. To believe this, one had to have some serious illusions about the Soviet system of domination, where progressive tendencies allegedly outweigh self-perpetuating and reproducing ones. It is to Marcuse's analysis of this system of domination and its developmental possibilities that we must turn.

Critical Social Theory: Forms of Domination and Development

In one respect, Marcuse's analysis certainly does not fall within the totalitarianism paradigm: He interprets the Soviet Union in terms of definite stages of development encompassing the past, present, and future of the system. Not only does he distinguish between Leninism and Stalinism—as did, in fact, some of the theorists of totalitarianism, notably Hannah Arendt—but unlike them, he also sees the post-Stalinist period as significantly distinct. Nevertheless, he also posits some essential continuities among these stages, and even a possible future one, hence they become developmental levels of *the same* social formation (whose nature, as we have seen, is never grasped either consistently enough or abstractly enough).

The first years of the Bolshevik revolution and "fully developed" Stalinism are, according to Marcuse, obviously different because of "the steady growth of totalitarianism and authoritarian centralization," a statement to which one will readily assent, and "the growth of the dictatorship not of but over the proletariat and the peasantry," which falsely presupposes that dictatorship under Lenin was somehow of the proletariat (and the peasantry?), a position at odds even with what Marcuse says elsewhere about Leninist substitutionism. He proposes that we should think of these differences not so much in terms of a "break," but as "the turn from quantity into quality."[32] In other words, put less bashfully, the fact of totalitarianism and authoritarian centralization marks the continuity between the periods, their dramatic increase marks the difference.

More fundamentally, according to Marcuse, Stalinism greatly accelerated Lenin's program of "civilization," that is, the priority of industrialization over socialist liberation through a revolution from above including vast terror. According to Marcuse, Stalinist civilization was successful, and its success makes possible and even necessary the emergence of a new stage of development.[33] He traces some of the formulations of post-Stalinist relaxation (new evaluation of capitalist development, the program of peaceful coexistence) back into the last years of Stalin's rule, and indicates that along with the successful creation of a sufficiently strong industrial base and postwar reconstruction, these are the presuppositions of far-reaching reform and liberalization.

> Administrative decentralization, emphasis on legality as against incalculable arbitrariness, shift in the enforcement of military discipline from brutality to persuasion, greater range of freedom for writers and artists, and critics, and, most important, gradual introduction of a reduced working day and increasing availability of consumer goods testify to this trend.[34]

Elsewhere, he adds the proclamation and even implementation of a "considerable democratization of the state . . . and self government,"[35] and "decline in the power of the secret police, . . . legal reforms, relaxation in censorship, liberalization in cultural life."[36] Again, however, we are not to conceive of post-Stalinism as an absolute break, the basis of continuity is and will be maintained: "the continued strengthening of the state and of the party agencies remains on the agenda, . . . intense regimentation from above seems to be required for the very success of the new efforts."[37] The changes are to be introduced exclusively from above, and "reform from above" has in one respect the same teleology as "revolution from above": the preservation and even extension of the full scope of the state's authority over society.

It is here, as against his flirtation with the notion of various versions of a transitional society, that Marcuse implicitly stumbles upon the true principle of identity of this social formation, which he never openly recognizes as a new and independent one *sui generis*. The next probable stage *or* phase of Soviet development, a post-Stalinist welfare state, in Marcuse's presentation will itself not escape this authoritarian principle of identity. In this context, he differentiates between minimum (welfare state) and maximum (liberated society) goals of development, the first being what he takes to be the actual program of the party leadership implied by the slogan to "catch up and overtake." The second is preserved on the level of the Marxian utopia the system cannot dispense with. For the moment we are interested only in the first, the post-Stalinist welfare state, which supposedly could and would be introduced fully from above, in conformity with the Stalinist doctrine of the strengthening of the state under socialism. Thus it will be "a direct heir of the Stalinist state."[38] Astonishingly (from retrospect), Marcuse refers to the components of its programs as "modest enough." In his own characterization, these "modest" features can go as far as:

> Rising standards of living up to a practically free distribution of goods and services, steadily extending mechanization of labor, exchangeability of technical functions, expanding popular culture, . . . the gradual assimilation of urban and agricultural, intellectual and physical labor . . . .Technical progress will overtake the repressive restrictions imposed in earlier stages. . . . [There will be a] transformation of political into technological controls.[39]

Even more astonishingly, all this should happen on the basis of existing trends, and can actually happen within an intact political system, whose variation may be restricted to relatively insignificant oscillation between different groups in charge (for example party and army), between personal and collegial leadership. We have seen that Marcuse postulates such a "minimum program" (along with its positive and negative aspects) to be not only inherent in a fully developed industrial society, but also implied by the Khrushchevist program of attaining the "civilization level" of the most advanced capitalist countries. It is, in turn, made possible by the relaxation of international tensions, and would further channel competition among the world systems in the direction of "peaceful coexistence." According to Marcuse, only the victory of socialism in this competition, *and/or* the collapse of the capitalist environment of the Soviet Union through "international revolution," would definitively put on the agenda the "maximal program" (whose details are more or less equivalent to the direct democratic producers' utopia of Marx). If we restrict this to the only relevant element, the democratization of political controls, which to Marcuse too represents the breaking point, the obvious question arises whether or not there are deeply entrenched forces and institutions that would counteract such a trend even in the context of international pacification, or better still, act counter to international pacification, in order not to make themselves superfluous. More immediately, would not even the political and social correlates of Marcuse's in fact entirely utopian minimum program bring attempts to actualize many of its elements through a concentration on a consumption-led program of economic development into conflict with the self-perpetuating tendencies of the contemporary system, which is anything but the technocratic rule implied by Marcuse's concept of a post-Stalinist welfare state?

In this context, Marcuse works with three fundamental tendencies of Soviet industrial society—one based on the common features of all industrial societies, the second and third based on the differentia specifica of Soviet society: its own proper underlying dynamic and its unique class structure. Industrial society in Marcuse's social theory, above all in *One-Dimensional Man*, contains two powerful and contradictory tendencies that penetrate the structure of "technics" itself. On the one hand, modern methods of production, and above all increasingly automatic machine technology, achieve for the first time in human history the potential conquest of all scarcity and toil. On the other hand, the same methods and the same machines are today everywhere penetrated by a specific historical logic of domination; they are used and utilized in such a way as to perpetuate superfluous labor, to manipulate needs, and to reproduce obsolescent hierarchy. Technological development makes human liberation in a new sense objectively possible,[40] but technological development in itself will not even lead to the full unfolding of the genuinely liberating effects of technology. Such a liberation would require transformation of the basic social and economic "institutions and relationships."[41]

As is well known, *One-Dimensional Man* is extremely pessimistic about such a possibility for all industrial societies, because of the supposed manipulation and reduction of all critical consciousness by an ideology that retreats into the one-dimensional world of science and technology. Characteristically, *Soviet Marxism* proposes a far more optimistic theory of Soviet society, a diagnosis that even *One-Dimensional Man* will in fact repeat if in a far more hesitant form.

According to Marcuse, the underlying objective dynamic of Soviet society tends to reinforce the positive side of modern technological development, and the class structure, instead of superseding such a trend, is itself vitiated by the same dynamic. To put it differently, it is the neutralization of the results of class division that implies a decisive difference between the trends of Western and Eastern development. (The result should be the inevitable realization of the minimum program of development, the aforementioned post-Stalinist welfare state, with more open possibilities than capitalist welfare states for the emergence of a liberated society.)

In this context, the train of thought is anything but convincing. First, there is a self-propelling trend of technical development toward "continuous growth of labor productivity and continuous rationalization."[42] But this is admittedly shared with the capitalist West, and the possibility that such developments will not be utilized to reduce labor and increase consumption is stressed by Marcuse. Then there is "the objective historical situation (i.e., the interrelationship between Stalinist power politics and capitalist consolidation),"[43] which supposedly drives the Soviet state toward "relaxation" and the redirection of growing productivity toward consumption. But why should relaxation have a different result for one of the two sides? Marcuse mentions the relative backwardness of the Soviet Union, and the need to "catch up and overtake" existing societies of high mass consumption. But where does his confidence come from that this *can* in fact be accomplished? And if accomplished, (i.e., if the extremely unlikely were to happen) why should the resulting society be especially open to revolutionary social change? We get the following answers to these questions:

1. While it is indeed international competition that forces the Soviet system to undertake automation, there are no internal limits here, as under capitalism, to automation and dramatic increases in productivity; no "fundamental reasons" for planned waste and obsolescence.[44]

2. Although the socialist base of production has not meant the exclusion of fundamental class distinctions, these are neither the motor of the productive process nor even intrinsic to it. As a result, the ruling strata are replaceable "without exploding the basic institutions of society,"[45] and will indeed become entirely obsolescent once their *raison d'être*, catching up with the capitalist world, has been fulfilled.[46] On this level, there are thus two trends: to prevent attainment of this level because of the self-interest of entrenched bureaucracy, and the need to do just this because of life-and-death competition with the capitalist countries. Marcuse bets on the second, because of what he takes to be the structural weakness of the new ruling class.

Regarding the first argument, even when it was written it flew dramatically in the face of all known facts (the Soviet Union was never a leader on any level or in any branch of industrial automation, the Soviet economy is the most wasteful in terms of labor and materials of any industrial society, its planned products are obsolete from the moment they are conceived, etc.). This false argument was evidently based on considerations derived from the fetishistic overestimation of the powers of a centrally planned society, present in so much of orthodox socialist theory, and the concept of profit derived from a rather crudely interpreted labor theory of value. The historical backwardness to which Marcuse refers[47] makes industrialization without waste and obsolescence and complete automation only desirable, hardly necessary. Total administration (which is a good name for what the Soviets call "planning"), contrary to Marcuse's belief,[48] was far better at providing technical development up to a certain level than beyond it. Finally, the idea that profitability in the economic sense fundamentally depends on the exploitation of constant or increasing quantums of real labor, and that automation is incompatible with this goal, is not only empirically untenable, but was rejected by Marx, at least the Marx of the *Grundrisse*, always one of Marcuse's basic sources. It is for reasons of the perpetuation of domination, according to Marx, that is, of the existing system of social controls, expressed by the subsumption of wealth under the value form, that labor time under capitalism cannot be fundamentally reduced.[49] But, whether or not one can interpret production in the Soviet system as penetrated by the value form, in a totalitarian society, as Friedrich Pollock already noted in 1940, the liberation of time along with the freedom to consume would be a far greater danger to social stability than in mass democracies.

This brings us to the second argument, on which the first depends. Marcuse needs to show that the logic of domination under Soviet conditions is structurally weak, and is therefore unable to maintain itself in the face of a combination of objective forces (peaceful competition with the capitalist world, the self propelling trend of technology) and subjective challenges that could emerge from the internal contradictions of Soviet Marxist culture and the spirit of Soviet society.

We have seen that Marcuse does in a way presuppose the supposedly *partially* socialist, transitional character of Soviet society as the basis of a decisive difference with late capitalism. This position, which he shares with classical Trotskyist analyses of the Soviet Union,[50] is elaborated in only one context, which, however, is exactly the one that divided Trotsky from some of his famous followers (Rizzi, Schachtman, Burnham). The master posed the question whether the Soviet bureaucracy was a new ruling class, and to the end of his life answered his own question with a resounding negative. The dissident pupils however replied affirmatively, if for different reasons. As always, Marcuse, a better dialectician than all of them, answered the question both affirmatively and negatively. While for a moment he seems to consign the question of whether or not the rulers of Soviet society constitute a "class" to "Marxist exegesis," and at times prefers, in the manner of Trotsky, to speak of a ruling group with a "caste character," on the whole Marcuse maintains the class character of Soviet domination. The exact identity of this class varies in his text from "government bureaucracy" to "political economic and military bureaucracy,"[51] and even "intelligentsia,"[52] and in fact he explicitly states that the replacement of one ruling group by another, in particular the party by the army bureaucracy,[53] would not essentially change the social system.

Two theoretical issues mingle in this analysis. Apparently, in Soviet society, the central institutional framework is primary with respect to the stratification system. And the hierarchical structure of rule, it seems, is based on a ruling group whose identities can shift as well as on a rather extensive privileged social stratum supporting it. (This is most likely the place of the intelligentsia, which as such is mentioned only once.) It is the first issue that Marcuse deals with, with results that in his opinion support his thesis concerning the structural weakness of domination in the Soviet Union. In fact, his avoidance of the second implies a fear, I think, of results to the contrary. Evidently, "the state as a system of political institutions" is the key to the nature and limits of the Soviet class structure. It is "the centralized authoritarian organization of the productive process" separating the immediate producers from the process of production that constitutes those who "control" (rather than "own") the means of production as a class, irrespective of the openness of ascent to it from below. The Soviet bureaucracy as a ruling class does not, in this view, stamp the production process by its own logic of reproduction. Rather, the logic of production emerges indirectly, as a result of the politicization of the economic system by a state that remains a hypostatized, reified, alien power over and against society.

Marcuse derives the following conclusion from this starting point: The ruling structure of Soviet society does not and cannot generate a self-perpetuating power, because (1) the power of the state has objective, economic limits;[54] (2) control, unlike ownership, is not an adequate principle for the self-identification and continuity of a ruling class that is kept fluid by countervailing political processes—planning and terror; and (3) the actual policies of Soviet society emerge competitively from the bureaucracy, and correspond to an (alienated) general interest, that is, "the basic trend of Soviet society."

While Marcuse utilizes the notion of the primacy of the political in deriving the stratification of Soviet society, he by no means accepts this principle in terms of its fundamental trends, which for him are necessarily economic. This historical materialist bias necessarily leads to a weakening of his admission that the bureaucracy is a class: It is a "political class," and as such, unable to root itself in and reproduce itself through the fundamental social process. The Soviet state has created from above an economic structure that has acquired its own immanent development merely to reproduce and fortify the ruling structure. The present foundation of this structure, however, is *doubly* uncertain. To begin with, "control" is directly exercised by agricultural and industrial bureaucracies. But the party's "social control" overrides this "technical administrative control." However, according to Marcuse, within the party "there is no separate homogeneous group to which social control can be attributed."[55] The top ruling group is subject to change, and others (the sub-bureaucracies) are in a competitive relationship vis-à-vis one another.

One might, of course, object that Marcuse has interpreted "control" in a much too voluntaristic sense, and that in order to maintain a "monopoly" of controls, the political bureaucracy need not, in fact, control the outcome of economic processes. Furthermore, political competition need not be any more of an argument against the common identity of the rulers in an étatist system of stratification than economic competition in a capitalist one. To this Marcuse replies with two arguments, one convincing, the other not. He points out that monopolization of power is counteracted by *terror* and *central planning*. As far as terror goes, his argument is identical to those of Hannah Arendt and Isaac Deutscher, according to whom the notion of bureaucracy as a ruling class is untenable in the face of the atomization and even physical destruction of enormous numbers of officials. Terror stands in the way of the crystallization of particular interests and group solidarities. Although Marcuse does not draw this conclusion, the argument tends to replace class analysis by focusing on a ruling institution that indeed reproduces itself either by terror *or* by bureaucratic domination *or* their combination.[56]

From the point of view of such an institution, the identity, particular interests, and even lives of its members are irrelevant, although, of course, in a more stable, more "normal" form it would protect these to an important extent. Such a normalization means and has meant the end of terror, at least *within* the ruling institutions. It is rather unclear what Marcuse means by its replacement by "technological terror." He is somewhat clearer but equally unconvincing when he counterposes the central plan to the monopolization of power. This is crucial, however, because his argument concerning the continued weakness of the structures of domination under post-Stalinist conditions depends on it.

According to Marcuse's rather plausible view, the central plan is not the result of the combined will of *the* bureaucracy, but rather a project arising *within* the bureaucracy as a result of the combined and adjusted interests and negotiations of the top bureaucratic branches (government, party, army, management). "The rate and mode of growth, and the priorities . . . are apparently determined through struggles and compromises between competing vested interests." So far so good. But according to Marcuse, the result is "a sort of general interest" that "must conform to the basic trend of the construction of Soviet society."[57] It is, of course, either tautological or nonsensical to call the result of interbureaucratic competition "general." While it is true that certain basic trends like the primacy of heavy industry, the centrality of the military sector, and the discrimination against agriculture are inevitable, confirmed through the "planning" process, one would be hard pressed to call these interests "general," or to assume that the continued monopolization of decision making will be any less confirmed by the "rate, mode and priorities of growth" that are chosen than by any of the others. If the decisions indeed are to be confirmed or canceled according to a variety of international and domestic "objective factors," including the international effectiveness of Soviet policy, it is hard to see how the maintenance and expansion of the power of "the economic, political and military establishment" is not one of these factors. Indeed, it is obviously the first among them, and as a criterion, outweighs even the international effectiveness of policy.

The arguments of Marcuse against considering the ruling structure of the Soviet Union in terms of the categories of class analysis deserve to be taken seriously, even if he himself in fact remains a prisoner of the orthodox Marxian class theory. This is ultimately the key to his argument against the existence of effective mechanisms of the self-perpetuation of particular interests. He quite evidently presupposes that only an economically based class structure could possess such mechanisms. This, of course, flies in the face of what we know about all precapitalist societies, and in fact societies of the Soviet type as well. Thus, the entirely paradoxical result: "A separate class which controls the underlying population through control of the economic, political and military establishments," must succumb to the "common interest," "a social interest in a hypostatized form." Correctly realizing that the Soviet bureaucracy as a whole is unable to serve its own purely economic interests, or those of its constituent parts, in a preposterous manner he deduces that it must therefore serve a social interest, alienated because society plays no role in formulating it. In fact, the Soviet ruling class *or* institution, the political bureaucracy or its possible replacements, need not serve anyone's economic interest, but only its own *political* logic of self-perpetuation.[58] This alternative in fact remains open in *One-Dimensional Man*, to the extent that Marcuse poses the question whether or not "material and intellectual growth" could be arrested at a level where the existing structure of domination would not yet be threatened. Clearly such an arrestation is in no one's economic interest, yet it has a definite logic. While Marcuse's answer is negative, his reference to a favorable, that is, a pacified international context driving the Soviet state in peaceful competition suppresses the obvious point that this variable too is not entirely independent of the actions of the Soviet state. Forces capable of arresting "material and intellectual growth" are also capable of negatively affecting international trends toward peace and disarmament.

This Marcuse did not want to admit, any more than did a Western peace movement thirty years later, during the Brezhnev era. Clearly, however, the overall Orwellian thrust of the analysis of *One-Dimensional Man* contains the alternative, in spite of the fact that this work too is still inexplicably interested in insisting on the relevant difference of the protosocialist Soviet Union and the late capitalist United States. In this respect, *Soviet Marxism* could be more consistently optimistic. Unlike *One-Dimensional Man*, it did not have to link the positive trend of development to some supposedly socialist features of the economic base alone, because on the side of the "subjective factor," the dialectic of Soviet ideology and morality, Marcuse was able to discern some potentially critical dimensions. These are in fact the bases of his attempt to integrate immanent critique into his overall analysis.

Soviet Marxism, Classical Marxism, and Critical Theory: The Step to Immanent Critique

Marcuse's reliance on a classical Marxist philosophy of history and class theory in his analysis of Soviet society ultimately reveals more about the weaknesses of these bulwarks of the classical theory than about the Soviet Union itself. As against his critical intentions, the results are *mildly* apologetic of Soviet society, which in spite of all appearances is seen as a more advanced stage of social development, a stage closer to an emancipated society than the capitalist mass democracies. Furthermore, there is no room in this analysis for the militarization of Soviet society, for the imperial character of the system as a whole. On the contrary, the society is seen for structural reasons to be potentially more pacific, less aggressive than its international rivals. The internally antagonist character of the society is to be admitted, to be sure, unlike in official apologetics, but it is not seen as *constitutive* for the society, even though the degree of the domination of the population is admittedly total and all-inclusive. Totalitarian domination, including terror itself, is in fact explained away on the preposterous grounds that its success implies at the very least a form of welfare state equal to and in terms of its underlying tendency even superior to that of the West. All in all, Marcuse's analysis inadvertently demonstrates the truth of his own statement, that key dimensions of classical Marxism have apologetic implications when applied "schematically" to the Soviet Union. But what about the method of critical theory proper, which has always implied a critique of classical Marxism? Indeed, Marcuse's and even critical theory's most synthetic work in immanent criticism *is* a Marxian critique of Marxism, and not only Soviet Marxism.

There are three participants in this confrontation: classical Marxism, Soviet Marxism, and critical theory. Their relation is presented in a series of changing combinations. Implicitly, Marcuse indicates five possible relations of the three versions of the theory.

1. Some Soviet Marxist revisions of classical Marxism are required by the historical changes of its object, above all world capitalist development. These revisions are accepted by critical theory and indeed they parallel in many respects the innovations of critical theory in the thirties and beyond.

2. Other Soviet Marxist revisions of classical Marxism are rejected by critical theory because they (at least temporarily) help the consolidation of a new form of (still?) antagonistic society.

3. There are areas of continuity between Soviet Marxism and classical Marxism rejected by critical theory either because of their self-deceptive quality vis-à-vis capitalism or because of their apologetic aspects vis-à-vis Soviet society.

4. There are also areas of continuity among classical Marxism, Soviet Marxism and critical theory, especially on the level of utopian concepts (Communism) and the distinction between real and empirical interests.

5. The three theories relate to one another as successive levels of immanent criticism that imply the critical appropriation of bourgeois ideology by classical Marxism, of bourgeois ideology and classical Marxism by Soviet Marxism, and of all three by critical theory.

I would like to examine the relationship of the three types of theory in Marcuse's presentation before examining the question of the *completeness* of his critique of Soviet society. In his characteristic conception, revision belongs to the essence of orthodoxy in Marxian theory. In a manner more satisfactory than Lukács, who rather ambiguously claimed that orthodoxy could be preserved on the basis of the application of the classical dialectical method, a practice that in the face of changing realities might leave behind all doctrinal substance, Marcuse insisted that

> The dialectical-historical structure of Marxian theory implies that its concepts change with a change in the basic class relationship at which they aim—however in such a way that the new content is obtained by unfolding the elements inherent in the original concept, thus preserving theoretical consistency and even the identity of the concept.[59]

Thus orthodoxy is compatible with revisionism if the original concepts are simultaneously negated and preserved. It is clear in Marcuse's presentation that *Soviet Marxism* to an important extent satisfies such a criterion. Above all this is the case with respect to the evaluation of the development of capitalism and its supposed agent of revolutionary transformation, the proletariat. In this context, the similarity, although not identity, of views between what Marcuse presents as Soviet Marxism and critical theory, especially of the 1930s, is rather striking.[60] First of all, both have registered the unexpected stability of late monopoly capitalism. Not only do they largely agree concerning the features of the new stage of capitalist development—governmental regulation of competition, monpolization, imperialism and even "the restriction or outright abolition of the democratic process, of civil and political liberties"—but Soviet Marxism, behind its orthodox desire to maintain the faith in the dramatic instability of this supposedly last stage of capitalist development ("state monopoly capitalism"), has in fact reconciled itself (as, of course, did critical theory) to the long-range perspective of the survival of this stage.[61] One of the keys to this stability is the neutralization of "the subjective factor," of the industrial proletariat, which critical theory has understood since the late 1930s as integrated, primarily because of the confluence of an increasingly economistic form of trade unionism and the ability of late capitalism to manipulate and satisfy the material wants of the organized sectors of the working class.

Soviet Marxism too has "adjusted itself to the factual situation" and has "put the Western proletariat on ice," at least until its supposed reactivation as "a revolutionary force," ultimately necessary again because of the canons of orthodoxy, which cannot be given up.[62] Of course, for Soviet Marxism, the revision of the classical doctrine of proletarian revolution was conditioned by a conception never fully accepted by critical theory: the shift of the context of world revolution to "the weakest link" in the world capitalist system, that is, Russia and more generally the East, and the corresponding emergence of the "external proletariat," that is, the peasant masses of the East, as a historical "subject."[63] The last quotation marks are supplied by Marcuse, because unlike the Soviet Marxists, he does not believe that the external proletariat is a revolutionary subject in the Marxian sense. According to him, the characteristic feature of all Leninism is "the shift in the revolutionary agent from the class-conscious proletariat to the centralized party as the avant garde of the proletariat," in other words, precisely the substitution never recognized by Marx and Engels.[64]

Here we apparently come to a feature of the Leninist revision of Marxism which Marcuse would condemn as a way of turning the theory into a source of legitimation for a new form of domination. Indeed, he is quite aware of the fact that substitutionism necessarily implies a situation in which dictatorship would be not of but over the proletariat. Nevertheless, his presentation ultimately represents a form of justification for this dictatorship, an acceptance at least of its historical even if no longer contemporary necessity. Marcuse, to begin with, accepts the premise of critical theory from the 1930s (later abandoned by Horkheimer and Adorno) that a new form of domination and subordination (even a terroristic one!) may be progressive if it initiates a new stage of development of the productive forces.[65]

However, his notion of liberated society was hardly exhausted by that of "electrification." Even the development of the productive forces is progressive, in his conception, only if it provides the foundations for a society in which the associated producers, free as individuals to satisfy their many-sided needs, control and dispose over the system of production itself. While substitutionism could easily be seen as the motor of industrialization in a backward country, Marcuse too cannot fully hide the strong possibility indicated by Franz Neumann, according to which a preparatory dictatorship might become a permanent one.[66] Evidently, however, Marcuse accepts the notion of a preparatory or educational dictatorship. He presents without criticism the Leninist development of the Marxian doctrine distinguishing between the immediate or empirical and the real or historical interests of the working class, originally a perception of the difference between the consciousness of the proletariat and theoretical analysis of the proletariat (1950), according to which the true interest (Lenin) and true consciousness (Lukács) of the proletariat could be "lodged in groups different from the majority of the proletariat," that is, the "centralistic organization." On an abstract level at least, this doctrine represents the main feature of identity, in his conception, among Soviet Marxism, classical Marxism, and critical theory. To be sure, the Soviet use of the distinction between immediate and real interests seeks to square the circle: It indicates how a dictatorship over the proletariat could nevertheless be of the proletariat.

Such sophistry is, in fact, avoided by Marcuse. But essential to his own doctrine are the intellectual immaturity and false needs of the members of all contemporary societies, factors that may make an educational dictatorship unavoidable. An educational dictatorship *over* workers (and peasants) retains its validity if it initiates processes that permit the spiritual development of its objects *and* establishes factors that block the way toward personal dictatorship. Marcuse, though extremely cautiously, does on balance postulate that the Soviet system has inhibited such processes (the end of internalization in the psychological sense), and has established such factors (national property, plan, terror, modern technology).

Nevertheless, Marcuse is quite insistent that the Soviet use of Marxism also reveals some extremely negative tendencies. These are expressed both through certain revisions of some doctrines, the direct application of some doctrines to a reality to which they are not applicable, and a rigid, ritualistic adherence to the body of doctrines as a whole. While Marcuse accepts the historical inevitability of the project of socialism in one country, whose Leninist origins he justly notes, he does strongly criticize the importation of nationalistic elements into Soviet Marxism.[67] Furthermore, he accepts no compromise in the area of social utopia: Both the idea of the continuation and even strengthening of the state under "communism,"[68] and the replacement of "the abolition of labor" by the formula of the generalization and glorification of labor in a communist society are seen by him as signs of some self-perpetuating tendencies in the present system of labor and domination.[69] The element of legitimating the existing Soviet reality, hence stabilizing it and guarding it from necessary internal challenges, is even stronger in the opposite procedure: Soviet Marxism not only revises certain elements of the Marxian utopia in an authoritarian direction, but also applies some utopian concepts to its own authoritarian reality. In particular Marcuse stresses here the notions of the abolition of alienation[70] and nonantagonistic contradiction,[71] in themselves orthodox, but when falsely applied to a nonsocialist society they involve the removal of the ground "from under the protest against a repressive organization of labor," and the elimination, or rather veiling, of all elements that might indicate progress beyond the established social order. The issue is somewhat more complex, however, because the theoretical adherence of Soviet Marxism to the whole body of classical Marxian doctrines, some of which, like the necessary instability of contemporary capitalism, and the revolutionary character of its proletariat, are in practice abandoned. Others, like the already mentioned end of alienation and antagonistic contradictions, violate everyday empirical experience of everyone in Soviet society. One must therefore explore how this contradiction is resolved. On the other hand, one must consider the consequences of this preservation of classical Marxism.

Marcuse does not actually tell us the reason for the doctrinaire and rigid commitment of the ruling party to Marxism; he indicates merely that it exists, that it is not merely a veil for other more mundane conceptions like the will to power, and that it is maintained and publicized at considerable potential cost to the holders of power.[72] We are left to surmise that the reason for this commitment has to do with an actual belief on the part of the rulers or even more a principle of identity, of self-identification. Be that as it may, in general these ideas "can be reconciled with reality only by a great expenditure of physical and intellectual force." The challenge is met on the level of empirical social science (especially when dealing with capitalism), by an Aesopean use of doctrine that subtly admits between the lines that the doctrines are no longer applicable, and in fact are no longer applied in practice. On the more difficult level of normatively charged theory, however, there cannot be even the minimum admission that the Marxian conception of socialism (i.e., the first stage of Communist society) is not applicable to the Soviet Union. Accordingly, the actual society is defined as identical with the prescriptions of the doctrine, which in turn necessarily loses its original relationship to social criticism, and even more significantly, truth itself. The doctrines become little more than instrumental directions for action; their language replaces the communicative dimension with magic.[73] While even in this context Marcuse seeks to assimilate Soviet Marxism to something like the Lukácsian philosophy of praxis (unwillingness to submit to the power of facts,[74] the criterion of truth is the ability to help realize what is stated[75]) in effect he winds up providing only a devastating criticism of Lukácsian theory itself to the extent that it anticipated the Stalinist destruction of theoretical reason.

Although Marcuse does nothing to disguise the tendency of Soviet Marxism to decline from genuine theory to a form of magic, he nonetheless shows a good deal of understanding for the origin of this state of affairs, that in his opinion contains the seeds of a reversal and a renewal. "The new form of Marxian theory corresponds to its new historical agent—a backward population which is to become what it 'really is': a revolutionary force which changes the world."[76] This claim is certainly a substandard one, since given the depiction of the theory as magic that manipulates its objects to action, it is very hard to see how these objects can be characterized as a "historical agent," and in particular, how they can become "for themselves" what the theory (falsely) claims they really are.

A second argument of Marcuse is more in line with his overall perspective: "The absurdity of Soviet Marxism has an objective ground: it reflects the absurdity of a historical situation in which the realization of the Marxian promises appeared—only to be delayed again—and in which the new productive forces are again used as instruments for productive repression."[77] Accordingly, Marxian theory is applied by an elite that believes in it under conditions when it cannot yet be true. Such a (false) application, however, according to Marcuse, can help bring about a condition when it will be true. This is especially the case because even "the ritualized language preserves the original content of Marxian theory,"[78] and under some conditions at least, we are to understand that this original content could once again recover its critical dimension vis-à-vis existing reality.

Clearly, this can happen in the overall conception only if the initial "absurdity of the historical situation" is overcome in a context in which the ruling institutions have not yet developed a rigid mechanism of self-perpetuation. I have already indicated my dissatisfaction with Marcuse's derivation of a smooth, necessary logic of the emergence of a higher developed and liberalized stage of Soviet society, and his deemphasis of the tendencies of this type of social system to reproduce its repressive institutional framework. Thus the preconditions of the reemergence of the critical dimensions of institutionalized Marxism are certainly not automatically produced. But assuming that the development of a new stage of Soviet society, a stage in which the ruling party-state institutions renounce the totalitarian penetration of society and culture, is at least objectively possible, the realization of this possibility would come to depend on the emergence of a critical consciousness dedicated to social change. In Marcuse's theory, this consciousness can emerge only in the context of the release of the critical potentials of the only form of social integration he discusses, Marxist intellectual culture. Given the ultimate weakness of his analysis of the "objective factor," all the more weight thus falls on the "subjective," whose logic is presumably anticipated by the immanent critique of Soviet Marxism.

But is an immanent critique of Soviet Marxism possible? The question is ambiguous, because while Marcuse's own work takes on the form of such a critique, this in itself does not indicate that such a critique can take place within the framework of Soviet society and culture.[79] After all, the Western critic, who can address Soviet politics directly, has at his disposal other Marxisms, classical and critical theory, which aid him in the recovery of moments of truth, deeply submerged (if there at all) in the ritualized and dogmatic Soviet Marxist canon. Are these moments genuinely reconstructible within Soviet society? Can there be a dynamic of Soviet society that would reduplicate the movement of concepts in Marcuse's critique?

Marcuse's own answer to these questions is profoundly ambiguous. On the one hand, he repeatedly portrays Soviet Marxism as incorporating immanent critique into its own methodology.[80] Marcuse depicts the method in the following manner: "to assume the validity of the adversary's ideas and objectives, to accept them, as it were, and to show that they are unrealizable within the theoretical and social framework in which the adversary operates."[81] On the other hand, Marcuse suggests that "the promulgation and indoctrination in Marxism may still turn out to be a dangerous weapon for the Soviet rulers."[82] This is because the use of the Marxian philosophy of history to justify divergences between reality and ideology, in the context of the actual developments of Soviet society, may cause a continuation of an older level of repression to appear irrational by the regime's own standards.

But may not changes in the content and structure of ideology remove this dangerous potential? Curiously enough, the above-cited lines of Marcuse's text refer back to the analysis of an earlier chapter, which in fact does not quite say what Marcuse later seemed to think.[83] Here Marcuse depicts only the explosive potential of the (genuine) ideological expression of unfulfilled individual interests. The justification of the new economic bases that presently require great renunciation as the way toward the total liberation of man under Communism keeps the critical dimension of this utopia in view. He also argues, however, that the regime will undertake a "life and death struggle against ideological transcendence," and will seek on all levels to deprive theory, art, and philosophy of their critical power. Several paragraphs indicate that this struggle has been or will be more or less successful. Marxian theory under Soviet conditions has certainly no longer the function, according to Marcuse, of being the lever that will break "determinism [the perpetuation of repression by and in the underlying population itself] and free the subjective factor, that is, the class consciousness of the proletariat."[84]

In *One-Dimensional Man* (1964), this argument is made even more generally, in reference to all potential opposition:

> the authoritarian transformation of the Marxist into the Stalinist and post-Stalinist language . . . leave[s] no time and no space for a discussion which would project disruptive alternatives. This language no longer lends itself to "discourse" at all. . . . The productive growth of the established Communist society also condemns the libertarian Communist opposition; the language which tries to recall and preserve the original truth succumbs to ritualization.[85]

Critique of Ideology and of the Spirit of Soviet Society

While *Soviet Marxism* was hardly as negative as *One-Dimensional Man* concerning Soviet developmental possibilities, its own doctrine of the transformation of ideology in fact anticipated the thesis of a one-dimensional intellectual universe. The anticipation, however, was counterweighed by a rather anomalous version of the Frankfurt thesis (and his own) of the decline of the individual (and of internalization), according to which the dialectics of repressive Soviet morality point in an emancipatory direction. The possibility of an immanent critique of Soviet Marxism in the fullest possible sense, in fact, rests on the theoretical outcome of Marcuse's juxtaposition of the simultaneous decline of genuine ideology, and of the internalization of morality.

The thesis of "the end of ideology" was born in particular to describe the exhaustion of Communist ideas and of intellectuals in the West. To be sure, Daniel Bell's conception involved a somewhat uncertain bringing together of two entirely different conceptions of ideology—Mannheim's "total conception," which was originally a perfectly general category describing comprehensive forms of consciousness ascribed to *all* forms of social existence (Bell restricts this to social movements), and the peculiar combination of chiliastic and instrumentalist use of ideas that characterized what the Communist movement (and some of its opponents) came to refer to as its "ideology." Nevertheless, he did perceive important changes in the intellectual culture of the West, whose positive side indeed involved the decline of the intellectual culture of the old left, even if the negative side of the same process largely disregarded by Bell came to mean—for a significant period at least—the decline and/or functionalization of *all* oppositional thought: Marcuse's "one-dimensional thought."

While not receptive to Bell's formula, the Frankfurt theorists—first Adorno, then Marcuse, and finally in the most comprehensive manner, Habermas—worked out their own versions of "the end of ideology" thesis. For the moment I will focus only on Adorno's conception, which I believe directly influenced *Soviet Marxism*. Adorno rejects the simplistic Marxian view (cited by Bell) according to which ideology is the expression of particular interests. Such is the case for "ideas" only when genuine ideologies, bodies of ideas with truth content, are replaced by an ultimate appeal to sheer force. Ideologies in the real sense of the word are two dimensional, their truth content is based on a necessity to "justify," through "rational argumentation," an order of things in need of justification. "Accordingly, the critique of ideology, as the confrontation of ideology with its own truth, is possible insofar as the ideology contains a rational element."[86] Ideologies thus conceived are "true in themselves," but become false when they "present themselves as already realized."[87] Ideologies exist when "something spiritual emerges from the social process." With Marx, Adorno refers to the falsity of ideologies, based on illusions of independence, but against Marx when he insists on an aspect of truth that "adheres to this independence" when consciousness seeks to transcend its societal preconditions. The critique of ideology preserves this truth on a cognitive level by reflecting on it and its relationship to society, and on a normative level when justifiable claims are turned against a reality that they in fact contradict.

According to Adorno, in contemporary society, both totalitarian and late capitalist, the traditional concept of ideology as well as the critique of ideology lose their subject matter. In totalitarian societies (including the Soviet Union) so-called "thought" (i.e., propaganda) is a mere instrument of power, which no one "ever believed or expected to be taken seriously."[88] This type of thought functions because of its hidden appeal to naked power. It glorifies this power, and is its "threatening face" rather than a veil. Under totalitarian conditions, the critique of ideology should be replaced by analyses of *both* the interests behind this power,[89] and the "human dispositions" that make others submit against their interests and without illusions.[90] Adorno extends these insights (won from the study of the mass psychology of fascism) to the capitalist mass democracies. "The anthropological changes to which totalitarian ideologies are tailored" are due to "the structural changes of society,"[91] the "crisis of bourgeois society."[92] What was once ideology is now the product of "planned and administered control" and not of the "autonomous spirit." In such a context, the critique of ideology retreats to self-critical, illusionless, but esoteric and important forms of truth (postauratic art and negative philosophy) and the critique of mass culture, the milieu in which the molding and constraining of mass consciousness takes place.[93] But in neither case can critique be an immanent confrontation of truth claims and the necessary falsehood that attaches to them. "Ideology" and "reality" converge: The "new ideology hardly says anything more than that things are the way they are . . . and could not be otherwise," and "reality becomes its own ideology."[94]

Undeniably, both *Soviet Marxism* and *One-Dimensional Man* are strongly influenced by this train of thought in Adorno. The linking of totalitarianism and mass democracies, on one level at least, is common to both of them. But unlike Adorno, Marcuse, however ambiguously, holds on to the possibility of the immanent critique of at least one totalitarian ideology, namely Soviet Marxism. This is all the more surprising because he depicts the change of the structure and function of Marxism as an ideology, its loss of rational discursive substance exactly in Adorno's sense. Marcuse faces a new problem, one that Adorno never faced, namely, the critique of Marxism itself as an ideology. In this respect Adorno's quick identification of Hitler, Mussolini, and Zhdanov forgets the demonstrable connection between Soviet Marxism and classical Marxism as well as critical theory, which as we have seen is the real basis of Marcuse's own immanent critique. However falsely, Soviet Marxism affirms its connection to values shared by both Adorno and Marcuse, and its concepts preserve, in however few contexts, some empirical claims to truth. Whatever the truth otherwise of the totalitarian thesis that Adorno seems to accept, in this context at least, there is no comparison between National Socialist and Soviet ideology. However this may be, Marcuse's relative justification to undertake immanent critique is undercut by its results. Precisely because the Marxist canon which the Soviets enshrine contains some truth claims dangerous to the system, the potential basis of internal challenges that could reduplicate and incorporate the movement of criticism in social movements, the status of this ideological whole has to be altered. What was a body of concepts representing the critique of ideology is thus translated into a ritualized canon that is no longer ideology. Even more, a bitter struggle is waged against all forms of ideological transcendence in art and philosophy—that is, two-dimensional thought, in the later terminology.

Marcuse explicitly takes up the Frankfurt thesis on the context and decline of ideology that he shares with Adorno in relation to Soviet society. His conception reveals that characteristic confusion of cognitive and normative conceptions of truth that marked all critical theory up to but no longer including Habermas. Ideology in the "classical" sense is defined as "necessary illusion" combining truth and falsehood. Truth in the first sense is cognitive "depiction" or "reflection" of social reality, false only in the sense that a historicist, transient, contingent order is seen as eternal, unchangeable, necessary. This is the Lukácsian side of Marcuse's definition, somewhat but not completely downplayed by Adorno. The characteristic Frankfurt shift of the latter involves a move to the second, normative level, where notions "true" in themselves—in particular, freedom, justice, and humanity—become false only as they are presented as already realized in an unfree, unjust, and inhuman reality.

Marcuse gives this side its full due: Images of justice, happiness, liberty, equality, and security have been historically preserved in the ideological spheres of religion, philosophy, and political theory, even if the intellectual misrepresentation of the real connection of these ideas to a social structure that violates them has made these spheres supports of established social order. As the statement reveals, Marcuse does not adequately distinguish the level of normative contradictions within ideologies with the cognitive one, that of ideology as containing true norms that are unrealized, and that of ideology as partly true, partly false cognitive expression or depiction of its own social reality. While the idea of cognitive misrepresentation of unrealized norms *as* realized is, of course, the link between the two levels, in the case of actual ideological complexes such as religion on the one hand and political economy on the other, either the normative or the cognitive level of concern obviously dominates. Marcuse's analysis of Soviet Marxism is in fact far better understood if one separates these levels. In the process, a characteristic distinction between the ideological context of the Soviet Union and the West emerges, a distinction that Marcuse needs to support his project of immanent critique in the context of the Frankfurt thesis concerning "the end of ideology." Instead of solving the contradiction between the two perspectives, immanent critique and end of ideology thesis (which amounts to that between critical theory of the 1930s and of the period after *The Dialectic of*

Enlightenment), he manages to reproduce the antinomy *within* his conception of Soviet Marxism as ideology. In turn, the political consequences of each side are developed in *Soviet Marxism* and *One-Dimensional Man* respectively.

On one fundamental level, in Marcuse's conception, *Soviet Marxism* is an ideology in the classical sense, falsely presenting itself as "the realization of reason," as the overcoming of the antinomies between "subject and objective" reason, between individual and society, particular and common interests, "is" and "ought."[95] The gap between these true (for Marcuse) norms and actual Soviet reality is so great that only the total surrender of the *cognitive* truth claims of all classical ideologies preserves the established order from explosive challenges. This is the first meaning of the "end of ideology" under Soviet conditions, with the obvious already mentioned consequence that entirely immanent critique of Soviet Marxism cannot satisfy the empirical-analytical claims of theory construction regarding Soviet society. Truth claims in Soviet Marxism are replaced by "prophetic" or instrumental directives to action, distinction between true and false is obliterated, sentences are uttered as parts of an ideological *ritual*, language reverts to magic. Paradoxically, however, the destruction of the cognitive ideological level, according to Marcuse, allows the preservation of the full original content of Marxian theory and its communication to a backward population. The ritualization of this theory *contains* its explosive potential in both senses of the word: On the one hand, in the face of a contradictory reality its force is suspended; on the other hand, the normative dimensions of a theory contradicting Soviet reality are preserved. Here the consequence is the preservation of an object domain for immanent critique that remains relevant, even if in a state of suspension, to a potential *crise de conscience* revolving around the unsatisfied claims of liberating norms.

We should note that if one were to accept both the general Frankfurt thesis concerning the decline of ideology in all contemporary mass society, and Marcuse's special claims concerning Soviet ideology, a characteristic difference emerges between the ideological situation in the West and that in the East. Celebrating the power of facts,[96] of the factually established, "bourgeois" ideologies have no reason to cognitively misrepresent *reality* except in the classical sense of blocking access to historicity, to alternatives. Here ideologies are deprived of their force, and critique of its object, by the systematic elimination of normative, contrary-to-fact elements from social science, for example, a dogmatic attachment to a classical ideology par excellence with powerful utopian elements. *Soviet Marxism* cannot follow this approach; instead, it blocks access to its own cognitive dimension. Herein lies the reason for the often noted subversiveness of independent empirical social research under Soviet conditions. In Marcuse's conception, however, the focus remains on those forms of cultural transcendence that could *reactivate* the contradiction between norm and reality. Whereas in the West, in the context of administered mass culture, the retreat of critical truth into the esoteric realms of art and philosophy means alienation from the possibility of action,[97] in the Soviet Union, ideological transcendence in the form of art and philosophy, in the context of Soviet Marxism as "the background ideology," becomes "a political factor of the utmost significance."[98] This argument, if valid, would begin to explain not only the high level of administrative coercion in art and the humanities in the Soviet Union, but also the historically crucial role of artistic and humanistic intellectuals as dissidents.

To be sure, Marcuse's argument with respect to the normative contradiction of Soviet Marxism as an ideology is itself antinomic. While ritualization preserves the full normative content of Marxism, other social processes deeply endanger it. Soviet Marxism not only shares the "characteristic of the present stage of civilization,"[99] that "the progressive notions of ideology are deprived of their transcendent factor," and that the *relative* independence of ideology from "established social needs" is increasingly canceled. The direct organization of the productive apparatus by the state, and the consequent unification of "the superstructure" and the base *means* also the assimilation of the superstructure to the base, excluding, as a result, all "functions which transcend and are antagonistic to the base."[100] In historical materialistic language, this argument is suspiciously like that of liberals like Hayek and Mises, who identify "economic freedom" and political and cultural freedom (and their loss) on the *logical* level. Nevertheless, empirically speaking, in relation to the Soviet Union, the argument is convincing. The authoritarian state that has finalized its form by becoming the one monopolistic firm of the national economy has indeed had the power and the will to fully monopolize all other realms of the production as well, for example, culture.

The reason for this, however, may not be so much the fusion of base and superstructure (which on the level of the fusion of economics and politics need not mean the disappearance of independent culture, and on the level of the fusion of all three spheres describes the process rather than explains it). It may have more to do with the internal dynamics of Marxism, when an ideology of an authoritarian order operates in context not only of the politization of the economy, but of society itself. Marcuse does not deal with the general problem of the politicization of society and the desire to exclude all forms of life, including culture, that can be the bases of independent challenges to the regime. Nevertheless, through the special medium of art, he takes up one aspect of the problem.

In both Adorno's[101] and Marcuse's[102] conceptions, the more the traditional realms of ideology are manipulated, coordinated by administration, "the more the ideological sphere which is remotest from the reality (and philosophy) becomes the last refuge for the opposition to this order." But only in the Soviet Union does this mean "a life-and-death struggle for the regime."[103] In the West, the culture industry either cannot or need not (or both) conquer these last brittle outposts of cultural autonomy. The unfulfillment and repulsion of the needs of the population are potentially more explosive under Soviet conditions than in the

West because here "the new economic basis is propagandized as insuring the total liberation of man under Communism." The immense contradiction is suspended by the ritualization of an ideology that would otherwise point to it, help "release" it. However, this suspension would be itself suspended by the demystifying power of critical art; the norms of the ideology might recover their motivating power under the impact of the utopian dimensions of genuine art whose cognitive functions may furthermore palpably recall the gap between norm and reality. Here is a fundamental difference between Soviet Marxism and technology and science as "background ideologies."[104] The Soviet regime must struggle against artistic transcendence and establish the humanistic/artistic fields as fully administered ones. But in the process, the ritualization of ideology itself seems to turn from a preservation to an abolition of critical controls. The dialectic of critical concepts seems successfully blocked. The conclusion of *One-Dimensional Man*, at least, seems to follow this logic. Here, the authoritarian ritualization of discourse is not presented in any sense as vitiated in the case of Marxian thought itself, which becomes, rather, the most striking example of the deformation of language.[105] The same leadership of the unified apparatus defines the requirements of industrialization, as well as right and wrong, true and false more generally. The desire to exclude the emergence of alternatives means that the very sphere of discourse is obliterated. In the process, a libertarian, Communist opposition becomes impossible; Marxian language fully "succumbs to its ritualization." Not only on the cognitive but also on the normative level, classical ideology thus comes to an end in Soviet society. Immanent critique is deprived of its object.

If *Soviet Marxism*, a work of immanent critique of Soviet society, did not draw this pessimistic, in part false conclusion, it was because of its peculiar conception of the spirit of "socialism" and its dialectic. If the chances of successful immanent critique were lessened by trends common to all industrial societies, and in the Soviet Union by the ritualization of Marxism, Marcuse seemed to believe that the Marxian ideology was nevertheless more resistant to such trends than liberalism, and even more importantly that its semantic potentials were somehow reinforced on the level of social psychology. This train of thought was to be the weakest in *Soviet Marxism*. Specifically, Marcuse seemed to believe, or at least so he said in this book, that the end of individuality in the traditional sense, as well as the end of the internalization of values had potentially liberating consequences under Soviet conditions. But in making this argument he was forced to violate the whole spirit of the Frankfurt critique of the decline of the subject that at all stages informed his own work.

According to Marcuse, the establishment of a repressive work ethic in the Soviet Union proceeded according to a different logic than in the West. Historically, he claims, the destruction of the private sphere as well as of the negative rights of the individual protecting this sphere create an entirely new context for Soviet morality.[106] What used to concern the individual in a separate, isolated social sphere is now externalized; all that was private becomes public.[107] Since in Soviet society, with the abolition of private property, privacy supposedly has no experiential content, its abolition is, astonishingly enough, declared not to be in itself oppressive, as it would have been under liberalism.[108] Totalitarianism is thus somehow its own justification. The only thing wrong with the elimination of the private seems to be that the public here is not a true *res publica* or a *polis*, but an oppressive state.[109] Marcuse, however, seems to show no regret for the loss of some of the most important protections against such a state. This is so because, according to him, even if the new, externalized ethic does serve as the instrument of the state, it has its own independent "momentum" as well.[110] With the diminishing of terror, the Soviet regime, in order to perpetuate its system of domination, would like to imitate the traditional bourgeois mechanism of internalization. Such internalization would lend dynamism to the reproduction of domination even when this has become superfluous from the material point of view. But, having eliminated the private sphere, having abrogated the foundations of traditional individuality, the Soviet regime, according to Marcuse, cannot count on internalization. Introjection of repressive values does not produce genuine internalization because "the 'human material' with which Soviet ethics works militates against a mere repetition of the process of 'bourgeois ethics.' "[111] Only given a separation of the individual from the state and the means of coercion, only with the existence of a developed private sphere does renunciation take the form of internalization. Under direct forms of state repression, and without a sphere where this can be psychodynamically reduplicated as self-repression, there is neither the need nor the possibility of repeating the patterns of Western ego formation. While in the West the ego declines under the impact of the abolition of the family and the rise of mass culture, the Soviet citizen does not become an individual in the first place.

I cannot here comment on the accuracy of this rather questionable speculative and undifferentiated description, but deal only with its supposed consequences. On the one side Marcuse admits that the argument has the implication that the weakening of internalization "impairs social cohesion and the depth of morality." This empirically plausible insight, however, is allowed to dangle in the text, without theoretical consequences. On the other side, in this analysis the weakening of the normative seems to foster in the Soviet population a purely cognitive-rational orientation with respect to social demands. Therefore, when the objective forces of production attained and the international situation would allow a relaxation of work discipline and repression, its continuation would have to appear completely irrational to the Soviet citizen. No internal psychic mechanism would call for the perpetuation of renunciation.[112] Whereas bourgeois internalization makes the individual morally "shockproof" toward the continuation of superfluous domination, surplus repression, the noninternalized Soviet ethic cannot produce such a shockproofing. Presumably, then, all that is needed for liberation under Soviet conditions is the dramatic development of the forces of production, the famous "catching up and overtaking." Through such complicated argument Marcuse manages to reconnect to a dogmatic premise of vulgar Marxism which needed neither critique of ideology nor analysis of morality to make its economic deterministic claims. The failure of the whole Soviet model of economic development never allowed a testing of this preposterous claim. But without such economic development, the theory, even if it were right on the level of social psychology, would have very different consequences than the one maintained by Marcuse. It would seem that without attaining an economic level capable of a dramatic reduction of work time and labor discipline, neither the repressive component of Soviet ethics nor the dissolution of normative ties and solidarities noted by Marcuse could ever be vitiated, within the terms of his own argument.

But the argument is wrong in its own terms, on the level of social psychology and sociology of morality. Here I can argue this point only by immanent criticism, namely confronting Marcuse's claims with some rather fundamental assumptions of his own school of thought. Indeed, it is extremely difficult to understand how Marcuse could permit himself simply to disregard in the Soviet context what the Frankfurt School and Marcuse himself wrote elsewhere on the decline of the individual subject and the end of internalization. While in the 1930s the emphasis of the Frankfurt school on the whole was on the link of the paternalistic, bourgeois family with an authoritarian character structure,[113] their analyses of both mass culture and of fascist movements in the 1940s convinced them that new and more destructive forms of authoritarianism and mass aggression are tied up with the decline of this type of family. From Horkheimer's 1941 essay "The End of Reason" to *The Dialectic of Enlightenment*, the Frankfurt writers repeatedly stressed that the end of private property and liberal competition deprive the classical bourgeois family of its economic foundations. This phenomenon was associated with the shriveling up of the whole private sphere and the end of the authority of the father. The latter is replaced by new agencies of socialization—the peer group, the statized system of education, and especially mass culture. In such a context the Freudian theory of identity formation, stressing the internalization of the norms of society through the intermediary of the father, has become obsolete. This is the point picked up by Marcuse in *Soviet Marxism*. But in the most important relevant texts of his tradition, the results of the decline of internalization were never considered beneficial, to say the least. For Horkheimer and Adorno, the free yet unfree individual of the bourgeois epoch is replaced by an atomized being, part of a mass, neither free nor individual, open to manipulation, incapable of resisting power, with a tendency of narcissistic identification with leaders who are no longer in the image of fathers. Instead of being freed cognitively by the end of the normative, such actors become irrational.

Adorno in particular traced Fascist mass movements to a postbourgeois character structure, beyond all internalized morality.[114] In his analysis the end of internalization leads only to psychic impoverishment and the reproduction of both group ties and identities on extremely weak grounds. This situation, prepared by the experience of manipulative mass culture, favors the project of ever more extensive social control. Instead of responding rationally to forms of authority, something that Marcuse's *Soviet Marxism presupposes*, mass individuals with weakened egos are perpetually under psychic threat. Thus they both crave the security the group or the leader can provide, and react irrationally to all threats, real or imagined, to this pseudosecurity. Their very psychic weakness makes them less able to resist even a symbolically weakened authority (a mere "brother") than were bourgeois individuals, who indeed were capable of resisting authority in the name of the father. Identification with a common "ego ideal" of the group makes the objective structure of authority less open to reflection than the internalized, individuated normative structures that constituted the classical superego. The release from the pressure of internalization here follows not the psychoanalytic path of id into ego, which presupposes the existence of an ego capable of (self-)reflection, but an unsublimated externalization of psychic energy.

Adorno and Horkheimer did not apply this analysis to Soviet society, even in its mobilized phase. But there was no reason, theoretical or political, why they would have denied at least its partial applicability. Of course, Marcuse's analysis presupposed the end of the movement phase of Stalinism which would have justified at least some comparisons with fascist movements. Nevertheless, he should have been quite aware of the argument that the phenomena of the weakening of the private sphere, the decline of internalized morality, the replacement of psychic repression of individuals by the management of atomized masses by large apparatuses which he found in the Soviet Union are foundations only for a new form of authoritarian personality, and hardly for a potential reflection concerning the obsolescence of domination. He ought to have realized that the politization of morality involving the abnegation of the individual cannot play the role once assigned to psychoanalysis, whose very presupposition is an individual capable of reflection.

Interestingly enough, in another context dealing with psychoanalysis a few years later Marcuse returned to the classical Frankfurt perspective on the end of the individual.[115] Now the decline of the private sphere and the end of internalization were linked only to the administration and manipulation of masses, without a foreseeable end. The decline of the authority of the father now was seen as giving place to alternative forms of societal conditioning. In turn, the decline of the bourgeois individual was linked to hostility rather than reflection. Instead of ending repression, the society of total administration only repressed it. It is from this concept that Marcuse developed his notion of repressive desublimation.[116] But while this later concept was applied to mass culture under capitalism, the general line of analysis was extended to Soviet society as well. The Soviet Union too had become, tendentially, a *vaterlose Gesellschaft,* whose fulfillment would lead not to the critique of super-fluous domination as he argued before, but to the release of tremendous destruc-tiveness.[117] This does not happen only to the extent that alternative if weaker forms of identification and normalization develop, which, however, are capable of reinforcing existing forms of domination. Neither the end of internalization nor substitute forms of socialization and control are now assigned the role of the genuine liberation of the instincts in the face of irrational authority. Indeed, while Marcuse again affirms the end of the age in which psychoanalysis could uncover the mechanisms of social control through the phenomenon of internal-ization, he nevertheless declares that the only hope today can be based on the insistence of psychoanalysis in taking the point of view of the autonomous individual, its needs, and potentialities.[118]

With this last argument Marcuse's case for the Soviet Union as a society still capable of realizing the utopian promises of Marxism collapses. We have seen that he was able to derive only ambiguous results from arguments having to do with the change of the international context, with internal patterns of develop-ment, and from the supposed fluidity of class structure. Even the assumption most important for his immanent criticism, namely the possibility of turning the claims of Marxism, even Soviet Marxism, against the existing forms of domina-tion, fell victim to the Frankfurt doctrine of the end of ideology in the classical sense. The same thing happened in the case of his incomparably cruder argu-ment concerning the supposed advantages of the destruction of the private sphere, the statization of morality, and the end of the autonomous individual. These features of totalitarian intervention into the psyche (which Marcuse of course recognized as such) could not be turned into preconditions of emanci-pation, at least not within the cadre of critical theory as established by Horkheimer and Adorno.

Thus it would seem that if the older critical theory did not in the end yield a viable understanding and critique of Soviet society, it nevertheless blocked the road to all shameful apologetics. Marcuse's *Soviet Marxism* marked the outer limits in such a direction. As his subsequent works show, in the last minute he was saved by the tradition he never wanted to abandon. But this tradition had no resources to block his alternative line of theorizing in *One-Dimensional Man,* according to which Soviet-type societies and capitalist democracies were simply alternative forms of totalitarian domination. Indeed, the philosophy of history in *The Dialectic of Enlightenment* seemed to favor this line of analysis, which Adorno and Horkheimer were too careful actually to produce on the level of social theory. Marcuse was less careful, both to his credit and to his debit. The price he had to pay for an uncompromising, if not particularly penetrating criti-cism of the Soviet Union in *One-Dimensional Man* was the systematic underval-uation of the elements of freedom, solidarity, and toleration in our own type of society, presupposed by his subsequent influence as a theorist and indeed the whole movement of the 1960s.

Notes

1. *Soviet Marxism* (New York: Columbia University Press, 1958). Marcuse's only rivals were two authors of the "Socialisme ou barbarie" group in France, Cornelius Castoriadis and Claude Lefort, whose positions were in fact far more critical of the Soviet Union than Marcuse's. This feature of their thought eventually projected both authors beyond Marxism, a move Marcuse never was to make. For an evaluation of Castoriadis's relevant work see chapter 7 below.

2. See *Soviet Marxism*, Part II, and the later Preface, and of course *One-Dimensional Man* (Boston: Beacon Press, 1964).

3. On his response to Bahro, see chapter 4 below.

4. It is actually the only work Habermas ever manages to refer to when he claims (wrongly) that critical theory and Western Marxism have done their homework with respect to the Soviet Union. He did this most recently in the essay "Die nachholende Revolution" published in the volume with the same title (Frankfurt/M: Suhrkamp Verlag, 1990). Six chapters of Part I of this book show the falsity of this claim, and indeed more chapters could have been written.

5. This method is extensively discussed by D. Held in his *Introduction to Critical Theory* (London: Hutchinson, 1980); by J. Cohen in *Class and Civil Society: The Limits of Marxian Critical Theory* (Amherst: University of Massachusetts Press, 1982); S. Buck-Morss in *The Origin of Negative Dialectics* (New York: Free Press, 1978); and in my introduction to the section on sociology of culture in *The Essential Frankfurt School Reader* (New York: Urizen Books, 1978).

6. See M. Rakovski (J. Kis and G. Bence), *Toward an East European Marxism* (New York: St. Martin's Press, 1979). The title of this work is a serious mistranslation of the originally published version: *Le Marxisme face aux pays de l'est* (Paris: Savelli, 1978).

7. This is the Lukácsian interpretation of Marcuse's critique of capitalism always presupposed by critical theory.

8. *Soviet Marxism*, pp. 108f, 138f. The claim of socialism for a nonsocialist society is hardly improved (as we will see) by the claim of a partly socialist society ("protosocialism") for one that is not one at all. For the concept of "traditional Marxism" see Postone and Brick in *Sozialforschung als Kritik*.

9. For this point see M. Merleau-Ponty, *The Adventures of the Dialectic* (Evanston: Northwestern University Press, 1973), and Rakovski, *Toward an East European Marxism*.

10. The last alternative is the most consistent with his overall treatment in *Soviet Marxism* and also *One-Dimensional Man*, if for no other reason than that his occasional stress on socialist or capitalist characteristics remains compatible only with this model. Clearly one-sided and wrong is David Lane's reading that places Marcuse exclusively within the "state capitalism" tradition of interpretation. The acceptance of the notion of a "transitional" society does not, however, commit Marcuse to the absurd parallel notion of classical Troskyist interpretation, that of a degenerated worker's state, of what obviously never was, nor is one according to any meaningful criterion.

11. *Soviet Marxism*, p. 134.

12. Ibid., p. xiii.

13. Cf. ibid., pp. 233–44.

14. The position, of course, is ambiguous. "All embracing" (as he notices in 1961) implies technological determinism, and therefore convergence. Hence he redefines the term in such a way that the all-embracing technological process in each case involves the penetration of different political criteria. If this is true, however, the affinity of the two systems remains unexplained.

15. *Soviet Marxism* p. 59; and pp. 235–36.

16. That is, totalitarian in the sense of a comparison to National Socialist Germany, which as we have seen above, even Max Horkheimer, the key figure of the Frankfurt School, at one time found convincing.

17. *Soviet Marxism*, p. 63. The explanation is itself amazing: The term is applied to different social systems and therefore loses its usefulness. But Marcuse himself will eventually apply it to both late capitalism and the Soviet Union!

18. Ibid., p. 67.

19. Ibid., pp. 197.

20. See *One-Dimensional Man*, p. 3: "For 'totalitarian' is not only the terroristic political coordination of society, but also the non-terroristic economic-technical coordination which operates through the manipulation of needs by vested interests. It thus precludes the emergence of an effective opposition against the whole."

21. Eastern Europe is mentioned only once by Marcuse, and only to indicate his fear that the events of 1956 in Poland and Hungary, themselves stimulated by Soviet de-Stalinization, are "likely to slow down and even reverse de-Stalinization in some fields" (*Soviet Marxism*, pp. 158–59). In this context, he not only accepts the legitimacy of a "protective belt" of East European states around the Soviet Union, but makes the rather astonishing claim, already falsified when he made it, that "while liberalization in the Soviet Union rested on the firm base of industrialization and collectivization this was not the case in the East European countries. Industrialization was still at a very backward stage, and the peasantry was not yet effectively coordinated with the national economy and its political institutions." What drivel! I wrote in the margin many years ago. It is amazing that Marcuse could imagine that industrialization and agriculture in the relevant countries were backward by comparison to the Soviet Union. It was utterly irresponsible to talk of collectivization in the neutral terms used here. Absurd as it was to imagine that these countries, unlike the Soviet Union, were not ready for liberalization, it was of course true enough that in many of them this could not be contained within the framework of the existing repressive system. These two very different ideas were apparently identified by Marcuse just as they were by the Soviet leadership, whose views (and implicitly, actions) he rehearses with understanding! These lines are the moral low points of the book. I wonder if Habermas ever noticed them, and if yes, why they did not dampen his periodic enthusiasm for Marcuse's *Soviet Marxism*, which earned only complete silence from other, older members of the school.

22. *One-Dimensional Man*, p. 42.

23. *Soviet Marxism*, pp. 83, and 60–61.

24. In one section only is this contradicted (ibid., p. 161): the Soviet Union can afford both!

25. Of course even this assumption could lead to alternative policies. The Soviet Union could hope to compensate on the geopolitical and military level for its deficiencies as an economic system, or on the other hand seek relaxation of international tensions (as Marcuse noticed for a part of the Khrushchev era) to relieve the pressures against the expansion of consumption and to provide space for economic reforms.

26. *Soviet Marxism*, pp. 63, 134, 138.

27. *One-Dimensional Man*, p. 43.

28. *Soviet Marxism*, p. 225.

29. *One-Dimensional Man*.

30. Ibid.

31. *Soviet Marxism*, p. 241.

32. *Soviet Marxism*, p. 58.

33. Ibid., pp. 59, 235.

34. Ibid., p. vi.

35. Ibid., p. 154.

36. Ibid., p. 159.

37. Ibid., pp. 164–65.

38. Ibid., p. 166.

39. Ibid., p. 172. I do not know what to make of the statement that the trend will involve both "a spread of bureaucracy and its privileges" and "a reduction of the gap between the top strata and the underlying population."

40. Cf. *One-Dimensional Man*, p. 3.

41. Marcuse's overall argument has been, rightly in my opinion, criticized for two opposite failings: technological determinism, i.e., the argument that in all industrial societies there is a *propelling* inexorable trend of technology determining structures and all other levels of social life; and the interpretation of all technology as politically structured (cf. Habermas in "Technology and Science as Ideology").

42. *Soviet Marxism*, p. 236.

43. Ibid., p. 158.

44. *One-Dimensional Man*, pp. 37, 39, 41–43; *Soviet Marxism*, pp. 241ff.

45. *One-Dimensional Man*, p. 43.

46. Ibid., pp. 44–45.

47. Ibid., p. 39.

48. Ibid., p. 37.

49. Cf. M. Postone, "Necessity, Labor, Time," *Social Research*, Winter 1978.

50. To which he never refers, with the exception of a single reference to Deutscher.

51. *Soviet Marxism*, p. 88.

52. Ibid., p. 91.

53. Ibid., p. 171.

54. Ibid., p. 51.

55. Ibid., p. 95.

56. *Or* new structures of selectivity, as I argue in chapter 3 below.

57. Ibid., pp. 95 and 97.

58. *One-Dimensional Man*, p. 44. The alternative Marcuse eliminates by spurious references to "power drive" or "will to power."

59. Ibid., p. 3. These entirely orthodox Hegelian remarks depend on the original concept having all the possible implications, as well as an internal developmental tendency that would be adequate to the changes of the object. As soon as this object is identified with empirical history, something the Marxist, unlike the Hegelian, cannot avoid, the conception turns into a species of theological history.

60. *Soviet Marxism*, p. 14; pp. 35–36. I should stress that I have in mind the Soviet Marxism presented through Marcuse's hermeneutic efforts, since on the face of it there can be no comparison between the sophisticated and original development of Marxian theory worked out by Horkheimer and his colleagues, and the impoverished official doctrine of the Soviet state, which to the end owed most of its form and substance to the works of Stalin. Marcuse, however, fully aware of this difference, seeks to show that buried in the Soviet Marxist canon lie many of the same insights as in critical theory concerning the need to revise orthodox Marxism in the contemporary world (necessarily buried, in his opinion, as long as the regime insists on holding on to the fundamental concepts of Marxism in spite of the difficulties it creates for itself). The dialectic of these concepts leads to a special relation of Soviet Marxism to reality.

61. Ibid., pp. 38–53.

62. Ibid., pp. 55ff.

63. Ibid., p. 20.

64. Ibid., p. 12.
65. Ibid., p. 181.
66. "Notes on the Theory of Dictatorship," in *The Democratic and Authoritarian State* (New York: Free Press, 1958).
67. Ibid., p. 143.
68. Ibid., pp. 85ff.
69. Ibid., pp. 167ff.; 219–20ff.
70. Ibid., pp. 219–22.
71. Ibid., pp. 138–39.
72. Cf. ibid., p. 24, for example.
73. Ibid., pp. 70–73.
74. Ibid., p. 74.
75. Ibid., p. 71.
76. Ibid., p. 73.
77. Ibid.
78. Ibid.
79. Marcuse himself, as we have seen, supplements immanent critique by philosophy of history, and a critical social theory that is in many respects constructed and not immanently unfolded from the categories of Soviet Marxism.
80. Ibid., pp. 187, 209.
81. Ibid., p. 209.
82. Ibid., p. 350.
83. Cf. ibid., p. 250 and chapter 6, especially p. 112. The two texts belong respectively to 1954–55 and 1952–53.
84. Ibid., p. 174.
85. *One-Dimensional Man*, pp. 101–102.
86. "Ideology," in *Aspects of Sociology* [1956] (Boston: Beacon Press, 1978), pp. 189–190.
87. Ibid., p. 198.
88. Ibid., p. 190.
89. Ibid.
90. Ibid., p. 191.
91. Ibid.
92. Ibid., p. 199.
93. Ibid., p. 201.
94. Ibid., pp. 202–203.
95. *Soviet Marxism*, p. 70.
96. Adorno, "Ideology," p. 202.
97. Ibid., p. 199.
98. *Soviet Marxism*, p. 111.
99. Ibid., p. 75.
100. Ibid., p. 109.
101. Ibid., p. 199.
102. Ibid., p. 110.
103. Ibid., p. 112.
104. J. Habermas, "Technology and Science as Ideology," in *Toward a Rational Society* (Boston: Beacon Press, 1971).
105. *Soviet Marxism*, p. 101.
106. Ibid., pp. 192, 196.
107. Ibid., p. 244.
108. Ibid., p. 198.

109. Ibid., p. 246.

110. Ibid., p. 203.

111. Ibid., pp. 236 and 247.

112. Ibid., p. 251.

113. See especially M. Horkheimer, "Authority and Family" (1936), in *Critical Theory* (New York: Herder and Herder, 1972).

114. "Freudian Theory and the Pattern of Fascist Propaganda," in *The Essential Frankfurt School Reader*.

115. "The Obsolescence of the Freudian Concept of Man" (1963), in *Five Lectures* (Boston: Beacon Press, 1970).

116. Ibid., p. 57.

117. Ibid., pp. 54–55.

118. Cf. ibid., pp. 53 and 60–61.

3

Critical Sociology and Authoritarian State Socialism

Jürgen Habermas has demonstrated the possibility in the West of a process of democratization that shows the limits of technocratic rationalization of polity and economy. Moreover, he has done this (however tentatively) while presenting advanced capitalism as a framework of political and cultural instabilities, potentially crisis- and conflict-laden. It is thus that he has reconstructed Marxism as a critical sociology. However, he has not *systematically* addressed the problem of the relationship of a Marxist critical sociology to those societies that use a version of Marxism as their "ideology" of legitimation. While it is not necessarily his task or that of his coworkers to produce a theory of the so-called socialist societies, it is nevertheless fair to ask if those approaches and concepts of his that have universal aspiration contribute to such a *critical* theory. For today most inherited Marxist theory, from Engels and Plekhanov to Lenin and Trotsky (and even Lukács, Gramsci, and Sartre), is either powerless in the face of the Soviet Union and Eastern Europe, or worse even contributes to their legitimation. In this essay I shall attempt to investigate the possible uses of Starnberg critical sociology for the study of these societies.

To begin with, I shall show (part I) that the problem of state-socialist society is not completely absent from Habermas's critical theory. Indeed, it will be possible to derive (part II) the principle of organization of state-socialist society from some clues in his works and those of his colleague, Claus Offe. Next, using concepts from the Starnberg theory of capitalist development, I shall argue (part III) that the inherent crisis tendencies of state-socialist societies can be "managed" in the long run only if, on the level of system integration, there is a transition from a high level of penetration of the social spheres by the political institutional core (positive subordination) to a lower level of penetration (negative subordination). I shall try to show (part IV) that negative subordination is

Reprinted with permission from *Habermas: Critical Debates* (Cambridge, Mass.: MIT Press, 1982), pp. 196–218, 309–11.

possible only if, within the political sphere, a relative "uncoupling" or "disjunctivity" of political and administrative functions can be achieved; but that this disjunctivity can be protected against tendencies threatening the organizational principle of the system only if, on the level of social integration, certain conditions of legitimation are met. Finally, using the Soviet case, I shall claim (part V) that the eclectic ideological mixture promoted in the administered public sphere can perform its function of legitimating the existing system only through some combination of economic success and activation of meanings rooted in the cultural life-world. The activation of meanings has hitherto proceeded in two directions: under the influence of legal development and under the revival of traditions and traditionalism. While the development of legality might threaten the stabilization of the existing organizational principle even on the basis of negative subordination, the process of "retraditionalization" points in a conservative direction: the reinforcement of a relatively high degree of positive subordination. It will be outside the methodological limits of this essay to determine whether a combination of these two tendencies can indefinitely support some version of a "dual state" in the different state-socialist countries.

I

Habermas never *completely* neglected the study of European social formations of the Soviet type. First of all they form, negatively, part of the background against which he has always sought to situate himself. His conception of Marxism (his critique of all objectivism and reductionism, and of the fetishism of technical development) and his concept of *Praxis* as *public* enlightenment and discourse (which led him to a critique of the Leninist-Lukácsian theory of organization) have blocked the way toward two of the major factors necessary for the Soviet-type synthesis: the core ideological and institutional structures. I do believe that this consequence was intended. Furthermore, from the very beginning his reconstruction of Marxism has sought to make possible a thoroughly autonomous treatment of what was formerly relegated to the superstructure (politics and culture), with the unintended consequence that the two other major factors necessary for the genesis and reproduction of Soviet society (the heritage of the bureaucratic state and of cultural traditionalism) could now become accessible to analysis. This means *in principle* a break with those elements of classical Marxist theory which confront the Soviet Union with the bad alternative of unintended apology and theoretical impotence. What I shall try to show is that this openness in principle can be maintained within the framework of Habermas's late social theory, in particular within the context of his crisis theory of advanced societies.

As far as I can tell, the problem of the analysis and evaluation of Soviet and East European societies appears four times in Habermas's work. I should like to indicate these briefly in chronological order.

1. In the important essay "Between Philosophy and Science: Marxism as Critique" (1960) the Russian revolution and the establishment of the Soviet system are characterized as perhaps the most important of four fundamental "facts against Marx"[1] that cannot be interpreted within the "old theory." Since this is Habermas's most extensive statement on the subject, I should like to present all of its points.

   According to Habermas:

   a. The October revolution, having no immediate *socialist* aims, was initiated by a weak proletariat with peasant support, and was directed by "Leninistically schooled professional revolutionaries."
   b. The latter established "a rule of functionaries and party cadres."
   c. On the basis of this rule, Stalin initiated a "socialist revolution bureaucratically from above, by the collectivization of agriculture."
   d. The system was finally stabilized after the Second World War as a world power.
   e. Nevertheless, in the face of postwar capitalist reform the system is at the very most a model for shortening the process of industrialization in developing countries.
   f. This is because its successes in raising the productive forces at a fast rate are outweighed by the periodic regression "from the constitutional rights attained under capitalism to the legal terror of Party dictatorship." Thus the Soviet Union is "far removed from the realization of a truly emancipated society."
   g. However, the development of the productive forces affects the social structure and the apparatus of domination, and a convergence with capitalism on "the middle ground of a controlled mass democracy within the welfare state is not to be excluded." Nevertheless, the Soviet system may possess the means of subverting the danger of all significant social change.
   h. Finally, a Marxist analysis of Soviet Marxism of the stature of, for example, Neumann's *Behemoth* has not yet been undertaken.[2] Marcuse's *Soviet Marxism*, the most extensive work of the Frankfurt School in this area, is not apparently considered as an acceptable alternative.

2. As is well known, in the 1960s and early 1970s Habermas thoroughly criticized and reconstructed the "old theory." What is the place of the Soviet Union in the "new theory" that emerged? The next mention of the problem is a brief but important one. In an extended critique of the technocratic systems theory of Niklas Luhmann,[3] Habermas maintains that a social technology which has no room for practical questions can play an important functional role in bureaucratic socialist societies, as well as capi-

talist societies, in the form of the "justification of the systematic limitation of practically consequential communication." Such an "ideological" role would be especially important because, in *both* forms of industrial society, genuinely ideological forms of legitimation become weaker and weaker as a result of growing system complexity, leading to an increasing legitimation deficit. Here Habermas indicates some steps toward a dynamic social theory, one that he himself only attempts to work out for advanced capitalism. No convergence theory is indicated, but the analysis points to a common possible future of all modern societies: technocracy, though not necessarily a single form of it, since the ideological sphere alone is understood as technocratic.

3.   The next mention of the problem is in *Legitimation Crisis*. It is worth quoting the whole passage:

> I think it meaningful to distinguish four social formations: primitive (*vorhochkulturelle*), traditional, capitalist, post-capitalist. Except for primitive societies, we are dealing with class societies. (I designate state-socialist societies—in view of their political-elitist disposition of the means of production—as "post-capitalist class societies.") . . . The interest behind the examination of crisis tendencies in late- and post-capitalist class societies is in exploring the possibilities of a "post-modern" society—that is, a historically new principle of organization.[4]

Here a few remarks are in order. Vis-à-vis the Soviet Union and Eastern Europe, Habermas seems to choose two strategies (or at least terminologies) simultaneously. On the one hand, he seems to depict them as transitional societies. The description *post*capitalist but not yet postmodern fits in well with the quasi-orthodox idea (supported by Marcuse in *Soviet Marxism*) that some supposed achievements like central planning, state or "public" ownership, and socialist ideological goals put the societies of the Soviet type on the road to socialism/communism, in spite of regressive phenomena (bureaucracy, terror, "bourgeois survivals," or whatever). On the other hand, and this is more important, Habermas seems to present late capitalism and "postcapitalism" as merely two modern forms of class society whose internal dynamics (crisis tendencies) must be analyzed if we are to evaluate the chances not of their convergence in either direction but of a "postmodern," truly emancipated society. This interpretation is supported by the essay "On Social Identity," where the party, along with the nation-state, are rejected as bases of a new and rational social identity for the modern world.[5] We should note here again that Habermas does not go on in *Legitimation Crisis*, even on the most abstract level, to derive either the principle of organization or the evolutionary crisis tendencies of "postcapitalist" societies.

4.   In two essays on the theory of social evolution, "Toward a Reconstruction of Historical Materialism" (1975) and "Historical Materialism and the De-

velopment of Normative Structures" (1976), the problem of the historical place of societies of the Soviet type returns and is posed in terms of a simple theoretical alternative.[6] "Bureaucratic socialism" (the so-called "socialist transitional societies") represents either a higher stage of social evolution than "developed capitalism," or the two are variants of the same stage of development. Here Habermas no longer considers (as he did in 1960) the convergence theory seriously. Nevertheless, it is the second alternative he inclines toward, because this would, according to him, demonstrate that the (late?) capitalist relation of state to economy is not the only possible version of *modern* society; and hence other possible alternatives *within modernity* would be conceivable, in particular a far more democratic one.

While the two societies undoubtedly share an enormous number of common characteristics as industrial-urbanized societies and welfare-warfare states, the theoretical grounds for treating them as two expressions of the same stage of development are doubtful. I am thinking of their specifically different institutional systems, and even more of their entirely "non-simultaneous" levels of legal development. As far as Habermas is concerned, we would be able to regard bureaucratic or state socialism and advanced capitalism in terms of a single evolutionary stage *only* if they could be understood as different expressions of *the same* principle of social organization. Following Adorno and returning to the technocracy argument, he tentatively proposes "the autonomization of instrumental reason" as a possible basis for such a principle. Klaus Eder dispenses with all doubt and asserts that the two formations are indeed two different contemporary expressions of the same developmental stage, one that he calls "society," that is, a social order "that achieves system integration through norms."[7] It seems to me that either of these proposals (aside from their empirical dubiousness) might mean a premature leap to a level of abstraction where the critical social theory of both social formations would become difficult to develop. Without dismissing the potential importance of evolutionary theory for the study of state-socialist societies, it seems to me that an immanent reconstruction (however ideal-typical) of the principle of organization of this social formation—the task of this study—has methodological primacy.

II

A theory of state-socialist social structure that starts out with the concepts elaborated by Habermas and Claus Offe might have several advantages over its most likely theoretical rivals. Unlike all versions of classical Marxism, Habermas and Offe do not assume the primacy of the economic (or any other sphere) in defining social formations and their logic. They have also come to reject all versions of the convergence theory, which amounts to something close to a bourgeois version of historical materialism. Unlike orthodox functionalist and systems-theoretical approaches, they neither treat social integration as merely the normative element of system integration nor do they have a methodological bias for conditions of self-adjustment, equilibrium, and stability. In particular, Habermas's concept of *organizational principle* attempts to map out the limits within which a system remains self-identical, while Offe's concept of *the crisis of crisis management* seeks to show the "limits of staying within those limits." Finally, unlike those who first utilized the social and system integration distinction,[8] Habermas does not dogmatically affirm the absolute primacy of system integration, nor do he and Offe restrict the notions of system and social crisis to conflicts involving global subjects, that is, classes; they do not, in other words, rush into a dogmatic stratification theory that could occlude all further independent analysis.[9]

It is in the pages devoted to the theory of social evolution that Habermas determines the concept of organizational principle in the most sophisticated manner. He defines the concept in *Legitimation Crisis* as the "capacity of society to learn without losing its identity."[10] An organizational principle limits three learning mechanisms in three social spheres: those of productive forces, of identity-securing interpretative systems, and of institutional steering capacities. From the point of view of a general theory of action, these spheres can be reduced to two levels: *social integration*, defined as "the system of institutions in which speaking and acting subjects are socially related," and *system integration*, "the specific steering performances of a self-regulated system." In his later essays we receive an important if slightly altered version of the concept that is even more adequate for our purposes: "Organizational principles of society can be characterized, *in a first approximation*, through the institutional core that determines the dominant form of social integration."[11] That is, social integration, "securing the unity of the life-world through values and norms," is regarded as the primary task of the institutions defining a principle of organization.

We are ready to consider the principle of organization of state-socialist societies. Within the domain of critical sociology, Habermas and Offe present us with two alternatives.

1. According to Habermas, state socialism is political-elitist class rule over a politically constituted but industrial system of social labor.[12] This definition focuses on the fundamental relation of class domination and implies a juridical relationship different from that of capitalism: the absence of "free" labor. If one proceeded from this perspective, one would have to elaborate the symbolic structures of self-identification that provide in this "socialized" society for the anonymization of "class" relations.[13]

2. Following Dahl and Lindblom as well as Etzioni, Offe gives us a three-term typology that allows us to locate "state socialism," as well as late capitalism, among industrial societies, a typology that corresponds to the

three domains of learning proposed by Habermas. Given the possibility of the functional primacy of three social spheres, exchange (economy), coercive relationships (bureaucracy), and political choice (normative structures), Offe defines capitalism as the primacy of exchange economy over bureaucracy and the normative sphere;[14] presumably he would not object if one defined state socialism as the primacy of an administratively or bureaucratically conceived political domain over both the economy and the normative-cultural sphere.

I prefer the version derived from Offe for several reasons. First of all, it is more abstract: It does not define social structure in such a way that one immediately tends to identify structural categories with those of social stratification.[15] As we shall see, it is especially useful to consider stratification in the Soviet-type societies as derivative from the specific institutional mode of domination. Second, Offe's form of the organizational principle clearly locates the three Habermasian spheres of learning under the more conventional names of economy, polity and culture. Although Offe's three-part model certainly suffers, as Habermas noticed, from an underemphasis on social integration, which potentially leads to a screening out of the independent dynamics of the cultural sphere, it nonetheless indicates the institutional core responsible for social integration. The system itself identifies this core as the party, and Offe's concept of bureaucracy as the sphere of coercive relationships points to the same institution. Nevertheless, we must modify these terms if we are to avoid identifying the functional moment of arbitrary and coercive political authority with either bureaucracy, as in the endless Trotskyist and neo-Trotskyist discussions, or even with the formally separate party institution proper (as distinct from the state, secret police, etc.). Following a distinction of Ernst Fraenkel,[16] which partially coincides with Offe's categories, the political element in question should be defined as that of the "prerogative state" (*Massnahmenstaat*), as distinct from the normative state; that is, it is the aspect of the party-state that exercises an arbitrary mode of political action unchecked by any legal limits and guarantees. The party indeed symbolizes and justifies the prerogative function (hence it must be retained as a formally independent institution); but it alone does not exercise this function. Therefore, it is more accurate to speak of the "party-state" as the structure in which the prerogative state is embedded. Accordingly, the organizational principle of state socialism is best defined as that mode of social identity that understands and legitimizes itself as *the domination of the prerogative state over society*. The way in which the organizational principle of state socialism is realized in the three social spheres of the economy, the administrative-normative state and culture is indicated in Table 3.1, along with key principles of legitimation, stratification, and the corresponding theories that have focused on one of the key domains in question.[17]

I cannot discuss here all the elements of this table. I would certainly maintain

Table 3.1

	Economy	State	Culture
Principle of political penetration (system integration)	Industrial-redistributive command economy	Dual state of party and state bureaucracies, fused at the top ("party-state")	Dictatorship over socialization and publicity
Key principles of legitimacy (social integration)	Rational redistribution of social optimum Welfare state	Substantive and formal justice Harmonization of interests of nation, class, or people	Social solidarity Collectivist ethics Empirical interest subordinated to "real" interests Social vs. individual, positive vs. negative freedom
Principle of stratification	(1) Redistributor-redistributed (2) Skills and educational levels of qualification	Hierarchical politocratic orders	Mass society Social atomization Classlessness
Corresponding theories	Managerial and technocratic theories Intellectuals as a new class Historical materialist and convergence theories	Monoorganizational society Bureaucracy as new class Theories of traditional (Russian) political culture	Totalitarianism theory One-dimensionality Dictatorship over needs

that it represents a plausible outline of Soviet and East European societies from the 1930s until the early 1960s, and perhaps including our time as well. In the 1930s, within the state-controlled sector of social life, the penetration and subsumption of economic, political, and cultural moments was already accomplished, but it was only in the cataclysmic formative period of the 1920s (in Eastern Europe in the late 1940s and early 1950s) that the same logic was violently extended to society as a whole. On the other hand, it is undeniable that gradually after the death of Stalin a process of partial yet significant depoliticization was initiated in some of the key social spheres. Since these have everywhere reached one sort of limit or another, we are justified to ask: At what point, if any, can these threaten the principle of organization, in other words the social identity of the system?

III

Using Offe's concepts, I should like to argue that the perhaps ultimately insoluble task of all directed social change in the Soviet Union and Eastern Europe is the replacement of positive subordination (of the cultural and economic spheres to the political) by a negative subordination that nevertheless preserves the original organizational principle, that is, the domination of the political over culture and economy.

Off offers *positive subordination* (for him of culture and politics to the economy, for us of culture and economics to politics) as both the positive contributions and the adjustment of the contents of subsystems to the dominant system, whereas *negative subordination* involves that partial growth of the subsystems to independence while retaining the functional primacy of the dominant system.[18] Habermas indicates the same differentiation in his conception of liberal capitalism, where a single institutional network (the market) takes on both steering and symbolic functions, with these reverting (in part) to different subsystems under late capitalism. Using both of their concepts, the Stalinist system can be understood as one of positive subordination that thoroughly politicizes the social spheres on the basis of the ability of a single institutional network (the party-state) both to control the redistributive-command economy and to mobilize immense reserves (vis-à-vis some strata at least) of revolutionary-charismatic and traditional legitimacy. An entirely new stage of the system would be one based on *negative subordination*, that is, the partial depoliticization of economy and culture and the distribution of steering and symbolic functions among different social spheres. This new stage would be that of the *same* system because it would preserve the functional primacy of a prerogative political sphere that has irrevocably given up its goal of the total penetration of all aspects of life.

Given the socially and politically dangerous overloading of the state sphere under Stalinism with tasks of steering and symbolic self-representation, the problems of administrative and economic rationality greatly endangered the system's "social identity." The first but necessarily temporary response was general terror. When the party was no longer willing or able to use large-scale terror as part of its "social cement," the task of the system became, in abstract terms, to protect its principle of organization from the dangerous linking of deeply embedded steering problems to an increasingly difficult legitimation problem, a protection attempted by the transition to some form of negative subordination of the social spheres to politics. The "motor" of this transition must be clarified before we can examine the possible patterns of negative subordination or "crisis management." Offe and Habermas have repeatedly and convincingly shown that neither voluntaristic nor systems-theoretical conceptions stressing self-regulation and equilibration can adequately account for such a "motor"; neither an agency nor a self-regulating system can account for *both* crisis management and "the crisis of crisis management." Aside from the problem whether such a thing is possible in principle, even Soviet theorists admit that self-regulation is absent from their social and economic system.[19] There is, furthermore, no way of ever showing that the process of self-regulation of a system of mutually dependent parts would protect an organizational principle based on centralization. Such protection must be and is under all state socialism a directed process. *But it is not consciously directed by a social agency*, whether the latter be a "class," an "order," or even the party elite itself.[20] The protection of the system's identity has an active center, namely an institution which is not the instrument of any social agency. While it may appear trivial to assert that this institution is the hierarchically organized party-state, it is less trivial to conceive of this institution as *a selection mechanism* having functional primacy in the system as a whole. From Castoriadis and Lefort to Konrád, Szelényi, and Rakovski, the historically novel unification of the partial bureaucracies of state, economy, and culture by a party has been the touchstone of "neo-" and "post-" Marxist analyses of the Soviet Union and Eastern Europe. It is, however, extremely important to stress (as have all of the interpreters just mentioned) that this unification is a successful one only in the system's ideology, that the societies in question are also the terrain of real and latent conflicts of interest.[21] Hence the concept of *selectivity*, developed by Offe, is more useful than that of unification. The party-state institution has a threefold screening function, in a sense analogous to the functions which Offe assigns to the capitalist state: to protect the existing political structure as a whole against individual bureaucracies; to eliminate the possibility of outside interests penetrating the structure of decision in any form other than their "representation" by bureaucratic sectors; and finally to produce the ideological justifications that disguise the party-state's "unifying" activity—to "screen" its own screening activity even from itself.[22]

Selectivity under state socialism means that the possible "events" that will result in administrative-political action will be drastically narrowed down. This process will be in part arbitrary but in part according to criteria determined by the party-state's factual power to penetrate and repress, its specific value and rule systems, and even more by its desire to protect its monopoly of the selectivity function against all quasi-institutions, groups, strata and elites, not to mention the underlying population itself. This protection, as well as the legitimation of the party-state summit as the ultimate instance of decision, is primarily the function of state ideologies that express in variously scientistic, *ouvrierist* and nationalist terms the one idea that the general and unified social interest is *represented* by this summit or even the "summit of the summit." In this representation, selectivity is veiled by entirely imaginary ideas of unity. The selectivity functions of the party-state must be disguised, veiled, and legitimized unless repression and terror are to replace all other procedures of deliberate action or inaction.

The Soviet system at its most repressive required immense reservoirs of meaning, stemming from its revolutionary heritage, its ability to activate the springs of nationalism, its revival of law, etc., that were subsequently reduced and even compromised by their use. The changing memories of different generations, to whom the symbolic events of past solidarity have no personal meaning, blocked the road to that kind of loyalty without which terror itself is impossible.

With the road back to Stalinism foreclosed, full *positive subordination* of society to politics became very difficult to achieve. The party-state institution of selectivity had to initiate some moves toward *negative subordination*, even if the attempted execution of negative subordination raises the question of the limits within which this very institution of selectivity—and with it the organizational principle of the system—could survive at all.

The reduction in legitimation reserves could have been compensated for initially by the increase of system rationality. Within the limits of the system, however, this increase was short-lived. The recent economic difficulties of East European state-socialist societies are now common knowledge.[23] Drastically declining rates of growth, continued and cyclical shortages, lagging productivity and technical efficiency serve as background to a period of reform which had begun in the early 1960s and which is still not exhausted in our time, at least in some countries. The system contradiction behind the economic difficulties has been interpreted variously, but I should like to single out one essential aspect. If one interprets the command-plan system as the key to the Soviet-type redistributive economies, it seems to me that perhaps the "fundamental contradiction" must be seen as that of the plan with itself, as the self-contradiction of planning rationality. More specifically, a totally centralized command system in an increasingly complex society seems to be able to achieve economic and social development only at a cost of increasing crises of information.[24] The more it attempts to bring under its control social and economic dysfunctions due to a bizarre combination of absence yet superabundance of information, the less its ability to discover the actual needs of the population *and* to process the increasing, *uncriticized* volume of information from its extended subsidiary organs.

The problem is not only that of information/communication. Since the planning agency is ultimately dependent on the party-state hierarchy whose key function is the "unification" and "harmonization" of latent and explicit social interests, the plan is unavoidably affected by various priorities adopted for the resolution of conflicts. Economic rationality is a relevant consideration, but so too are other political and social priorities. A plan that tries to integrate all of these considerations cannot be rational (according to any one criterion of rationality), or even consistent with previous or future plans that may express somewhat different constellations of interests and priorities. Furthermore, the resistance to authoritarian planning by enterprises and working operatives penetrates the plans through the distortion of information and the deliberate misinterpretation of directives. The more the plan seeks to encompass these dysfunctions, the more authoritarian and irrational it becomes.

IV

Rationality crises have a character which is entirely different from cyclical economic crises. As Habermas has shown: (1) rationality crises disorganize social life on a continuum with an uncertain threshold of tolerance; (2) bargaining and reciprocal adaptation can contain many of the disruptive consequences, some of which can be anticipated and avoided, others of which can be retroactively corrected by shifting the results toward the weakest possible strata, regions, or institutions; (3) the agents of planning can be shielded from political dissent through a closed system of technical expertise supported by a full-fledged technocratic ideology.

While the state-socialist systems have already benefited from the first two of the "advantages" of rationality crises, the third involves an internal "disjunctivity" (Offe) between the state as planner and the party as representative of the collective interest that no Soviet-type society has been able to achieve.[25] Yet the dynamic of the whole reform period, associated above with all "market socialism" and the proposals of Liberman, Brus, Šik, Kornai, and other economists seemed to point in this direction. What the reformers and their partisans in the West did not consider systematically were the limits presented to their efforts by the organizational principle of the system, limits that were indeed incorporated in their own works in the form of a gap between market socialist ideology—with all the usual economistic assumptions about the necessarily and generally democratizing consequences of a market economy—and an actual program of rather cautious decentralization that in no way challenged the existing institutional core of society on which *all* structures of existing privilege and authority depend.[26] To be more precise, there are two types of reform ideology in state-socialist systems, one that banks on the full scientization of the existing institutional network of planning, control, and information, the other that ties any possible rationalization of the whole to decentralization, that is, to some form of negative subordination. The first alternative has little importance beyond reinforcing the integration of the party itself, putting its original hyper-rationalist dreams of a totally controlled, transparent society on supposedly scientific foundations.[27] It is the second type of reform program that expresses, however ideologically, a permanent option for the system, which must somehow rationalize its social and economic procedures and integrate an increasingly complex society without recourse to the terroristic methods of the past. Let us state a basic thesis of this essay: for the leading strata and institutions of the system which are seeking their own security, not only a return to Stalinism but also the two extremes of no reform at all and a reform involving the full decentralization and democratization of all social spheres are impossible and undesirable. Given the organizational principle of the society *and* minimum requirements of administrative rationality, there are two dangerous extremes for the system: too much reform and too little. Some outer limits of reform must therefore be provided by the necessity of shielding the institutional core of the prerogative state. Hence we may regard the actual reform programs, whatever the ideologies and even intentions of individual reformers, as means of *crisis avoidance* for a system whose presuppositions cannot be threatened.

The Starnberg conception of the "crisis of crisis management," or of "second-order" crisis phenomena, here reveals its methodological value. In relation to capitalism Offe has repeatedly stressed that (a) there is a maximum and a minimum threshold of state intervention in the contemporary capitalist economy, and that (b) the possible extension of these thresholds depends on the degree of social integration, that is, on the availability of necessary symbolic resources of legitimation. The adoption of this scheme for increasingly developed forms of state socialism is justified because here, too, the problem is definable as moving from positive to negative subordination—even if in the case of capitalism negative subordination means increasing state intervention in the economy, and in the case of socialism decreasing state intervention. For state socialism the *maximum* possible level of state intervention would be primarily defined by the depth of existing steering-problems, by the political problems of the existing forms of adaptation to rationality crises and, finally, by the ideological resources that would allow a regime to weather through economic stagnation. The *minimum* permissible level of intervention would be defined, above all, by the maintenance of the integrity of the core institutional complex that specifies the identity of the system, and only secondarily by the economic dysfunctions produced by the decentralization of controls.[28] In fact, I believe that the economically dysfunctional effects of reform have been greatly exaggerated by its opponents, who fail to distinguish between dysfunctions due to reform and those due to the incomplete nature of the reform (e.g., the resistance of workers to a new wage structure when they do not acquire independent organs of interest representation).

We may be in a position to evaluate the problems of crisis management or of second-order crisis phenomena if we turn to the problem of managing the links between economy and party-state on the one hand, and party-state and culture on the other. It has been persuasively argued that economic reform, in the manner of a significant degree of decentralization, must involve a partial emancipation of the economic from the political hierarchy. The emancipation can be effective only if institutionalized through legal guarantees of horizontal links between economic units and of some freedom for economic interest groups. The advocates of this argument expect those achievements to "spill over" from the economic sphere to the spheres of political administration and culture, in a sense "reconstituting" *civil society*.[29]

The constitution or reconstitution of civil society is manifestly incompatible with the organizational principle of the state-socialist societies. Thus the problem of the successful management of the crisis of economic-administrative rationality is the problem of the successful avoidance of the spillover of administratively executed depoliticization. The argument for the plausibility of spillover depends on four assumptions. The first is the unavoidability in the long run of further attempts at economic decentralization. The second is the necessity of institutionalizing the effects of decentralization in terms of legal reform that, among other things, eliminates arbitrary political interference in the activities of economic agents. The third is that legal reform cannot be restricted to the economic sphere, because a law that purports to protect individuals cannot merely protect them as economic subjects. The fourth assumption is that the withdrawal of the party from the economy and the legalization of the rights of economic subjects will permit the formation of interest groups. The existence of a plurality of interest groups in the economy requires a transformation of political institutions, establishing a pluralistic process of decision making on the state level. Moreover, since these groups are not merely economic but also *social*, so too their economic rights cannot be protected unless their *human* rights are as well. The end result of the series of assumptions is that the depoliticization of the economy leads to the formation or reemergence of civil society.

However attractive the projected outcome of such a spillover may be, it seems clear that it *can be avoided*. It is possible for the political-administrative system to execute a withdrawal from the economic sphere, and even to institutionalize this in terms of legal reform, without depoliticizing the sociocultural sphere and without genuinely pluralizing the political sphere itself. The possibility exists of restructuring the "dual state," within which the prerogative state must remain predominant over the normative state. Its restructuring would combine the features of a *Rechtsstaat* in relation to a reformed economy with the elements of the political prerogative state whose limits of intervention in culture, everyday life and the noneconomic dimensions of administration would be defined only by itself. In other words, in order to establish a high degree of depoliticization of the economy without "spillover," the party-state structure must execute the kind of "uncoupling" (Habermas) or "disjunctivity" (Offe) of administrative and political institutions, or rather of those institutions that would protect the link between the prerogative state and the sociocultural sphere from the demands of legality, rationality, and publicity.

Under what conditions can the necessary internal disjunctivity of the party-state yield a stable combination of an administrative *Rechtsstaat* with its face toward a depoliticized economy and a political party-state controlling the sphere of social interests and forms of cultural discourse, self-expression, and learning? As we shall see below, the very possibility of disjunctivity depends on the autonomous resources of the cultural sphere. With the prerogative state withdrawing from the economy, not only the pressure of legitimation on the party-state but also the sources of the legitimation of the party as a formally separate institution would be drastically reduced. The party's claim of being the agent of both substantive justice and *total* social welfare originally rested on its supposed *global* knowledge of all society, and its supposed representation of the *general* (national, popular or working-class) interest. With the partial abandonment of the commanding heights of the central plan (that would now be left to the relevant state ministries) and the tacit admission of selective sectoral lobbies into the party-state itself, these foundations would be decisively weakened; and the weakening of the legitimacy of the party endangers the legitimacy of the prerogative state. The outcome of this process would certainly depend on what new or old sources of legitimation could be tapped by the reconstructed institutional system. If the bulk of available cultural traditions point in the direction of the democratization of politics and liberalization of culture, the new institutionalization of the party-state based on disjunctivity must be an extremely precarious one. In other words, "spillover" is not to be interpreted literally; it is possible only when it is met half-way by the autonomous logic of the sociocultural sphere based on differential historical sources.

Thus the logic of the cultural sphere determines whether the most plausible strategy of crisis management is: (1) the reinforcement of positive subordination (i.e., a level of state intervention resembling the Stalinist epoch); or (2) the depoliticization of the economy in the context of the uncoupling of administrative and political systems; or (3) an oscillation between the two. Whether a process of uncoupling or disjunctivity, if it does occur, will or will not release dysfunctional demands in the sociocultural sphere depends on the logic of cultural traditions. Hence neither the strategies of crisis management nor their outcome can be evaluated without considering the dynamics of the sociocultural sphere.

V

To speak of the *independent* dynamics of the sociocultural sphere is one of Habermas's key contributions to the development of critical social theory. He initially defined this sphere as "the cultural traditions (cultural value systems) as well as institutions that give these traditions normative power through processes of socialization and professionalization."[30] Of course, the sociocultural sphere is the key terrain of social integration. In this essay I shall focus on the Soviet Union, not only because it is the key political system within the constellation of states and because it is the only complex on which some of the necessary preparatory work has been done, but also because it is one of the only systems in Eastern Europe where one does not have to effect the impossible separation between integration through military occupation, through political-social compromise with the occupying power, and through indigenous mechanisms of social integration.

I have argued that any degree of disjunctivity between political (prerogative state) and administrative (legal and normative state) institutions would relieve the combined party-state from some of its burdens of legitimation, but that the same development would also tendentially endanger the already precarious legitimacy of the party, which symbolizes the powers of the prerogative state based on substantive justice. Without disjunctivity in the sense that I described it, there can be no economic reform that does not risk great political dangers; and without economic reform the slowly expanding system of socioeconomic rewards (consumption) can most definitely not be secured. It is Habermas's thesis that "value" (economic) and "meaning" are mutually substitutable within certain limits. Hence what we must discover is the capacity of the sociocultural system to produce meaningful motivations in the context of either continued social conservatism (which endangers socioeconomic rewards and indirectly the legitimacy of the party-state based on welfare and rationality) or progressive liberalization (which endangers the party and therefore the social identity of the system). Ideally we would have to determine not only the available functional and dysfunctional motivations in the present, but the relationship of political ideology and motivation in the context of three developments: (1) the irreversible consequences (if any) of urbanization and industrialization for the traditional component in motivations; (2) the consequences for motivation of the reform/ conservatism cycle itself; (3) the consequences of drastic expansion of the ideological-administrative apparatus into culture, along with the administered development of the official ideology itself.

Only four major ideological complexes are officially and semi-officially promoted in the unfree administered public sphere of state-socialist societies. One of these, Marxism-Leninism, is the symbolic system that justifies the formally separate existence of the monolithic party (defined above as the institution by which the prerogative state, the actual institutional core of the whole, identifies and justifies itself). Nevertheless, because this ideology is today entirely empty and ritualistic, it can perform its symbolic functions only by containing in ever-shifting combinations the other three, genuine ideologies: an ideology based on memories of the Leninist New Economic Policy (NEP), a nationalist-traditionalist ideology, and the already-mentioned authoritarian-technocratic ideology.

The basic continuity (in spite of a transformation of function) of Marxism-Leninism as the hegemonic complex is a matter of record. Nevertheless, the classical dogmas of Marxist-Leninist orthodoxy, especially those concerning the transition to communism, are held increasingly cynically.[31] Thus Marxism-Leninism cannot be the *sole* means for the ideological legitimation of society: as a ritualized dogmatic quasi-religion, it is too impoverished; as a rational ideology, it is constantly endangered by the reality to which it is increasingly irrelevant. But it is still an indispensable component of the identity of the institutional core, and its dominating role in philosophy and political theory guarantees the exclusion of serious public discussion about society.[32] Thus, within the limits of the system, it can only be supplemented, not replaced.

The ideology of the NEP, based on a legally established mixed economy and the famous Leninist *smychka* between peasant and worker, was never formally renounced, even when the economy was fully politicized and the peasantry defeated and crushed. At two junctures, various ideological aspects of the NEP were revived even more dramatically: in 1936 when the "normative state" based on law was reconstructed (largely on the precedent of late tsarist and NEP law), and in the 1960s during the period of economic reform.[33] The idea of a reformist "return" to Lenin implies the Lenin of the NEP and not that of *War Communism* or *State and Revolution*, a Lenin that strategically combined the monolithic party with an authoritarian state and a mixed economy. We know furthermore that the NEP, conceived as a mixture of a benevolently authoritarian-welfare politics, reasonable rates of economic development, and decollectivized agriculture, retained an astonishing level of normative validity for the generation of the Second World War.[34] The Soviet system as we know it cannot survive without maintaining this ideological complex, and yet the NEP also cannot be allowed to become the ideological center of the whole. A consistent version of the NEP would be open to all of the dangers of "spillover," especially in a society far more developed than that of the 1920s. To maintain some minimum resemblance between the ideology of the NEP and contemporary reality, the regime must (a) gradually improve the standard of living *both* in terms of public welfare and private consumption, and (b) slowly improve an atmosphere of public security and even legality. It is almost certain today that the first of these conditions cannot be satisfied without further steps (and serious ones) in the direction of reform. It is my belief, however, that NEP ideology is not *in itself* hostile to the self-identity of the system. The economists, planners, jurists and intellectuals who promoted it sought indeed to preserve this self-identity in a rationally reconstructed society. Rational reconstruction carries the risks that we have attempted to describe above, and after the experience of 1968 these risks appeared intolerable, though it is not at all certain that the same reforms would everywhere have the same consequence as in Czechoslovakia. As a result, the partisans of the NEP have remained ultimately weak and in the 1970s were exposed to conservative counterattack. Such conservative counterattacks are possible only because (and so long as) the remaining two ideological complexes retain some mobilizing power among ruling strata, as well as some power to secure a significant degree of popular loyalty to the established state—or at least to secure its best replacement: apathetic, privatistic, depoliticized adaptation.

The authoritarian-technocratic ideology of extending the results of the "scientific technological revolution" in the direction of more sophisticated socioeconomic planning and control seeks to mobilize key sections of the technical intellectuals, some originally reformist and others more conservative. This ideology, representing "reform" without any substantive economic and legal concessions, could affect the population at large only by some extremely improbable level of expanding economic growth rates and above all public and private consumption. Most economists in Eastern Europe and even the Soviet Union seem to believe, however, that technocratic-authoritarian "reform" would have the opposite consequence: namely, a continuation of the rationality crisis. So the only purpose of the ideology in question is to keep the technical and political sectors of the "ruling elite" united—or, better still, to represent their common desire to avoid all strategies that would threaten the institutional core of the system (in particular, the selectivity which secures their relative powers and privileges). In this context the experience of 1968 once again represents the ideological watershed in the Soviet Union and most East European countries.

Finally, the most important terrain of ideological legitimation is a nationalist-traditionalist complex that has also penetrated Marxist-Leninist and NEP ideologies. It hardly needs to be recalled that Marxism was "Russified" in the process of becoming Soviet Marxism;[35] and it is perhaps even more important that the legal development of both the NEP and the post-1936 period represented a development of a complex within which Russian legal traditions (significantly different from those of the West) were a key component.[36] Indeed, whatever popular power these ideologies have in our day is shared by their rational and traditional components, which have now become inseparable. It may be completely futile to try to decide whether, as Berdyaev believed, Marxism was Russified or, as Solzhenitsyn now maintains, Russia was Marxianized. We are dealing in fact with an entirely original statist ethos that combines features of one side of Marxism (statism as against democratic socialism), one side of Russia (caesaropapist autocracy and authoritarian bureaucracy as against popular anti-statism), the Leninist self-definition of anticapitalist intellectuals, as well as a work ethic derived from capitalism itself. So far as the Russian traditions are concerned, even its discarded populist and antistatist components are preserved by the ruling party itself. As a result, one may speak of a nationalist-traditionalist ideological complex sustained by the combination of two sets of traditional elements: On the one hand, the heritage of "autocracy, nationality, and orthodoxy" that survives as the compulsory service state,[37] as the celebration of the imperial heritage, as an aggressive military-political ethnocentrism, as the ritualization of orthodox dogma, and as the cult of the autocratic personality; and on the other hand, the antiauthoritarian heritage that focuses on communitarian anticapitalism, the ethics of collective solidarity, ideas of substantive justice and welfare, as well as the celebration of the Russian people, who supposedly possess all these qualities.[38] In the Soviet period the two sides were inseparable. Populism was the mask of autocracy, and especially during the period of the "heroic socialist construction" and the "Great Patriotic War"—that is, in moments of real or supposed external and internal danger—both worked sufficiently powerfully for the population as a whole. Yet autocracy could not do without the populist mask and was therefore forced to preserve and even to develop it. In moments of external danger this was done rather easily. It is only with the emergence of the Soviet Union as a great industrial and imperial power that the two moments became genuinely separable. Without genuine external threat, without the obvious necessity of enforced self-sacrifice, populism could again rediscover its antistatist spirit; and with the autocratic center promoting social atomization and a puritanical work ethic,[39] the mythologies of the Russian people and of the benevolent autocracy have become to some extent unstuck. Today, the opposition between the Solzhenitsyns and the ideologists of official Soviet nationality is potentially more radical than the clash between "tsar and people" in the nineteenth century.[40] The imagined solution is, however, still the same: the synthesis of the poles in a virulent militaristic, ethnocentric, anti-Semitic, Great Russian nationalism. In a very real sense the possible success of this strategy represents the ultimate alternative to what we described as the realization of negative subordination between state and society. What then are the chances of this synthesis?

The sustenance of the eclectic ideological mix of Marxism-Leninism, NEP reformism, authoritarian technocracy, and traditionalist-nationalism, and even more the displacement of the weight of the whole in the direction of virulent nationalism, depends on the cultural elements internalized through the family and education. For the bulk of the population we presume that explicit ideologies of legitimation did not play the sole or even the crucial role of social integration during the cataclysmic process of the 1930s: "a mixture of traditional ties, fatalistic willingness to follow, lack of perspective, and naked repression (above all)"[41] have been far more important ways of ensuring the subordination of the collectivized peasantry and the newly created proletariat than "the convincing force" of statist ideologies. Nonetheless, for social integration to be successful there must be a complementarity between the ideologies that mobilize leading economic, political, and cultural strata and the forms of motivation, loyalty, subordination, and adaptation that emerge from the cultural life-world of the population. This complementarity cannot be maintained if four Habermasian theses are correct. The first asserts the impossibility of the administrative creation of meaning; the second proclaims the erosion of all dogmatically held traditions in the modern world; the third alleges the impossibility of constructing a rational social identity in the modern world around the nation-state or party elite; and the fourth acknowledges the survival of only postauratic art, scientism, and universalistic morality (embedded in legal institutions and structures) as forms of social integration that are able to withstand the critical rejection of petrified traditions.[42]

I accept the first of these theses on the basis of epistemological assumptions drawn from both Habermas and Gadamer which cannot be presented here. What I should like to argue, however, is that the second thesis is partially false, and that this deprives the third and fourth theses of some of their main force. In other words, we are obliged to consider the continued possibility of prerational or irrational identity formation around the nation-state; and that even if scientism, modern art, and morality indicate the terrain where genuinely contemporary forms of cultural creativity must be located, in modern Russia at least this terrain hardly exhausts the symbolic systems relevant to social integration.

If we take the 1930s as our starting point, two already-mentioned contradictory developmental tendencies can be registered in the sphere of social integration. There was first of all an obvious process of "archaization," the Stalinist "resurrection of the historic Tsarist pattern of building a powerful military-national state by revolutionary means [from above] involving the extension of direct coercive controls over the population and the growth of state power in the process." But there was also a great need, from the mid-1930s onward in the

context of a shattered fabric of traditional society and the craving of both officials and people for security, "to regularize, to consolidate, to reinsure, to ensure
a ruly and predictable working of the responsible institutions, some kind of
constitutionality."[43] It is easy to agree with Lewin that it is the clash of these two
tendencies that produced the second phase of the terror, namely Stalin's violent
attempt to prevent the consolidation of the power of those normal bureaucratic
agencies that showed their influence in the explosion of constitutionalism and
legality in a sphere previously dominated by revolutionary, substantive justice.
What must also be stressed, however, is that the duality of law and terror was not
abolished by the post-Stalin consolidation of law, but rather was replaced by the
duality of law and politics that penetrated the structure of both law (e.g., in the
form of vague, unspecific definitions of political offenses) and politics. Even if
the legal reforms of 1936 and especially 1953 and after were determined by
needs of stability, security, and rationality, even if from 1936 onward the Soviet
bureaucracy rediscovered the power of legal legitimacy, nevertheless the continuation of the "dual state" required resources of legitimacy other than legality. In
other words, the fundamental trend of legal reform would have destroyed the
dual state unless the extralegal political element could draw on a combination of
charismatic-revolutionary and traditional symbolic resources. Given the terroristic trappings of charismatic autocracy, there was, after 1953, a decisive shift in
the direction of tradition and even more of "traditionalism" or traditional legitimacy. The possibility of this shift grounds the dominant, prerogative element of
the dual state, and with it the organizational principle of the Soviet system.

We should not underestimate the significance of the return to law that was
obviously pushed by rising *modern* social strata (bureaucrats, technical intellectuals, etc.). Today, moreover, the defense and extension of legality is the "project" of an enormously important pressure group of modern jurists, the size and
influence of which is almost entirely new in Russia.[44] Nevertheless, the reemergence of law *was* from the outset paralleled by the revival of traditions all along
the line. From the regime's side, the tsarist slogan of "nationality, orthodoxy,
autocracy" well expresses what was sought and what was in fact revived. But
what was revived on the side of the population undergoing enormous sacrifices?

For the Stalinist period we are not without some empirical material. Whatever
its weaknesses, the results of the "Harvard project on the Soviet social system"[45]
show that renewed traditionalism remains an important part of the social psychology of the Soviet "citizen." The model of the ideal society, held by the great
majority of the displaced persons interviewed by the researchers, was indeed a
slightly rationalized welfare-statist version of traditional Russian autocracy. The
respondents had little interest in formal law, political participation, and even civil
rights, with the exception of the right of privacy and family against political and
administrative interference. They were also deeply imbued with the traditional
attitude of the superiority of collectivistic Russia over the individualistic West.
Though they revealed much dissatisfaction with the regime, their alternative

loyalties based on familial *and* occupational privatism led in most cases to passive acceptance of the regime.[46] Most surprisingly, the values of those interviewed concerning family education with respect to general socialization and occupational goals turned out to be deeply and even increasingly "traditionalistic," in Weber's sense of the term. Inkeles and Bauer are of course right when they maintain that the regime has been successful in suppressing some of the traditional components of education, since they mean the particular traditions (strong patriarchy, orthodox religion, etc.) of the Tsarist period. These, however, do not exhaust the meaning of "traditionalism," which I construe as the uncritical elevation of the reproduction of an existing mode of life to normative validity. What the data of the Harvard project show is that the motivation structure of their sample did not unambiguously shift from "traditional" to "modern" orientations, but that there was instead a noticeable rise in *traditionalistic* motivations of adjustment to a pregiven situation, as well as traditional personalistic motives (turning activity increasingly inward) in the context of a significant and remarkable fall in the level of motivations based on modern norms of achievement.[47]

As many interpreters have indicated, the effect of the regime on the traditions it fostered has always been highly selective; the only traditions which have been allowed official expression are those which reinforced the regime's political and economic goals. What the regime did not promote, at least originally, was the emergence of a traditionalistic, family-based ethic that stressed the protection of fundamental human ties through passive acceptance, adaptation and sociopolitical fatalism, even after the traditional religious values of the past have been discarded. This attitude is, however, greatly reinforced by the still existing extremes of political and economic centralization and the total administration of the public sphere, which together exclude *intimate* solidarities on all except the family level. Of course, in the context of economic growth and legal security, this form of traditionalism would also be compatible with a vocational achievement ethic linked to civic privatism.[48] But in the past all traces of legal security were missing, whereas in the present and foreseeable future it is likely that economic growth will remain a problem. Hence in the Soviet Union we may count on the reinforcement of the traditionalistic features of privatism.

Can we also assume that the traditionalism of everyday life in Russia is open to the ritualistic aspects of Marxism-Leninism and to the semi-official traditional-nationalist ideology? With respect to the first of these, the answer is probably negative, since here we are dealing with an ideology whose connection to actual communities—the substance of all traditionalism—is very remote. The official institutions of Soviet society are merely illusory communities. It may be otherwise with respect to the traditional-nationalistic ideology. In moments of military, political, and social crisis related to the outside world (China, the West, Eastern Europe), the regime can probably once again activate the nationalistic and patriotic resources of legitimation that were so important in overcoming the apathy, cynicism, and anomie of the population during the Second World War.

But without identifiable enemies, it is at least questionable whether the atomized, privatized, family-orientated majority of the population can be indefinitely shielded from the social criticism of schools of dissidents by a massive propaganda campaign defending the existing "Soviet way of life."[49] While Great Russian nationalism may justify a community of interests against outside and inside "enemies," the same ideology also represents a potential danger to the stability of the system. For Great Russian nationalism reinforces the self-consciousness and resistance of other nationalities that will soon represent over half the population of the Soviet Union.[50]

Although the actual ideological-political setting is full of dangers and ambiguities, on Habermasian grounds one would have to adopt a generally hopeful attitude. It is his belief that, in the modern world, institutions cannot be consolidated on the basis of regressive forms of legitimation. The development of law in the Soviet Union seems to bear out the point. Today the existence of a significant civil-rights movement in Russia is possible because of the large-scale replacement in civil and criminal law of traditional, substantive considerations by formally guaranteed rules and procedures. No matter how conservative jurists are personally, their work prepares the ground for a *rechtsstaatliche* transformation in the future, one that would have to be fought and suffered for by courageous individuals whatever their immediate political ideology, since legal protection of speech and assembly is desperately needed by all dissident tendencies. But to return to our own hypothesis: Even the creation of some kind of modified socialist *Rechtsstaat* may still, under certain conditions, be compatible with the system's authoritarian identity principle and organizational core. To believe that legal development must necessarily overshoot this mark requires Habermas's confidence in the erosion of irrational, traditionalist structures of consciousness and the moral development of the human species. It requires, furthermore, a single logic of legal development in history, one that may be disputable in light of the continued viability of the "dual state" in state-socialist countries, as well as the persistence and reappearance of traditionalistic structures of consciousness. In the spirit of a slightly modified version of Habermas's theory of moral development,[51] I would claim that so long as the universal moral-legal achievements of the West are preserved, the penetration of these into other contemporary settings is at least possible. But this penetration necessarily depends on what Weber called historical *Wahlverwandtschaften*, that is, on the prior development of particular national cultural constellations and on the institutional mechanisms of the preservation or elimination of those traditions which favor or inhibit the emergence of civil society. These two aspects can be evaluated only in a framework of analysis which is both abstract-systematic *and* historical-comparative, one that would necessarily assess the possible futures of societies with the *same* state-socialist organizational principle according to their deep-seated historical *differences* and according to the developmental tendencies which are necessarily common to them all.

Notes

1. J. Habermas, *Theorie und Praxis* (Neuwied: Luchterhand, 1967), pp. 161–63 (*TP*, pp. 184–86).

2. In later editions of this essay, the partial exception in the Polish context of Modzelewski's and Kuroń's "Open Letter" is noted.

3. J. Habermas, "Theorie der Gesellschaft oder Sozialtechnologie," in J. Habermas and N. Luhmann, *Theorie der Gesellschaft oder Sozialtechnologie—Was leistet die Systemforschung?* (Frankfurt: Suhrkamp, 1971) pp. 265–67.

4. J. Habermas, *Legitimation Crisis* (Boston: Beacon, 1975), p. 17. [Hereafter *LC*.]

5. J. Habermas, "On Social Identity," *Telos* 19 (Spring 1974).

6. *CES*, pp. 152, 158.

7. K. Eder, "Zum Problem der logischen Periodisierung von Produktionsweisen," in *Theorien des Historischen Materialismus*, ed. U. Jaeggi and H. Honneth (Frankfurt: Suhrkamp, 1977) pp. 511, 520.

8. D. Lockwood, "Social Integration and System Integration," in *Explorations in Social Change*, ed. Zollschan and Hirsch (Boston: Houghton Mifflin, 1964); and F. Parkin, "System Contradiction and Political Transformation," *European Journal of Sociology* 13 (1972).

9. N. Mouzelis, "Social and System Integration," *British Journal of Sociology* 25 (1974).

10. *LC*, p. 4; see also pp. 7–8, 16.

11. J. Habermas, "History and Evolution," trans. D. J. Parent, *Telos* 39 (Spring 1979) pp. 144, 148, 156.

12. *LC*, pp. 17ff.

13. Cf. A. Arato, "Systems of Reproduction and Histories of the State," *Telos* 35 (Spring 1978), under the heading of "Understanding Bureaucratic Centralism."

14. C. Offe, "Crisis of Crisis Management," *International Journal of Politics* 6 (1976), p. 33.

15. C. Offe, *Strukturprobleme des kapitalistischen Staates* (Frankfurt: Suhrkamp, 1972); J. Cohen, "System and Class: the Subversion of Emancipation," *Social Research* 45 (Winter 1978), and "The Problem of Class Analysis in Advanced Capitalism," New York, New School for Social Research dissertation, 1979.

16. E. Fraenkel, *The Dual State* (New York: Oxford University Press, 1941).

17. The categories used, in a slightly altered form, are drawn primarily but not exclusively from recent works by M. Rakovski, "Marxism and Soviet Societies," *Capital and Class* 1(Spring 1977); M. Rakovski, *Towards an East European Marxism* (London: Allison and Busby, 1978), an incomplete translation of *Le Marxisme face aux pays de l'est* (Paris: Savelli, 1977); G. Konrád and I. Szelényi, *The Intellectuals on the Road to Class Power* (New York: Harcourt Brace Jovanovich, 1979); F. Fehér and A. Heller, "Forms of Equality," *Telos* 32 (Summer 1977); and F. Fehér, "The Dictatorship over Needs," *Telos* 35 (Spring 1978). In my opinion all of these suffer slightly from a one-sided extension of the structural principle of politics, culture, or economy to the whole.

18. C. Offe, "Crisis of Crisis Management," pp. 35–36.

19. M. Lewin, *Political Undercurrents in Soviet Economic Debates* (Princeton University Press, 1974); and R. Laird, " 'Developed' Socialist Society and the Dialectics of Legitimation in the Soviet Union," *Soviet Union/Union Soviétique* 4 (1977).

20. This is true especially because there is not and cannot be (except in the ideology) an agency in Soviet society to whom the society as a whole and the relationship of its parts to the whole is transparent. Cf. C. Castoriadis, " The Social Regime in Russia," *Telos* 38 (Winter 1978–79).

21. Cf. essays in *Interest Groups in Soviet Politics*, ed. H. Skilling and F. Griffiths (Princeton University Press, 1971).

22. Offe, *Strukturprobleme*, pp. 65ff.

23. Cf. Lewin, *Political Undercurrents*.

24. Ibid.; and F. Parkin, "System Contradiction and Political Transformation," *European Journal of Sociology* 13 (1972).

25. Yugoslavia is the possible exception, and perhaps this proves that it is not a Soviet-type society.

26. Cf. Rakovski's excellent discussion in *Towards an East European Marxism*.

27. C. Lefort, *Un homme en trop. Reflexions sur "L'Archipel du Goulag"* (Paris: Seuil, 1976); Fehér, " The Dictatorship over Needs"; but see Laird, " 'Developed' Socialist Society and the Dialectics of Legitimation in the Soviet Union."

28. I do not believe the crisis of crisis management can be sought in the demonstration (on the level of system integration) of the inevitable coincidence of permissible maximum and minimum levels of political intervention (where even the maximum would be too little from the point of view of maintaining the primacy of the political, and even the minimum too much from the point of view of economic rationality); rather, it must be sought in the analysis (on the level of social integration) of the difficulties of legitimating either or both a strategy based on undiminished levels of intervention and/or one based on reform.

29. Lewin, *Political Undercurrents*, pp. 164–65, 178, 236–38; and Konrád and Szelényi, *The Intellectuals*, pp. 231–32.

30. *LC*, p. 149, n. 15.

31. Compare H. Marcuse, *Soviet Marxism: A Critical Analysis* (New York: Random House, 1958) with Castoriadis, "The Social Regime in Russia," and V. Zazlavsky, "The Problem of Legitimation in Soviet Society," in *Conflict and Control*, ed. Vidich and Glassman (Beverly Hills: Sage, 1979).

32. M. Vajda, "Is Kadarism an Alternative?" *Telos* 39 (Spring 1979).

33. H. Berman, *Justice in the USSR: An Interpretation of Soviet Law* (Cambridge, Mass.: Harvard University Press, 1963); R. Sharlet, "Stalinism and Soviet Legal Culture," in *Stalinism*, ed. R. Tucker (New York: Norton, 1977); and Lewin, *Political Undercurrents*.

34. R. Bauer, A. Inkeles, and C. Kluckhohn, *How the Soviet System Works* (New York: Knopf, 1956).

35. R. Dutschke, *Versuch Lenin auf die Füsse zu Stellen* (Berlin: Wagenback, 1974).

36. Berman, *Justice in the USSR*.

37. R. Tucker, "Stalinism as Revolution from Above," in *Stalinism*, ed. Tucker.

38. F. Barghoorn, *Soviet Russian Nationalism* (New York: Oxford University Press, 1956).

39. V. Zazlavsky, "The Problem of Legitimation in Soviet Society" and "The Rebirth of the Stalin Cult in the USSR," *Telos* 40 (Summer 1979).

40. M. Cherniavsky, *Tsar and People* (New Haven: Yale University Press, 1961).

41. *LC*, p. 22.

42. *LC*, pp. 70, 79, 84–89; "On Social Identity," pp. 98–99; "History and Evolution," pp. 115, 197.

43. M. Lewin, "The Social Background of Stalinism," in *Stalinism*, ed. Tucker.

44. D. Barry and H. Berman, "The Jurists," in *Interest Groups in Soviet Politics*, ed. Skilling and Griffiths.

45. Cf. Bauer, Inkeles, and Kluckhohn, *How the Soviet System Works*; and R. Bauer and A. Inkeles, *The Soviet Citizen* (Cambridge, MA: Harvard University Press, 1959).

46. Bauer, Inkeles and Kluckhohn, *How the Soviet System Works*, pp. 138–42, 236–39, 150–54, 171–78.

47. Bauer and Inkeles, *The Soviet Citizen*, pp. 220–26, especially pp. 221ff.

48. *LC*, pp. 76–77.
49. Zaslavsky, "The Rebirth of the Stalin Cult in the USSR."
50. H. Carrère d'Encausse, *L'Empire éclaté* (Paris: Flammarion, 1978).
51. Cf. A. Heller, "Habermas and Marxism," in *Habermas: Critical Debates* (Cambridge, Mass.: MIT Press, 1982).

4

From Western to Eastern
Marxism: Rudolf Bahro

Western Marxism is Maurice Merleau-Ponty's name for a post–social-demo-cratic, post-Bolshevik, primarily philosophical tradition of Marx interpretation in Europe and America.[1] The term can be made sense of only if we keep in mind the self-constitution of Western Marxism against the double background of a successful Marxian revolution in the East and the corresponding "Eastern" Marxist theoretical and philosophical synthesis. "The Russians . . . act philosoph-ically, but philosophize like mad dogs";[2] the 1924 description is Ernst Bloch's, one of the founders of Western Marxism. Initially a philosophical justification of the October Revolution whose Eastern self-understanding did not meet either West-European theoretical criteria or political needs, and hence a form of Left Communism, since 1940 at least, Western Marxism has become a critical theory of *all* contemporary forms of domination including the societies of the Soviet type. Since the 1960s various trends of Western Marxism have constituted an important, oppositional intellectual stream also in Eastern Europe, first under the rather nonsensical name of "revisionism" and later, referring to the common thread of the various positions, under that of the more exact but lesser-known term "philosophy of praxis." In the 1970s especially—in Yugoslavia earlier— Western Marxism in Eastern Europe began to yield a series of theoretical analy-sis of "really existing socialism," alias "despotic state socialism," alias "bureaucratic collectivism" or "centralism," alias "rational redistribution," alias "statism." Of these, the work of Rudolf Bahro, *The Alternative in Eastern Eu-rope* (hereafter: *Alternative*; New Left Books, 1979) is not only the best known but also the most extensive and synthetic. Nevertheless, of his major competitors Bahro is the least able to provide a genuinely critical theory of his form of society.[3]

We are indeed fortunate to have in translation Bahro's book as well as the volume *Rudolf Bahro: Critical Responses* (hereafter: *CR*; M.E. Sharpe, 1980)

A version of this essay was published in *Telos* in 1981.

edited by Ulf Wolter, which includes essays by Herbert Marcuse, Rudi
Dutschke, Jiři Pelikán, and others. It is now possible not only to consider Bahro's
contribution to the study of authoritarian state socialism (my own choice of
terms), but also the limits of the classical tradition of Western Marxism from
Lukács to Marcuse as they reveal themselves in the distorted mirror of the Soviet
Union and Eastern Europe. For in spite of his pedantic, scholastic style reminiscent of DIAMAT and HISTOMAT Bahro *is* a Western Marxist,[4] both in terms of
many of the resources he draws upon and the overall aim of his synthesis. His
stress on the role of the subjective factor, the historical subject of social transformation, as well as his concept of social objectivity as reification come from
Lukács (perhaps mediated through Lucien Goldmann). His conception of the
active role of consciousness, at times reversing the so-called materialist premise,
is reminiscent of the early Korsch. He explicitly draws upon Gramsci for a
theory of intellectuals and to indicate the task of the party, the collective intellectual: the achievement of cultural hegemony. He adopts the Marcusian theory of
true and false needs culminating in a vision of emancipation as the reconciliation
between culture and nature; his contempt for "repressive tolerance" comes from
Marcuse as well. He draws his idea of cultural revolution from Westernized
Maoist models (first stage) and from Marcuse and Reich (second stage). He
utilizes the results of new working class theories. He even hazards some (vague)
references to Habermas's model of an emancipated public sphere as that of communication free of domination. Finally, he seems to be familiar with some of the results
of the most up-to-date Marxology. In short, he fully earns the praise of Herbert
Marcuse (*CR*, p. 25) who called him the author of "the most important contribution to Marxist theory and practice to appear in several decades." The only
problem is that the Trotskyist leader and theorist Ernest Mandel has referred to
the *Alternative* in only slightly less complimentary fashion (and less modestly) as
"the most important theoretical work to come out of the countries which have
abolished capitalism since Leon Trotsky's *Revolution Betrayed*." Why a problem? Because Trotskyism has always been "only" the most sophisticated version
of *Eastern* Marxism.[5]

Both Marcuse and Ernest Mandel are right to claim Bahro, and not only
because of the latter's eclectic combination of different theoretical traditions. It
is the thesis of this review that in the face of authoritarian state socialism the
theory of cultural revolution that emerged in the 1960s as one of the three main
self-interpretations of the New Left (the others being participatory democracy
and "third worldism") reveals itself in spite of all its emancipatory elements as
Eastern Marxism as long or as soon as its link to theories of radical democracy is
vitiated by a renewed Marxist orthodoxy. The problem, in other words, is not the
survival of "Eastern" elements in an otherwise "Western" work. The elements
we may recognize as Eastern themselves belong most directly to the Left Communist tradition of the 1920s and later, as Hermann Weber has noticed. As far as
the most questionable of these go, notably Bahro's defense of a single-party

system, it is paradoxically Mandel (who also would like to be a practical European politician) rather than Marcuse (who could afford to be more consistent) who finds them suspicious. Indeed the latter dramatically and aggressively defends the theoretical supports of just such authoritarian features, in particular the distinction between immediate and real interests and a dictatorial relationship of the plan to the development of needs. Thus it is quite impossible to neatly separate out the emancipatory, Western and authoritarian, Eastern features of Bahro's work. The opposition between his willingness to undertake a critique of all his classical sources including Marx, Engels, and Lenin (a sine qua non of Western Marxism established by Lukács) and his desire to present the Soviet ("noncapitalist") road to industrial society as on the whole progressive, is only apparent. The fundamental charge against Marx and Lenin is, indeed, that they did not fully understand or at least admit the necessary shift of the theater of world revolution to the East and the need for an authoritarian, statist, bureaucratic formation *sui generis*, produced by an intellectual vanguard rather than the proletariat, as the preparation of the industrial but noncapitalist foundations for a future socialist social formation.

There is indeed an important axis of contradictions (or rather antinomies) in Bahro's book, but it is not between Western and Eastern Marxism. His antinomies have another source: the opposition of what he deduces from his synthesis and what he is presented with as historical clues by contemporary struggles for liberation in his part of the world. Many of these primarily political antinomies are worth listing. At times Bahro considers political democratization (in the sense of formal democracy) in Eastern Europe as a step backward toward "political restoration" and at times as a necessary if small step forward, the presupposition of other steps. The struggle for civil and human rights he sees alternately as the crucial recovery of what should be realized and preserved under all socialism and as the concentration of the movement on something inessential. The achievement of a relatively free public and cultural sphere is the foundation of all that is to follow but it also expresses the suspicious, corporate, immediate interests of intellectuals who seek to shine amidst repressive tolerance. The national dimension of the opposition he sees variously as fully justified, as justified but backward looking, and as backward looking and dangerous. Correspondingly, he understands the stabilizing functions (for Russia) of the imperial structure of the whole and yet uses its partial survival as a bargaining point with the existing parties (who are threatened with the eventual collapse of the whole system of states). He attacks the monolithic aspects of the existing system, but seeks to split the ruling parties only temporarily. Essentially he too wants a single-party system but on the basis of a renewed party, a league of communists. At times he points to free trade unions as a necessary and even paradigmatic element of plurality in a single-party system, but at least in one crucial place (*Alternative*, p. 190) he argues that the desire to "restore" free and independent unions is a confirmation merely of the subaltern role of wage workers in bureaucratic socialism. He proposes a system of dual power between society and state, but he insists on a unified center of ideological hegemony for both society and state, again his reformed communist party. He accepts the necessity of economic decentralization but he continues to assign all really fundamental choices to the central plan. He sees how the old party has imbued the old plan with the dimension of its particular interest in maintaining power, but he proposes to repeat the same structural relation with a new single party, a new plan and without indicating serious control mechanisms or even informational devices from below. Finally, he calls to account in a manner similar to Szelényi, Konrád, and Gouldner, the avant-garde party intellectuals of the original revolution for masking the particular interests they managed to impose as general, but ingenuously claims that the new, collective intellectual needed to guide the transformation to socialism would and could suppress its own particularity. Indeed, when he claims that this particularity consists in the interest in completely unlimited and uncensored forms of public expression, he manages to distinguish his "alternative" from a society in which the intellectuals as such constitute a ruling class but not from the contemporary societies of East Europe.[6]

It should not be very difficult, especially after the Polish summer of 1980, to distinguish the strand in Bahro's antinomies that expresses the practice and the theory of the "really existing" East European opposition. What, of course, needs to be explained is why in each instance he is also committed to the contrary, to something authoritarian, and against his intentions, conservative. Bahro is the only theorist I know who *both* fully demystifies Bolshevik ideology, seeing the continuity between Leninism and Stalinism, and accepts the necessity not only of the authoritarian turn of the October Revolution, but also of the Stalinist revolution from above. He furthermore maintains the necessity and legitimacy of a neo-Leninist political strategy for the present. In this context his reasons are as different as the outcomes are supposed to be. While his apology vis-à-vis classical Leninism is the consequence of his acceptance of the Eastern Marxist theory of the shift of the world context of anticapitalist revolution, his neo-Leninism follows from his acceptance and interpretation of the Western Marxist theory of cultural revolution. I would like to deal with these two—connected—trends in his thought in two separate steps in order to once again ask the question: To whom does Bahro speak? For whom was the *Alternative* written?

Asia and the Formation of Industrial Despotism

The application of the theory of the Asiatic mode of production *cum* Oriental despotism to the Soviet Union, though its antecedents are in Marx, Engels, Lenin, and Plekhanov, is classically Western Marxist in its conceptual strategy. Using the best in Marx against deterministic and unilinear versions of Marxisms,[7] interpreters from Wittfogel to Dutschke were able to greatly relativize the schematic, evolutionary model of historical materialism accepted by all the movements from Social Democracy to Maoism. Surpassing the original theorists of Western Marxism, Lukács, Ernst Bloch, Karl Korsch, who could be collectively called the philosophers of the October revolution, the theorists of the Asiatic mode of production sought to specify the historically unique characteristics of the new antagonistic society the Bolsheviks set up: in their view neither capitalist, socialist, or even transitional between the two. In this tradition of analysis (in spite of his totally uncharitable and unreasonable attitude to Karl Wittfogel) Bahro uses the theory of the Asiatic mode of production as a building block of his theory of history in general, and in particular as the key to his understanding of the Soviet Union as a form of industrial despotism representing the modernization of agricultural (Oriental) despotism. The structure of Soviet history (and rather strangely of East European history as well) is here grasped as that of a noncapitalist road to industrial society—one that has up until now been able to produce only a new form of antagonistic society (form of domination) *sui generis*. Bahro rejects the Trotskyist notions (degeneration of the worker's state and that of bureaucratic counterrevolution) used to sustain the conceptually and historically implausible and implicitly apologetic idea that the Soviet Union is somehow a transitional mix between capitalism and socialism.

Given this start, it is astonishing that in the political-ethical sense Bahro regresses behind the intent of the Trotskyist formula, coming up with a model this time openly apologetic of Stalinism. His criticism of the idea of partial degeneration is not motivated by a more critical stance toward the Leninist (and Trotskyist) origins of Stalinism but by a clearly more affirmative relationship to the Stalinist formation of the Soviet Union. Bahro believes that the socialist ideology of Leninist intellectuals was from the beginning only the false consciousness of an elite—so far so good, but now the disaster—"called upon" to lead a very different process historically necessary and unavoidable: an authoritarian, bureaucratic, modernizing revolution from above. Reopening the door to extreme determinism,[8] of Stalinism he considers only the most outrageously terroristic features bypassable—and at times not even these (*Alternative*, p. 90). He never seems to tire of repeating (deliberately echoing the views of Marx concerning the merits of capitalism) that the Stalinist period of forced industrialization and collectivization was fundamentally creative and progressive both on a world historical scale and in the context of Russian history. To be sure, his arguments are (unfortunately) familiar to Western readers. Bahro's Stalinism interpretation is to be located somewhere between Dobb and Deutscher who, of course, had little use for the concept of the Asiatic mode of production.

And yet it is only half right to claim as does Hassan Givsan (*CR*, pp. 79ff) that Bahro's analysis of Soviet development could have been made without relying on the Asiatic model altogether, locating early Soviet history in a world capitalist context marked by the relation of developed and dependent milieux. Half right, because the model has different consequences on the *diachronic* and *synchronic* levels. On the level of historical explanation the concept of the Asiatic mode of production is rather superfluous because Bahro clearly reinterprets it in terms of *the* classical Eastern Marxist doctrine (connected to the names of Parvus, Trotsky, Lenin, and Mao) of the historical change of the locus of world revolution to the East. Thus agricultural despotism is, however implausibly, simply a synonym for underdevelopment. In this context, instead of indicating either a historical dead end, or better still the emergence of an open-ended evolutionary line that for no immanent reason leads to anything like socialism—which is, after all, the conceptual child of Western civil society—Bahro maintains that the outcome of the only possible noncapitalist road to industrial society, "industrial despotism," will necessarily put the Marxian model of socialism (indeed, a rightly utopian variant), increasingly impossible in a Eurocentric and privileged West, back on the agenda. Bahro's revolution, too, is "permanent," even if it takes far longer than originally expected. It is therefore not surprising that he returns *sub rosa* to the notion of the transitional society, to be sure not a "degenerated" or "deformed" one.[9] His *industrial despotism* is transitional but between Asiatic, agricultural *despotism*, and *industrial* socialism. It leads to socialism for classical reasons, the "protosocialist" nature of industrial despotism consisting in two halfway steps to socialization: étatization ("socialization in an alienated form") and the reduction of social antagonism (ultimately based on the hierarchical division of labor) to its pure, quasi-classless form of the state against society. What separates the developed versions of Bahro's industrial despotism from socialism is therefore "only" the self-perpetuating, authoritarian, bureaucratic state, a view quite analogous to that of Engels (Anti-Dühring) concerning the supposedly last, statist phase of capitalist development today enshrined in the state monopoly capitalism thesis of some of the European communist parties, including the SED. Nevertheless it is in this context, on the level of structural analysis, that the model of the Asiatic mode of production really yields something that the orthodox historical materialist models had to do without: the étatistic or statist principle of organization of an antagonistic system in which neither property nor any other economic criterion is the fundamental clue to social structure. Thus Bahro fruitfully refers to those (he thinks all) Asiatic empires where the political-bureaucratic structure defined and perpetuated a form of domination without private powers of disposal over agricultural property. One may, of course, legitimately ask, as does Lombardo Radice (*CR*, pp. 143–44) for party political (Italian Communist Party) reasons, whether the argument should represent a genuine historical lineage or only an analogy. Neither is historical Russia Asiatic, nor are concepts like "semi-Asiatic" terribly useful. Furthermore, one needs no doctrine of the Asiatic mode of production to ascertain that very few (if any) societies are definable as modes of production in the first place. The schools of Max Weber, Émile Durkheim, and Karl Polányi have of course represented this view in terms of an enormous wealth of conceptual and empirical detail. But Bahro tended (in the GDR at least) to read only Marxist success, and it is paradoxically the doctrine of the Asiatic mode of production (or its political side, Oriental despotism) that led him to the thesis that societies of the Soviet type, at least, are not definable either as modes of production or by the primacy of the economic sphere but by the primacy of the political. Furthermore, there can be no question of mere analogy if we see the notion of semi-Asiatic agricultural despotism as an attempt, however inadequate, to conceptualize the specificity of Russian despotism, that is, Tsarist autocracy.[10] Bahro maintains not only that the two forms of domination ("Oriental" and Soviet) are comparable, neither being definable by possession of private property, but he insists on the actual continuity between Tsarist autocracy and the Soviet period, in his language between agricultural and industrial despotisms. Nor is his argument merely a historicist one in the manner of the political culture school in the West, deriving one phase from the structure of the previous one; instead he demonstrates the convergences of several factors in the revolution-restoration (Antonio Gramsci) of étatist bureaucratic power. The autocratic Russian heritage is only one factor in this context; the social, rational, geographic fragmentation of the empire inherited by the Bolsheviks,[11] the superior power of the capitalist environment encircling the Soviet Union, and the dynamics of the revolutionary situation itself—that is, the availability of overwhelming state power in a political vacuum—are the others. We will soon see why he does not add two others still: the authoritarian *structure* and *theory* of the revolutionary party itself.

Bahro, of course, defends the necessity of the étatism that has emerged; he is an enthusiastic apologist in the manner of Gramsci of the civilizing mission of the state. But he *is* critical of the logical outcome, namely that institutional structures necessary for the phase of modernizing, industrializing agricultural despotism turned out to be self-perpetuating even when no longer relevant economically. Such renewed conservatism appears according to him in a conservative dress—the unity of state and ideological power under industrial despotism is that of a quasi-theocracy; the political bureaucracy is a church hierarchy and secular officialdom in one. It is furthermore self-reproducing in the form of a new, political principle of stratification—though not in the form of a new, collective, possessing class.

To be more exact, Bahro presents us with two principles of stratification for authoritarian state socialism, which he does not seek to unite under a single concept in the manner of Konrád and Szelényi.[12] The differing levels of education provide the basis of a nonantagonistic social hierarchy in his conception. In other words, as long as different levels of education exist (Bahro seeks to abolish them in the long run), stratification according to knowledge is functional from his point of view and serves "the general interest." It is the political division between the party state bureaucracy and those it administers that represents the only fundamental form of antagonism of this society, the only contemporary bases of interest conflict. In fact, the two principles of stratification—technical education and politics—are in conflict with one another, and Bahro similarly to Szelényi tends to regard the triumph of the first, which he too interprets in a technocratic sense, as necessary for genuine social progress. To be sure, the political bureaucracy presumably defined not as a class but as the hierarchic structure of state institutions defends to the end an economic and social structure that helps to reproduce its monopoly of power.[13] Its key instrument according to Bahro is a monopoly over socially and politically relevant knowledge and information. It is this combination of power and knowledge that makes industrial despotism a conservative theocracy in a historical period in which its dogmatized knowledge no longer corresponds to general social needs. It is, however, the insistence on knowledge that makes the present system according to him ultimately vulnerable. Deeply apologetic of its past, Bahro nevertheless seeks to work out a critical conflict theory for the present of the system. But it is in this context that he will yet again become apologetic; this time only implicitly of an authoritarian regime.

Cultural Revolution and the Return of Authoritarian Politics

If the formation of "really existing socialism" is not determined economically, no immanent economic necessity will produce its transformation. Here Bahro has a distinct advantage (also of post-1968 hindsight, but not only) over the bulk of reform economists in the 1960s who have deduced the unavoidability of reform on the bases of historical, materialistic, economistic analyses of the supposedly fundamental contradiction between modern forces of production and the existing relations of production, that is, the politico-bureaucratic straitjacket of modern industry. He believes, however, that he has an alternative explanation of developmental possibilities. It is here that well known Western Marxist themes play an intrinsic role in his presentation: A bureaucratic state whose power rests on its ideological monopoly above all can be transformed on the bases of a new kind of consciousness leading to an antibureaucratic, *cultural* revolution that has a new revolutionary subject or agent.

Bahro's alternative is derived as "objectively possible" on the bases of the dialectic of consciousness. Even a system based on the principle of bureaucratic monopoly of knowledge, in economic and military competition with late capitalism where expert knowledge has become a force of production, cannot help developing an increasingly educated, expert population on all levels of society. The fundamental contradiction of really existing socialism is therefore between the monopoly of knowledge and the necessary development of forms of consciousness that tend to overshoot it, surplus consciousness. Even here, however, we do not get a mechanical, deterministic model of revolution; within the dialectic of consciousness there is room for four types of development (*Alternative*, p. 314; *Lecture*, p. 18). Two complementary forms of "subaltern" consciousness—what he calls absorbed (the fatalistic consciousness of the dominated) and bureaucratic (the consciousness of the dominators)—belong to the reproduction of the system as it exists. Two forms—contradictory to each other—belong to surplus consciousness. These are defined by either being directed to *compensatory* interests the concern of which is private, atomized need satisfaction compensating for being dominated, or to *emancipatory* interests and needs that aim beyond the existing system toward a genuinely free and egalitarian society. Compensatory consciousness refers to an interest and need structure that represents the success of the state to reorganize and redirect surplus consciousness in a conformist direction; emancipatory consciousness can be preserved as a system transcending one only when self-organized. The self-organization of surplus consciousness is what Bahro refers to when he uses the Western Marxist concept of the revolutionary subject (*Lecture*, p. 19). This revolutionary subject does not exist; it must constitute itself. Question: from what materials? Answer: from sociologically plausible carriers of emancipatory consciousness. Who are these; what class, stratum, or group? Bahro's answer, however ambiguous, points to a new revolutionary intelligentsia, one recruited supposedly from all social strata and in any case not equivalent to all of the intellectuals of the present. How are they to be organized? As a new league of communists.

Let us proceed more slowly, and above all more critically. Bahro without any hesitation whatsoever accepts the Leninist thesis that the working strata (for socialism he rejects the concept of class) are capable of developing only economistic interests: here subaltern consciousness or at best compensatory needs. For him this argument supplies ample justification for the historical dictatorship of the Bolsheviks over all strata, including industrial workers—indeed he defends just that atomization of classes that others like Hannah Arendt and even Isaac Deutscher tended to consider the hallmarks of totalitarianism. The breaking up of *all* corporate interest formation was necessary, he argues, in the interest of modernization, industrialization. Among the results of this atomization of all historical classes is a new form of stratification based fundamentally on the supposedly nonantagonistic, classless principle of levels of knowledge and expertise. In such a social system, both system-transcending needs and organizational abilities are more than ever generally available only to the higher, more educated, and expert strata. The argument, to be sure, contradicts the claim that the revolutionary intellectuals will be recruited from all strata, but Bahro sticks to his guns. The last did not become first in the October Revolution, and today they can become so even less—and least of all, on the bases of their own self-activity. To Bahro, 1953 (a confrontation over norms), 1956 (an attempted comeback of counterrevolutionary elements), 1968 (a glorious revolution of intellectuals, a slightly ironic description despite his support), 1970 (proletarian cultural revolution from above—an utterly misleading description), and even 1976 (though he doesn't say why) all demonstrate that the self-organization of industrial workers remains a myth. Let us not delude ourselves, the author of *The Alternative* (who may not be identical to the Bahro of today) could have found equal reasons to explain away 1980 as well. Perhaps he would have spoken mainly about the role of the intellectuals, perhaps the emergence of Polish Meanys and Kirklands; perhaps he would have stressed the ambiguous role of the church.

In a sense Bahro is right: The working class as the revolutionary subject is the product of conceptual mythology in Marx, Rosa Luxemburg, and above all György Lukács.[14] Along with Alvin Gouldner, Ivan Szelényi, and György Konrád, most recently, he is justified in arguing that exactly the myth in its Leninist form allowed the revolutionary intellectuals to substitute themselves for workers, whose consciousness remains hopelessly empirical (i.e., reformist), in the name of the historical interests of the class known only to them. But once again, as in the case of the Asiatic mode of production, Bahro turns a critical doctrine into an apologetic, affirmative one. Like Gouldner apparently, but most emphatically unlike Szelényi and Konrád, he believes that the solution is the realistic, or nonmythological acceptance on the part of a self-recruited intellectual elite of itself as the revolutionary subject. To justify this belief he offers several supportive hypotheses:

1.   Intellectuals possess by far to the greatest extent system-transcending, emancipatory interests and needs. This view he does not hold consistently because he is also suspicious of the corporate, immediate interest of intellectuals in a completely free culture.
2.   The nonantagonistic character of social (as against political) stratification under state socialism allows for a homogeneity of interest representation. This position is merely asserted, dogmatically. One may justly wonder whether Bahro is not taken in by the appearances of a system where all open interest conflicts are suppressed, or internalized by the ruling institution. Also, stratification according to expertise may itself be political as Szelényi insists, even if not in the sense of the same political principle which constitutes the ruling institution.
3.   The intellectualization of the work process on all except the lowest levels allows the recruitment of revolutionary intellectuals from all strata. Yes, but according to his own argumentation in (1), the bulk of these would be recruited from the best educated.
4.   The historical, general interest of the body politic can be absolutely known and substantively embodied in a fully developed socioeconomic-cultural (hence total) revolutionary program. It is this last hypothesis, never explicitly stated, but always assumed by Bahro, that is the most questionable and most dangerous. The idea of the absolute knowledge of history is absurd enough when assumed by a speculative, contemplative philosopher like Hegel; when joined to a theory of action as in the notion of the revolutionary subjectivity it becomes disastrous. In such cases an epistemologically absurd conception of knowledge is replaced by that of absolute will. Whoever is appointed as subject, political action from above is legitimated, from below deemphasized. Modern societies are differentiated and at least

tendentially plural; no single, homogeneous will can emerge from them. Such a will can be imposed only from above. The train of thought inevitably leads to the idea of a single party with state power as its goal, and Bahro is not afraid to draw the conclusion. Not only does he resolutely defend the single-party dictatorship of the past, he also believes that a single party—if a new one—must lead the work of socialist transformation today.

Here we reach what seems to be the limit of toleration of even Bahro's most sympathetic critics.[15] Nevertheless it is Bahro who is consistent with his own premises. To him the only justification of a many-party system is the structural presence of interest conflict in society. But he has systematically argued that in developed, really existing socialism, because of the absence of private property (the classical Marxist criterion) and of a polycentered, market economy (the Weberian criterion), and because of the intellectualization of much of physical work (the new working class assumption) social stratification is nonantagonistic, and the levels of the social hierarchy are fluid. The social whole, of course, *is* antagonistic, the line of social contradiction being drawn by the possession of political and administrative power between the party state hierarchy and the rest of society. As a result, Bahro is convinced that if political power (i.e., the party state) in such a society were democratized or even if "transitionally" it would be ready and willing to represent the *real* interests of those below, the last class feature of the society would be abolished. With the present one-party system pluralistic representation is impossible; with its reformation it would become unnecessary; this seems to be Bahro's point. The thrust of his critique in the tradition of the 1960s seems to be aimed at the party itself: Democratize yourself, and, from above, political life.

Of course, Bahro is not this naive. Fully conscious of the neoconservative response of the various parties to the threat embodied in 1968, he is nevertheless not ready to renounce the Communist party, to be sure the ideal as against the actual one. The existing hierarchy is beyond hope; its consciousness and interests are tied to the preservation of their power. Nevertheless, *individuals* within the party and maybe even in the apparatus itself could be recruited for the new Communist party that he calls "league of communists" after the Yugoslav example. On this basis the existing party must be split (echoes of Lenin and the twenty-one points) so that it can be rebuilt on new but completely unified foundations. When a church is hopelessly corrupt (Bahro actually uses this analogy and not only because he believes in the theocratic character of really existing socialism), a reformation can be successfully institutionalized only as a new, purified church. The party is dead, long live the party, because outside the party there is no salvation.

Bahro is a very decent man and personally not authoritarian even if he is not a little religious. He indeed hopes to preserve *his* new party from the bureaucratic fate of the old not only by a series of organizational reforms (possibility of factions, restoration of the principle of election from below, free and open discussion and debate) but because he believes in the relevance of three historical assumptions, the first already given, the other two to be consciously instituted:

1.   The conclusion of the capitalist road and the end of the international threat to really existing socialism; hence the features of a despotic, bureaucratic revolution from above and of a militarized, bureaucratic system of preparedness are no longer required.
2.   The putting into motion of a culturally revolutionary program tendentially abolishing the split between manual and mental labor, division of labor proper according to Marx, the supposed foundation of all state domination over society.
3.   The split of the party-state dyad along the lines of ideology and political power and the organization of power as *dual* and as *democratic*.

The first point could be readily accepted if one believed in the first place in a historical correlation between development and democracy, and in the "threatened fortress" rationalization of Stalinism. Even here we should not underestimate the ability and willingness of the existing system to perpetuate underdevelopment and international tension. The second, a programmatic argument, derived from Chinese and some New Left models, reopens Bahro to authoritarianism, this time in the form of a pedagogic dictatorship, while the third, derived from the East European opposition, is vitiated both by the idea of a single, vanguard party and that of a mono-organizational socialist state.

It is, of course, the stress on the program of cultural revolution that made Herbert Marcuse (*CR*, pp. 25ff.) so enthusiastic about Bahro. In this context he was far more willing to draw out the last consequences than Bahro himself; to accept what has been recently called the dictatorship over needs.[16] Bahro's own program is neatly divided into Chinese and New Left stages.[17] The first has obviously nothing to do with actual East European reform attempts from above or from below; neither market, independent social organization, or political democratization play any role here. Bahro's models instead are the French Jacobins (nonsensically enough) and the new Jacobins of the Soviet War Communism period as well as the Maoists. The only aim of this stage seems to be the economic equalization of the population, from above, in four steps: (1) Liquidation of bureaucratic corruption, (2) abolition of piecework and work norms, (3) general participation of all in single operative work, and (4) equalization of wages according to labor time (upward adjustment only for the most unpleasant types of work).

While the first two steps are unobjectionable, the next two recall the worst excesses not only of Maoism but also of Eastern Europe at the heights of the Stalinist period. They entail in any differentiated society incredible burdens for significant parts of the population, or at the very least significant parts of the population (and hardly only an upper stratum) will interpret such equalization of work and consumption as an incredible burden—politically the consequences are the same. Economically, the living standards of perhaps a third and the aspirations of perhaps two-thirds would be dramatically lowered. After the experiences already mentioned no one has the right to assume that the relevant strata will willingly and without repression consent to such measures. Interestingly enough, while Bahro seeks to justify the equalization of consumption as a necessary prelude to future democratization (the only conceivable argument here, which, however, puts the cart before the horse), far more realistically Marcuse (*CR*, pp. 32, 35) insists on the suppression of false needs (i.e., the bulk of material needs) for the majority of the population as the only way of breaking the *past-present* continuum of domination. He is unafraid (*CR*, p. 32) of the repression entailed in such a process. Assuming (but not admitting), however, the desirability of a society of homogeneous need structure, the only possible road to this form of equality vitiates equality on the political level. The result can be achieved only with the strengthening of repressive, bureaucratic institutions of execution and enforcement, and a bureaucracy is by definition not the equal in power of those it administers. And more, as Lukács in a prophetic moment in the crucial year of 1919 already realized, it is precisely the institutions needed to discipline a population from above that have a tendency toward self-perpetuation. The price of planned, enforced social equality is institutionalized political inequality,[18] the unavoidable consequence of Bahro's first cultural revolutionary stage that could be best described in his own words (used incorrectly to describe 1970 in Poland) as a "cultural revolution from above."

The step from Stalin to Mao is, of course, in many respects not a very great one and in any case it is well within Eastern Marxism. It is, however, completely against the grain of the democratic aspiration of the East European opposition that Bahro, however ambiguously, shares. On a theoretical level he hopes to democratize his conception, however, by a model derived not from such sources but from Western Marxist conceptions of cultural revolution. The aim remains the total transformation of the structure of needs, according to the canons of Marxism anthropology of human nature itself. The instruments: the complete abolition of the division between mental and manual labor on the one hand, and the abolition of all alienated, quantitative, in a word "false" needs. The result, the rich individual of Marx's dreams, is to be accomplished through a centrally planned determination of needs and the tightly related labor time schedules. This fetishism of planning painfully if residually present in so much of Western Marxism (e.g., in Marcuse's *Soviet Marxism*) has been repeatedly described by East European critical theorists as the fundamental structural characteristic of the *existing* East European systems.[19] Bahro may be more conscious of the dangers involved than, say, Marcuse, but he is more afraid of another: the complete determination of needs from below leading to an anarchy of needs that can be mediated only by the market, a process that will lead to new inequalities. Hence he proposes what I take to be the classical Leninist solution: on the one hand the central planning of needs and labor time from above (minimum program), on the other the democratic choice of communally organized collectivities among various plans submitted by the center concerning different ways of organizing needs and time schedules (maximum program). I call this the classical Leninist solution because of the specific time relationship between the two programs implied by the terms minimum and maximum. Given an already formed need structure of the population, obviously Bahro wants to implement only the minimum program in the immediate present, though his language hides the fact that it is the minimum program that must involve the maximum of coercion. Between minimum program and maximum program, or maximum coercion and democratic self-administration, lies the planned development of individuals capable of exercising democratic functions, in other words, a pedagogic dictatorship. It is again to Marcuse's "credit" that he fearlessly draws out the implication, which in any case is part and parcel of his own theory:[20]

> Bahro's analysis falls back on a position that has been tabooed by both Marxism and liberalism: Plato's position (an educational dictatorship of the most intelligent) and Rousseau's (people must be forced to be free). In fact, the educational function of the socialist state is inconceivable without a recognized authority; for Bahro that authority is grounded in an elite of intelligence. However consistently Bahro may insist that the league as well as the party leadership must come from all social groups and remain accountable to the people at all levels, the scandal remains and must be sustained. (*CR*, p. 32).

As Marcuse knew when he was writing this, he is, of course, opening himself and Bahro to some serious charges of authoritarianism. His answer to his critics on this point was ever ready: One must be able to distinguish between false and true needs, ones engendered by existing systems of domination and ones pointing beyond them, otherwise real emancipation can in no way be imagined. I do not believe, however, that we are stuck with the dilemma that either all individually felt, perceived, and claimed needs are valid ("true") or that those needs are "false" (invalid) which appear so from the heights of the sophisticated culture critiques of industrial civilizations.[21] What hides behind the first claim is a relativistic, normless social analysis. What hides behind the second with its implication of pedagogic dictatorship is a dogmatic, objectivistic conception of absolute philosophic knowledge. The alternative to both is the definition of those needs as valid and true which can be defended as such in procedures of public, democratic participation and will formation involving conflict and compromise. If such procedures are to truly involve *communication free of domination*, a phrase Bahro uses but without understanding, they must be institutionalized in the self-organized and managed cells of social life. Instead of seeing such forms of direct democracy as results of pedagogic dictatorship, we must understand them as necessary and possible from the outset if a dictatorial outcome is to be avoided. The road to a society democratically organized from below (undoubtedly Bahro's utopia too) cannot in principle be achieved by nondemocratic means.

Bahro does not unambiguously consent to the authoritarian implications of his social philosophy. Clearly he hopes to incorporate some democratic elements in his program from the very beginning. His league of communists is to be distinguished from the old party because of its democratic communication with popular organizations. From the outset councils, committees, cooperatives (the seeds of future council democracy) are to be established; in the context of pedagogic dictatorship they are to be "the schools of the masses," in Marcuse's reading, the only consistent one. How do things stand with Bahro himself? The term "dual power" or "dual supremacy" appears two or three times in his work. Marcuse, in line with his own conception, clearly misinterprets the letter of the conception when he understands it as a duality at the summit between the communist party and the league of communists (*CR*, p. 31), a split that Bahro seeks only temporarily. With a bit of wishful thinking one is tempted to accept Dutschke's interpretation (*CR*, p. 202), which refers back to the period between February and October 1917 when Russia was temporarily "the freest country in the world," or Pelikán's (*CR*, p. 181), who reinterprets Bahro's conception according to the Polish developments toward (as we now know) August 1980, leading to the establishment of independent, competing social institutions from below, what the members of KOR have very accurately called the reconstitution of elements of civil society. In point of fact Marcuse's textually incorrect interpretation is closer to Bahro's thrust than Dutschke's philologically accurate derivation of the term "dual power," or Pelikán's projection of the theory of new evolutionism into Bahro. Demonstrably, he is throughout his work rather skeptical about the advance represented by the recovery of civil rights, cultural freedoms, and institutions of autonomous interest representation. These he considers *at best* a detour necessary only because the extreme resistance of the systems to genuine communist reformation pushes the opposition into the minimal program of the restoration of bourgeois rights, and *at worst* the expression of particular, separate interests of intellectuals (cultural freedom) and workers (free trade unions). While it would be possible to find lines in the *Alternative* more positive about such innovations, it is ultimately Bahro's conception as a whole that speaks against a principled defense of the duality of society and state:[22] his insistence on the leading role of a single party, albeit a reformed one, and the even more fundamental definition of all interest formation from below as merely compensatory. With this notion in mind, we can give the various interpretations of his conception of dual power their due. Bahro's league of communists is first constituted as a social movement, against the existing state. Thus, in context of the overthrow of the present system there may be indeed initially a duality of power between the representative of society, the league, and the party-state. Here is the source of Marcuse's misreading, except that Bahro does not for a moment seek to institutionalize any division at the summit. In terms of a rather loosely interpreted history one may be able to divine some sort of relationship to the October Revolution as well in the manner of Dutschke, except that the Bolsheviks did not succeed in reducing the independent action of the councils until the very end; they were not hegemonic in society. In any case Bahro is in a hurry to recomplete the steps from February to October and beyond when even in his own testimony Russia was hardly the freest country in the world. The party in the end must be reunited with the new league as its core, and state power must be preserved as a unity (*Alternative*, p. 350). It is true that the oppositionists of the Polish KOR, to name the most relevant contrast, are also unwilling to challenge the unity of the institutions of the party-state, although, of course, for strategic reasons. For now they accept the leading role of the existing party in the state, although not in society. Being ready to deal with the existing unreformed party-state, they may indeed seem less radical than Bahro. Of course Bahro himself continues to believe in the possibility of a genuine mono-organizational socialist state. It is paradoxically thus that he negates the idea of a genuinely self-managing, repoliticized society. Unlike KOR, and contradicting Pelikán's interpretation, he insists on the ideological hegemony over society, the *leading role in society* of the very same element, the new league of communists (i.e., the reformed communist party) which must aim at becoming (or already is) the leading spirit of the state as well. It is this step that completes the journey to October. Bahro's alternative is at best a replay of the Russian Revolution under contemporary circumstances. It is thus that a Western Marxist program of cultural revolution turns Eastern in his hands.

Bahro's Audience

For whom is the *Alternative* written? Paradoxically Marcuse's enthusiastic reading seems to support Szelényi's implication that we are dealing with an ideological defense of the road of intellectuals to class power, which on the structural level will be this time the transition from an industrial to a "scientific-cultural" despotism.[23] Though persuasive, this thesis should be challenged. Bahro continues the classical suspicion of Bolshevism (in this respect the heir of Jacobinism) against all class or even interest group formation on top as well as bottom, including very explicitly the stratum of the intellectuals as a whole. To be sure, rather more carefully than in his other works, Szelényi himself states only that Bahro's "alternative from above" is an alternative *of and for* the Bolshevik intellectuals, a statement in itself hard to contest. On the other hand, it is quite evidently not *for* the Bolshevik intellectuals as a whole, present or future. Whether we accept Leszek Kołakowski's often repeated thesis concerning the end of the possibility of revisionism in the context of parties now cynical concerning their own ideology, or the contradictory claim of Hermann Weber (*CR*, pp. 17–19) based on the ever-reproduced internal contradiction between the theory and practice of official communism, or even the stress of Pelikán on a necessary combination of reform orientations within the existing parties with a process of democratization from below (*CR*, p. 172), we must nevertheless realize that Bahro's book, written by a man of the apparatus, reveals *in itself* an internal tension within at least the SED. This tension cannot be simply understood as that of technocrats versus politocrats (in a sense Bahro is neither) nor especially in the GDR as that of decentralized or centralized versions of socialism. Bahro does not belong to the reform generation of the 1960s whose activity as the Czech example shows tended to release forces from a society formed before the imposition of Stalinist dictatorship, forces that could no longer be integrated in any version of a one-party rule. Politically he is, moreover, further away than they from the actual movements of Eastern Europe; as Pelikán notes,[24] a good deal further than his nearest analogue, András Hegedüs, whose own acceptance of a single party is at best pragmatic, at worst historicist, but who nevertheless decisively supports all movements for the reconstruction of the state-society duality.[25]

While it may be rather difficult to directly point to specific groupings or strata in the generally deideologized East European parties who would identify with Bahro's alternative, it may be nevertheless possible to indicate the political trajectory of his proposals in terms of existing structural possibilities. Bahro's program of cultural revolution—legitimated by a new egalitarianism above all, but also by a proposal for participation from below that would fully respect the ideological hegemony of a "new" Communist Party—is translatable into part of the solution of a yet unsolved problem of the East European parties of hoping to keep the system's identity intact in the context of contemporary modernization, rationalization.[26] This process involving some solution of the now chronic rationality crises of the regimes will be possible only if the centers of power in East Europe and the Soviet Union manage to move from the positive, direct subordination of all forms of social life to the party-state, to a negative, less direct, less homogeneous form of subordination that might permit rather different spaces for movement in the various social spheres of culture, polity, and economy.[27] This transition, which may unite the hopes of the most conformist remnants of market socialism with those of more conservative elements, is possible only in the context of a rather significant increase of the party-state's ideological resources. Here is the possible role of the revival of nationalism all along the line, but in the GDR in particular—where the national issue cannot be revived for several obvious reasons;[28] the "reformation" of orthodox Marxism in a necessarily neo-Leninist form may be a possible replacement. Whatever Bahro's personal intentions, it is only in such a context that his work (or some other version of a similar thesis) could have and may yet find its political importance.

The Alternative is addressed to the party, yet Bahro was jailed and expelled. From 1924, and the attacks on Lukács and Korsch, the *Eastern* Marxist Communist parties resolutely fought against *Western* Marxist interpretations and even justifications of their politics. The reason is perhaps still the same: The authoritarian socialist house of power cannot afford to legitimate as its own two-dimensional, internally antinomic ideologies, open to immanent ideology critique. Bahro's antinomies are from this point of view especially dangerous, because at variance with the central thrust of his book some of them express the aspiration of today's opposition. Furthermore, his insistence on the need for a new church in a Communist reformation could not, of course, be any more pleasing to the orthodox than to those who wish for a genuinely secular politics. If it is true that rather conservative reformers in the party are in fact addressed, it is also true that Bahro tells them that their aims cannot be ultimately carried out without a temporary institutional break in the party, necessary for a full-scale purification and reconstruction. The idea recalls 1956 and 1968, the only precedents for such a thing in the history of authoritarian state socialism. After 1968 especially (and 1980 has not falsified the point) the ruling parties have realized that any internal institutional split would endanger their very survival.[29] This is the context of the new strategy of the opposition in Poland at least, structural reform from below.

The actual audience of Bahro turned out other than intended. Because of its mixture of Western Marxist and Left Communist foundations we should not be surprised about the intellectual success of *The Alternative* in the West. The Eastern Marxist outcome of the book makes it irrelevant to contemporary struggles for liberation in East Europe. To fully realize the reasons is a necessary condition for the renewal of the desperately needed dialogue between critical theorists East and West, who must free themselves from all apology concerning one another's systems of domination.

Notes

1. M. Merleau-Ponty, "The Adventure of the Dialectic," (Evanston, 1973); P. Anderson, *Considerations on Western Marxism* (London, 1976); A. Arato and P. Breines, *The Young Lukács and the Origins of Western Marxism* (New York, 1979) as well as F. Fehér's forthcoming review of the last, in *New German Critique*; also see: R. Jacoby's and M. Jay's forthcoming books on Western Marxism.

2. E. Bloch, "Aktualität und Utopie: zu Lukács' *Geschichte und Klassenbewusstsein*" (1923), in *Philosophische Aufsätze* (Frankfurt/M., 1969), pp. 597–600.

3. Cf. among other works J. Kuroń and K. Modzelewski, *Monopolsozialismus* (Hamburg, 1969); M. Rakovski, *Toward an East European Marxism* (London, 1978); G. Konrád and I. Szelényi, *The Intellectuals on the Road to Class Power* (New York, 1979); A. Heller, G. Márkus, F. Fehér, *The Dictatorship over Needs*, forthcoming; S. Stojanovic, *Between Ideal and Reality* (New York, 1970).

4. Here I must slightly revise an earlier judgment expressed in A. Arato and M. Vajda, "The Limits of the Leninist Opposition," *New German Critique* (Winter 1980), where we argue that at most Bahro's position corresponds to the left communism of the 1920s but not to Western Marxism as here defined.

5. F. Fehér, cited in note 1.

6. Thus Ivan Szelényi's brilliant critique of Bahro, based on his own thesis, is right

but for the wrong reason. Cf. "Whose Alternative," *New German Critique* (Spring/Summer 1980). Szelényi would perhaps defend himself against this criticism by saying that only in the liberal societies of the self-regulating market is the interest of intellectuals definable in terms of free publicity and culture, while in the state socialist societies participation in "rational redistribution" on the political, technical, or ideological level replaces this. Nevertheless, even this argument would indicate that the October revolution was carried out in the name of the historic interest of intellectuals against their immediate empirical interests. The existing intellectuals would therefore be in the same position *vis-à-vis* the revolution as the existing workers. Should we therefore believe that the historical interests of one of these were *really* represented by the vanguard? The role of intellectuals in opposition to the existing systems from the 1920s to today certainly speaks against such a claim. It is Bahro who seems to be right here—the intellectuals do preserve their interest in free publicity and culture also under state socialism. However, it is not *only their* interest, as workers from Budapest to Gdansk repeatedly showed.

7. A remarkable (and convincing) critique of this conception in Marx and others is in P. Anderson, *The Lineages of the Absolutist State* (London, 1974), doubly remarkable because of the depth of its analysis and learning but also because the results are used to reintegrate Russia within a single model of European development required by the Trotskyist apologetics of the October Revolution. To justify the continuity of the October Revolution with European socialist traditions, the permanent revolution must begin in Europe, if in an underdeveloped part of it. But if, as Anderson rightly believes, one must separate the historical lineage of Turkey from China because of the inability of *any* concept of Asiatic mode of production to contain both, should we not separate the lineages of England and France from that of Russia because of entirely analogous difficulties with the overblown Marxian concept of feudalism that he relies on in spite of his excellent sources in non-Marxist historiography?

8. If a multilinear one. Bahro's conception of history—in spite of the use of the Asiatic model—is that of orthodox historical materialism. His biological analogies, his use of the economistic model of the dynamic of forces and relations of production, his attachment to the famous womb metaphor, which he rechristens as the larva stage, all point in this direction. The multilinear adjustment lies in his insistence that a new historical stage follows from a previously less developed line. It is in this form, as we will see below, that the idea of transitional society creeps back into his analysis.

9. Noticing the contradictions, in an article summarizing *The Alternative* (*New Left Review*, November-December 1977, hereafter: *Lecture*), he adds that late capitalism is also a society transitional to socialism, presumably because of its own étatistic features.

10. Bahro mixes this stress with another because he needs to represent Russia as really Asia. Otherwise, the October Revolution and its aftermath might not provide the lesson for Asia that he has in mind.

11. Bahro never asks whether an empire should have been inherited in the first place; genuine federalism is hardly an alternative in his work. Recently it has been argued rather convincingly that the fundamental features of the social model and an anticipating of the post-1945 situation were cemented as the consequence of the resynthesis, recentralization of the imperial heritage in the 1920s. See Hélène Carrère-d'Encausse, *L'empire éclaté* (Paris, 1978). The argument is present in Bahro but under the mask of inevitability. It is useful to recall for all analysts of the Soviet Union that it is neither a centralized nation-state nor a federation, but a centralized, multinational empire. V. Zazlavsky's otherwise excellent analysis, "The Ethnic Question in the USSR" (*Telos*, Fall 1980) is marred by the false alternative, unitary state or federation.

12. For them, "rational redistribution" is that single heading, tendentially uniting the political bureaucracy, the technocracy, and even the whole of the intelligentsia. However,

tacitly a second principle, political status, is introduced by them as well when they define the institutional core as a closed ruling order or estate. (This point—analogous to Bahro's definition of the party as a closed corporation—is lost in the English translation of Szelényi and Konrád as revised by Richard Allen). On the other side Bahro himself uses knowledge as a principle legitimating both the antagonistic and nonantagonistic principles of stratification, even if knowledge of fundamentally different kinds is meant. The fundamental difference between these views is that Bahro does not integrate the whole of the intellectuals as the tendential ruling class of the present, nor does he assign to them hegemony (this belongs to a renewed party) under his own technocratic alternative. He does accept the legitimacy of a functional hierarchy according to education; this leads Szelényi to accuse him of being an ideologist for intellectual class rule.

13. Bahro is by no means so clear as some of his interpreters would have him (cf. Alain Touraine, *L'après socialisme* [Paris, 1980]) concerning the primacy of political state to antagonistic stratification relations. At times he seems to claim indeed that the political bureaucracy is a possessing class, but what it possesses is the state. The question whether we are dealing with a class, or a closed political status group (order or state) organized around the political institutional core of the society is hardly trivial. I will return to the issue of social stratifications, and Bahro's contribution in this regard, elsewhere.

14. On Marx cf. Jean Cohen, "System and Class: The Subversion of Emancipation," in *Social Research* (Winter 1978) as well as her forthcoming book on the same subject. On Lukács cf. Arato and Breines, op. cit.

15. With the exception of Marcuse, as we will see. Paradoxically the generally negative critic, Szelényi, says that one party is already one too many. The witticism bypasses the issue; one or many is the alternative, not one or none, unless we are to believe (as Szelényi does not) in the immediate possibility and desirability of an entirely direct democracy. Actually, Szelényi, more in a manner of KOR and perhaps Hegedüs to whom he refers, seeks to introduce some realism into his own proposal. For the moment East Europe is stuck with a single party; this, however, does not mean that no elements of pluralism and self-administration can be introduced in society.

16. Cf. the forthcoming book by A. Heller, F. Fehér, G. Márkus as well as two articles: F. Fehér, "The Dictatorship over Needs" (*Telos*, 35), and F. Fehér, A. Heller, "Forms of Equality" (*Telos*, 32).

17. Marcuse denies Bahro's relationship to the Chinese cultural revolution, which is, however, decisively proven by the testimony of Dutschke regarding Bahro's original manuscript (cf. *CR*, pp. 33, 192, 205, 208).

18. See F. Fehér, A. Heller, "Forms of Equality."

19. On the most sophisticated level under the complementary rubrics of rational redistribution (Konrád, Szelényi) and dictatorship over needs (Fehér, Márkus, Heller).

20. Cf. M. Bookchin, "Beyond neo-Marxism," *Telos*, 36; H. Marcuse, J. Habermas et al., "Theory and Politics," *Telos*, 38; and J. Cohen, "The Legacy of Herbert Marcuse," *Dissent* (Winter 1981).

21. On the theoretical problem of needs cf. A. Heller, *Marx's Theory of Need* (London, 1977) and C. Castoriadis, "From Marx to Aristotle, from Aristotle to Us," *Social Research* (Winter 1978), pp. 724ff.

22. We should note here the fundamental identity between the ideal of dual power demanded in many of the council experiments from Petersburg 1905 to Budapest 1956, and the imperfect and perhaps temporary achievement, as the result of "democratic" revolutions in at least some Western European countries (and the United States), of a form of separation between state and civil society that did not deprive society of its own mode of political public life. The classical work on this topic remains, in spite of its pessimism and overly global analysis, J. Habermas's *Strukturwandel der Öffentlichkeit* (Neuwied,

1963). The point concerning the Hungarian councils is made by C. Lefort in "The Age of Novelty," *Telos*, 39.

23. Bahro's alternative, in Marcuse's words (*CR*, p. 30), "would demolish the privileged position of the intelligentsia by universalizing it." In Szelényi's depiction: "The solution to the Platonian dilemma is found: in order to ensure that philosophers do not represent a privileged class, you make everybody a philosopher. . . . But what are poor intellectuals to do until everybody becomes an intellectual?" They will of course rule in the lengthy "transition." Szelényi, op. cit., pp. 119–20.

24. Cf. also C. Heuberger, "Neue Wege zur Überwindung des osteuropäischen Sozialismus," *Rundbrief des Sozialistischen Büros* (May 1979), and A. Arato, M. Vajda, op. cit.

25. Cf. the interview with Bahro in *Der Spiegel* after his release and arrival in West Germany.

26. On the economic level this process has been described first by Jánossy as the transition from extensive economic development (i.e., drawing in of ever newer sectors of society into urban industrial production and consumption), to intensive development (i.e., expanding the need structure of the existing population and the productivity of the existing labor force).

27. In this context see: A. Arato, "Critical Sociology and Authoritarian State Socialism," chapter 3 of this volume, for an analysis of the problems involved in such a transition. While the experience of Poland 1980 requires a thorough revision of this as well as most other theses on East European societal alternatives, I still consider the abstract model of development presented by this article defensible.

28. See A. Arato, M. Vajda, op. cit.

29. The argument is brilliantly made, against all historical materialist interpretations of East Europe implicitly including the thesis of Szelényi and Konrád, by M. Rakovsky in *Toward an East European Marxism* (a ridiculously inaccurate title of the British publishers given to *Le Marxisme face aux pays de l'est*).

5

Immanent Critique and Authoritarian Socialism: On Konrád and Szelényi's *Intellectuals*

I

Is a critical social theory of authoritarian state socialism, one not apologetic for any contemporary form of domination, possible at all? The question and the theoretical efforts to which it is relevant have two identifiable origins, one Western and the other Eastern European. Born as a set of efforts to understand in a practical and meaningful way the forms of domination characteristic of our epoch, the critical theory of the Frankfurt School—the Western contribution—is today apparently exhausted. Aside from a whole series of brilliant analyses of German fascism, as well as a number of imposing studies concentrating on the cultural sphere of late capitalism, the older critical theory in New York and Frankfurt, I do not believe, has ever fulfilled its self-defined social-theoretical tasks. And while the newer critical theory in Frankfurt and Starnberg had at its highest point developed the foundations for a sophisticated, many-strata conflict model of the legitimation crisis of late capitalism, the representative product of this type of analysis contained some partially hidden doubts about the possibility of critical theory in the sense of immanent social criticism. Subsequently, the factual antinomy of practical philosophy and evolutionary social science in the work of Habermas (and his colleagues) expressed the new embarrassment of this tradition in a far more serious way than did his few increasingly skeptical remarks concerning the chances of an immanent critique with a communicative,

Reprinted with permission from *Canadian Journal of Political and Social Theory/Revue canadienne de théorie politique et sociale*, Vol. 7, Nos. 1–2 (Hiver/Printemps, 1983), pp. 146–62.

practical relation to its audience. Independently of the value of the work done on the foundations of a discursive, communicative ethics and the theory of social evolution, no one today assumes anything more than at best indirect gains for a critical social theory of contemporary forms of domination from these primarily methodological, metatheoretical projects.

The viability or impossibility of critical theory can be established only by actual efforts of analyses (philosophically informed, it is to be hoped) of contemporary social formations. Of these, quite obviously late capitalism and authoritarian state socialism are the most important. In the latter context the relatively minor part played by the study of the Soviet Union in the history of critical theory is more or less scandalous. While Horkheimer in 1940 pointed to the potentially apologetic function of classical Marxism vis-à-vis the most authoritarian of the regimes of his time ("integral statism"), there are only two works in the Frankfurt tradition—one by Herbert Marcuse and the other by Oskar Negt— which, as far as I can tell, try to apply the methods of this school in this domain.[1] While it would not be easy to prove that this omission played a role in the exhaustion of critical theory, it is now clear that no version of this theory is worth reconstructing if it remains in part apologetic (as was Marcuse) or conceptually powerless (as was Negt) in the face of authoritarian state socialism.

The same question can also be approached from the angle of independent Eastern European theoretical efforts to deal with their own social reality. Significantly the major form of oppositional thought in the 1950s and 1960s began with a Marxist (i.e., anti-Stalinist) revision of the ruling ideology and thus was never intrinsically connected with the democratizing and liberalizing political goals of many members of this reform generation. On the other hand, the full-fledged renaissance of Marxian philosophy (as a philosophy of practice), as well as the revival of serious economic analysis during the second half of this period, also bypassed the social-theoretical inheritance of Marx for a different but very good reason: the painful evidence of a personal experience with the weakness of a whole set of policies based on classical Marxian doctrines, i.e., concepts such as underdeveloped socialism, transitional society-degenerate workers' state, state socialism, and bureaucratic collectivism.

And yet, as contemporary post-Marxist intellectual ferment in several countries seems to show, the abandonment of all possible Marxian methods in favor of one or another well-known Western liberal or conservative approach can easily lead to theoretical impotence and, at worst, to apologies for forms of domination other than their own. Indeed, many Eastern European oppositionists today face the same danger against which they have justly warned Western radicals for fifteen years: producing ideological justification for the form of domination faced by the other. In this context the project of a critical theory of Eastern European societies which might involve something more than the revision of official Marxism, or even the return to the classical Marxian social theory, surely offers some hope. Even if it should turn out that all of the doctrines of classical theory involve apologetic or irrelevant consequences for the study of authoritarian state socialism, it might still be the case that the original practical intentions can be well served. Such would be the program of a *neo*-Marxist critical theory of authoritarian state socialism and would require a reconstruction of historical materialism.

Yet if the practical intentions themselves could not be adequately distinguished from *both* state socialist forms of domination and irrelevant and incoherent social utopias, it still might be possible to relate a new project of emancipation to a dynamic social theory that would at least preserve as its regulative principle the Western Marxist relation between philosophy and social theory. Such would be the program of a *post*-Marxist critical theory.

Such theoretical programs have indeed already emerged in today's Eastern Europe, especially in Hungary, even if the two types of critical theory—the neo-Marxist and the post-Marxist—have not yet been clearly differentiated. Actually, all significant efforts until now have made some serious use of, or concessions to, at least some dimension of classical Marxist social theory. And next to the projects of the reconstruction and transcendence of Marxism, those of revisionism and renaissance also continue (if decreasingly) to inform the meaning of critical theory in Eastern Europe. As a consequence, in addition to my original question concerning the possibility of any critical theory of authoritarian state socialism, I will also want to ask to what extent and in what sense such a theory can and should remain in the Marxian tradition.

II

The history of critical theory in the West has, of course, involved a series of changing relationships to Marxism. The two works of the Frankfurt School dedicated to the critique of Soviet Marxism thus reveal two different types of theorizing. Both Marcuse and Negt used a method of immanent ideology critique, confronting Marxist norms preserved—even in their Soviet deformation—with the existing socioeconomic structures which were unable to satisfy them. But while Negt carefully avoided, in the manner of Adorno, the support of all positive theory construction concerning the social structure, Marcuse (as usual more "affirmative") embedded his ideology-critical theses in a series of dogmatic assumptions, most notably, one involving the independent socialist logic of central planning and state ownership of the means of production guaranteed an outcome consistent with the relevant Marxist norms. And when in *One Dimensional Man* he produced his own end-of-ideology thesis denying the tension between norm and reality in all advanced industrial societies, he moderated but did not abandon the affirmative and implicitly apologetic theses. However critical of this effort, I must also admit that Negt (then still under the influence of Habermas) produced nothing more than a static confrontation of Soviet norm and reality without any further theoretical and political consequences. In other words, neither a purely negative ideology critique, nor the affirmative linkage of critical theory to the body of classical Marxian doctrines, produced a dynamic and nonapologetic social theory of authoritarian state socialism.

Today after a decade of discussion, some additional and perhaps more import-ant reasons for the failure of the older critical theory in the face of the societies of the Soviet type can be adduced. The program that critical theorists from Horkheimer and Marcuse to Adorno and the early Habermas believed to have discovered in the Marxist critique of political economy was indeed an ambitious one. In this conception an immanent critique of formal ideological systems, first of all, combined the hermeneutic task of philosophy (by pointing to culturally significant norms embedded in social institutions and practices) with the empiri-cal-analytical task of the best of the social sciences (by establishing the system-atic interconnections among and within the spheres of social life). But secondly, its position between philosophy and science allowed critique to go beyond each by demonstrating the dynamic tension and opposition between norms and social institutions and practices, as well as the self-imposed, self-reproducing contra-dictions of the social system itself.

When made conscious, the opposition between norm and reality is the basis of social action for the realization of the norm. On this level the relationship of critique to its audience is that of practical enlightenment and motivation which works only if, in a discursive process, the addressees of theory recognize the norms as their own. The self-contradictions of the social system are, on the other hand, raised to the level of consciousness for the sake of theoretical orientation of already constituted social actors. The method was supposed to work because of the double sense in which the criticized ideologies embodied "true" and "false" consciousness: the unity of a valid norm with false claims of its actual realization, and the unity of accurate or adequate scientific description with false claims of necessity and transhistoricity. Is such a theoretical program in any sense defensible today? Can prospective critics of authoritarian state socialism relate to it at all?

Implicitly, but clearly, Habermas himself has recently restricted the general applicability of critical theory in the sense of immanent critique to classical capitalism, where, according to him, a market-based economic system has taken on the primary task of social as well as system integration. A value-theoretical critique could thus simultaneously operate on a normative and empirical or more exactly (since both levels involve norms) action and system theoretical levels. With the partial repoliticization of the economy under late capitalism, social and system integration are again institutionally differentiated, and the social sciences dealing with the various spheres of reproduction no longer have to be either totalizing or normatively overburdened.

Analogously, it could be argued that the transformation of authoritarian state socialism might undermine immanent critique.[2] There are, nevertheless, perhaps even weightier objections that do not assume a fundamental transformation of its object, ones that all contributions to the critical theory of authoritarian state socialism should take into account. The status of "critique" independent of philosophy and social science (which it supposedly absorbs) turns out to be difficult to sustain. If one does not assume a quasi-Hegelian logic of the development of thought for which every epoch is best expressed in a single system of ideas, and for which every such system reflexively absorbs its predecessor (something Marx assumed even more definitively than Hegel), it becomes logically possible that the number of ideologies relevant to immanent critique will be one, several, or even none. If there are several which may indeed embody different normative claims, critical theory cannot dispense with the services of practical philosophy dealing with the foundations and validity of norms. I believe, at least in principle, that the same would be true in the case of the existence of only one theoretically significant social ideology.

The objection that immanent critique always needs philosophical justification is in itself surely not fatal. Such was Marcuse's position with reference to the philosophy of the past in the 1930s; Adorno too insisted on the antinomic complementarity of immanent and transcendent critique. It may also be the case, however, that in a given social formation no generally significant system of thought exists with philosophically defensible normative claims, and/or that the intellectual schemes with normative claims that do exist have no implications whatsoever for grasping the systemic interconnections of societies.

In the one case the hermeneutic claims of critical theory and in the other its social scientific (systems theoretical) dimension would be endangered. In reference to the first I should mention one version of the end-of-ideology thesis in the writings of Marcuse, Adorno, and now Habermas, according to which genuine, two-dimensional ideologies involving tension between empirical and normative claims are dead in a period (advanced capitalism) in which the bourgeoisie has become cynical about its values. This thesis has its parallels in at least three Eastern European countries (Kołakowski: Poland, Zaslavsky: USSR, Budapest School: Hungary) with one addendum: Not only are the normative claims of the ruling ideological ritual, Marxism-Leninism, philosophically empty, but, given that their purpose is to exclude all serious discourse about society, they are not even believed by the ideologues themselves.

Assuming the necessity of social integration for all societies, one may, of course, argue that forms of symbolic life with implicit validity claims will necessarily exist even in such a context, if on a deeper level, embodied by institutions (often small-scale), practices, objectivations, beliefs. But theory building in the sense of immanent critique requires something more: genuine two-dimensional ideologies. Their supposed decline may drive one to a resigned social philosophy, though it should not—as it unfortunately did for the older critical theory—exclude the rehabilitation and critical appropriation of those methodologies (hermeneutical, phenomenological, interactionist, "genealogical") that are our only access to the institutions, objectivations, practices, and beliefs responsible for social integration.

In reference to the second problem, the absence of systematic interconnections in the case of existing ideologies or even social-scientific approaches, the answer after the recent work of Habermas is simple and somewhat tautological. Given such a quandary, only the application of the concepts of systems theory gives us a key to systems integration. Such a step may be unavoidable, even assuming the existence of genuine ideologies (in the sense of the Frankfurt School) with both normative and systemic implications. We ourselves should not accept too quickly the global claims of such ideologies, or, worse, attribute much significance to them. There may not be a single road, even in principle, to the study of the "totality" of the social spheres, and those in the tradition of critical theory perhaps ought to learn methodological pluralism, even at the potential cost of being charged with eclecticism. In other words, not only philosophy but the action and system theoretical social sciences need at the very least to complement immanent critique, with the boundaries among them depending on the gradually reconstructed structure of the social formation in question.

The reason for continuing to insist on immanent critique in the context of such an expanded theoretical program is the special relationship of this type of theory to its addressees. In the present context this relationship also has its problems. The linking of the critique of ideology with the enlightenment and motivation of the addressees of theory assumes, I believe, a homogeneous value system between the ideology and the relevant social agents. Under some conditions of social integration (given certain national contexts) such an assumption may be empirically defensible. But we should recall the latitude given by Max Weber (on very good empirical grounds) to the conditions satisfying political legitimacy: A form of domination is indeed strengthened by the relevant beliefs of a whole population, but the conditions of legitimate domination are minimally satisfied by referring to what he misleadingly called the administrative staff (*Verwaltungsstab*). Moving from the concept of legitimacy to that of ideology (in some respects a precarious move), we might therefore admit that in some societies immanent critique will address only ruling elites (to use another inadequate term). Such indeed has been the partially justified claim of Kołakowski and members of the new Polish opposition concerning the social critique of the revisionist reformers of the 1956 generation. This claim is usually followed by another one—based on the end-of-ideology thesis—concerning the end of revisionism. Here too the response of critical theory would have to be based on the analysis of social integration without any self-restriction to the critique of ideology in the strict sense. The raising to the level of consciousness of those institutionalized beliefs and enforced practices that symbolically integrate systems otherwise perceived as oppressive, hierarchical, and exploitative preserves the enlightening and motivating role—especially for authoritarian state socialism—that critical theory restricted to the critique of more formal ideological doctrines. The critique of the latter will, however, retain its relevance wherever significant sociological strata or groups continue to be motivated, at least in part, by values shared with dominant ideologies (in some countries not necessarily the official one).

III

The question concerning the conditions leading to the possibility of a critical theory of authoritarian state socialism fortunately does not have to be posed in an intellectual vacuum. Although in Eastern Europe itself no relevant theoretical project has, as far as I know, directly taken its point of departure from the older or newer critical theory, several have been noticeably affected by this tradition as well as some of its methodological difficulties. The entirely new dimension linking the approaches in question is the common desire to undertake a critique of ideology of classical rather than merely Soviet Marxism. In this context several historical precedents should be recalled. From the point of view of the imperatives of his own theory construction, Marx himself always distinguished between political and "vulgar" economy. An analogous relationship between classical and Soviet Marxism becomes theoretically plausible in the context of the already mentioned end-of-ideology thesis. Not only is classical—unlike Soviet—Marxism genuinely suitable for further construction theory if critically appropriated, it may indeed embody a normative project continuous with at least some aspects of institutionalized symbol systems under authoritarian state socialism.

The idea of a Marxian critique of Marxism, of turning historical materialism against itself is, furthermore, one of the constitutive dimensions of the tradition Merleau-Ponty named Western Marxism. First proposed by Lukács in 1919, then by Korsch and later by Mannheim, and accepted by members of the Frankfurt School in their various replies to Mannheim, the self-critique of Marxism had not been fully carried out until now. While on a metatheoretical level, Habermas and Wellmer achieved much in this regard, they most definitely did not explore the potential connections of the theory they criticized to a new form of domination. While this was in part attempted by Negt, the critical thrust of his argumentation was turned back on Soviet rather than classical Marxism.

Given these precedents, the current Eastern European efforts at a critical theory of authoritarian state socialism, which engage in serious confrontations with some of the strongest versions of Marxian theory, represent both a continuation of and a new departure within Western Marxism. In the context of this essay I can only list a series of such efforts (perhaps unavoidably stressing Hungarian theorists, given my own background), but will select one—that of Ivan Szelényi and György Konrád—for closer scrutiny.[3] The objective will be to indicate the differences among five representative approaches by pointing not only to the various notions of critique, but also to the different types of relationships to social scientific theory construction, both Marxist and non-Marxist.[4]

1. Rudolf Bahro's position in the spectrum of critical theory in Eastern Europe is indeed unique: He is the only neo-Leninist. It is in large part from this

point of view that he criticizes classical Marxism. His conception of critique involves using parts of the theory against other parts (at times correcting revolutionary expectations through what he takes to be historical evidence); he nowhere steps outside the Marxian tradition for sources of constructive theory building. He rejects the norm-reality model of immanent critique as useless or even dangerous utopianism; classical Marxian norms he (inconsistently) considers historically irrelevant and Soviet Marxist ones apologetic, at least in the context of an already modernized version of state socialism. From classical Marxism, he accepts a version of its deterministic theory of history; from Leninism, its political substitutionism, although in a new and openly elitist form; from Western Marxism, the program of cultural revolution. It is not hard to show the perhaps unintended political and theoretical conservatism of his approach.

2. The work of Ivan Szelényi and György Konrád represents an immanent critique of Marxism as an ideology of revolutionary intellectuals, a motif also present in Bahro. The critique remains a historical materialist one to the extent that it is built around the model of the Marxian class theory (reinterpreted through concepts drawn from Weber, Polányi, and Mannheim), but it is post-Marxist to the extent that it breaks (more radically and consistently than Bahro) with the philosophical dimensions of the original project. While explicitly rejecting a normatively motivated critique, this theory—unwilling and perhaps unable to reflect on its norms—oscillates between populist (*ouvrierist*) and democratic socialist political conceptions. Recently, the program of a socialist civil society has acquired equal weight in Szelényi's essays to that of a society where the immediate producers exercise control over the economic surplus, but the relationship between these utopian conceptions has been nowhere clarified.

3. The authors of *The Dictatorship over Needs*, Agnes Heller, Ferenc Fehér and György Márkus, work with a somewhat antinomic combination—analogous and indeed related to the newer critical theory—of the philosophy of praxis and critical social science. In the case of two of these authors, Heller and Fehér, the combination is that of a philosophy continuous with the Renaissance of Marxism of the 1960s reinterpreted as a radical communications theory within a formal sociological, in large part Weberian, framework mobilized for social criticism. In the case of the third author, Márkus, while the philosophical perspective—his own version of a radical communications theory—is shifting in a post-Marxian direction, his project of a critical economics relying on a variety of sources (Robinson, Kornai, Kalecki, Brus, et al.) is built up around Marxian principles of organization. For Márkus, also coauthor of an unpublished 1972 critique of *Das Kapital*, critical theory must discover the specific rationality ("goal-function") of a socioeconomic system from the point of view of another possible society.

4. The work of Mihály Vajda increasingly represents a break with all dimensions of both the philosophy and the social theory of the Marxian tradition. The program of a democratic civil society remains regulative for the post-Marxist critical political theory of Vajda, who, somewhat like Kołakowski, has concen-

trated his critique of Marx on the intended abolition of the state/society duality which can be realized, as both argue, only by the state-absorbing society. Unlike Kołakowski, Vajda is a critical theorist insofar as he explicitly seeks to work out a perspective, without, however, utilizing Marxian categories of a new type of social formation that would be a postbourgeois, but democratic (radical democratic?) version of civil society. In his recent work he has sought in a somewhat historicist manner, to ground the chances of such a society in the differing historical traditions of the several Eastern European cultural complexes.

5. Another project of a post-Marxist critical theory is that of János Kis and György Bence (Marc Rakovski), coauthors with Márkus of the *Das Kapital* critique and authors of *Le Marxisme face aux pays de l'est*. They have now definitively broken with the philosophy of praxis, and more recently—seeking to establish an adequate communicative relationship with today's actual or potential democratic movements—with all Marxian language. Nevertheless, their desire for a dynamic social theory necessary for the clarification of the issues faced by existing or possible social movements make them post- rather than anti-Marxist, even if their conception of another desirable society is increasingly restricted to liberal parliamentary democracy not distinguished from the existing capitalist democracies. The presence of socialism in such a society is neither thematized nor rejected by Kis and Bence.

IV

The book by Szelényi and Konrád, *The Intellectuals on the Road to Class Power*, is of particular interest because it is the most explicitly relevant to critical theory in terms of the very self-definition of the authors. In the book, as well as in Szelényi's subsequent essays, the terms "immanent critique," "critique of ideology," "critical social theory" repeatedly appear whenever their own method is discussed. They define "immanent and transcendent critique" and the, for them, parallel (if ambiguous) terms "critique of ideology" and "ideological criticism" by a rather scientist reference to the value-fact problem. The immanent critique of ideology, as against transcendent ideological criticism, does not evaluate premises, but interprets societies wholly from within their own context. Thus the aim of immanent critique is to discover the interests, conflicts, and alternatives hidden by ideologies and especially by universal normative claims which are not further explored for their dimension of truth. While one of the requirements of the Frankfurt School critique of ideology—the "defetishization" of false appearances—is thereby satisfied, it is not at all clear that something important is not lost here by the easy abandonment of a second requirement, the bringing of valid norms and their false claims of realization into explosive tension. In effect, as I will try to show, this conception of critique inadvertently vindicates Adorno's refusal to make a clear-cut decision between immanent and transcendent critique. The difficulty is not solved by self-reflection alone. Szelényi and Konrád do interpret the critique they are interested in as self-critique: as Marxists of Marxism, as intellectuals of the ideologies of intellectuals, indeed as immanent critics of immanent criticism (identified as empirical sociology in Eastern Europe, at least, in other words with the authors' own background). Only it is not at all clear how and whether they get out of any of the logical circles involved. Indeed, they say as much when denying that even self-critique can divest intellectuals of their social character and ethos as intellectuals.

The aim of the two authors, and here they are the direct heirs of Mannheim, is to clarify or uncover the particular empirical interests behind all norms, projects, and values. Szelényi, in particular, vehemently denies all attempts (Habermas, Budapest School) to justify, validate or even seek the universal. If in one place Szelényi somewhat inconsistently confesses to be within "the broadly defined value framework of Marxism," this can mean only (for the sake of even minimum consistency) that the value of the interests of one particularity—the direct producer—is implicitly affirmed by this framework, though in a contradictory fashion. It is the continuity of this otherwise ungrounded and surely transcendent valuation that links the three apparently different formulations of this project to criticize Marxism as an ideology: Marxist critique of Marxism-Leninism, historical materialist critique and post-Marxist critique of Marxism. All three formulations presuppose the *ouvrierist* value premise, the application of class analysis and the rejection of the point of view of the universal.

If the direct producer and the power of class analysis are the elements that remain valid for Szelényi and Konrád in the theoretical heritage of Marx, its original sins, to the authors, are teleology and universality (or more exactly the subsumption of *techné* under *telos*, of technical reason under the claims of goal-setting or teleological reason) and the sacrifice of particular interests to supposedly universal ones. Applying the method of class analysis to the two ideological doctrines, they argue that these correspond very well to the interests of a new intellectual class. These interests converge to create a social structure (itself not wholly unprecedented in Eastern Europe) around which the new class can be constituted and consolidated, a structure based on the economic dominance of teleological (in other words, centrally planned but elsewhere ambiguously identified as "rational") redistribution of the produced surplus under the cover of supposedly general interests. To be sure, they argue that the ideology did not produce the new social structure; indeed the dirigistic and étatistic ethos of late nineteenth-century bureaucracies preexisted, if not also penetrated, the Marxism of the time in which intellectual and worker interests were both embodied. Nevertheless, the continuity of Marxism as a pre- and postrevolutionary ideology indicates the deep elective affinity between the classical doctrines, the desire of the intellectuals for a scientifically planned and organized society, and the bureaucratic ethos.

It is of course admitted that in the postrevolutionary period Marxism indeed degenerated from a critical theory of capitalism to a set of apologetic, affirmative doctrines—a state religion. But Szelényi and Konrád do not stress its consequent demise as a genuine ideology suitable as the object of immanent criticism; obviously they do not consider the issue important. The best-developed ideology of intellectual class rule (however ambiguous internally) remains the classical Marxian system, and for the Soviet Union and some of the Eastern European societies the point retains at the very least its historical significance. More importantly, the knowledge of its open and hidden dimensions justifying domination by intellectuals allows the thematization of those features of the social integration (Szelényi and Konrád call it "ethos") which symbolically embody these ideological dimensions if (Szelényi and Konrád do not admit this) a ritualistically preserved Marxism-Leninism were to be unable to do so. According to Szelényi, some of these dimensions, existing in the form of the consensus of beliefs, are:

1. The necessity and legitimacy of a direct proportion between inequality and different levels of intellectual qualification.
2. The necessity of scientific allocation of resources and of long-term planning.
3. The priority of societal and long-term over individual and short-term interests.

The three points correspond to the symbolic requirements of the conception of intellectuals as a new class. The first (coming more from functionalist sociology and only indirectly justifiable by the classical Marxian conception of the first postcapitalist stage) validates a gulf between intellectuals and the rest of the population without, however, pointing to a principle of unity and coherence for the "new class"; the second legitimates the structure around which it is supposedly organized, that of central planning ("teleological" or "rational" redistribution) but at the possible price of conflicts among competing technocracies and alternative plans; the third validates the unity of the class around the claims of a scientific knowledge of history possessed by the center of the politocratic party.

It would surely be possible to claim that the three points validate the privileged position of three differently constituted and in part overlapping strata capable of both conflict and concerted action: intellectuals, technocracy, politocracy. On the other hand, the ideological coherence and continuity among these doctrines provides the best argument for Szelényi and Konrád that ideological/technocratic/bureaucratic intellectuals constitute the unified ruling or dominating class of an authoritarian state socialism still in the process of its final crystallization. To be sure, they seem to prefer a combination of statistical arguments drawn from stratification theory and research, and structural arguments stemming from the Marxian class theory. Yet no statistical arguments about income, living conditions, and other forms of material privilege that show the relatively privileged condition of intellectuals under state socialism can establish,

I would contend, the *interest* of intellectual individuals or groups (or anyone except the upper apparatus) in a society in which the economic interests of almost all individuals and most groups are daily compromised and sacrificed. At most, one could speak of the constitution of such an interest within a structure of power that appears as given and unchangeable, imposed objectively (or externally) and not through the will of the social stratum in question. But what is the sense of treating the intellectuals as a whole (however defined) as the ruling or dominant class within such a social structure? Szelényi and Konrád must insist on similarities of income and privilege because only these criteria (unlike status or power) homogeneously relate to the presumed class as a whole. Even in their conception the whole does not rule, only what they suggestively call its politocratic estate. (The analogy to the bourgeoisie, a dominant but not necessarily ruling class, would be of no use here because it presupposes the state-civil society separation and the consequent existence of a form of power that is in itself not political.)

"Rational redistribution," the structure of economic planning legitimated by claims of rational knowledge, also does not point to an unambiguous future class position of intellectuals. Although the legitimating principle of redistribution was originally understood largely as expert, instrumental, means-end rationality (which would be fully developed only as technocracy), the term "rational" was later reinterpreted by Szelényi according to Weber's few remarks defining substantive or material (i.e., goal-positing) rationality. It is not so important that Szelényi does not as a result reverse his prediction concerning the triumph of the technocracy over the politocratic order; the conception as a whole stressing the fusion of *telos* and *techné* implies the mutual dependence of the two, given the structure of teleological planning. As long as there is such a dependence, the central structure of domination remains that of hierarchical orders (*Stände*) and not classes, according to the logic of the conception.

But even if a technobureaucracy came to appropriate all the key positions around the planning structure all the way to the very top of decision making, reducing the remnants of the politocracy to a political administration, it would still not be clear how, in a society where all power is exercised through the state structure (here identified with rational redistribution), intellectuals outside this structure could possess class power in any meaningful sense of the word. And to produce ideology for such a structure from which they are directly excluded would not distinguish the cultural, artistic, academic intellectuals from their analogues under capitalism, which, the authors hold, forms an independent stratum and not a class. Unless, of course, being censored were to be interpreted as a special sign of power, a point they actually make, but never too seriously.

If, however, the only argument for the unity of the intellectual class is the ideological content of the ethos of state socialism (which especially in an earlier period also embodied an *ouvrierist* content), then the case for an intellectual ruling or dominant class is only slightly better established than that for the dictatorship of the proletariat under Stalinism. One can claim participation in direct rule for neither, and all explicit (workers) or implicit (intellectuals) claims to rule would be falsifiable by pointing to (as do Szelényi and Konrád) the unification of particular interests, politically defined status and actual power in the party-state structure itself. To the extent, furthermore, that the ethos of state socialism has been investigated from the quasi-functionalist point of view as the ideology of intellectual class power, one develops the suspicion that the domain of ideology (or rather of social integration) is itself seriously shortchanged by the class analysis of Szelényi and Konrád. I am thinking of such obvious issues as nationalism, traditionalism and neotraditionalism, religion and quasi-religion, of the key ideological differences between imperial center and its various peripheries; there is no way (except entirely negatively, by referring to the identity problems of intellectuals unable to identify a form of class rule as their own) to integrate these theses in the model of ideologies, legitimating intellectual class domination in a period of transition between politocracy and technocracy. If we were to claim that the ideological dimensions stressed by Szelényi and Konrád are constitutive of class structure (not their position but perhaps more defensible), should we not also admit that these other dimensions of the state socialist ethos might be constitutive of social realities as well?

To sum up: Not only does the utilization of classical Marxist class analysis as the foundation for the critique of ideology lead to unjustifiable sociological analyses and projections, but the very content of the ideologies is in the process illegitimately narrowed down with further potentially damaging consequences for the analysis of social structure. I do not believe that the situation is any better concerning the political conclusions of the analysis, or, rather, it is better only because they (especially Szelényi in his more recent essays, but implicitly also Konrád in his new volume of essays and fragments) bring another rather different perspective into their account.

V

Whom does Szelényi and Konrád's immanent critique of ideology-*cum*-class analysis propose to address? Whose alternative does it represent? In his response to Bahro, to whom he directed the second question, Szelényi insists on a "sociology from below" articulating the interests of the oppressed and exploited. The idea consistent with his own inconsistently held value-premise is that the alternative in question is that of the immediate producer based on a new principle of legitimacy, that of the right of productive workers to control and dispose of the produced surplus. On the other hand, when the cowritten book discusses the oppositional "marginal" intellectuals, who are clearly enough its actual addressees, we get a somewhat different picture. Of the first of the two general types, the "transcendent" revisionists or ideological critics—the theorists of the renaissance of Marxism (Praxis school, Budapest School) are criticized because their insistence on a new society realizing the original *telos* of Marxism can lead only to a new or a renewed version of the rule of the politocratic estate. At the same time, the second type, the empirical revisionists or immanent critics of ideology—hence the empirical sociologists who are generally non-Marxist but also Szelényi and Konrád (as indicated by their earlier works)—are defended because of their unmasking of the actual interest structure and actual inequalities of state socialism. They are also defended as having aims that—because of the unavoidable limits of immanent intellectual criticism of intellectual class power—necessarily converge with those of technocracy. It is here, I believe, that Szelényi and Konrád hope to break the circle of all sociology of knowledge. Because they themselves are immanent critics, they defend technocracy as a higher, more rational stage of the existing system. But as critics of immanent criticism, they defend technocracy because they believe that among the unintended consequences of technocratic rule, given the need of technocrats for new allies and new legitimations, will be the greater and perhaps institutionalized possibility of the articulation of the interests of workers. Accordingly, Szelényi and Konrád propose that marginal intellectuals should, in such a context, become the organic intellectuals *both* of technocrats and of direct producers, formulating the interests of both. Clearly enough, they see their book as doing just that.

It is here that the political proposal of Szelényi and Konrád, based on class analysis and supposedly on the point of view of the direct producer, shows its problematic side. When they actually formulate what they take to be the content of working class interests, they come up with little more than the "monetarization" and "marketization" of all economic relations, a demand identical to those of the more radical technocratic reformers of the 1960s. While on the whole I accept these suggestions—though one needs to discuss their limits, and in particular Szelényi's argument that under state socialism it is redistribution that is the source of fundamental inequalities, with the market being the partial corrective—I am nevertheless still a bit amazed about such easy identification of two potentially opposed strata or "classes." While Szelényi and Konrád admit the possibility of future conflict, *it is evident that this very idea tends* to exclude the possibility of being the organic intellectuals of both sides. In their book at least, the representation of workers' interests seems somewhat deficient beyond the point already mentioned; workers' control over the surplus, for example, is more or less identified with the free-market sale of labor power as well as of the products of small-scale producers, necessary but hardly sufficient conditions of the self-management they often mention. But they do not ever really indicate that the principle of workers' control over management (the economics of which are, to be sure, hardly understood) is in immediate conflict with technocracy once anything resembling a genuine market—something both sides do need—is established.

It is not at all clear, as a result, whether Szelényi and Konrád have avoided that "substitutionism" with which they have charged other radical intellectuals.

A universalizing guise may not be the only form in which substitution can occur; for example, Szelényi and Konrád use the famous Marxian critique of the French revolutionary bourgeoisie not only to characterize the project of the original Bolshevik intellectuals, but also to represent the alliance politics of technocracy.[5] The very idea of the *representation* of the interests of those who cannot articulate these themselves leads to substitutionism unless it is coupled with some kind of communicative, discursive model of interaction between theory and its addressees. In the absence of institutions that would permit such interaction, theory—if it is to avoid substitutionism—ought to restrict its political claims to the establishment of such institutions, which are logically prior and in a formal sense constitutive of the interests in question. Having rejected the communication model (of a critical *Öffentlichkeit*) of practical, normative justification in Habermas and the Budapest School, Szelényi has unfortunately closed, on the methodological level at least, this avenue to another, more democratic politics. But fortunately in his writings after 1978, probably under the impact of the new Polish opposition, he opened another, equally fruitful approach in the same general direction: the idea of a socialist civil society.

Already in their book, Szelényi and Konrád point to the project of a new political society, abolishing the duality of state and civil society, as one of the elements of the classical Marxian ideology that could foreshadow and eventually justify the étatist synthesis to come. While their connection of this idea to the desire of intellectuals for a scientifically planned society is at odds with their insistence on the necessarily beneficial effects of the victory of technocracy for the restoration of civil society (plurality, legality, publicity)—a thesis otherwise based on an unconvincing hypothesis of the unavoidable spillover of the consequences of economic reform—it is nevertheless this idea, presented in a deterministic and politically doubtful form, that already definitively connected the book to the political opposition of the 1970s. It was important that, contrary to the ideas of Bahro, Szelényi and Konrád saw the next stage of state socialism not only as a form mixing two forms of "legitimation" (rational redistribution and workers' control), but also as (at least) a mix between two sets of state-society relationships. Some of the confusions pertaining to this latter notion were dispelled as the development of the opposition helped to reverse Szelényi's stress upon the economic and political dimensions to the benefit of the latter. While he became somewhat less willing to spell out exactly the contents of workers' interests, he more and more clearly affirmed that—without civil society—self-management, political self-determination, workers' control, participation in planning, etc., remain empty slogans. As a result, the shape of the next possible and desirable stage of state socialism could be better conceptualized as a form of rational redistribution in which the important utopian (and contradictory) element of workers' control would still have only a corrective function, while the genuinely new aspect would be the institutionalization of articulated and organized conflicts. While Szelényi does not propose a political solution for the achievement of this stage of state socialism (a kind of determinism continues to plague his writings), he clearly states what would be at stake if such a stage were institutionalized: the extension of yet unpredictable forms of direct democracy. (But he continues to be skeptical about the relevance of representative democracy in Eastern Europe, as does Hegedüs.)

On an analytical level, Szelényi continues to this day to link the idea of a socialist civil society to the full (and therefore more flexible) unfolding of the class domination of intellectuals. He simply refuses to notice that if he accepts the emergence of civil society as a world-historic gain, he must more consistently rehabilitate some of the (always precarious) universal dimensions of the great democratic revolutions that, following Marx, he calls "bourgeois." But, so changed, the model would suggest an entirely different process of emancipation than one going through a fully modern variant of the class domination of intellectuals. Alternatively, if one conceptualizes the transition to technocracy on the basis of a falsely understood dialectic of universal and particular in the bourgeois revolutions (the universal as an ideological mask rather than the partially contradictory project of definite groups and movements)—or even on the basis of the alliance of two particularities (technocrats and workers) and their "organic intellectuals"—the project of a socialist civil society would be irrelevant to this transition. The model of Marxian class analysis and the theory of civil society have apparently different analytical and normative consequences; in this version, at least, a post-Marxian critical theory could not be successfully complemented by orthodox Marxian theory construction.

Nor is the project of a socialist civil society compatible with the rather peculiar notion of immanent critique put forth by Szelényi and Konrád:

> rational redistribution finds it easy to appropriate any transcendent analysis for its own purposes just as the capitalist elite can integrate immanent critique to its own uses . . . in our day only that which is immanent can be transcendent, but only that which transcends the existing order can be immanent.[6]

Forgetting for the moment that the last phrase restores a normative intention toward another type of society, denied at the beginning of the same book but of course implicitly assumed elsewhere, it is evidently true that the idea of a socialist or any other civil society cannot be generated from the immanent critique of the ethos and ideology of rational redistribution. At best, the already present or systematically engendered interests, conflicts, and alternatives hidden and distorted by this ethos can be so uncovered. And whatever the meaning of the statement that the capitalist elite can integrate immanent criticism, the idea of civil society is available today only as a result of an immanent critique of civil-bourgeois society. On the other hand, a transcendent critique here would wipe out, and in practice always did wipe out, the civil along with the bourgeois. The point of view of civil society, justifiable on the basis of the criteria of a radical communicative ethics, is transcendent vis-à-vis the dominant ethos of state socialist societies, not to speak of the ruling ideology. It may not be so, of course, in the context of fragments of tradition preserved and available in perhaps most of these societies. In such a context, immanent critique is necessarily split: the method that opens up the crisis phenomena of the existing social integration (most relevant to ruling strata) will not be the same as the one establishing a communicative relationship with the actual or potential democratic opposition.

Notes

1. Cf. Herbert Marcuse, *Soviet Marxism*, New York: Vintage, 1961; and Oskar Negt, "Marxismus als Legitimationswissenschaft, Zur Genese der stalinistischen Philosophie," introduction to A. Deborin and N. Bucharin, *Kontroversen über dialektischen und mechanistischen Materialismus*, Frankfurt am Main: Suhrkamp, 1969, pp. 7–50.

2. If it were possible to work out a stage model of authoritarian state socialism in which the political system (or subsystem) played the role of double integration (i.e., social and systemic) in the first, more authoritarian stage, then the same partial shift from immanent critique to positive theory construction would be applicable here too. Although I have written an essay claiming such a transformation and theoretical shift, I must admit that the analogy to capitalist development may not strictly hold. It is not yet possible to say certainly and unambiguously that any national variant of authoritarian state socialism has already reached or even can reach such a second stage.

3. Cf. György Konrád and Ivan Szelényi, *The Intellectuals on the Road to Class Power*, trans. A. Arato and R.F. Allen, New York and London: Harcourt Brace Jovanovich, 1979. The original manuscript was completed in Hungary in 1974.

4. Here I cannot go into all the reasons for the important omissions in my short survey, i.e., Hegedüs, Medvedev, Havemann, the Polish and Czech émigré generation of 1968 whose relationship to critical theory was negligible when they were still in Eastern Europe, and the Praxis school whose important works on the subject at hand belong to an earlier period of Marxist discussions.

5. Here to be sure, given the changed evaluation, an element of historical correction is smuggled in: the universalistic claims of the bourgeoisie issued in a legal system that had to allow the formulation and defense of interests other than their own. Disregarding the historical oversimplifications involved here, and also that such a conception of universality is diametrically opposed to everything else the authors say on the subject, it is highly unlikely that the correction applies to a project, which, unlike that of the eighteenth-century revolutionaries, is formulated in purely economic rather than in political-legal terms. The argument therefore saddles technocracy with the logic of substitution without the unintended democratizing consequences. The step to substitutionism seems to be grounded in the very approach of the two authors.

6. Konrád and Szelényi, *The Intellectuals on the Road to Class Power*, p. 250.

6

The Budapest School and Actually Existing Socialism

We have now traveled at least part of the road ahead. *Dictatorship over Needs* by Fehér, Heller, and Márkus, together with works by Szelényi and Konrád,[1] Kis and Bence,[2] Castoriadis,[3] Vajda,[4] and Zaslavsky[5] represent a very solid beginning for a critical social theory of the societies of the Soviet type. These works go beyond a mere application of classical Marxian concepts, and reconstruct theory itself in the process of analyzing its objects. Using many analytical instruments entirely new with respect to the classics, they seek to attain at least a part of what Marx himself sought: a theory of the dynamics of the society in question in relation to a normatively better and at the same time possible society. Thus they take the point of view, even if on a theoretical level, of movements for emancipation. Of the works mentioned, *Dictatorship over Needs* is most self-conscious about its place in the tradition of critical social theory. Its authors, Ferenc Fehér, Agnes Heller, and György Márkus, are members of the Budapest Lukács School who have wound up teaching and working in Australia. While They have come a long way from any of Lukács's theoretical positions, they nonetheless affirm that in some meaningful sense they are "still" Marxists. And indeed in one sense at least they are, more than some of the others mentioned: They resolutely work with an abstract structural model of the reproduction of Soviet-type societies in general; their concessions to a plurality of traditions, histories, and even structural positions within the Soviet system of states are minimal (cf. 39–40). This is ultimately both a source of strength and weakness: The authors are unrivaled in exploring the structures and problems common to all of the societies, but cannot really do justice to the dynamic possibilities either of differentiated single units or of the whole that contains heterogeneity as well as uniformity. In what follows I present the thesis of *Dictatorship over Needs* in reply to the following questions: (1) What is the nature of Soviet-type societies?

Reprinted with permission from *Theory and Society* 16 (1987): 593–619. © Martinus Nijhoff Publishers, Dordrecht, Netherlands.

(2) How are they legitimated? (3) What is the relationship of structure and history? (4) Are these societies truly modern? (5) What are the relevant contradictions and crisis tendencies? (6) What are the perspectives of conflict and change?

What are the societies of the Soviet type? As György Márkus brilliantly demonstrates, the historical answers of the left—underdeveloped socialism, deformed workers' state, transitional society between capitalism and socialism or Asia and socialism, state capitalism, modernized Oriental despotism, bureaucratic collectivism—all based on a dogmatic class theory or a philosophy of history, do not carry much conviction today. But neither do the older theories of academic scholarship: totalitarianism and industrial society, the former postulating the ultimate identity of the Soviet Union with Nazi Germany, the latter its eventual convergence with the capitalist world. The polemical revival of the concept of totalitarianism in our day even if understandable from the point of view of political mobilization, carries great analytical risks. What we need clearly is a new concept. In this context Szelényi and Konrád produced something entirely original, even if synthesized from the works of Weber, Polányi, and Marx. According to them, societies of the Soviet type are or claim to be those of the rational redistribution of the social-economic surplus: rational in the sense of Weber's type of a specifically modern form of domination; the stress on "redistribution" and "surplus" comes from Polányi and Marx respectively. Every element of this definition could be and was attacked: the societies in question are not formally rational nor even claim to be; here étatism represents an organization of production and not only of distribution, and the surplus cannot be specified without a true price system. Whatever the merit of these objections (and they are considerable), they should not disguise the true achievement of Szelényi and Konrád: namely the definition of Soviet-type societies in terms of an abstract principle of organization that refers simultaneously to the self-identity of the ruling institution (the claim of rationality as the basis of a *legitimate* dictatorship) and the social structure (global control operating in terms of the maximization of the surplus product available for redistribution). Even if the original terms of the Szelényi–Konrád analysis cannot be accepted—and now Szelényi has himself replaced formal rationality with Weber's substantive or *materiale* rationality— no future analysis can forget the double requirement of their proposal; that we must deal with both social and system integration (in the sense of Habermas) if we want to understand the principle of organization of Soviet-type societies.

The three authors of *Dictatorship over Needs* seem to solve the question of the system's principle of organization in three different ways. Márkus, focusing on the economic structure, (leaving questions of social integration to his colleagues) works out the economic "goal function" of the regime as "the maximization of the volume of the material means (as use values) under the global disposition of the apparatus of power as a whole" (65). Heller, turning to politics (both on the level of social and system integration), postulates a totalitarian identity that moves through "Jacobin," "charismatic," and "traditional" historical forms, that is realized through the unified penetration and control of political, social, cultural, and economic life. Finally, Fehér, dealing with the dynamics of the system, works with a concept of an all-embracing paternalism as the key to the system's identity both from the point of view of the rulers and the ruled, and argues that the dictatorship over all free need articulation by individuals and groups, "dictatorship over needs," is the expression of this principle on the level of the social structure. All three authors use, however, the concept of the dictatorship over needs, and it might appear that the abstract principle of identity that defines the system is to be located on this level. Actually for all three it is only a derived principle. For Márkus, it is not the "dictatorship over needs" but "the expropriation and monopolization (in principle) of all means of socialization and social organization by a single apparatus of power" that is the basis of the goal function of the system that represents "only" the material basis for the operation of this deeper or more general principle (66, 70, 83). In other words, the mono-organizational society (see the Australian scholar Rigby, as well as Kis and Bence) can operate only if control over productive activity is maximized. In its pure form (but only in its pure form) such a system seeks to deprive even the atomized consumers of all independence; it is then that the "system tends to act as a brutal dictatorship over needs" (89, 98). In Fehér's analysis too, where the concept of the dictatorship over needs plays its greatest nominal role, the principle is in turn derived from the establishment of a political society that logically enough suppresses "the individual person and his free associations, communities, his Kommunikationsgemeinschaft"; in other words, civil society, and one is tempted to add not only on the level of instances of need articulation (253–54). The abolition of the market, which is after all the actual economic basis of a dictatorship over needs, is in this analysis "only derivative" (254) of the abolition of civil society along with all of its associations of which some, *but only some*, had the purpose of need articulation. Finally, Heller points to the dictatorship over needs as the specific practice of the Soviet bureaucracy, whose power, however, in her analysis, is a derived one (177–78). For her, too, Soviet-type societies are political societies abolishing the differentiation between state and civil society (167–68). Moreover, according to Heller, a modern political society is inevitably totalitarian, whatever the specific forms of legitimation (Jacobin, charismatic, traditional) and forms of rule (aristocracy, autocracy, oligarchy), presumably because modernity implies plurality and political societies are mono-lithic or mono-organizational.

Is the common, even if implicit, definition of Soviet-type societies by the three authors that of a totalitarian state-society? Even Agnes Heller, who uses this concept most explicitly, warns that totalitarianism is compatible with different socioeconomic structures, hence there is no question here of a return to the thesis of the identity of Soviet and Fascist regimes. Totalitarianism is now apparently confined to the system of domination but in the Soviet case, it is precisely this system that in the form of monolithic and mono-organizational structures penetrates the rest of society (political society) including the economy (the maximization of control over production of use values, the dictatorship over needs). One might thus say that for the authors there may be several types of totalitarian states, but only one type of totalitarian society, that is, Soviet-type society. Can such a concept even in its revised form account for the richness of the experience we now have in time and space of Soviet-type societies?

It has been recently argued by several Polish critics of the concept of totalitarianism[6] that even if the regimes of East Europe have a totalitarian self-understanding, the actual project of the abolition of independent society inevitably fails in the face of the persistence and reemergence of social forms, stretching from networks of small and informal groups and circles of friends and colleagues to various associations and agencies explicitly created to represent rights and interests, to exercise pressure. Many of these writers stress the difference therefore between the "pays légal" and the "pays réel," the legal or official society and the real one. Márkus's analysis lays the groundwork for an analogous distinction implying "an ever-growing cleavage between the official and the actual reality of economic life" (103). In order to work at all in the context of its existing goal function (maximization of control over use values), the economy must involve operations (second economy based on legal and semilegal private market oriented activities, third economy based on the reciprocal if illegal services of units of the first economy) that escape this goal function. It seems to me therefore that, just as Szelényi and Konrád before him, Márkus implicitly postulates a development from a point when the goal function implied the maximization of *the proportion* of party-state commanded economic activities to all others to a point when it implies *only* the maximization of its absolute volume. The second notion, however, is no longer compatible with that of totalitarian controls. Once the pure form of the system is no longer viable, under the post-Stalinist stabilization of Eastern Europe, the "dictatorship over needs" is also significantly relaxed through the extension of consumer choice in the official economy and the appearance of "various segmental markets of the price-fixing type" (89). The point reappears in various forms in Heller and Fehér, with the former conceding that "it is not completely out of the question that in the economic sphere the ruling elite at least tries to replace totalization by the hegemony of the state in society" (166).[7] Fehér, however, warns that, strictly speaking, there can be no developmental stage in the history of Soviet-type societies, which are in particular incapable of executing a transition from "extensive growth" based on constant increase of the size of the labor force, low levels of consumption, and monolithic steering institutions to one of "intensive development" based on increases of productivity and consumption along with mixed economic steering structures (263). However, it may be with the problem of developmental stages to which I will return, obviously Soviet-type societies have developed in the direction of economic detotalization. In fact, however, while in some societies this restriction of detotalization to the economy may be practicable, in others such a reform is sure to "spillover" into other social spheres or lead to centrifugal tendencies. In other societies still, the reconstruction of independent forms of noneconomic social life (alternative public sphere, associations of interest representation) has already taken place from below, even if no more than extremely recalcitrant toleration (and never legalization) could be extorted from the authorities. Can the same totalitarian principle of identity be applied, to name only some examples, to the almost fully unreformed Soviet Union, to Poland with its church, alternative public sphere, and social movement, and to Hungary with its quasi-legalized second economy (and some would say "second society" as well)? The answer is, of course, that this principle works best for the historically early version of the system in its home country, the Soviet Union, as well as in Eastern Europe and that today it works somewhat better for some societies than for some others.

Obviously the criticism just presented is nothing new, and is today the staple for the immense majority of even former totalitarianism theorists. Nevertheless it seems to have one serious drawback: the inability to establish the thread of obvious continuity, that is, the identity, of formerly totalitarian and now to various extents detotalized societies. The obvious basis of this continuity remains some kind of totalitarian identity, which, however, only used to be expressed in a totalitarian project that was historically a failure. After this failure something does survive of it, that is moreover common to all the countries. Evidently this is the fundamental insistence on the need to preserve the ultimate power to decide the limits of detotalization, of reversing the trend if need be, of restricting it to specific spheres of social life. No East European regime has ever surrendered the power of the prerogative state to penetrate any area of society at will, to define the limits of its nonpenetration by the criteria of power politics alone. From the Russian peasants of the NEP regime, that involved significant detotalization in its own right, to Polish peasants, workers, and intellectuals and Hungarian participants in the second economy today no one can be sure, there are no institutional guarantees concerning the fact that what is permitted today will be permitted tomorrow. However, the actual penetration and control of society and economy can in the context of an undiminished prerogative power be rather variable.

The primacy of prerogative power over society predates the actual totalitarian regime, and postdates it as well. Nevertheless, it is itself a totalitarian principle, if only potentially so. We can speak of the next stage of Soviet-type systems only if in one crucial social sphere at least (e.g., the economy) the power of the prerogative will be replaced by legality (*Rechtsstaatlichkeit*). No transition to an economy of intensive development, for example, is possible without such a fundamental shift. There is, however, good reason to think that such a shift cannot in turn occur without pressure from below—because the one thing the regimes will never institute without pressure is a break with the existing principle of identity. Such pressure and the regime's ability to resist it is highly dependent on conditions of legitimation.

The category of legitimation refers to the same level of social reality as identity, the level of social integration. Nevertheless, an abstract identity might operate through a succession or even a mixture of different forms of legitimacy (in Weber's sociology of domination the two issues are somewhat confused). There is, however, some question whether or not legitimation is at all a relevant category in Soviet-type societies. Leaving aside for the moment theories that reject the category altogether as too voluntaristic (structuralist Marxism, Castoriadis's theory of the social imaginary) in particular, Habermas's explorations of the communicative and normative foundations of even empirical legitimation[8] have occasioned some serious doubt about whether a concept presupposing actual or at least implicit consensus is applicable to Soviet-type societies that exclude precisely any meaningful public sphere. Mihály Vajda and even one of the authors of *Dictatorship over Needs*, György Márkus, incline toward this view.[9] At the other end of the theoretical spectrum, nearer to the assumptions of functionalist sociology, Victor Zaslavsky[10] has not only insisted on using the concept of legitimation for Soviet society, but has included terror and identity of interests (explicitly against Weber's warnings) under one all inclusive concept. Atomization itself or "accepted atomization," that is, the absence of communicative relations is a form of legitimacy for Zaslavsky. As against these two extremes Heller returns to a generally Weberian position, but in an original way that allows her to account for the perspectives of the two extremes by placing them on a different level of legitimation. Like Weber and Habermas, but unlike Szelényi and Konrád, she restricts the problem of legitimacy to the state, to the political order. As Márkus's analysis already shows, "the goal function" of the economy can be described without a reference to legitimation, in terms of a set of constraints operating on the level of system integration, beyond the will of individual or group actors. The political order in Heller's conception cannot operate on such bases alone. Nor can it survive over a long enough period of time on the bases of "various types of interest, including the imposition of fear." Following Weber's important distinction between administrative staff and population, she goes on to the original position that "a social order is legitimated if at least one part of the population acknowledges it as exemplary and binding and the other part does not confront the existing social order with the image of an alternative one as equally exemplary" (138). This conception would allow Heller to account for a level of quasi-consensus for the first part of society, and a level where precisely the absence of communication relations blocks the emergence of all alternative conceptions of society. Thus her conception of legitimation is potentially the most synthetic, and is thus quite applicable to Soviet-type societies, given the empirical phenomena to which consensus and functionalist theories call attention.

Heller differentiates her analysis of legitimacy both in time and space. Against Szelényi and Konrád, but like Zaslavsky, she calls attention to the transformation of legitimation during the course of Soviet development and the variability of legitimation problems and resources among Soviet-type societies. In her developmental schema, Soviet society has moved through periods of Jacobin nonlegitimacy, Stalinist charismatic legitimacy, and finally traditional legitimacy. In a Weberian style, she maintains that each form is mixed and contains traces of the others; moreover, they contain substantive rational legitimacy as a subsidiary form of legitimation. The only attempt to enthrone substantive rational legitimacy as the primary principle, in the Khrushchev era, was a dismal failure.

As Ivan Szelényi has realized,[11] the validity of Heller's schema depends on the evaluation of the concept of substantive rationality, which he at least continues to propose as the major legitimating principle of the whole Soviet era. Weber has defined this (*materiale Rationalität*) not as a concept to be compared to both formal (means–ends) and value rationality as Heller maintains, but as the wider genus into which value rationality itself belongs. What is common to all types within this genus is the application of "certain criteria of ultimate ends" ("of which the socialist and communist standards constitute only one group"!) irrespective of means–ends calculations.[12] Weber (and we must stress this against both Heller and Szelényi) was not convinced that substantive rationality was "rational" at all except in the cases where the ultimate end, as in natural law versions of value rationality, contained the value of formal rationality itself. It may, of course, be an important, necessary correction of Weber to introduce a concept of substantive rationality that is based on claims of a scientific analysis of society and even history rather than the formal rationality of any procedures. In Soviet ideology this claim comes together with the dimension Weber stressed, the representation of the *interests* first of a class, later of classless society,[13] but the priority is always given to the claim of scientific knowledge. The question is only whether such a claim *actually* legitimated Soviet society in any of its stages, which as Szelényi notes in his review of *Dictatorship over Needs*,[14] is not identical to the question of whether the society actually embodies substantive rationality of any kind.[15] Following the analysis of Zaslavsky (in some respects parallel to Heller), it is evident that the claim of substantive rationality (and legitimation is first of all only an accepted claim) did legitimate the Lenin period for at least the politically active part of society. Heller's own discussion (as against her definition) points exactly to such a state of affairs, but she is sidetracked by the question of whether the society was actually rational (to Weber substantive rationality could not have rational consequences!), and by her selective stress on the Weberian texts speaking of the legitimacy of an *order* (there was no established order in Soviet society during the Lenin period according to her) when of course Weber has not in fact, nor should he have, so restricted his concept. Furthermore, her plausible definition of the structure of rule of this period as an aristocracy (to be sure: the relation of Weberian, Aristotelian, and Marxian categories in Heller's work remains somewhat unclear) itself excludes the notion of the absence of legitimacy as does the concept of authority (versus domination) itself. Nevertheless Fehér (242) and Heller (143) are on very strong footing indeed, and are supported by Zaslavsky, when they discuss the brittleness and instability of substantive rational legitimation in a context in which formal and discursive processes of rational decision making were increasingly excluded. The claims of scientific knowledge of history, of a superior form of rationality are either to be redeemed by the actual (or at least partial) fulfillment of original claims and predictions (which is not possible without formal rationality) or must be dogmatized, ritualized, and indeed traditionalized. To be sure, this happened in the Stalin era, when, however, as all interpreters point out, charismatic legitimation became dominant. Actually charismatic legitimation (which as Zaslavsky points out also began under Lenin) could on its own sustain a decrepit substantive rationality (what is the relevance of reality testing in the face of charisma?) except of course for the fact of its own notorious instability. With the end of Stalin's cult, substantive rationality (Zaslavsky's rational ideological legitimation) stood alone and could not, as it is well known, deliver on its grandiose Khrushchevist claims. It is extremely problematic, as a result, to maintain its present dominance (as against its continued presence) in the Soviet Union, as does Szelényi, or argue for its replacement by some kind of rational nonideological legitimation, as does Zaslavsky, which reduces, however, only to necessarily unstable and labile constellations of common interests. Heller's argument for the new primacy of traditional legitimacy is therefore superior to at least these competing alternatives.[16] However two very difficult problems arise for her given this postulate: (1) Even if the traditions of the Soviet Union, above all of Russia, could help sustain a traditional or retraditionalized legitimacy, can such a structure of legitimation work where the system is externally imposed and is not an indigenous local product, where given traditions may not be consistent with its functioning? (2) How can we conceive a modern society that operates according to traditional legitimation?

The charge of a structuralism insensitive to history and especially histories has been recently leveled at the whole class of neo-Marxist theories of Soviet-type societies by Mihály Vajda.[17] According to this charge, theorists from Bahro and Szelényi–Konrád to Kis–Bence construct single, abstract models of all Soviet-type societies, leaving aside that there is a great difference between the countries where the system is an indigenous product and where it is imposed, and that there are further important differences among countries of the latter variety as well. When using history at all, structuralist theorists (in particular Bahro and Szelényi–Konrád) work out a single lineage of development the aspects of which may be put together from various actual histories in an eclectic manner. Only residually do they pay attention to the historical differences among, for example, East and Central Europe.[18] General projections about the future are derived from single particular instances (which however are dependent on national contexts), for example, Bahro, from Czechoslovakia in 1968, Szelényi–Konrád from the Hungarian reform. Does the objection apply to *Dicta-*

torship over Needs? The work, to be sure, is rather frankly of the abstract and structuralist genre; it is the study of a social formation in Marx's sense. The authors are implicitly (and rightly) concerned with the dangers of a version of historicism that would leave no room for a theory of those structures and institutions that make the various societies of the Soviet type the same. Nevertheless, on the level of legitimation in particular, Heller points out that the societies of the Soviet type are in fact not the same. According to her, East European societies and in particular Hungary, Poland, and Czechoslovakia are in permanent legitimation crisis, because the number of subjects for whom the system is directly valid is small, while the rest of society does have an alternative social model: Western liberal democracy (137–38). She notes that the present legitimacy of the government even in Hungary for unusually large strata is not that of the system of domination, but of the government that achieves the best possible deal under a rejected system of domination. The argument on this level, however, does not leave the structuralist method, but rather implicitly postulates a structure of structures, the imperial system with an implication of differences between the problems of integration in the center and the peripheries. The center (whether we see it as the Soviet Union or even more properly Great Russia) cannot be integrated through force or identity of interest alone, according to an argument as old as the first book of Plato's *Republic*: The internal stability of rulers must be guaranteed according to other mechanisms than those used to dominate the ruled. Here conditions of legitimation must pertain that need not pertain wherever the imperial center can exercise a surplus of force for integration. Thus, the countries of East Europe can be in a permanent legitimation crisis, yet be stabilizable. In other words, the proportions of domination and hegemony, to use Gramsci's language, can be structurally very different in the center and the peripheries.

Nevertheless, the element of legitimation, at least with respect to a small group, is not absent in the countries of East Europe, even according to Heller's argument. In this context she asserts on the one hand (holding on to a structuralist paradigm) that the types of legitimation in Eastern Europe are "miniaturized imitations of those in the Soviet Union" but on the other hand that there is a main divergence between center and periphery on this level, which turns out not to be entirely confined to the problem of positions in the overall structure. Or rather with respect to the development of the Soviet stages of legitimation the divergence seems to depend on structural position only with respect to the first two drastically contracted stages of Jacobinism and charisma (and even the attempted but failed third stage of substantive rationality), while with respect to the third (or fourth stage), traditional legitimacy, a divergence appears that is no longer confined to the problem of for whom the system is legitimate, but is related to the very model of legitimation.

Traditional legitimacy is, of course, based on the claims of validity of traditions, of patterns, rules, and beliefs considered binding because of having been valid over a (usually very long) period of time. In the Soviet Union gerontocracy, political conservatism, and even more the disappearance of a political language along with the annihilation of the public sphere and the declaration that socialism is what exists and not something in the future are the marks of such legitimation. Leaving aside for the moment the issue of how strictly a Weberian concept of traditional legitimacy can be applied to Soviet society, it is evident that when one is dealing with only a sixty-or-so-year-old "tradition," the element of willful choosing *of* tradition and *among* traditions, that is, "traditionalism," must be stronger than in traditional societies in general (among which the authors of *Dictatorship over Needs* do not in any case include Soviet-type societies!). In order to link Soviet legitimacy, however, to a more traditional temporality, much older Russian national traditions had to be affirmed, no matter how selectively. In particular the autocratic, paternalistic, and ethnocentric features of this tradition have been chosen, ever since Stalin, to validate both the internal structure of domination and the imperial system as well. Nevertheless, according to Heller, Russian tradition had to be combined with an even more important traditionalization of Soviet history, in order not to challenge the other nationalities of the Soviet Union unnecessarily. Heller sees the revival of the Stalin cult above all in the need to reestablish the unbroken validity of the Soviet period with the October Revolution and "the Great Patriotic War" as the two modal points of the tradition.

Nationalism and traditional legitimacy: the two concepts are not obviously compatible, because the former is a specifically modern ideology.[19] Soviet "traditionalism" represents an attempt to revive traditions of autocracy and paternalism and a specific national identity. The authoritarian relation of state and society throughout Russian history, the relative absence of civil society along with its various forms of autonomy, has created both institutional and personality structures receptive to autocracy *and* a great storehouse of historical precedents that could be used to justify autocratic rule (152–53). Nevertheless, not all Russian traditions could be appealed to in this context: neither the liberalism of the nineteenth century nor the indigenous institutions of the workers' movement. In particular traditions of authoritarian acceptance of the status of mere subject, and paternalistic renunciation of economic independence were attitudes, as Fehér shows in some detail, common to Russia's past and to a major dimension of socialist thought along with the requirements of the system constructed by Stalin and his heirs in particular. A good deal of empirical evidence from the Harvard studies of the 1950s to present immigrant studies demonstrates that paternalism in fact is accepted and desired even by those who disapprove of the regime on other grounds. Similarly nationalism, even if a modern ideology, already belongs to Russia's prerevolutionary past. It was modern once but now, along with other modern ideologies including Marxism itself, it can be dogmatized and ritualized. It can be turned to conservative and defensive purposes. Thus it can become material for "traditionalism" if not necessarily in the form of traditional legitimacy. To be sure, when the regimes appeal to this ideology the reasons are not always conservative. Once again ideology and domination are in a relation of elective affinity: As the multinational empire of the Tsars was reconstructed, a national-imperial relation of Russians to non-Russians and Soviets to East Europe emerged that has made the retrieval of traditions of national legitimation almost mandatory. Nevertheless it remains an open question to what extent a dynamic form of nationalism that would emerge wherever this ideology is put to aggressive purposes can be contained within traditional legitimacy or even traditionalism.

While the imitation of Jacobin–Bolshevik or charismatic forms of legitimation was a relatively easy matter all over East Europe, even if generally unsuccessful vis-à-vis the population as a whole, the imitation of an appeal to national traditions in the various senses just discussed had to present formidable difficulties. In this context, Vajda's argument, according to which the histories of East European states must be systematically differentiated even among one another, carries much weight.[20] If we stay with the simple (but not the only possible) variable of state-civil society relations, these are in particular extremely different among the East European countries. Different religions and cultural histories, different relations to Western Europe, different histories of non-European occupation, different types of states to begin with, and different versions of state autonomy during the centuries of imperial absorption, different experiments with estate and parliamentary forms of representation all play a role here. Most of the countries, however, have had enough autocratic and étatist traditions to make the imitation of this aspect of Soviet legitimation at least plausible.[21] It is obviously otherwise with nationalism, which could be apparently connected to equally unacceptable power ambitions with respect to various neighbors and anti-Russian defensive postures. As Heller argues, it is above all the lack of genuine or (with the crucial exception of Romania) even apparent independence that makes national legitimation of the Russian type ultimately untransferable to the regimes of Eastern Europe. Thus, according to her, these regimes must either accept their permanent legitimation crisis or continue (in the Hungarian case) a necessarily unsuccessful Khrushchevist experimentation with substantive legitimacy (154–55).[22]

It would seem, however, that traditions of national identity may replace explicitly nationalist traditions as the prop of new, not necessarily or entirely traditional legitimation. The "historicist" atmosphere of Hungary, East Germany, and (without much success) the Polish regime has of course been noticed by many observers. A selective use of national tradition can imply choosing other than nationalist foci of identification. One can thus focus on authoritarianism and religiously based obedience (as in the case of East Germany) or on the identity of a small and threatened nation, depending on the structural situation and on what is available.[23] All appeal to national traditions carries important risks; this is true even within the Soviet Union itself and is even more true for countries without full national sovereignties. But there may not be a risk-free strategy for the integration of Soviet-type societies. The question is only whether the risks of such legitimation in traditional or traditionalized forms would be acceptable for an apparently modern social formation.

In his review of *Dictatorship over Needs*, Szelényi decisively contests the primacy of traditional legitimation under any existing version of Soviet-type societies. This he does consistently enough, because he himself maintains that substantive rationality, a principle of legitimation as modern according to him as formal rationality, is characteristic of these societies. Leaving aside Heller's justified remarks concerning the instability of substantive rationality divorced from formal rationality or even Weber's own doubts concerning the modernity of such a principle, we must ask whether the notion of traditional legitimacy or even that of traditionalism is itself consistent with the modernity of Soviet-type societies otherwise postulated by the authors of *Dictatorship over Needs*. It turns out, however, that it is the postulate of modernity that is itself a contradictory one within the framework of the book, and not only because of Heller's concept of traditional legitimacy.

It is Márkus in particular who insists on the modernity of Soviet-type societies, during the course of his devastating argument against interpretations based on the concept of the Asiatic mode of production or Oriental despotism. His own definition of modernity is, however, astonishingly limited to a structural condition in which "relative scarcities tend to characterize economic development even after the satisfaction of elementary human needs became at least a possibility" (93). In other words, modernity for him implies a dynamic relation of expanding production and needs expanding at an even faster pace. To be sure if "dictatorship over needs" has any meaning at all, it implies an attempt to reverse the two rates of development. Thus if the need structure proves to be more dynamic than the development of production this must have other origins than the specific characteristic of such a system. Leaving this issue to the side, we would note Márkus's (somewhat inconsistent) admission that the system "has a tendency to restrict the phenomena of modernization to definite spheres, especially that of economy (both production and consumption)" (43). Apparently then modernity is not exhausted by its economic definition and the nonmodernity of noneconomic aspects of society becomes possible to thematize. The admission is all the more serious, because aside from extreme voluntaristic interpretations of such a thesis, Márkus affirms "the primacy of the political" for Soviet-type societies.

To be sure there are strong reasons, empirical and normative, to insist on the modernity of Soviet-type societies. The systems are, to begin with, effective competitors of the West, unlike traditional or semitraditional societies, on the military-diplomatic level. Secondly, the model offers a method of modernization to the third (and fourth) worlds even if less effective than Western methods. Furthermore, on the normative level, all concepts interpreting Soviet society as backward, or premodern seem to occlude, as Márkus argues, the very real historical responsibility of socialism—a specifically modern ideology and movement—in the genesis of the Soviet system and its satellites.[24] Fehér notes the same problem in reference to the totalitarian tendencies of other features of Western modernity. Indeed, Hannah Arendt's early concept of totalitarianism was rightly insistent on the difference of the new phenomenon from all traditional autocracy, because the historical despotisms (including the Russian) were in fact (if not in law) dualistically or dyarchically organized. However all these arguments imply only the necessity of considering certain aspects or spheres of Soviet-type societies "modern"; they need not exclude the possibility that others are traditional or at least nonmodern.

The authors of *Dictatorship over Needs* in fact amply document such aspects. Aside from the already mentioned stress of Heller on traditional legitimacy and Fehér on paternalism, and even Heller's difficult-to-justify choice to describe the system of rule in terms of "antediluvian" categories (aristocracy, autocracy, and oligarchy), Márkus too is forced to admit features that are analogous to those of premodern societies (forced labor, semibondage to land, covert political privileges in the social hierarchy, the *nomenklatura* system as well as his choice to describe the ruling institution as an *Anstalt*, or a close corporate entity, cf. 69)[25] and that represent links to traditions of the past (38 and elsewhere). He is further ready to note that while the types of traditions that are preserved differ from country to country, and in some countries the regime exists in distinctly nonbackward cultural environments, these very differences (based on the pre-established, traditional patterns of national histories) are clues to the differentiation of the societies in question (40). Nevertheless, he insists on two points: Despite this differentiation, the societies of the Soviet type are varieties of the same structure and what is the same, the essential set of characteristics, is indeed modern. "The specifically precapitalist features . . . are inscribed in, and subordinated to, such mechanisms of social-economic reproduction which have no analogies in history and ought to be regarded as unique" (40). Moreover, even if precisely the common structure was externally imposed in most of the relevant countries, by now it has become indigenous even in the historically modern settings: "the framework within which the population articulates its plans, expectations, and even its desires" (40–41).

The uniqueness of the Soviet model in history is not yet its full modernity. In spite of his general thesis Márkus admits that the weight of many traditionalist elements is actually on the increase in East European societies (38) along with social conservatism (40). Thus he leaves room, at least in principle, for Heller's and Fehér's stress on traditionalism and paternalism as the key features of the legitimation of today's system. If modernization is restricted above all to the economy, the preservation of traditions and retraditionalization might apply to the sociocultural context of Soviet-type societies. The implication (in Habermasian language) is a modern form of system integration and a nonmodern form of social integration (especially plausible because substantive rationality and cha-risma are neither modern nor traditional in the Weberian scheme!). To be sure, Habermas, who has done more than anyone to give us a differentiated concept of modernity, has always postulated the modernity of "bureaucratic socialist" socie-ties. In response to critics he has further refined his view, arguing that bureau-cratic socialism and late capitalism represent two modern alternatives developing out of liberal capitalism.[26] This argument is, however, neither historically nor systematically acceptable. Soviet society did not develop out of or as a response to the crisis of liberal capitalism. Nor, on the level of system integration, are its degree of institutional differentiation (in particular the absence of differentiation among economics, politics, and culture) and, on the level of social integration, its moral-legal-ideological structures *modern* according to Habermas's own criteria. On the bases of some of these, Talcott Parsons, for example, has logically enough considered Soviet society to be incompletely on the path of moderniz-ation, which for him, to be sure, is a simple teleological path. One could at most argue that, capitalism and Soviet-type societies being in general con-temporaries, the latter has still not transcended a level of development analo-gous to the earlier classical stage of capitalism.[27] This argument, however, would still leave one on the level of system integration and in itself could account for elements of tradition only as temporary residues but not as reviv-als, not for retraditionalization as a tendency in the reverse direction. Within modernization theory, however, even in one less linear and teleological than that of Parsons, it is possible to postulate failed models that are unable (1) to overcome all traditional elements and (2) to produce adequate forms of modern social integration. The first feature can be then applied to those societies of the Soviet type where specific aspects of the national tradition were always pre-served, the second to the process of retraditionalization and the recent emergence of historicist and national forms of legitimation, relevant even to those societies where the social context was initially modern or was apparently successfully modernized in the early years of the regimes. The parasitism of Soviet-type societies with respect to capitalism postulated by Márkus in the footsteps of Castoriadis speaks for this interpretation.

Even the model of failed modernization must, however, take account of the fact that Soviet society and the Soviet system of states are the contemporaries of the West in the sense of its viable competitors. The idea of distinguishing be-tween nonmodern social integration and modern (but noncapitalist) system inte-gration would accomplish this except that no modernization theory from Parsons to Habermas could possibly admit that the viability of economic and political steering could be unaffected by the persistence of a premodern, or the emergence of a nonmodern "life world." Indeed Márkus's depiction of the economic struc-ture indicates that while Soviet-type economies may seek some kind of rational-ity based on minimizing what counts as costs and maximizing what counts as useful results, this cannot be a goal rationality, that is, a rationality of equal effectiveness to the one of capitalism, because costs and benefits cannot be brought under a homogeneous measure of any kind. Only in the area of military production, where the presence of the army as consumer imposes a very different logic on production and where cost restraints are not allowed to count at all (97), are the effects of production comparable to those in the West.

The fundamental incongruity of military and civil production has been one of the bases of Castoriadis's recent reformulation of his theory of Soviet society. Especially relevant to my concern here is his division of the economy itself into modern (the military economy, which according to him is the basis of a "sub-society") and inadequately modern (the civilian economy) sectors. The argument is based not only on the fundamental differences between two classes of products, but also on those between the form of production characteristic of closed and open enterprises.[28] Thus is it possible, using Castoriadis's results, to argue that the bifurcation between nonmodern social integration and modern system integration does penetrate the level of system integration, that is, the economy itself, but that the uncoupling of military production has contained the results in such a way as to allow the Soviet Union to compete with genuinely modern societies on the international terrain. The bifurcation, however, reappears on the level of social integration too, between two dimensions of legitimation drawn from the Russian national tradition: Conservative traditionalism[29] (increasingly including what is left of Marxism ideology) and the national imperial imaginary stressed by Castoriadis.

Two consequences follow from this analysis that do not entirely correspond to the conclusion drawn by Castoriadis himself. (1) Either of the two ideologies, nationalist-expansionist or conservative, can become the bases of Soviet policy for the future, and it depends among other things on other actors in the world system of states, American and European, which of the two will be reinforced. (2) The long-run stability of the dualistic organization of the Soviet economy depends, excluding decentralizing reforms, on the international payoffs of some possible strategy based on it. Without such payoffs the (nonreformed) inadequately modern civilian sector will affect the modernity of the military sector in a negative way. As Szelényi has shown, it is possible to see the development of the military sector as a version of the transition between extensive and intensive modes of development.[30] But in a context far less modern than that of Nazi Germany or especially that of the postwar American welfare–warfare state (Szelényi's two examples), the extra-economic and in part retraditionalized components of the environment of the Soviet warfare-state are likely to affect the rationality of the whole in a very adverse way. Thus the solution outlined by Castoriadis does not affect the thesis of a failed modernization, even if under some condition for which ultimately its opponents must be at least coresponsible, Soviet society can continue to compete effectively in the international political-diplomatic-military area. That is, at least if its *internal* crisis tendencies and those of the outer periphery of the empire can be successfully managed or contained.

Perhaps the most problematic feature of Castoriadis's analysis is that he seems to postulate a stable outcome for Soviet society no longer apparently threatened by structural crisis of any kind and open only to a revolutionary overthrown from below, one not in any way rooted in the immanent tendencies and dysfunctionalities of the given system. The authors of *Dictatorship over Needs*, in this respect resolutely in a neo-Marxist tradition of analysis, seek to work out on the other hand a theory of immanent contradiction, crisis, and conflict. There seems to be division of labor in this context, with Márkus working out the fundamental contradiction along with the resultant economic dysfunctionalities, Heller postulating the condition of possibility of legitimation crisis, and Fehér producing an analysis of the actual conflict potential. While there is no question here, unfortunately, of fully integrating these levels of analysis, as, for example, in the theories of late capitalism in Offe and Habermas, the sequence of concepts nevertheless does reflect the latter's *Legitimationsprobleme im Spätkapitalismus*, to be sure excluding the distinction between economic and rationality crisis. This distinction, however, is specifically irrelevant to Soviet-type societies, where there is no differentiated self-steering economy and where even what appears as economic dysfunction is in reality an aspect of the fundamental problem of administrative rationality with regard to origin and in most cases, outcome.[31] Rationality problems in other words originate from the failure of administration adequately to control or steer the social system, and in general do not (like the classical economic crises of capitalism) lead to a simultaneous break in system and social integration, but the accumulation of difficulties on a continuum, which is threatened only on the bases of relatively independent tendencies in the sociocultural "lifeworld." Thus we should in general not speak of rationality or legitimation *crises* but only *problems* unless the two phenomena actually converge.[32]

Márkus's analysis of the structural socioeconomic "contradictions" of Soviet-type societies is a masterful one, unique in the whole literature on the subject. He first poses the problem on the level of the goal function itself, which is a principle of maximization (of the values controlled by the apparatus), but cannot be one of effectivity, or effective maximization, because in the absence of real economic prices (70–71) what are defined as "real costs" and "useful results" as physical magnitudes are not comparable in a homogeneous manner. Thus from the very outset the goal of production and the actual results diverge. According to Márkus the apparatus of power, in spite of its enormous powers of control, is by no means actually able to overcome the spontaneous logic of economic life (given the absence of a differentiated economy one should perhaps say social system!). This contradiction between *command* and *"economic"* logic, is precisely the basis of rationality problems, and Márkus develops the link in two complex chains of argument. The command system as "an integrated system of binding orders" (77) actually operates as a process of semi-institutionalized competition and bargaining between the various horizontally and vertically articulated bureaucracies (79). Systematic overstatement of objectives, along with over- *and* understatement of costs at different stages of the process, is a function only of the structural strengths of the partial-bureaucracies making claims. The shape of the "plan" will in turn depend only on the desire of the economic planners to maximize the system's goal function, and even more importantly the ability of the most powerful bureaucracies to affect the internal distribution of the goal function to the benefit of their area of control and responsibility. The already strong must always get organizationally stronger in such plan bargaining. The actual economic outcome, given systematic overstatement of costs in the final stages of plan bargaining, is constrained not by the ability to use resources effectively but only by the ability to fight for these and, of course, by the availability of physical resources that are by definition always scarce. The unavoidable result is the otherwise inexplicable coincidence of waste (unutilized factors) and shortage, based on hoarding of all factors of production irrespective of the structure of internal demand for these (84–86).

From the side of the logic of the "economy" as a whole, it is evident that the command structure is based on a systematic fiction: on the assumed but unreal identity of the official economy and the actual one. Here the contradiction is ultimately based on the dictatorial powers of the command system and "the unpredictable character of the global outcome of the innumerable consumption choices and of the decisions taken in the pseudo-market of labor" (87). The absence (in principle) of reliable information about consumer preferences here again leads to the coexistence of waste (unsalable products) and shortage. What the politicized command system gives to the units of production and consumption they do not necessarily need; what they need, however, they do not get. Actually, as Márkus shows, the second and third economies are needed to make the system function at all. The second economy based on market and profit principles fills some of the gaps between production and consumption (99); the third economy based on reciprocal services fills the gaps between branches of production itself, helping to redress the balance of waste and shortage by the "exchange of generalized equivalences." While they help to iron out some of the dysfunctionalities of the first economy, the second and third economies—unmeasurable and uncontrollable by their very nature—help to widen the increasingly enormous cleavage between the official and actual economies, thereby exacerbating the coming crisis of the latter (103). In this context Márkus rightly notes the analogy with late capitalist societies where in order to manage internal crisis tendencies, system-foreign, redistributive elements are incorporated. Here too, as in the analysis of Offe and Habermas, the management of rationality crisis leads to the crisis of crisis management itself.

Is it valid, however, to speak of economic or rationality *crises* when speaking of Soviet-type societies? Márkus disputes the idea of long-run stabilization on the basis of a segmentation between civilian and military industry. On the one hand, the backward nature of the former will affect the latter, which is already having difficulties "keeping pace with the newest technological advances." On the other hand, the cost of armaments will eventually affect the until now perceptible rise in living standards and with it, possibly the minimum bases of social compromise—especially on the Western peripheries of the Soviet empire (103–104). Does this argument return us to the classical logic of economic crisis in Marxist theory? Márkus is, to be sure, rather skeptical whether, especially in the Soviet Union, sufficiently organized social groups can emerge to impose a new logic on social economic development. His argument in this context returns to his conception of the foundation of the socioeconomic goal function of the system: the monopolization of all power and means of organization (105). Even if the regime fails "economically" (in the Western sense of that term) it succeeds in its own proper aims: to reproduce the existing power relations by denying an economic basis to all activities outside the corporate ruling order.

To be sure, the contradiction of the system as presented by Márkus could be reformulated as the project of suppressing civil society, which cannot function without reconstituting civil society. However the residual autonomy of consumers, sellers of labor power and the reemerging independence of producers in the second economy represent only a minimal civil society, the system of needs, one whose social solidarity is threatened by the specific forms of the second economy itself. Atomized consumers, workers, and producers are not capable of supplying the subjective moment required for crises in the full social scientific sense of the term.[33] Without the action of relevant social agents from below, the structural problems of an unreformed Soviet society can continue, and social-economic stagnation itself may not for a long time affect the freedom of the regimes to act as long as a truly modern military establishment can be maintained, and as long as in the center of the system of states, conditions of legitimation can be met.

Clearly the issue of legitimation is extremely relevant to the problem of crisis. If we can postulate, following Márkus, the chronic rationality deficit of Soviet-type societies along with the decreasing likelihood of significant structural reform from above as a form of crisis management, the actual possibility of significant transformation (however partial) is in some important measure the function of the dynamics of social integration, in particular legitimation. In this context Heller's analysis yields little that is hopeful. Defining legitimacy *crisis* (what should perhaps be "problems") as the absence of one of two poles of legitimation: validity of the regime for a significant part of society *and* nonexistence of alternatives for the other part, and *collapse* (but should be "crisis") of legitimacy as the absence of both poles, she comes up with the following gloomy picture. The regime has legitimacy *problems* in East Europe, but is fully legitimate in the Soviet Union. In this context, of course, it should be added that the legitimacy problems of the other countries can be contained, and even peculiar types of negative legitimacy (as in Hungary) may emerge. Under what conditions are these negative and positive forms of legitimacy under threat? Without being able to answer this question directly, I would like to suggest that the recent events in East Central Europe might justify a less pessimistic analysis, which, unlike Heller's, extends the notion of legitimation linked to national traditions also to the countries of East Central Europe, while in part questioning the possible *stability* under partially modern conditions of an appeal to traditions, not to speak of traditionalism, in *any* of the countries including the Soviet Union itself. In particular the dialectic of tradition has in the key instance of Poland led to a reconstruction of symbol systems in a direction compatible with a resurgent civil society and even its democratization.

It is, of course, unfair to criticize Heller for providing an analysis without open perspectives, because it is Fehér's task in the book's division of labor to present "the conflicts and the perspectives" of the regime. The only two valid questions to raise therefore are whether this last part of the analysis is sufficiently linked to the first to and whether or not these restrict somewhat its theoretical imagination. With respect to the first question the answer is yes, but it is yes with respect to the second one as well. It is my opinion that some key assumptions of Márkus and Heller that they share with now classical totalitarianism analyses do restrict Fehér's treatment of conflicts and perspectives.

The starting points of Fehér's analysis are in fact strongly linked to the final conclusions of his coauthors. On the one hand, following Márkus, he asserts that, given the unlikeliness of a reform allowing the successful transition from extensive to intensive development, both the maintenance of social compromise based on slowly rising living standards and the development and rationalization of the military-industrial-imperial complex become decreasingly possible (263, 278). But, following Heller's analysis of legitimation, he argues that the imperial periphery, Eastern Europe, will be "the epicenter of the gathering storm whereas in the Soviet Union itself the course of events will be more peaceful even if not free of conflict" (281).

The first premise to examine here is the one concerning the impossibility of structural reform. Upon closer examination this thesis is even more radical than it seems: in line with the classical totalitarianism thesis, the authors of the *Dictatorship over Needs*, unlike Szelényi on the one hand and Castoriadis on the other, reject in principle the idea that Soviet-type societies can have any fundamental *stages* of development. Thus, to begin with, the transition to a consumption-oriented intensive stage of development is denied, because this is incompatible with the dictatorship over needs. Márkus's point too seems to be that irrespective of the growth of the second and third economies and the resulting rationality problems, the first economy will always be under the original goal function that maximizes control over use values. Secondly, the postulate of military-oriented rationalization is accepted as an option within the given system, but the viability of a new stage of consolidation based on this is denied (Fehér 262, 278). I believe, however, that the alternative principle of identity as the minimum definition of the "sameness" of the system introduced in this essay, based on the priority of the prerogative state over society, allows both types of alternative developments. The consolidation of a military-political stage of the given system would be extremely compatible with such an identity involving only a replacement of the institution exercising the prerogative by a new one that would need direct penetration even less than its predecessors. Nevertheless, such a transition would require the consolidation of a new type of symbiotic relationship with some key capitalist countries, given the probable negative long-range effects of the backward civilian economy on the military one. This may be, however, the very point of the Soviet armament drive and political-diplomatic offensive. The development of a nonmilitary consumption-oriented stage, because it would be *less* compatible with the system's identity, would require the external blocking of the development of a military one. The mixed-economic structures of steering intensive development would require, and the necessary freeing of not only the consumers but a large number of units in the first economy from stage tutelage, would imply that the systems' principle of identity would have to be preserved in some other than the economic sphere. This would be the case especially because genuine economic decentralization could not work without some measure of *Rechtsstaatlichkeit*, some surrender of precisely prerogative power at least with regard to the economy. The economic goal function, too, would in this case have to be altered, possibly from the maximization of use values under state control to a maximization of "merely" budgetary resources. Such a change would amount, to be sure, to radical, structural reform. The argument of the *Dictatorship over Needs* as well as experience of all relatively recent East European "reforms" (with the partial exception of the Hungarian) indicates only that such a reform will not be introduced without pressure from outside the core of the system. Even if it could be made compatible with the regime's identity, the risk appears to be too great (possibly because of a false generalization of the Czech experience) and there is no force within the structure of power that today would take this risk without a greater alternative risk. (It is otherwise with the military-oriented alternative of development, of course.) Thus a genuine structural reform of the systems can be introduced only on the basis of significant pressure from below or outside. Paradoxically, then, only a process incompatible with the system's identity could introduce a new stage of this identity.

In this context, Fehér's typology of conflict potentials is extremely helpful. He indicates the struggle for economic rationality to be a significant force within a spectrum that includes struggles for national sovereignty and for civil society (publicity, legality, collective forms of autonomy). But it is fair to say that no perspective for genuine social change emerges from his analysis. First, he is skeptical in principle about *all* strategies of rational change, not only reform from above (which will not be undertaken), revolution (which is structurally possible only in the Soviet Union where conditions are, however, much more stable) and reform from below, the creation of counterpowers from below, which can lead only to cooptation or repression (297). But even more importantly, with the decline of oppositional Marxism he does not see any significant ideology cementing a truly viable, long-range strategy of opposition. In this analysis the problem of fundamentalism (nationalist and religious) looms large, and much of the argument hinges on it. My own postulate of the possibility at least in principle of a new, nonmilitary stage of the system on the basis of the given identity vitiates to be sure the claim that reform from below is in principle impossible, that the regimes can never put up with some counterpowers in any significant social sphere. I would even argue that such would be in fact the only means (outside of the military option) to manage their structural problem. But even if in principle possible, a fundamentalist opposition cannot be the agent that achieves such a stage.

According to Fehér, nationalism is a natural product of the systems in Eastern Europe, because of the loss of sovereignty to the Soviet Union, the existence of (mutually) disadvantageous economic relations between center and periphery and ideological resistance to the inept Soviet attempts to impose their own cultural hegemony. To an extent he neglects here, as does Heller, the utilization of nationalism as a negative legitimation, which in turn further opens the national issue for a potential opposition on the level of immanent critique. To Fehér, the new nationalism is a form of fundamentalism and as such a direct enemy of democracy. Equally important, "the reciprocal national hatreds in this region . . . directly play into the hands of Soviet imperialism using the millennial 'divide and rule' technique" (295). Leszek Kołakowski, over ten years ago, issued a similar warning[34] adding that East European nationalism greatly reinforces the only long range social integration of Soviet society: Great Russian nationalism. Indeed if the term "fundamentalism" absolutely describes one nationalism in the region, it is the Russian. But here we should again recall the structural difference between center and periphery: Fundamentalist nationalism, in the age of the decadence of Marxist-Leninist ideology, is a new positive legitimation in the imperial center. The situation in at least some of the countries of the periphery is different: Here fundamentalist-aggressive forms are on the whole less important (and increasingly less important) than fundamentalist-defensive forms on the one hand and democratic ones on the other. Above all in Poland, the struggles for democracy, national independence, and workers' rights were tightly linked.[35] Only in the moment of decomposition did negative, fundamentalist traits of nationalism appear—but even then it is remarkable, given Poland's past, to what a small extent. There were no anti-Soviet slogans or provocations and, whatever the private view of many participants, in the public sphere there was very little anti-Semitism.[36] Interestingly it was the regime, or parts of it, that sought to address what is most negative in the Polish tradition, and in this (unlike in 1968) it was almost completely unsuccessful.

It is evident that national tradition cannot be treated as a given and unchangeable factor of a political culture. Nationalism itself as we have seen has different potential forms, dynamic or traditionalistic in the case of Russia itself. In this respect, the otherwise different analyses of Vajda and Fehér are both historicist, in the sense of positing a given historical, national tradition that structures the culture of the system (Vajda) or at least that of the opposition (Fehér). But national tradition, to begin with, created by collective actors operating within the culture, can also be (and generally is) transformed when taken up again. In the context of the manipulated public sphere of partially sovereign East European states, national tradition can supply the cement of a negative legitimacy based on *raison d'état.* Within the traditional public sphere of the Polish church seeking to preserve a minimalist version of civil society that guarantees above all its interests, the same tradition is transformed to support an organic, evolutionary doctrine of change. In the milieu of the alternative and critical public sphere of the democratic opposition (which Fehér otherwise supports: see his remarks on KOR, 296) national tradition reemerges in forms that truly imply moral development. The symbols, the traditions to be sure are not entirely plastic, and they do determine the range of possibilities, the possible language in which projects can be articulated. In Poland, for example, Catholicism is such a nonplastic constant. But within its range there is, as we have seen, room for free cultural creation. Catholicism itself can be, and was in Poland, interpreted in traditionalist and hierarchical or modernist, personalist, and democratic terms. Astonishingly enough, furthermore, in a country without a tradition of democratic political culture, the experience of workers and intellectuals in the last thirty or so years has achieved much in this regard, broadening the very meaning of national tradition, and affecting the interpretation of Catholicism itself, for many in a democratic direction. There has been a veritable three-way struggle over the national tradition with the regime as the only clear loser in the sense of losing some of the basis of a negative legitimacy connected to *raison d'état.* Hence the regime's inability, for example, three years after Jaruzelski's coup to undertake significant reform, to control the sphere of culture, to fully smash the social movement whose last great victory[37] was the amnesty of summer 1984, or even to control its own security forces. In this context, the opposition to be sure also gains little except further opportunities for building its alternative culture and public sphere.

It is of course not possible—unfortunately—to argue that the Polish example refutes Fehér's argument, or the generally dark outcome of *Dictatorship over Needs.* The same could be said about the reluctant reformism of the Hungarian regime, which is the only historical basis of Szelényi's and my own arguments concerning the abstract possibility of a new reformed stage of Soviet-type societies based on mixed economic steering, decentralization, and modified *Rechtsstaatlichkeit.*[38] Above all, neither the Polish nor the Hungarian examples tell us much about Russia, where there is neither a broadly based democratic opposition nor any trace of reformism from above. The negative diagnosis of *Dictatorship over Needs* is backed up not so much by the unchanging totalitarian essence of Soviet-type societies as by the specificity of Russia.) Here the long-range hope lies in (1) the defeat of all attempts to establish existing West European capitalist countries as Soviet imperialism's cultural *cordon sanitaire* supplying its missing economic dynamism and (2) reluctant Soviet acceptance of a reformed Eastern Europe precisely in this new role. To put it simply: Eastern Europe can be Finlandized only if Western Europe is not. Such an outcome is, however, not independent of the activities of autonomous social actors East and West. Without their relevant efforts the verdict of *Dictatorship over Needs* will unfortunately stand. The most a critique of the work could show is that some of the contexts analyzed are more open than it proposes. No one would be more happy if this were true than the three authors themselves.

Notes

1. I. Szelényi, G. Konrád, *The Intellectuals on the Road to Class Power* (New York: Harcourt, 1979).

2. M. Rakovsky (pseudonym for Kis and Bence), *La Marxisme face aux pays de l'est* (Paris: Savelli, 1978).

3. C. Castoriadis, *Devant la guerre* (Paris: Fayard, 1982).

4. M. Vajda, *The State and Socialism* (London: Allison & Busby, 1981).

5. V. Zaslavsky, *The Neo-Stalinist State* (Armonk, NY: M.E. Sharpe, 1982).

6. K. Wojcicki, "The Reconstruction of Society," *Telos* 47 (Spring 1981).

7. This conception is close to the general model of Szelényi and Konrád concerning stages of probable development.

8. J. Habermas, *Legitimationsprobleme im Spätkapitalismus* (Frankfurt: Suhrkamp, 1973).

9. Personal communications with this author.

10. Zaslavsky, "The Problem of Legitimation in Soviet Society," in Vidich, Glassman, eds., *Conflict and Control, Challenge to Legitimacy of Modern Governments* (Beverly Hills: Sage, 1979).

11. See Szelényi's review of *Dictatorship over Needs* in *Telos* 60 (Summer 1984), 166ff.

12. M. Weber, *Wirtschaft und Gesellschaft*, fifth ed. (Tübingen: J.C.B. Mohr, 1972), 44–45.

13. Ibid.

14. Szelényi's review of *Dictatorship* in *Telos*.

15. Actually Szelényi and Konrád confuse this issue as well in their book, *Intellectuals*.

16. See my own argument for retraditionalization, "Critical Sociology and Authoritarian State Socialism," in Held, Thomson (eds.), *Habermas: Critical Debates* (London: Macmillan, 1982), Chapter 3 in the present volume.

17. M. Vajda, "Existing Socialism in the Light of the Traditions," *The State*.

18. Cf. Szelényi, Konrád, *Intellectuals*, 91–92.

19. Among recent works see: B. Anderson, *Imagined Communities* (London: New Left Books, 1983); J. Szücs, *Nation und Geschichte* (Budapest: Corvina, 1983); E. Gellner, *Nations and Nationalism* (Ithaca: Cornell University Press, 1983).

20. Cf. Vajda. His conclusions are supported by authors such as M. Raeff, R. Pipes, R. Bendix, R. Tucker, and S. White.

21. See the volume edited by A. Brown and J. Gray, *Political Culture and Political Change in Communist States*, second ed. (New York: Holmes and Meier, 1979).

22. F. Fehér, "Kádárism as the Model State of Khrushchevism," *Telos* 40 (Summer 1979).

23. Vajda, "Is Kádárism an Alternative?" in *The State and Socialism*.

24. This argument however is specifically not relevant to Vajda's and Szelényi–Konrád's use of models of traditional society, Asiatic Mode of Production or Russian traditions since these authors specifically stress the responsibility of revolutionary socialism, because of its *Wahlverwandschaft* with the authoritarian aspects of the given traditions and given forms of backwardness.

25. The concept of *Anstalt* represents a refinement of Szelényi and Konrád's *Stand*, except that Márkus's version indicates a permanent quasi-traditional feature of the system while Szelényi and Konrád restrict theirs to early stages only. Thus Márkus in spite of his stated intention, gives a greater stress to some of the traditional features of the system than some of the authors he implicitly criticizes. To be sure the idea of redistribution in Szelényi and Konrád, drawn from Polányi, establishes the traditional analogy especially deeply on the structural level if one treats the rationality of the system (i.e., the idea of *rational* redistribution) as a myth, as does Szelényi in his review in *Telos*.

26. See *Theorie des communikativen Handelns* II (Frankfurt: Suhrkamp, 1981), 563ff.

27. Arato, "Critical Sociology and Authoritarian State Socialism." In a "Reply to My Critics" in the same volume Habermas seems to work with a similar version.

28. In *Devant la guerre*.

29. To be sure "traditionalism" and even more "conservatism," as Martin Jay—referring to the work of Mannheim—kindly pointed out to me, may be in general modern or at least "posttraditional" ideologies. Weber does, however, use the term "traditionalism" in contexts like classical China at points where traditions were challenged in one way or another. The apparent contradiction can be solved if we distinguish, unlike Weber, between legitimation and motivation. Traditionalism *as an ideology* (as all ideologies) is a modern form of legitimation that hopes to restore or respond to a traditional pattern of motivation. Unlike traditional legitimation it is, however, dependent on an argumentative and discursive structure, which for specific *reasons* it wants, however, to suppress on the level of motivation. My own concept of "retraditionalization" is closer to "traditionalism" as here redefined than to "traditional" legitimacy in Weber's strict sense.

30. R. Manchin, I. Szelényi, "East Europe in the Crisis of Transition" (manuscript).

31. Arato, "Critical Sociology"; Szelényi in his review of *Dictatorship* in *Telos*.

32. I agree with Szelényi on this point. Habermas originally distinguished between problems and deficits, crises and systems crises. Today he adds the possibility of conversion into politically issueless social pathologies as well.

33. M. Vajda and J. Kis have also stressed this consequence of especially the Hungarian second economy, the latter in the samizdat publication *Beszélö*, no. 9.

34. "Thèses sur l'espoir et désespoir," in *La Pologne: une société en dissidence* (Paris: Maspero, 1978).

35. A Touraine et al. *Solidarité* (Paris: Fayard, 1982).

36. M. Wieviorka, *Les Juifs, La Pologne & Solidarność* (Paris: Danoël, 1984).

37. The present essay was written in 1984. See my article in *Journal of International Affairs* (Winter 1985), "Some Perspectives of Democratization in East Central Europe" (Chapter 11 in the present collection). M. Vajda has been the first to stress this point in relation to the alternative public sphere in Hungary, most recently in the manuscript "Kelet-Középeurópai perspektivák."

38. On the last issue see J. Kis's article in *Beszélö*.

7

Facing Russia: Castoriadis and the Problem of Soviet-Type Societies

Among the major representatives of critical Marxism, a tradition to which he once belonged, Cornelius Castoriadis is without peer as an analyst and critic of the new social formation of the Soviet type. The others have produced only sophisticated apologies (Lukács, Sartre), ambiguous and self-deceptive criticisms (Gramsci), repetitions of Trotskyist illusions (Marcuse) or exercises in avoidance (the Frankfurt School). Even the members of the Budapest School began their various creative analyses of the social structure and dynamics of the society they lived under only in the 1970s. Castoriadis has been on the job since 1946 and remains committed to it down to his latest writings. To be sure, of the four distinct theories of Soviet society he produced, the last two could not be contained within even the most critical and self-critical Marxian perspective. The challenge of the Soviet Union drove him beyond Marx, thus deeply influencing his whole intellectual development. In the face of new unfreedom he created an entirely new and original philosophy of freedom.

The following lines will concentrate on the development of Castoriadis's theory of Soviet society and will not attempt to do justice to his philosophy as a whole, which owes an important part of its genesis to both the successes and the unsolved problems of this theory. For the first three versions of the conception the focus will be on the reasons for the impossibility of working out a Marxian critical theory of the new social formation. For the last version, presented in *Devant la guerre*, the issue will be its own theoretical adequacy in the present situation.

The USSR as a "Third Historical Solution"

The first original conception of Castoriadis concerning the nature of Soviet society emerged in 1946 directly from his confrontation with Trotskyism.[1]

Reprinted with permission from *Revue européenne des sciences sociales*, 1989.

Deeply troubled with the politics of the "defense of the Soviet Union" and its implicitly pro-Communist West European implications, he came to see the theoretical roots of the official positions of the Fourth International with uncommon clarity. In the process he produced a conception different from even that of various Trotskyist dissidents from Rizzi and Schachtman to James and Dunayevskaya. According to Castoriadis, Trotsky and his orthodox followers confused genesis with structure, and juridical form with social relations. To be sure he accepted the notion that the October Revolution degenerated, but this fact, he argued, does not in itself describe the structure and the dynamics of the new type of regime, which could be introduced without degeneration or indeed any kind of proletarian revolution. The emergence of the so-called people's democracies demonstrates the point. Furthermore, the Trotskyist notion of degeneration involved a single historical line between capitalism and socialism; thus it is equivalent to the introduction of capitalist elements into a socialist context. To Castoriadis, however, whatever individual elements the new regime shared with socialism and capitalism, its essential features and forms of coordination belonged to neither system, but to a third, one also modern, a "third historical solution." This solution did presuppose a revolution in its origins; either a proletarian one, as in the original case, which did degenerate thereby producing a new type of bureaucratic regime, or a directly bureaucratic if anticapitalist revolution as in all subsequent cases. Either way, the result was a new social formation—neither socialist nor capitalist, nor even a form of transition from one of these to the other. In this context, Castoriadis had to face the theses of both the orthodox, who postulated some kind of "workers' state," and those dissidents who argued in terms of a state capitalist system.

The orthodox Trotskyists confused, according to Castoriadis, the "juridical appearances" of nationalization and planification, which hid a new system of class domination and exploitation in a manner parallel to the forms of legal equality in both private and public law in the bourgeois epoch. Using a version of the classical Marxian method of the critique of ideology, Castoriadis undertook to demystify the common "fetishes" of the Stalinists and the Trotskyists. Behind the appearances of state ownership and central planning identified with workers' ownership and coordination by so much of orthodox Marxism, Castoriadis discovered a new, politically constituted bureaucratic ruling class privately, if collectively, owning and controlling production, and new forms of domination and exploitation different but more extensive and intensive than those of capitalism.

Evidently, however, it was the identification of planning with worker interests that was ideological, not the claim that the system involved planning and centralization leading to the abolition of the laws and regularities of capitalist economies. Against the revisionist Trotskyist thesis of state capitalism, Castoriadis argued that a system where the forms of automatic functioning and the types of crisis tendencies discovered by Marx no longer applied "bears no resemblance to capitalism."

Indeed, like some Frankfurt School theorists, notably Friedrich Pollock in

1941,[2] Castoriadis argued that in the new system both a differentiated economy and its functional primacy in society disappear. As against Pollock, however, Castoriadis denied at this time that the immanent tendencies of capitalism can lead to such a system of the primacy of the political. Thus, unlike Pollock and Horkheimer, or for that matter Rizzi and Burnham, Castoriadis was not a theorist, in 1946 at least, of the totalitarian convergence of all late industrial societies. Indeed, for him, the Soviet Union, produced by revolution, was the best representative of the new type of noncapitalist *totalitarian* society, a point Pollock inexplicably denied.

Castoriadis's method that led to his original conception of the character of Soviet society involved a utilization of the work of Marx against the various brands of Trotskyism. This meant a rather orthodox use of the methods of ideology critique as well as the Marxian political economy. Remarkably enough, however, the results he attained tended to challenge the limits of the classical Marxian philosophy of history itself. To be sure, the form of ideological criticism he adopted from Marx's critique of the ideas of equal exchange and legal equality was not really appropriate to explore what he called "the juridical forms" of nationalization or statization and central planning. As he recognized somewhat later when he still used a modified version of this argument,[3] what he called bourgeois equality had a true as well as a false side. This adequate side could not, however, be restricted to the mere expression of the interests of the dominant class. If one is to recognize any truth or adequacy in the form of equality one must look beyond class interest, to the normative implications of the form itself. Since Castoriadis's concern was only the demystification of the norm, he did not pause to consider why the norm of equality had the power to mystify, with the consequences of this power in part pointing beyond mystification. He did not, in other words, notice that ideological critique in Marx had a double aspect of a critique that defetishizes forms of appearance on the one hand and on the other confronts norms with their violations in actuality.[4] From the point of view of this double critique, however, the fetishes of Soviet society turn out to be different from those of liberal capitalism. State ownership and planning are facts in Soviet society and not norms at all; they do not in themselves imply expressions of workers' interests, and their bureaucratic consequences follow from them without any contradiction. In the Soviet Union itself, moreover, the normative claims that these forms represented workers' democracy at its highest level were entirely empty, similarly to those made in the Constitution of 1936. No critical analysis of such claims, unlike those of liberalism, could have any theoretical or practical consequences. Castoriadis was perhaps misled by the fact that he himself indeed worked out a critique of a genuine ideology, namely Trotskyism, and this did have important consequences for his theory and politics. But significantly this ideology was not that of the system itself, and was banished from the Soviet Union along with its advocates. The mistake led, however, to a false parallelism between classical capitalism and Stalinism, even though

Castoriadis knew that the totalitarian nature of the latter was an important element of asymmetry between the two.

In any case he strongly maintained the nonidentity of Soviet society with capitalism. Here, interestingly enough, Castoriadis's insistence on a second dimension of the classical Marxian theory, the critique of political economy in a completely orthodox version, played an important role. Simply presupposing that the law of value and at least some of the crisis theorems based on it applied to contemporary capitalist society in spite of some tendencies toward state interventionism, and even fusion between state and economy, Castoriadis registered what was to him obvious: The same dynamic description does not apply to Soviet society. Therefore, in terms of the Marxian theory of social formations, the two systems had to be fundamentally different types of industrial societies. This recognition brought him right up against the limits of the Marxian philosophy of history, which did not recognize the possibility of a third form of industrial society besides capitalism and socialism. To simply identify the new with Rosa Luxemburg's term "barbarism," which she in turn linked to Marx's own notion of the possibility of the mutual ruin of both contending classes, supplied only a verbal solution to the problem, especially since Castoriadis at this time believed that the new social formation was the more stable version of industrial society. Without clearly recognizing it, he was close to the discovery that the reality of the Soviet Union does not allow the uncritical acceptance of all dimensions of Marx's own theoretical synthesis: Either the economics or the philosophy of history had to be abandoned.

Keeping the economics but restricting it to the West was his solution. This move revealed that the only dynamic theory of contemporary society Castoriadis could then conceive of was the Marxian political economy. This limitation had two consequences, which turned out to play a role in his transition to a new theoretical paradigm: failure to understand the nature of a changed capitalism in the West, and inability to conceptualize any theory of crisis and conflict for the Soviet Union.

The Theory of Total Bureaucratic Capitalism

It would be tempting to argue that Castoriadis worked out his second model of Soviet society in order to save the Marxian philosophy of history that his first model brought under threat. One may even harbor the suspicion that he was disturbed by one possible political implication of postulating two different but parallel industrial societies, only one of them totalitarian: the abandonment of the defense of Russia in favor of the defense of the West. What his own texts point to, however, is rather the theoretically well motivated doubt concerning the validity of the Marxian political economy in the context of a changed and changing capitalism. Thus Castoriadis had good reason to seek a new dynamic theory of society to put in place of the old. Instead of seeking further, however, he believed that he already had the foundation of such a theory in his own conception of bureaucratically ruled industrial society. Thus he came to rediscover, in a rather similar form, the theory of the totalitarian convergence of late industrial societies worked out by Friedrich Pollock and Max Horkheimer a few years before. Unlike them, however, Castoriadis was supremely conscious of the fact that the new theory represented the opposite procedure from the doctrine of state capitalism, namely the analysis of private capitalist societies in terms of the social model of the Soviet Union and not the reverse. As he put it later, the study of bureaucratic Soviet society became for him "the royal road for the comprehension of the most important problems of contemporary society."[5]

The new conception first made a partial appearance in the article "The Concentration of the Forces of Production," published in 1948, and was further elaborated in the same year in one of the founding texts of the new group and journal with the same name, "Socialism or Barbarism," and was fully developed in the major theoretical essay of 1949, "The Relations of Production in Russia," as well as in the slightly later piece "The Exploitation of the Peasantry Under Bureaucratic Capitalism." It is still fundamentally the same conception that we find in his writings on the "thaw" and on 1956, in 1960–61 when it led to a major theory of contemporary capitalism in the essay "Modern Capitalism and Revolution," and even as late as in his 1972 introduction to his political writings.[6]

Here we cannot deal with many of the differences among these various writings, which would be all the more important from the point of view of Castoriadis's general theoretical development. One should note, however, especially at the outset a certain reluctance to fully identify the two societies of private capitalism and bureaucratic regime. In the two transitional essays of 1948 Castoriadis notes significant asymmetries and differences, such as partial versus complete emancipation from the laws of the classical capitalist system; economic versus military integration in the capitalist world system; evolutionary versus revolutionary trend toward bureaucratization; incomplete versus complete assimilation of satellites. Throwing some inadvertent doubt on his earlier analysis of the similarity of juridical mystification under the two systems, Castoriadis even mentions the existence of juridical limits to exploitation under contemporary private capitalism as an essential difference.[7] Nevertheless, in spite of all this, he speaks in the very same writings of the one fundamental trend in all industrial societies toward concentration and centralization of capital, the fusion of state and economy, the replacement of the bourgeoisie by the bureaucracy as the dominant class, and the étatization and above all bureaucratization of all spheres of life. These trends, we are told, are completely realized in the Soviet Union and perhaps Nazi Germany whose essential similarity is now affirmed, and only incompletely in American and other postwar private capitalist societies. Nevertheless, Soviet society now represented something like the common totalitarian future of all industrial societies, one still identified with barbarism but also with the internal logic of capitalist development, a necessary and inexorable future that only socialist revolution can reverse or avoid. Hence the choice of the name "*socialisme ou barbarie.*"

To be sure, Castoriadis remained conscious of the different origins of bureau-cracy and statism in the two types of society in question. Indeed, he has now refined his conception of the degeneration of the Soviet regime in terms of the failure of the establishment of workers' management of industry at the very outset. Nothing like this dynamism of proletarian revolution and degeneration is, of course, to be found in the case of the capitalist countries; the distinction of Castoriadis between genesis and structure does not require it. Nevertheless, as he developed this conception he came to argue that it is above all the resistance and struggle of the working class that forces private capitalism to centralize, concen-trate, and rationalize production, and the bureaucratization of the reformist labor unions and parties plays a major role in making such transformation of the system possible. Thus the key elements of the two processes of the genesis of bureaucratic capitalism are not as dissimilar as he first assumed.

Although he invented the term later, the Soviet Union in the new conception was understood as "total bureaucratic capitalism," as against the "fragmented" bureaucratic capitalism of the West. In most respects the analysis of Russia simply continued and built upon his earlier model; the fact that he now identified it as capitalist did not change things to the extent that the tendencies of capitalist development were themselves derived from the model of Soviet society. And yet, the new terminology involving different terms of comparison meant the gradual erosion of some of his earlier positions. He again took up the issue of juridical appearance and social relations as before,[8] but in a somewhat self-con-tradictory manner he now also maintained in a different context that the juridical freedoms of the proletariat under private capitalism are indeed important limits on exploitation that are absent in the Soviet Union and Nazi Germany. While the first use of the concept of juridical form as mystification pointed to a similarity of ideology and social relations and hence a global parallelism in spite of essen-tial structural differences between *liberal* capitalism and Soviet society, the argu-ment now gravitated toward an identification of the latter with *late* capitalism, which Castoriadis saw as the *totalitarian* future potentially of the whole indus-trial world.

Similarly he again rejected the neo-Trotskyist theory of state capitalism, be-cause he maintained as before that the classical description of capitalism was inapplicable to Russia, and that it was a "silly joke" to see the forms of distribu-tion here as bourgeois. Yet when he introduced the Leninist conception of state capitalism he did so only to show that nationalization and planification do not in themselves mean socialism even in Lenin's theory. He argued, furthermore, that the organization of society in the Soviet Union was the extension of the model of the bureaucratized, rationalized, and indeed planned capitalist factory to the whole. The term bureaucratic capitalism itself implied not so much the abandon-ment as the deepening of the concept of state capitalism.[9] Above all, Castoriadis's argument now for the first time tended to share an essential feature with the state capitalist thesis, namely the claim (which he did not abandon till the 1970s in spite of obvious inconsistencies) that the whole general orientation of production and the situation of the worker under the two systems involved the same objectives as well as the same processes of control and rationalization.

The exploitation and oppression of workers is the same in Detroit and Leningrad, at Renault and Csepel. It is this idea that best characterizes Castoriadis's attempt in the 1950s and 1960s to give substance to his theory of bureaucratic capitalist convergence. What was still a future projection in 1949 became very much a diagnosis of the present a few years later. The reduction of workers to mere objects of managerial direction, the extraction of the greatest possible surplus labor, the methods of direct coercion, speedup, piece-rates, bonuses, and the denial to workers the least right to organize the work process are the same, according to him, in both systems.[10] Two caveats should be mentioned to put the argument in perspective. Castoriadis was battling first and foremost against opponents who claimed that whatever else may be wrong with the Soviet Union, the "situation" of workers is fundamentally better there than in the countries of private capitalism. In relation to them, at least, he was supplying an important, if insufficient corrective. Second, his fundamental intellectual honesty allowed him to suppress nothing that he knew about the Soviet Union. Thus he supplied, without being conscious of it, important correctives to his own argument. Thus he mentions in the case of Soviet and East European workers the nonexistence of the rights to strike, to organize, and to form unions and even of the ability to talk and read freely, and to listen to anything but official propaganda. Yet he says all this without drawing the conclusion that their rather different situation in these respects makes the condition of workers in the West fundamentally better. In general his conception of identity of the two systems on the micro (workshop) level was rooted in a macroeconomic conception according to which Soviet bureaucratic coordination and planning was simply the extension to the level of society of precisely the model of coordination of the giant capitalist firm as well as the methods of social control of the modern capitalist workshop. This conception seems to imply that the firm and the workshop are the same in the two systems, and to a Marxist it is this dimension that ultimately matters. Thus Castoriadis maintains that the bureaucratic plan is "the most highly perfected realization of the spirit of capitalism."[11] And though he significantly adds "pushed to the limit," he does not seem to realize that even within his own conception it might make a great deal of difference for the microstructures themselves that a model of macrocoordination is organized according to the model of the giant bureaucratized capitalist firm, or according to a very different model, which need not be that of "perfect" competition. Put provocatively, the organization of the whole of economic life according to the model (or perhaps at best the metaphor) of the capitalist firm may make it impossible for actual firms to function as capitalist ones.[12]

To be sure, Castoriadis did add the qualification "pushed to the limit" to his remark about the realization in the Soviet Union of the spirit of capitalism. This idea leads him, however, in two opposite directions. First, in context of his thesis of the fundamental identity of the two systems, he wanted to demonstrate that in private capitalist societies too the same limit is in the process of being reached. And second, he was sure that he could show that reaching the limit would be a source not of stability but of new types of dysfunction and conflict.

After the postwar scare of McCarthyism Castoriadis no longer wanted to be on record predicting the coming of any type of the authoritarian state in the West. Instead, in the work "Modern Capitalism and Revolution" he drew up an indictment, a few years before Marcuse, of capitalist mass democracy as a new form of totalitarianism:

> modern societies, whether "democratic" or "dictatorial," are in fact *totalitarian*, for in order to maintain their domination, the exploiters have to invade *all* fields of human activity and try to bring them into submission. It makes no difference that totalitarianism today no longer takes the extreme forms it once took under Hitler or Stalin. . . . "Peaceful" manipulation of the masses and the gradual assimilation of any organized opposition can be more effective.[13]

This highly polemical claim is built upon a sophisticated argument whose parts involve the well-known thesis of the fusion of state and society in the context of state interventionism, the Weberian-Lukácsian argument about the bureaucratization of all spheres of life—now including even culture and leisure, a series of points anticipated by Kirchheimer and later made popular by Marcuse about the vanishing and integration of forms of bureaucratized (party and union) opposition, and finally a set of arguments concerning full employment, demand management, and mass consumption by Keynesian welfare states reducing needs to narrow economic ones that could now be satisfied.

The coming and stabilization of the new capitalism points according to Castoriadis to the (excusable) error of past Marxists of projecting the forms of classical capitalism into the future, inexcusably continued by orthodox Marxists even after the changes have already occurred. Nevertheless, in one respect he continued to rely on Marx's methodological model, more so than did Marcuse in *One Dimensional Man* that in many respects parallels his thesis. Aside from discovering possible new forms of opposition (in particular, new movements especially of the young) Castoriadis resolutely sought to discover the new forms of dysfunction and crisis of bureaucratic capitalism. Here the idea of "pushing to the limit" had the meaning that a capitalist system cannot function at all when its principles completely triumph in all spheres of life. Thus bureaucratic capitalism seeks only to realize what has already failed on the shop level, precisely as a response to this failure: the total reduction of human beings to objects. Here once again Castoriadis insisted on the idea of a common fundamental contradiction and crisis tendencies of both types of systems, private or fragmented bureaucratic capitalist and the Soviet-type or total bureaucratic capitalist systems.

The claim is most plausible on a fundamental level that points to the tension between modernity and all its heteronomous forms. According to Castoriadis the deepest contradiction of both types of society is that between the requirement of autonomy and participation needed to make complex modern societies function at all, and the tendency to reduce all human persons, relations, and functions to purely objective, calculable, rationalizable entities. When it came to analyzing the actual institutional tensions and crisis tendencies linked to this contradiction, it is evident that Castoriadis has succeeded far better in the case of the Soviet-type societies, which always remained the target of his analysis, than in the case of the private capitalist ones to which he tried to extend his model of totalitarianism.

Castoriadis was deeply impressed by the Hungarian revolution of 1956, which he considered the most advanced form of workers' struggle for a genuinely self-managed society. To be able to derive the universal lesson from this experience, he used the occasion to develop a crisis theory of Soviet-type societies that was both synthetic and original, and which remains in many respects valid to this day, in spite of the problem of the overextension of this theory.[14] In general he saw two sources of dysfunction, the conflict of bureaucracy/plan with workers/executants and the contradiction of bureaucracy/plan with itself. The resistance of workers to exploitation, generally informal and spontaneous, as well as the killing of autonomous forms of workshop coordination and self-regulation, have dramatic effects on both the quantity and quality of what is produced. This resistance makes the expansion of productivity in all of its senses impossible; in particular the system lacks and does not reward forms of spontaneous technical innovation and adaptation on the shop floor. Given the insatiable hunger for all components of production, whose source Castoriadis does not actually discover, unemployment is not a threat and workers cannot be deterred from absenteeism, lateness, and lax work tempo, at least not without terror, which cannot, however, be the cement of modern production, and which is too dangerous for the bureaucracy itself. Low productivity in the area of energy production leads to underutilization of productive capacity; thus the combination of waste and shortage. This train of argument, it should be said, one that Castoriadis considers the central source of the crises of bureaucratic society, is hardly applicable to the contemporary capitalist societies which are not "economies of shortage" constrained by the physical availability of productive resources.

I believe, however, that a second strand in Castoriadis's argument concerning the internal contradiction of bureaucratic planning deals with a more fundamental problem in Soviet-type societies. Here he points to three areas of difficulty: (1) the crisis of information, (2) the conflict of bureaucratic levels and instances, and (3) the problems of political recruitment and promotion. The first source of information distortion is from workers hoping to underestimate their productive capacities. They are often helped by the managerial levels closest to them, whose own ability to fulfill plans is thereby enhanced, and who are in any case dependent on a minimum of shop floor goodwill. The problem is, however, more general in a hierarchical top-down management structure, where each level and especially the managers of firms overestimate their costs and underestimate their potential product. Later writers like Kornai and Márkus understand precisely this tendency as a clue to the peculiar bargaining structure of command economies that produces the shortage phenomena already mentioned by allowing only the physical availability of resources to constrain investment. Castoriadis too understood the conflict among bureaucratic instances as an important element of distortion of planning decisions, even if he did not clearly indicate political weight in the absence of reliable information as the criterion deciding between alternative assessments of needed inputs and potential outputs of firms, along with the destructive consequences of this. Where he did thematize this criterion was in context of the peculiar "civil service" structure of managerial and planning bureaucracies, leading to the superimposition of expertise and politics. Here he had in mind the nomenklatura system of appointment and promotion that replaces efficiency and innovation by loyalty and clique membership as the standard of success, leading to a system of veritable counterselection.

The overall system of bureaucratic command produces both opacity and anarchy. Castoriadis rightly stressed that the problem of information or rather "mendacity" is so radical that it is impossible for the planning bureaucracy to have any kind of overview of the economic system. Thus it remains hostage to its own distorted statistics even in the post-Stalin period when data are not deliberately falsified. One might think that along with differences in productivity, this factor points to a significant difference with Western capitalist economies, leading to far greater strains and potential dysfunctions. But Castoriadis tends to insist only that the plan is *as chaotic, as wasteful* as the market, that the bureaucracy is just *as incapable* of rationally directing the economy as private capitalism.

Indeed, when it came to the private version of bureaucratic capitalism, Castoriadis repeated in rough outline the same crisis tendencies he discovered for the Soviet model. To be sure, now an analysis that was powerfully concrete in its original context became rather unspecific and abstract.[15] Or rather, as he is speaking of the two systems simultaneously, the analysis remained concrete only to the extent the reader referred back to the societies of the Soviet type. Whereas in the case of these societies the train of argument points to blockages that tendentially eliminate all real dynamism, in case of Western societies Castoriadis could link the abstract crisis potential to a heterogeneity of empirical "crisis events" that could interrupt the existing dynamism only if coupled with unanticipated forms of global and conscious mass action. This rather Lukácsian conclusion is not supported in the case of private capitalist societies either by the type of crisis theory that Lukács presupposed, or by a theory that Habermas and his collaborators were to work out ten years later, or even—despite appearances—by Castoriadis's own crisis theory of Soviet-type societies.

Castoriadis's efforts to work out a crisis theory of all contemporary industrial societies was part of an effort to reconstruct and thereby save the Marxian theory of society. In the late stages of this effort the doubts grew; Castoriadis came to the conclusion in particular that the Marxian economic theory presupposed the same reification of human activity and relations, and the same deemphasis of the class conflict constitutive of structural changes as was capitalism itself. To be sure, this criticism applied a good deal less to the rather Lukácsian Marxism Castoriadis utilized and managed to deepen. But a second objection could not be escaped even by this version of the theory: Namely that the Marxian critique of capitalism in all its varieties actually implied that nationalization and planning could overcome the anarchy and crisis tendencies of capitalist society. Similarly to Horkheimer in 1941, Castoriadis was in 1960–61 on the verge of arguing that a new capitalism requires an entirely new version of critical theory. That he did not do so just yet had to do with at least two elements of orthodoxy in his social theory.[16] He seemed to believe first of all that centralized global planning without markets, plus nationalized property, plus workers' management of industry could be made to work in context of a global, pyramidically organized council-type democracy. Not only was this notion, a version of the classical Marxian utopia, entirely untested according to him by the Soviet experience, but more importantly it committed Castoriadis himself to an evolutionary philosophy of history in which the existing trends toward centralization and concentration represented important components of progress. It was indeed this philosophy of history, continuous with that of classical Marxism, and not any lack of human sympathy nor especially any misunderstandings about the exploitative, inefficient, and oppressive kolkhoz system, that was responsible for some rather unfortunate early remarks concerning the carrying out of the verdict of history against small-scale private producers, that is, the Russian peasantry by the Stalinist bureaucracy.[17]

This philosophy of history, which was more or less the only doctrinal element of what he called "traditional" Marxism still lingering on in Castoriadis's conception in the early 1960s, produced some incoherence within his thought. Assuming again the existence of only two forms of modern industrial society, socialism and capitalism, and also that the Soviet Union and the Western countries were both capitalist, the question which of the two types is more advanced, inevitable for the Marxist, could not be answered. In terms of the common trends of concentration and centralization, and the inauguration of central planning and state ownership (for Castoriadis, only the negative side of socialism), Soviet-type societies would have to be judged more advanced on a single evolutionary line. In terms of productivity, ability to avoid loss of dynamism, and most other economic indicators, however, the opposite would be the case. And if one is to try to get out of the difficulty by arguing, as Castoriadis often did, that getting close to the limit of realizing the fundamental tendencies of capitalism must mean decay, decline, and loss of dynamism, how are we to explain the powerful expansion of state interventionist private capitalist systems in the postwar period and their relative freedom from global crisis compared with liberal capitalism? Castoriadis could think of an answer to this line of questioning only when he openly broke with Marxian social theory.

Totalitarian Capitalism or Capitalism Minus Democracy

As early as 1956 Claude Lefort took Castoriadis to task concerning the evolutionist and economistic bias of the conception of bureaucratic capitalism.[18] Although admittedly producing no rival, global conception of his own, Lefort hammered away at the following points:

1. The economic perspective focusing on global trends of concentration and centralization makes the Stalinist party merely the "personification" of total capital.
2. Such a line of analysis misses the revolutionary break needed for the emergence of bureaucratic domination.
3. The political processes of violence, purges, and terror are required for the self-constitution of the party as a new type of bureaucracy that is the collective apparatus of appropriation as well as power.
4. Within capitalism the fusion of state and civil society cannot be realized.
5. The whole conception, in the name of a "historical pseudonecessity," misses the creative role in modern economies of market, competition, and decentralized enterprise.
6. In spite of every reservation Castoriadis's theory comes close to the theory of state capitalism, abandoning the insight that the Soviet Union represents an entirely new type of modern, totalitarian social formation.

What Lefort himself missed was the greater consistency of Castoriadis, who, like himself, wanted in 1956 to remain within the classical Marxian conception of history. The objections, however, were significant in spite of this reservation. Castoriadis was to build several of them, or their analogues, into his theory when he broke with this classical conception. A mature document representing the third distinct position of Castoriadis on the Soviet Union is the major 1978 essay "The Social Regime in Russia."[19] It is astonishing how much of his previous conception of "total bureaucratic capitalism" he is able to build into the new one. He himself plays on this theme by introducing a streamlined version of the earlier theory as a paradigm of real (also the best?) Marxian analysis. But now this analysis is pronounced incomplete and abstract, because it equates the situation of Russian and Western workers by not integrating the absence of political and civil rights, the right to organize, and the presence of totalitarian controls into the presentation of the condition of the former. Indeed, these social and political differences referring to juridical forms that are hardly only formal, affect also the economic aspects of the lives of Russian workers. They lose important instruments for the reduction of their exploitation and even more importantly cannot limit the wasteful irrationality of bureaucratic domination that diminishes and deforms their consumption in particular and quality of life in general. And while the absence of juridical freedoms does not eliminate the possibilities of resistance to exploitation, these are forced into paths that only increase the irrationality of the system.

With all this said, the fundamental contradiction of the system is analyzed as before in terms of deactivization and the need for participation, as are the resulting tensions and dysfunctions having to do with the lack of information, and intrabureaucratic conflicts. But now, freed of the weight of an indefensible philosophy of history and in the midst of the conservative Brezhnev era, the balance sheet of a failed society could be drawn up. Not being able to reform itself because of the fear that the most timid of significant steps might lead to explosions or the gradual loss of bureaucratic power, the Russia of the apparatus (1) cannot feed itself; (2) cannot satisfy solvent demand; (3) can maintain military parity with its main competitor only by spending an exorbitant part of its resources; (4) cannot effectively respond to the national question; and (5) cannot even deal with the problem of orderly political succession, saving itself only through gerontocracy. There can be no doubt that the Western capitalist countries represent a social formation more successful in dealing with these problems; indeed it was they rather than some conception of a new type of socialist society that were used as yard sticks.

To be sure, Castoriadis maintains the terminological link between total and fragmented *bureaucratic capitalism*. But now the Soviet-type system is once again pronounced as world-historically new even if the supposedly unchanged institution of the firm is said to be its essential link with capitalism. More importantly, Russia is said to be a part of capitalism's social historical universe because sharing and even bringing to a paroxysm its self-contradictory social imaginary, the striving for pseudorational mastery. What remains to be explained is why the original private capitalist contexts of this imaginary do not organically produce the culmination of its inherent tendencies, with all the attendant irrational and destructive consequences. Why, in other words, is a revolution needed to bring to a climax principles that already dominate in the old society?

Once again Castoriadis indicates that it was Marxian theory, this time that of bureaucracy and bureaucratization, that has made an answer to this question so difficult. Accordingly, within a consistent Marxian theory he himself has made bureaucratization in his earlier writings only the social side of capitalist concentration and centralization, and bureaucracy the personification of capital. And indeed such explanation retains its validity as a purely economic, production-oriented analysis. The trends toward concentration and centralization do have the implication of the abolition of the private capitalists, of capital and even economy in the strict sense—that is, a society of the Soviet type. But the trend cannot reach its "ideal limit" because it cannot spontaneously produce one of its indispensable driving forces, the bureaucracy itself. According to Castoriadis's new analysis, modern bureaucracy has two origins, states and armies, and it is from these that the capitalist enterprise inherited the model, in the process rationalizing it. The new version was then readopted by its original sources, as well as modern political parties. While the argument is not clear or complete at this point, it would seem that while the four modern bureaucratic structures (preserving the mark of their different origins?) may penetrate most or all spheres of life under advancing private capitalism, they do not gain the unity under this system required for full-fledged bureaucratic domination. For this, Castoriadis says, an essentially political process, in particular a revolution, is needed. Capitalism engenders only a specific type of bureaucracy, the "standard" (presumably the Weberian) type that, if we extend the argument, is not suitable as the undifferentiated center of political-economic-cultural-military domination. Only a political process, not derivable from economic trends, can accomplish the needed transformation.

Our question does not thereby disappear. After all, the new bureaucracy is not in this analysis, at least, supposed to be less modern than its capitalist forerunners; it is merely a different modern type. Moreover, it is more capitalist than are bureaucracies under capitalism itself, bringing to culmination the deepest trend of capitalist society itself, the drive to unlimited mastery. Why cannot the political processes of capitalism itself produce a bureaucracy adequate to its own concept? What must, in other words, be overthrown in capitalist society to produce unification among otherwise increasingly homologous and interchangeable bureaucracies?[20]

The seed of the answer, to be unfolded in the subsequent writings of Castoriadis, is already there in this essay. For a long time he considered working-class resistance to be one of the motors of a development toward increasing rationalization and centralization of controls. Now, however, we get the following contrast. In Russia worker resistance increases the irrationality of the system; in the West it saves it from precisely this. The two contexts, however, are not on the same level. In Russia resistance decreases the efficiency of an already established bureaucratic plan; in the West the emergence of just such a planning is blocked. Has Castoriadis simply reversed himself on this point? Actually, it is the form of working-class protest organized around civil, political, and union rights put in relief here that distinguishes the new argument from the old. While protest as such interferes with exploitation, and thus promotes rationalization, protest in the framework of rights blocks the bureaucratic-authoritarian options of rationalization. Given, however, the irrational consequences of such rationalization, it can be indeed said that the workers' action within the forms provided by legality saves the system from greater irrationality. Thus, private capitalism is forced to put up with elements of nonidentity that actually institutionalize some participation and thereby preserve the system from reaching the culmination of its destructive tendencies.

Such would be one reconstruction at least following the sense of Castoriadis's own analysis. It contains one possible implication that was surely unintended, namely an ambiguous attitude to the legalization of labor struggles, as both providing a space for freedom and the possibility of stabilizing an otherwise self-destructive system of domination. Shortly after publishing the essay under analysis this political implication involving some lingering hostility to existing forms of democracy disappeared, as Castoriadis began generalizing the original argument by speaking about a double institutionalization as the foundation of Western modernity, that of democracy and that of capitalism. Accordingly, a bureaucratic revolution would be needed to free the drive toward unlimited pseudomastery from its institutionalized democratic impediments. A new, democratic, antibureaucratic revolution would then self-consciously do exactly the opposite by building on existing institutions of autonomy that would not have to be, in the West at least, invented ex nihilo.

But is it democracy as such that stops bureaucratization in societies that Castoriadis rightly considers "oligarchic"? I believe that another contrast to be found in "The Social Regime in Russia" provides a better starting point for a theory of double institutionalization. I have already referred to Lefort's distinction between the surviving duality between civil society and state in the West and its abolition under Stalinism. Lefort also maintained that even in Russia the antagonism of the two spheres would be reproduced, "in a more aggravated form."[21] This analysis, hardly clear when first developed, received new and important elaboration by Castoriadis. Parallel to Habermas's *Strukturwandel der Öffentlichkeit*, Castoriadis took leave of the simple dualistic model of state/civil society and spoke of three spheres characteristic of bourgeois society: the private, the public-civil, and the public-governmental.[22] Even in the West the extension of the state has reduced the independence of the other two domains. But total bureaucratic capitalism involves a "qualitative break" by obliterating the distinction between the two "public spheres" and reducing the private to a minimum. Nevertheless, the state, controlled by a "part" of society, cannot actually unify and homogenize the "whole"; cannot obliterate the social, which reappears in the form of both the resistance of subjects and divisions within the apparatus. This analysis, representing an important contribution to a theory of civil society, explains how social division can return "in a more aggravated form" without automatically reconstituting the "public-civil" sphere. With this argument Castoriadis indeed points to the "qualitative" difference between Western and Soviet-type societies, and to the institutions that must be eliminated in a "qualitative rupture" if the latter is to be established at all. It is precisely the institutions of private and public autonomy that workers utilize when in the West they challenge capitalist exploitation and reification on the basis of their rights. And at the same time it is these institutions, in their bourgeois form, that within the terms of Castoriadis's theory stop capitalism from realizing its most irrational consequences, thereby helping to stabilize this system and to preserve its dynamism.

Castoriadis's third theory of Soviet society preserved to a residual extent its links with Marx's project as a whole by working toward a crisis theory. Even more, the revolutionary aspiration is maintained: "Among industrial countries, Russia is the prime candidate for social revolution." This statement can be interpreted in terms of a Marxian evolutionism that would locate revolution in terms of the final realization, or "pushing to the limit" of the tendencies of a system, with all dysfunctional and irrational consequences. Such, however, was no longer Castoriadis's perspective. First, we should notice that his conception of revolution can no longer be the same for the Western capitalist countries and the Soviet Union. Both in turn would have to be structurally different from the Bolshevik one, which wound up eliminating in the new conception the institutional complex of democracy (or civil society) in order to allow the unfolding of the other, the bureaucratic one (that Castoriadis at least identifies with capitalism). This depiction involves the sobering thought for Western revolutionaries that the Bolsheviks too did not seek to abolish civil society in order to strengthen the bureaucratic tendencies of their own society, and that precisely this abolition led to the unintended result. Whatever revolution can now mean in the West, it would follow that it must in any case preserve and build upon the existing structures of freedom. Yet paradoxically these structures reinforce today a relatively stable and dynamic form of capitalism. It is fair to say that Castoriadis did not solve this paradox, and therefore could no longer easily reconcile his new conception with his never-abandoned call for radical revolution. In the case of Russia, however, the same difficulty did not apply. Here the institutions for the pursuit of reformist activity similar to that of Western labor did not exist. Nor, according to Castoriadis, was reform from above with serious structural consequences to be expected. Russia is a "prime candidate for social revolution" to Castoriadis, not because he is predicting such a thing on the bases of any existing trends including the tensions he analyzed, but because he saw nothing in this society worth preserving from the normative point of view, and because of his belief, that there was no other option for serious change for the system that had to be untenable under the conditions and challenges of modernity.

Stratocratic Dual Society and its Instability

In the Brezhnev era serious interpreters of the Soviet Union confronted a paradox. How can it be that a society so irrational from the economic point of view, one that repeatedly cannot carry out its own projects of reform, nevertheless appears to be so stable? Only Castoriadis worked out in 1980 a sociologically important answer to this question leading to his important 1981 book, *Devant la guerre*.[23] On the basis of his rather Weberian conception that a society organized on the basis of the totalization of bureaucratic reason must be deeply and *increasingly* irrational, he now proposed that stability can be regained through dualistic reorganization. The argument had a certain analogy with his conception of the capitalist democracies as products of dualistic institutionalization, except that in the Soviet Union he saw dualization in terms of the creation of a military "subsociety," genuinely modern, within the larger, increasingly conservative bureaucratic society to which he continued to apply most of his earlier depiction. In effect he postulated a division within the bureaucracy itself as the fundamental form of the detotalization of a system that could not otherwise reform itself. Dualistic organization and the creation of the military subsociety were seen as the solution of the problem of *the simultaneous necessity and impossibility of reform*, as the Brezhnev era's functional substitute of reform.

Castoriadis's argument for the impossibility of the self-reform of the system was forceful and direct. Since all serious decentralization requires the significant pushing back of the apparatus, this body, entirely intact in the Soviet Union, will sabotage either the emergence of a global reform program or its being put in effect, or both. There is in the Soviet Union at least no new political cadre capable of overcoming the resistance of various bureaucracies that is most efficient on the societal microlevels. Even if it were possible to institute partial reforms, furthermore, these could not possibly affect the overall functioning of society, and would be certainly reabsorbed by the system. Thus, reforms that might work always represent a danger of spilling beyond their original bounds, and will therefore not be instituted from above, while reforms that are easily containable might perhaps be instituted, but will not work.[24]

Castoriadis's thesis concerning the actual reorganization of Soviet society begins with two established facts. First, he stresses the great disparity between a country being capable of establishing and maintaining a military-industrial complex of at least equal efficacy (not efficiency) with that of the most advanced capitalist country, and at the same time not being able to satisfy the minimum demands of modernity in all nonmilitary-related sectors. Second, he points to the well-documented division of Russian industry into closed and open enterprises, the former more or less coinciding with the industrial component of the military-industrial complex. The relative, but significant, success of this complex is then explained both by the systematic monopolization of the best resources including labor, and a different mode of social organization. This second aspect, which justifies the use of the term "military subsociety," is based on a significant restriction of mobility of the workforce coupled with important material and nonmaterial privileges. Furthermore, on the basis of several actual studies, Castoriadis shows the prevalence of chauvinistic attitudes on the part of the Soviet working class found in the military subsociety that has, in other words, a distinct economic, social, and ideological identity.[25] The higher efficacy and the relative modernity of the military subsociety is, according to Castoriadis, related to a structurally differentiated, privileged and better motivated sector of the workforce. To be sure, he does not notice that in itself the built-in priority of investments earmarked for this sector, would, in terms of the standard pattern of the Soviet economy, actually diminish efficiency as well as quality. Nevertheless, the much higher quality of inputs would distinguish this sector from civilian heavy industry, which would be the second preferred candidate for investments. Even more important, in the case of the military-industrial complex, the consumer (the army), actually present on the plant level, is indeed sovereign as against the whole Soviet pattern; thus the quality of the output can be controlled. Because of this feature, as well as the symbiotic-exploitative attitude to the civilian economy, the model of the military subsociety cannot be transferred to the rest of Soviet society in spite of continual calls urging this.[26]

Castoriadis speaks not only of a military subsociety but also of a veritable *stratocracy* in the Soviet Union. He warns that he is not implying a takeover by or even the preponderant influence of a military clique, but rather of domination by the army as a social body. And yet when he asks how it was possible for the military-industrial complex to absorb the best resources (which he inconsistently considers the reason why the civilian economy cannot be "moderately prosperous") he easily slips into the following answer: "because for some time the effective power over decisive orientations has belonged to the army, to the heads of the military bureaucratic apparatus."[27] Thus a structural argument is converted to an empirical one concerning the dominant class, a conversion that too easily exposes Castoriadis to empirical questions concerning his evidence for such a claim. In fact, he does not need this type of hypothesis resurrected from his Marxist past; the structural argument would have sufficed at least with respect to economic choices. The structure of plan bargaining in the Soviet Union of which he is aware systematically favors the sectors with the best established political power position;[28] the military gets the most and best resources because it is de facto already the most powerful. To be sure, this argument does not yet explain the qualitative difference in privileges that Castoriadis detects between the military sector and all the rest, including the most privileged sectors of the civilian economy. Here, however, his own argument concerning the decay of the official ideology and its gradual replacement by a national-imperial imaginary supplies the missing theoretical link. This ideological transformation does not have its source in the rise of military subsociety or stratocracy; its analogues are to be found in all East European countries without the dualism Castoriadis analyzes. Even the uniquely imperial form of the new ideology can be traced to the special relation of Russia to its various peripheries, which do not allow for a merely nation-state version of nationalism. The new imaginary however, in context of a superpower role, explains not only the better motivation of the workforce in the military subsociety, but also a bargaining position qualitatively superior to all others for the bureaucratic apparatus of this sector. What I am arguing, in other words, is that Castoriadis's theory is best understood as that of the military subsociety *cum* national-imperial imaginary, and that the polemical, proto-Marxian notion of the stratocracy is unnecessary.

The critics of Castoriadis's thesis rarely understood it. Characteristically, arguments pointing to the potential instability of the new dualistic structure were used to deny its existence.[29] Castoriadis shares some blame for this misunderstanding to the extent that he, against the grain of his all previous analyses especially in his Marxian period, seemed to presuppose not only the existence, but the overall stability of the structure. To be sure, he does tell us that "skimming" by the military economy "aggravates the chronic debility of the civilian economy, which is essentially the result of the resistance of producers and the profound irrationalities inherent in bureaucratic management."[30] Thus Castoriadis in effect builds his whole theory of dysfunction and loss of dynamism into his conception of the military subsociety that on the economic level, unlike the elements of dualism under capitalism, only lowers the performance of the whole. However, this economic result does not homogeneously affect Russian society; the inhabitants of the military sector gain where the others lose. More importantly, the new ideology along with the actual power of an internally stable and corporately distinct military are capable of integrating even a society with declining overall growth rates and standards of living.

This last answer is not convincing, because it seems to point only to the options of continued social integration. What remains unclear, however, in context of the necessarily symbiotic relation of the two economies, is how long a declining civilian economy can produce the minimum required for a military sector depending less on its own efficiency than the exploitation of the rest of production. It would seem certainly that the decline and decay of the civilian sector would have to affect the military subsociety's own success. The Brezhnev era's alternative to reform could not supply the missing answers in the longer run.[31]

While it is not easy to comprehend outside the testimony of everyday events why exactly Castoriadis ascribed an expansionary policy to the "stratocracy," it might very well be that he had in mind (among other things) the search for substitutes of a missing internal economic dynamism.[32] Actual conquest or even more importantly new types of politically dominant relations with more dynamic economies (preferably capitalist ones) could, of course, renew the resources for the Russian military subsociety indefinitely.[33] What this proposal, of course, did not count on is the superior ability of the capitalist countries to vastly increase the technical pace of military competition.

And it did not count on Afghanistan. Castoriadis's thesis, to be sure, as he himself tells us, was born in a conjunction of events in which the invasion of Afghanistan figured prominently. It is interesting to speculate to what extent the impending defeat in Afghanistan, where sophisticated American rocket technology played a key role, prepared the atmosphere for a new attempt at reform. While it would be possible to argue that it is merely the external challenge symbolized by Star Wars that is the source of Gorbachev's reform attempt, Castoriadis does not take this easy way out in a recent article.[34] Rightly he understands that the external challenge would not be as serious if the internal structure would be functioning successfully, although, given the risks for the regime, the internal loss of dynamism would not in itself lead to reform. In any case, Gorbachev and his supporters faced both internal decay and external dangers at the moment of his accession to power. Castoriadis now stresses that the dualistic solution was no longer working, and that the stagnation and decay of the civilian sector threatened the efficacy of the military sector as well. All the same, to Castoriadis the present regime and policy represents only an "interlude" between stratocracy and something in any case completely different from the present reform project, which Castoriadis considers deeply flawed. To begin with, he is not entirely sure that the real strategy of at least part of Gorbachev's support has anything to do with changes of economic structure. In this context he stresses what could be called a "short-cut" solution: cutting down commitments, public relations, making deals, buying time. In his estimation this strategy is already brilliantly successful.

And yet, he is unsure whether such a strategy, which would not run the risk of internal conflicts, can accomplish enough in context of the continuing processes of economic decline. Thus he does seem to attribute a serious reform intention to at least a part of the Gorbachev team. Of course, he remains convinced of the built-in limits of structural reform from above. He now includes new arguments specific to the current Russian context such as the total absence of a coherent and comprehensive reform conception, the potentially extreme and uncushioned dis-locations for the population that would be caused by price reform as well as the discontinuation of obsolete enterprises, and, based on his own conception, the potential conflict of the reformers with the military-industrial complex if the command-bargaining structure so favorable to the latter were abolished. But in relationship to the central issue—the resistance and sabotage by the bureau-cratic apparatus—Castoriadis like other analysts is now willing to recognize, at least implicitly, that the Gorbachev team itself has become conscious of these limits, even if several years after the best known formulations in Poland and Hungary. Thus he interprets *glasnost'* as yet another Westernizing drive in Rus-sian history hoping to create, from above, elements of a self-active civil-political society capable of fighting the resistance of the apparatus.

Such a drive, he argues, is a contradiction in terms. To begin with, he does not see how the mainly intellectual constituency mobilized so far could be "a social historical movement for reform . . . ready to fight for reform and invent on the innumerable spots of life whatever is necessary for its successful implementa-tion." To be sure, he wrote this before the emergence of new types of reform movements in the Baltic and the vast mobilization in Armenia. Nevertheless, he sees the paradox of reformism from above, even in a form that seeks to constitute independent social actors, in terms of the basic contradiction of bureaucratic society that requires autonomous participation and at the same time deactiviza-tion and passivity. Accordingly the attempt to create an autonomous movement for reform from above within powerful but never strictly defined limits is antino-mic and self-defeating. Thus the Gorbachev team will either water down its own reform and constitute the new conservative backlash to its earlier efforts, or it will be defeated by others. These two options, to be sure, presuppose the failure of the creation of a genuine movement for reform. But if such a movement capable of reversing reaction did emerge, it would not be able to stay within any of the limits required by the reformers from above. In this case Castoriadis foresees an explosion, military intervention, with an entirely uncertain outcome.

Two years after Castoriadis first presented this trilemma its terms remain suggestive. To be sure, either version of conservative backlash leads only to decay and stagnation. There is no basis for the reconstitution of the dynamism of a military-civilian dual society, and even military intervention against autonomous initiatives would have no other socioeconomic alternative than that of the conservatives. Thus it is not absurd to assume that the present regime will continue, with all its ambiguities and indecisions about the structural questions. This means time for the formation of new actors whose perspectives and orientations cannot be easily anticipated. Certainly, a clash initiated from below cannot be excluded, with predictably conservative short-term outcome. But can we exclude the possibility that the time will be used by a multiplicity of new actors to learn the difficult art of radical, self-limiting reform from below? Such would be the most promising outcome of the time that Gorbachev's "reform" still may have. But it seems certain that if the reformers do not manage to step over the Hungarian or Chinese reform thresholds,[35] which could lead to a learning process within reform and its possible acceleration, the outcome (or plurality of outcomes) of the growth of movements will above all resemble the stalemate leading to the Polish martial law regime. And yet, given the present state of the Soviet economy, that solution would solve as little as that of General Jaruzelski. If the regime of Gorbachev is an interlude, it can only be, in order of likelihood, that to further decay, renewed reform, or the complete overthrow of the existing system. Of these options Castoriadis seems to exclude only successful or even continuing reform. For him the choice remains "autonomy or barbarism." The trouble is, however, that in the Soviet Union only radical, structural reform that builds for the first time a genuine civil society seems to be an alternative to the variety of imaginable barbarisms.

Notes

1. "On the Regime and Against the Defense of the USSR" and "The Problem of the USSR and the Possibility of a Third Historical Situation," both in *Political and Social Writings* (Minneapolis: University of Minnesota Press, 1988) (hereafter: PASW) I.
2. PASW I, 39.
3. "The Relations of Production in Russia" (1949) in PASW I, 114–16ff.
4. See Jean Cohen, *Class and Civil Society: The Limits of Marxian Critical Theory* (Amherst: University of Massachusetts Press, 1979).
5. PASW I, 7.
6. *La societé bureaucratique* (10/18; Paris, 1973). English version in PASW I.
7. PASW I, 71–72; 84.
8. In a Postface written in 1972, this whole train of thought coming from classical Marxism is described as "almost completely meaningless."
9. PASW I, 135.
10. PASW II, 57–58, 75–76.
11. PASW II, 62.

12. The work of János Kornai supplies today the best demonstration for this thesis. To be sure, his model of the whole is based on the conception of a paternalistic politically self-constituted bureaucracy and not the bureaucratic firm. See *The Economics of Shortage* (Amsterdam: North Holland, 1980), and more recently *Dilemmas and Prospects* (Cambridge, Mass.: MIT Press, 1986). For an important extension and elaboration still within a neo-Marxian framework see György Márkus in *Dictatorship over Needs* (New York: St. Martin's Press, 1982), chapter 2.

13. PASW II, 266–67.

14. PASW II, 60–61.

15. PASW II, 286–87.

16. I am neglecting the internal evolution of his philosophy that did bring him to the actual break with all Marxism in the mid-1960s.

17. PASW I, 169–71, 173; 175.

18. "Totalitarianism Without Stalin" (1956), originally published in *Socialisme ou barbarie*, now in *Political Forms of Modern Society* (Cambridge, Mass.: MIT Press, 1986), pp. 64–68, 72–73. Castoriadis often cites this article without, as far as I can tell, directly replying to the criticisms.

19. *Telos* (Winter 1978–79).

20. This question presupposes Castoriadis's own framework. As for myself I consider the bureaucracies of party, state, and enterprise more disparate than they are in his analysis, and for me the issue becomes the conditions of possibility of the victory of one, originally state-centered, bureaucratic logic over another that is capitalism-centered.

21. "Totalitarianism Without Stalin," op. cit., pp. 73–75.

22. "The Social Regime in Russia," *Telos*, op. cit.

23. Published by Fayard in Paris.

24. *Devant la guerre*, pp. 154ff. See also the entirely convincing "Rejoinder" to P. Piccone and V. Zaslavsky in *Telos*, 53 (Fall 1982). Hopefully, Zaslavsky will not today cite the highly ambiguous Gorbachev experience in his own defense, since soon after the debate with Castoriadis he was ready to pronounce the Soviet Union of the Brezhnev era well integrated and in need of no reform. See the debate with me in *Telos*.

25. *Devant la guerre*, pp. 139–44ff.

26. See D. Horowitz; also see A. Amerisov in *Soviet-American Review* (Chicago), vol. 4, no. 1 (1989).

27. "Facing the War," *Telos* 46 (Winter 1980–81): 50.

28. *Devant la guerre*, p. 148.

29. See, for example, G.T. Rittersporn in *Telos* (Spring 1981), who also confuses the issue of military power as the medium of a military-political-diplomatic strategy with the ability to fight a traditional, Clausewitzian war.

30. "Facing the War," p. 47.

31. Cf. my 1985 article "The Budapest School and Actually Existing Socialism," chapter 6, this volume.

32. I remain unconvinced by the argument that the well-demonstrated "national-imperial" imaginary is equal to a virtually empty ideology of "brute force" for its own sake. The new ideology strongly links itself to many of the traditional symbols of Russian and even Soviet history, and allows a conservative-imperial as well as an expansionist-imperial posture.

33. It is in this sense that Jean Cohen and I interpreted Castoriadis's thesis in "The Peace Movement and West European Sovereignty," in *Telos* 51 (Spring 1982).

34. "The Gorbachev Interlude," in A. Arato and F. Fehér, eds., *Gorbachev: The Debate* (Oxford: Polity Press, 1989).

35. See my introduction to ibid.

Part II

The Rise of Civil Society and Democratic Theory

8

Civil Society vs. the State:
Poland 1980–81

Civil Society?

The categories of civil society do not represent a conceptual scheme brought into the Polish events from the outside. The participants themselves and their Western collaborators have declared their struggle as that of society against the state. "The state has not been able to successfully dissolve civil society," writes Alexander Smolar in his preface to a 1978 volume coming from the Polish opposition, "the texts . . . are manifestations of the existence and vitality of civil society in a country ruled by a communist party."[1] "Society organizes itself in the form of a democratic movement and becomes active outside the limits of the institutions of the totalitarian state,"[2] states Jacek Kuroń. KOR (worker's defense committee) is renamed KSS–"KOR" (social self-defense committee–"KOR") to indicate the goal of the *self*-organization of *all* parts of society, pioneered by industrial workers, and the support of *all* (worker, peasant, student, intellectual) initiatives for both interest representation and the defense of civil rights. In one form or other, the idea of the reconstitution or reemergence of civil society involving variously a struggle for the rule of law and the guarantee of civil rights, for a free public sphere and for a plurality of independent, self-organized, democratic forms of associations, is present in all the documents of the opposition. For KOR, their ensemble is definitive. According to Adam Michnik, the state can today desire a minimum of legitimacy only if it rigorously carries out three implications of the August 21 Gdansk agreements, which would then begin to function as a genuine "new social contract": protection of the civil rights of citizens, toleration of an actual plurality of public opinion, and the acceptance of a structure of compromise "crossing the totalitarian power structure with a democratic mechanism of corporate representation."[3]

A version of this essay was published in *Telos* 47 (Spring, 1980–81), pp. 23–47.

The secondary literature has also taken note of the new stress of the Polish opposition. While before 1980 at least most writers generally spoke of a human and civil rights movement (somewhat one-sidedly; the definition is more accurate for the Czechoslovak opposition around Charter 77), others have been more all-encompassing: Jacques Rupnik, following Kołakowski in particular, defines the transformation of Polish dissent from 1968 to 1978 as "the end of Revisionism and the rebirth of the Civil Society."[4] In describing the events of 1980 two German writers, Reinhard Fenchel and Hans-Willi Weis,[5] are forced to coin a German term, *Zivilgesellschaft*, to introduce a meaning no longer present in *bürgerliche Gesellschaft* (today the equivalent of bourgeois society), that is, the organization of a plurality of social interests outside the state in an (increasingly) independent social sphere. Indeed, Fenchel and Weis, as Jiři Pelikán elsewhere,[6] speak of the emergence of a form of dual power, between the existing state and a new, self-managing society. To be sure, in Poland itself under the given conditions of 1980–81 the concept of dual power is rarely mentioned. One of the few to have actually used the concept, first secretary Stanisław Kania— whom no one has ever accused of any knowledge of history and political theory—declared in January 1981 that history has no example of dual power and, of course, no such thing will be permitted in Poland. The leadership of Solidarity, however, seems also emphatic, if less direct, on this point, repeatedly stating that their goal is only the defense of worker interests and not any form of participation in *political* power. On January 19, upon his return from Rome, Lech Wałesa stressed above all the *nonpolitical character* of the union. Periodically, the members of KOR *seem to* affirm the same point: The democratic movement is not challenging the power of the state *in its own sphere*, or even the leading role of the party *in the state*; it is not building a new party or seeking to capture and exercise or even participate in state power.[7] While there is a crucial tactical point involved here, since a direct, militant challenge to the leadership of the rather shaken single party in the state-political sphere would certainly bring Soviet intervention, the issue goes as far as the underlying premises of the democratic opposition concerning the type of society it wants, and thinks possible in the short run. These premises are not always articulated clearly or consistently, perhaps deliberately so. When Michnik, for example, argues that the new union will be political only in the sense of unions in England, Italy, or the United States, one immediately recalls the distance separating these political roles and organizational types from each other, not to speak of the new, independent Polish labor union. While the long-range goal for the whole democratic opposition is certainly parliamentary mediation between state and society,[8] for the present it is hard to say whether the renunciation of participation in state power is only tactical, or belongs to the very principles of an entirely new type of movement that seeks to build or rebuild structures of social solidarity and participation, bypassing state power altogether or relating to it only on the level of negotiation and compromise. If the latter is the case, and for KOR and the whole milieu around Solidarity I believe it is, there is nevertheless a gap between minimal and maximal interpretations of what is to be the institutional starting-point of a long road that may eventually lead, in Kuroń's formulation at least, to a parliamentary state and a directly democratic society. The latter goal is not shared by the whole democratic opposition, and, as we will see below, there is a great deal of difference among the alternative self-interpretation and strategies that have emerged from a revived society, "from below." One point, however, unites them all—the point of view of civil society against the state, in other words, the desire to institutionalize and thereby preserve the new level of social independence achieved.

Civil Society, West and East

It is rather amazing that all of the proposed alternatives of independent Polish development are compatible with the idea of the resurgence of civil society. Because let us not hesitate to admit that we are speaking of the relevance of a category of *early* modern Western political theory, to most no longer relevant in a transformed West itself, to a modern, *industrial East* European context. Differentiating what from the Greeks to the eighteenth century has been considered one, the political and the social dimensions that are united both in *politike koinonia* and *societas civilis*, the constitutive political symbolism of Western modernity, with important national and chronological differences, has been *institutionalized*[9] as the duality of (political) state and civil society. In the social systems that emerged this institutionalization was in all cases contradictory,[10] bearing the structural marks of a differential genesis in which to greatly varying extents the bureaucratic administrations of absolutist states, liberal and later democratic social movements, and the agents of the new, capitalist economy have played the decisive role. Under the weight of this contradictory institutionalization, in context of the industrialization of the West the duality of state and civil society, and above all its normatively central mediating element of an emancipated public sphere, have proved fragile.[11] Nevertheless, as the history of nineteenth- and twentieth-century movements against capitalist economy and nondemocratic state indicate, the same contradiction has also given projects of *social* emancipation its meaning. It may indeed be the case that the differentiating, rationalizing tendencies of modernity itself as well as the need for new forms of social integration constitute the objective possibility of the autonomy of society from both state and economy.[12] However that may be, it is certainly possible to interpret contemporary social, auto-gestionaire movements in the West as clues to the possible reemergence of civil society.[13] Only in Eastern Europe, however, and in particular Poland, do the social movements themselves see their struggle in these terms. Are we facing here a belated development[14] that, if against all odds successful, will recapitulate the development of the contradiction of civil society in the West, or the possibility of something genuinely new, that indeed may offer some clues toward the future meaning of emancipation also in the West?

In West European history, the constitution of the state–civil society duality would have been unthinkable without the generating activity of the state, "from above," which to be sure took on extremely different proportions in different countries.[15] On the other hand, the range of freedom of an emancipated, critical public sphere mediating between society and the state, everywhere more or less a characteristic of early modern development, depended on the nationally varying strength of social movements and institutions generated "from below," in struggles of the elements of the new more egalitarian society not only against the old society of estates but also against the new state. To be sure, the "struggle" against the limitations of the old society, and against economic tutelage of the state, was carried on most effectively and with the most permanent results by the increasingly powerful interests of a free-market economy themselves reinforced (in some places constituted) by the rationalizing efforts of modern state bureaucracies; nevertheless the elements of social autonomy expressed in the political sphere and parliamentarianism in Europe (and also in social and regional self-administration in America) were generated by social strata among which the new bourgeoisie represented only a part, at times a relatively small part. Thus the force field between state and society in Western Europe including the Germanys (with Prussia as the boundary case) was constituted by three sets of actors, of which in terms of institutional results, depending on the country, the economy, or the state turned out to be strongest, society the weakest—but not everywhere equally weak.

The situation in Eastern Europe was historically considerably different.[16] Until 1917, at least, we may nevertheless speak of a comparable constellation of forces, which, however, did not manage to execute a state and society separation *even* in the purely economic sense. The overwhelming superiority of state power is everywhere characteristic, although seeking its own modernization, this state power did seek to organize from above some independent social and economic institutions. While the determination of East European autocracy as a form of feudalism[17] or even *Ständestaat* remains unacceptable precisely because of the overwhelming weight of state power, we may readily admit that this state power derived its strength from social compromises that left the society of the old regime (in some East European countries or empires resembling a true society of orders, in Russia not) far more intact here than in the Western parts of Europe. Including Prussia, there is again a good deal of differentiation in the respective strengths of state, economy, and society among the three empires dividing up the geographical area that constitutes today's Eastern Europe. We may nonetheless argue here that everywhere the state was strongest, society by far the weakest. Still, the Tocquevillean thesis about the continuity of absolutism, revolution, and postrevolutionary étatism should not be applied too mechanically in this context;[18] it needs the additional stress that the destructive leveling of the old society of orders occurred in a less continuous fashion across the three periods—the task was achieved to a greater extent than in Western Europe by the postrevolutionary (1917) or postwar (1945) states.[19] The new state power that everywhere (with the exception of Czechoslovakia) achieved or completed the destruction of the *old* society was powerful enough either to destroy, or to inhibit the very emergence of new structures and institutions of social autonomy. Of the constitution of a modern civil society it achieved exclusively the negative side; its very principle of identity, the social, economic and cultural primacy of the prerogative state[20] (if not its actual ability to fully realize this principle) implied the nonexistence of the parameters of civil society: systems of needs (excluded by the idea of the imperative central plan), institutions of plurality (excluded by the monopoly of the one party), rule of law (excluded by the idea of substantive justice, hiding the prerogative state), networks of publics (excluded by the idea of absolute knowledge).

The absorption of society and economy in state structures is in my opinion not fully modern.[21] The incomplete differentiation of state and economy makes societies of the Soviet type unable to compete economically with the developed countries of the capitalist world or to satisfy the economic needs of the population in those East European countries where the need structure is affected by Western standards. If the first statement can be sustained only on the level of the philosophy of history, the second is overwhelmingly demonstrated by the economic picture of Eastern Europe for the last ten to fifteen years, as well as the reform attempts in several of the countries. These attempts (which should be treated under the category of crisis or dysfunction management) can be summed up under a single phrase: to constitute, from above, an economy at least partially (in some places: to a large extent) differentiated from the state without allowing or contributing even indirectly to the emergence of forms of social autonomy. This attempt to contain *the social* need not have been everywhere equally unsuccessful, as some historical-materialistically inclined reform economists secretly must have hoped; under some conditions even laissez faire economics (of which there never was a question here) is compatible with autocratic political institutions. Nevertheless, in the Czechoslovakia of 1968, for reasons to be sought in the political traditions—rather unique in Eastern Europe—inherited from the interwar period and even before, economic and only limited social reform "from above" dramatically released democratizing energies "from below" that indeed captured the ruling party itself "from within," threatening to reconstitute civil society, that is, to abolish the existing system altogether.

The lesson of 1968 was well learned by the ruling parties, henceforth—with the exception of Hungary, where 1956 and its defeat created entirely favorable circumstances for the regime both internally and externally[22]—reform attempts from above in the direction of any significant level of even purely economic autonomy were to be drastically limited. Two roads toward the constitution or reconstitution of civil society were now dramatically closed. After Hungary 1956, the revolutionary overthrow of the authoritarian state from below is a road open only to the imperial center itself, where the conditions of social integration are unique, defined by its very being the imperial center and by its relatively great isolation from the rest of the world. After Czechoslovakia 1968, the reformist, initially economistic attempt from above, that is, through the ruling parties themselves, is considered the functional equivalent of the first road by almost all of the ruling parties, and in particular by the party of the imperial center, which will tolerate neither the overthrow from below nor the conquest from within of any of the other ruling communist parties. Today there is before us the possibility of a third road. The theory and practice of the Polish opposition from 1976 to 1980 has shown that there is *at least the possibility* of a structural reform of authoritarian socialism from below.

Can such a model from below lead to a contemporary reinstitutionalization of civil society? Can it lead to a form of civil society that no longer labors under its historic contradiction? Before turning to the first question, I would like to indicate three general reasons for saying a preliminary yes to the second: (1) In Poland, unlike the West, or for that matter interwar Eastern Europe, the struggle for civil society is occurring after and not before industrialization, hence imperatives of economic growth (given especially the contemporary world dilemmas of growth) do not have to play the same kind of role as in the West. The results of a civil society not adequately separated from a centrally placed economy are known to Poles from Western experience. (2) In Poland, as I will argue, the constitution of civil society is not in any sense occurring from above. Neither is the state interested in playing such a role, which is contradictory to its principle of organization as it was not for West European absolutism, nor is it desired to play this role by anyone below. The results of various forms of étatist modernization are also known to the Poles, to say the least. (3) In the relative absence of the other two potential agencies for the constitution of civil society (capitalist logic of industrialization, étatist logic of modernization from above), the social movement in Poland can make an emancipated public sphere (or spheres) far more central in the civil society in formation than anywhere before. Of the three possible institutional centers of modern society—state, economy, and societal public sphere—we have until now only experienced the primacy of the first or the second; Poland represents an experiment in the third.

On the other hand, the necessity of some kind of compromise with the existing state power, and the potentially powerful influence of the existing Western model of civil society are certainly reasons for some pessimism in this context. Can a social movement achieve a workable model of civil society alone through structural reform from below, and if so, what kind of civil society, given a formally intact, authoritarian state?

Structural Reform from Below

In the 1970s critical East European intellectuals in general[23] came to accept and operate under the thesis that the possibility of a reform of the systems based on the transformation or even democratization of the ruling parties "from within" has become impossible as a result of the experience of 1968. Whether the argument was derived only pragmatically, empirically, or theoretically,[24] the political alternative seemed to be revolution or resignation.[25] In a brilliant 1971 article, Leszek Kołakowski showed that stemming from the classical Marxian tradition this alternative (even assuming what cannot in all countries be assumed, a democratic outcome of a total revolution) reduces to one—namely resignation.[26] Indeed it is not hard to see that revolution (the 1956 model) on the periphery of the empire would be crushed by the center, while in the center itself it is implausible precisely because of the legitimating advantages provided by an empire organized around a national core. It was in this context that Kołakowski first proposed a concept of partial, yet structural reform from below aiming at the reconstruction of dimensions, spaces of the social realm. The thesis certainly better corresponded to the forms of East European opposition in the seventies than the choice revolution or resignation. The period indeed was to be rich in forms of dissent. In several countries a defensive civil/human rights campaign (e.g., Charter 77, the Russian Helsinki Watch Committee) reinforced by international publicity became a factor in dissident politics. In a few countries at least the seeds of a second, alternative public sphere were planted in the form of *samizdat* literature. And in Poland in the wake of two major and partly successful working-class eruptions a new offensive strategy was formulated: that of reform from below, different from both reform attempts initiated from within the parties and revolutionary challenges coming from the outside. Significantly, the major articles explicating this strategy, Kołakowski's "Theses" and Michnik's "New Evolutionism," as well as Kuroń's "Thoughts on an Action Program," were written in the wake of each of two great working-class challenges, 1971 and late 1976. The new strategy came to be dramatically applicable to 1980 not because of the provision of those intellectuals, but because of what was presupposed in their thesis: the continuity of the historical experience of workers and from 1976, other groups and strata. Nevertheless, the conceptualization was to contribute form to the challenge from below between 1976 and 1980, at least in the form of the organized activity of KOR, along with a new consciousness of what can be attained and within what limits.

If one moves through the three essays of Kołakowski, Michnik, and Kuroń in this order, there is on a theoretical level a movement from system to action, anticipating the events to come. Kołakowski begins with a model of the totalitarian system as that of a society deprived from all forms of social self-defense, a model that he seeks to relativize on a general philosophical basis. If the systems were successfully totalitarian, they could be overthrown only as wholes. If totalitarianism is, however, only a tendency, a project laden with internal contradictions, then it can be *partially* reversed by another tendency, another project—the self-defense of society. Though the essay represents a step toward Kołakowski's final break with Marxism, we should note the praxis philosophical bases of his argument. We can never know purely theoretically the plasticity, the limits of a system which among other things depends on the consciousness of social actors of this plasticity, these limits. Theoretically, we can indeed discover that the totalitarian project in East Europe is on many levels self-contradictory (the desire for unity *against* the desire for security, the practical irrelevance of its ideology *against* the need for ideological continuity, the necessity of technical development *against* political limits on technical development, need for national legitimacy *against* the surrender of parts of national sovereignty) but it depends on the actions of those below whether these contradictions will become opportunities for the system's limitation. Without resistance the systems can be, according to Kołakowski, successfully totalized. But on the basis of constant resistance and pressure "by society," which becomes in this context *partially its own subject*, a society more in harmony with purely social needs can be wrested from the state. Neither national nor popular sovereignty are in this framework all-or-nothing propositions. Contrary to the theses of revolutionaries, structural if partial reforms that weaken the existing system are possible. But those who want all will get nothing.

Kołakowski's 1971 arguments form an implicit philosophical background to Michnik's 1976 article on the "new evolutionism."[27] Nevertheless, five years and one uprising later it was possible to restate the position in far more political terms. With the transformation of the cultural picture and the reactivation of the intellectuals (totally shaken in 1968 by the anti-Semitic attacks on them, inactive therefore in 1970–71), it was *possible* not only to say that the party should not be addressed as an agent of reform (the error of so-called revisionism) but also to turn to an independent public opinion. Furthermore, in the wake of the reabsorption of the results of 1971 (a compromise, "a social contract" between two parties only one of whom was organized) it was also *necessary* to say that the pressure from below must receive independent organizational forms. Closer to the possibility of action its limits could be more clearly defined. Society can relearn to organize itself and to act, great concessions can be wrested from the Polish power structure, but neither the existing links of Poland to the Soviet Union nor the control of state institutions by the *one* party can be challenged without inevitable Soviet intervention. Indeed, the self-democratization of the party à la Prague 1968 is also in this context dangerous. It is thus "the international context" that eliminates both reform from above and revolution, and points to structural reform from below as the last hope of democratization as long as the Soviet system itself is intact.

That such a strategy is not doomed from the start is demonstrated according to Michnik by two "accomplished facts": the achievement of the first form of continuous self-organization by Polish workers after 1976 and the intransigent defense of civil rights as well as its own interests by the powerful Catholic church. It is on these two pillars that Michnik erects the new strategy of constant struggle for reforms that will enlarge the spaces of civil liberty and guarantee respect for human rights. Certainly these key aims informed the founding of the organization KOR. But once the organization was off the ground, its strategy could be seen in more ambitious terms. Jacek Kuroń, another cofounder of KOR, has clearly enough always represented the most radical trend within it. It is in his own 1976 pamphlet on oppositional strategy[28] that we first see a systematic program for the recovery of all dimensions of civil society. The struggle for reform from below is for the reestablishment of the rule of law, independent publicity, and freedom of association. These would naturally issue in a struggle for parliamentary democracy—Kuroń tries hard to show the compatibility between parliamentary rule and socialized property—except under the given Polish circumstances. In this context Kuroń found himself in a paradox. While from his famous coauthored "open letter to the PUWP"[29] he clearly remained an advocate of direct, self-managing forms of democracy, he now has come to believe that such forms would not be meaningful under a totalitarian system and that they ought not to exhaust democratic politics, even ideally speaking. And yet, while he believes that a democratic parliamentary system is clearly outside the limits constituted by the threat of Soviet intervention, that is, a one-party *state* system, he is indeed proposing that autonomous forms of *social* self-management be the goals of reform from below. It is his conception of social movement that seems to provide him with a solution of this paradox; these are to be the loci of new social autonomy; it is indeed a multiplicity of equally important social movements (peasants, workers, Catholics, and intellectuals) each operating on the basis of already "accomplished facts" (decollectivized agriculture, de facto compromises concerning price structure and the emergence of the first forms of worker self-organization, freedom of several levels of church activity from religious to cultural, de facto toleration of a second public sphere) that is to progressively restrict the sphere of decision of the party-state.

In this context three major questions arise. First, should one put such a strong stress on social movements in a presumably totalitarian context where no form of social independence, not to speak of independent movements, are permitted? Second, will not the movements from below, if they are indeed possible, need some support from above, from within the ruling party, in order to be successful? Third, if some combination between actions from below and from above can be coordinated, will not the role of reform from below amount to next to nothing in its minimal interpretation and to a struggle for parliamentarianism in any serious interpretation? These questions were indeed debated by Polish and other East European dissident intellectuals in the period 1976–80. A positive answer to the first presupposed a strong relativization of the totalitarian thesis, which has been reintroduced at this time primarily for polemical rather than theoretical reasons. As long as one seriously expected liberalization or even democratization of the systems, the totalitarian thesis presupposing a completely unified power hierarchy remained unacceptable for critical East European intellectuals. Its acceptance theoretically speaking signified the end of one strategy before the birth of another. With the political stress on social reform movements from below, one had to reexamine another fundamental premise of the totalitarian thesis, the one concerning the total atomization of society. We have already seen how Kołakowski represented this premise as a statist tendency, which will be as successful as countertendencies defined by political resistance will allow it to be. In the literature seeking the foundations of the strategy after 1976, this point was deepened by a reference to informal, familial, in other words, small-scale private networks of social relations that represent social self-defense even when formal movements and open struggles are absent. Indeed it is this largely spontaneous, defensive response that is the condition of social movements, which represent a higher, more organized level of social plurality. Initially, circles of family and friends represent the protection of the private sphere from an administered and controlled public one. They are means that permit the defense of a given society, its customs, mentalities, its national and local identities. The reconstruction of society is possible in such countries because the foundations are there; social ties as such do not have to be reconstituted, only their more complex forms.[30] We can, within the limits of this paper, avoid a rather necessary polemic with the conception (that would have bleak consequences in Poland too) that the totalitarian thesis in its original version *does* apply to countries where the system was not imposed from the outside.[31] The thesis of the survival of society and of its potential political significance in any case applies to several other East European countries. In Hungary, for example, where no one at the moment banks on the possibility of social movements of the Polish type, András Hegedüs has stressed the implicit, in part only potential plurality of social forces (interest groups, etc.) that seek some kind of autonomy and, in particular, independent public expression.[32] To the extent, however, that one is referring to partial interests significant from the point of view of macropolicy, Hegedüs is forced to admit that the ruling party can integrate them, though it cannot abolish them. Going somewhat further, János Kis and György Bence, speaking from direct experience, have clarified under what conditions private life becomes the foundation for a new public life.[33] Stressing the complicated networks of personal ties among intellectuals (communication possibilities) and workers (workplace conditions), which stood in the way of the emergence of atomized, "lonely crowds," they have argued that these conditions of adjustment under normal conditions can become bases of collective expression under condition of crisis. In Poland, such, according to them, are the foundations of lasting social movements, but even in Hungary—where the opposition is almost exclusively intellectual—the existing network of personal ties is the foundation of a second, alternative, critical public sphere, now in formation.

Thus the rediscovery of society under the conditions of state socialism in itself can lead to a program of opposition more limited than that of social movements for reform. But even concerning the Polish situation, there is room for the question whether such movements from below are *adequate* bases of a reform program. In several essays Jiři Pelikán has addressed this question to the Polish opposition.[34] But the idea of the necessity of a split at least, or a differentiation of the ruling parties even after 1968 is present in the work of Bahro and Hegedüs as well. For Pelikán the model of 1968 remains in any case fundamental. For him any successful democratization of systems of the East European type presupposes significant action from both above and below, and only the Prague spring represented an adequate model of the coordination of these, the beginning rather than the end of an epoch in which democratization has become possible. Even if significant changes since 1968 have strengthened the conservative potential in the ruling parties—and in particular, neo-Stalinist forces as well as the forces of the military-industrial complex—and have eliminated all forums of serious intraparty discussions, the fundamental situation remains unchanged. No movement from below has the power to alone carry out significant programs of reform nor are the ruling parties at least in the longer run in principle closed to reform ideas. If after 1968 the initiative for reform has passed to outside these parties, if the building of parallel institutions has become necessary and possible, the opposition must not overlook the possibility that its activities can "work inside" the ruling parties causing a new differentiation at the very least between rationally thinking functionaries and the conservatives. Pelikán hopes to reunite all oppositions under this formula, Bahro (representing the neo-Leninist extreme), after all, admits the impossibility of changing the ruling party from within, while Michnik (representing the extreme anti–avant-gardist position) recognizes the necessity of having "partners" if not "allies" within the Communist party. Two essential political differences, however (not to speak of the fundamental philosophical ones), cannot be reconciled in this context. The first concerns the source of long-run initiative. Is it to be above (older communist reformism) or an "alternative above" (Bahro) or is it to be below, in a plurally conceived society (KOR)? The second concerns the basis of cooperation. Is it to be identity or similarity of goals ("alliance"), or merely compatibility or complementarity of fundamentally different goals ("partnership")? As Kuroń once put it, KOR believes only in the pragmatism of those in power and not in the existence of a liberal wing in the party.

After 1968, in any case, there are two reasons to doubt the existence of such a wing; the first is the often noted de-ideologization of the parties, closing off the possibility of a purely immanent critique, and the second is the actual experience in 1968 of the apparent incompatibility of genuine liberalization and the organizational principles of the system. Nevertheless, presented within the *faits accomplis* of an organized movement from below, there is reason to hope that a pragmatic wing of the party will realize that what to them is the necessary crisis management of the existing system can only be successful on the basis of these new facts. Such a realization may, for example, lead to the reinvigoration of the for-the-moment moribund experiments of economic reform. This can be the basis of "partnership" between the opposition and a section of the party, leading to a new social compromise between state and society. Such has been the position of KOR from 1976 to today.

The idea of a "historic compromise" has also repeatedly come up in the writings of Hegedüs after 1977, but with a somewhat different stress, at least before the events of 1980. This brings us to our next question. Is there a third possibility in Eastern Europe between two forms of compromise between society and state, each of which is valueless from the point of view of one of the two sides? On a theoretical level, at least, this issue was debated in the Hungarian opposition between Hegedüs, seeking to move from one form of reformism (from above) to another (from below), and Kis and Bence, representing the position of KOR as they interpreted it. In reality, the disagreement expressed two different interpretations of the kind of society–state duality that is possible and worthwhile to establish in Eastern Europe, a disagreement that—as we will see—also came into the open in Poland during the 1980 events. It should be said that Hegedüs, often the target of criticisms by other oppositionists for his party-directed reform strategy in the 1960s, was one of the very first outside of Poland who raised the perspective of the restoration of civil society as a state–society duality. Indeed, he proposed his own version of social duality in a form that transcended the traditional liberal division of the public and the private without accepting either the dissolution of the private or the social in the state sphere. Utilizing Habermas's double conception of critical Öffentlichkeit as the "political" dimension of the nonstate, "private" sphere and the social, communicative dimension of the state sphere, he goes on to say that both the social and the political need to be public,[35] indeed as foundations of a genuine, protected privacy as well. This is what he claims on the most abstract level, and the formula is indeed sympathetic. But when, without the benefit of an immediate knowledge of Polish developments, as his critics point out, he goes on to concretize his proposal, and in particular the strategy of its realization, we see the emergence of what could truly be called a minimal program for the realization of civil society. He indeed assigns the task of initiation to social movements from below, but it is also clear that he expects an unusually high degree of tolerance and even support from above. And although he defines the task of the social sphere as "authority" over the political bureaucratic sphere (bureaucracy being in any case unavoidable in a modern society) that continues to exercise "power," the control functions of which this authority is to consist are left extremely vague. It is even unclear whether we are dealing with only a new form of legitimation of the existing form of power. Moreover, since he rejects both societal interest representation (e.g., independent trade unions)[36] and especially (party) pluralism in the political sphere, it is not exactly clear whether his societal plurality would be organized at all, although only this would distinguish them from the latent interest groups of Soviet and East European societies that—he stresses—are already there. To be sure, the charge of conservatism would not be a fair one here, since Hegedüs indicates also from the point of view of the system in what manner the societies must change to recover their socioeconomic dynamism, to solve their endemic rationality, and information crisis. Nevertheless, he is open to the charge of Kis and Bence that the apparent plausibility of his program rests on an ultimate compatibility of his proposal with the existing organizational principle of the system. There is not, they stress, an identity of interest in system-transcending reform, above and below. What Hegedüs's analysis ultimately lacks is an element of pressure—organized pressure for the power structure to allow something *not* compatible with its interest. Finally, he does not evaluate the existing movements in Eastern Europe in a realistic way:

> These movements are at the same time stronger and weaker than Hegedüs thinks. Stronger, because it does not depend on the good intentions of the power structure whether or not they are capable of realizing their goal. Weaker, because they cannot replace independent institutions of representation.[37]

Yes, stronger and weaker. But certainly—and this is the meaning of the new evolutionism—also not strong enough to replace the existing one-party structure of the state by a multiparty one, assuming that this were desirable. Hegedüs has a point, of course, and it is thus that his position avoids apology for contemporary Western societies, that without the direct democracy of significant social movements a multiparty system can be also seen as "monolithic." But the response of Kis and Bence is also to be taken seriously; without representative institutions there are no mechanisms of compromise (interest integration) *among* social movements. We might add: except of course the existing state, which imposes such an integration from above. Hegedüs's insistence, paralleled in detail by Bahro, by the way, that the interest structure of state-socialist societies is more integrated than in capitalist countries, takes this de facto integration from above for granted. Here lies the true weakness of his position. Its strength, however, is its acceptance of the state–society duality while the struggle for the transformation of the state sphere itself, proposed by Kis and Bence, bypasses this in the direction of maximalism. The two authors do stress rightly that without the institutionalization of some kind of pluralism, even in political crisis situations (which, in fact, they tend to consider undesirably dangerous), the unity of the power structure will be reestablished (or maintained) and the room of movements to maneuver for independent social spaces will be severely limited. But does it follow that the plurality of social movements can be institutionalized and coordinated only through the establishment of a multiparty, parliamentary form of political pluralism? We should recall once again the implications of maximalism in Eastern Europe pointed out in the Polish context by some of the very sources Kis and Bence consider definitive.

The minimalism–maximalism polarity concerning the interpretation of the new evolutionism is not merely a function of an intellectual debate (in Hungary, that is) itself removed from the real political terrain of this strategy (i.e., Poland). I believe that it was precisely absence of immediate political relevance that allowed Hegedüs on the one hand, and Kis and Bence on the other, to draw out the ultimate implications of two diverging interpretations also found in Poland, which were, however, suppressed or veiled for political reasons. On the other hand, the actual evolution of the strategy, and in particular its many successes from 1976 to 1980, were to narrow, temporarily at least, the distance between interpretations; on the political level in this period there was increasingly little difference between the statements of theorists as different as Kołakowski and Brus, Pelikán and the spokesmen of Charter 77, Hegedüs and his two younger compatriots, who are former disciples of the Lukács school. On the one hand, many of the unnecessary paradoxes of both maximalism and minimalism were solved in practice, on the other, many real questions were temporarily suppressed or forgotten. There was, as a result, increasing consensus around the following four points, at least among Polish and Hungarian intellectuals (the political reference point being, however, Poland alone, except as noted):

1. The limit of reform from below is constituted by the given state institutions, in other words the single-party system that cannot be overthrown (1956) or democratized—hence abolished—from within (1968).
2. The means of pressure from below are organized, but open and public, nonconspiratorial and non–avant-gardist social movements, each representing one constellation of interests.
3. Pressure from below can force the existing system to adhere to its own constitutionality and legality (also relevant to Czechoslovakia) as well as to tolerate in fact the plurality constituted by the social movements themselves.
4. The organization of plurality, in particular of a second, alternative, critical public sphere can bypass the state altogether by setting up parallel institutions (this is also relevant to Hungary). Of course, here too, national and/or international pressure is implicitly necessary for the survival of parallel institutions.
5. Legality, plurality, publicity, though important means of the organizations of pressure on the state, are to be seen above all as ends in themselves!

Point five, of course, is the definition of what constituted the important string of successes of the social movement in Poland between 1976 and 1980 but also its limits. The three categories are, of course, constitutive of the classical nineteenth-century concept of civil society—only the system of needs is missing. The opposition, in other words, succeeded in achieving tolerance for the various levels of its activity, but did not succeed forcing the state to change its overall policy—in particular no proposals toward an economic reform were forthcoming.

Facing an unfolding civil society it was forced to tolerate, the party-state power structure chose self-isolation and immobilism. The results: the partial victory of the movement of 1976 defending the old constitution against changes that were to formalize the leading rule of the party and the existing relationship to the Soviet Union, the partial victory of the defense of the rights of workers prosecuted for their role in 1976, the relative success in creating foundation committees at least for organizations of worker, peasant, and student self-defense, and the surprisingly high degree of success (in spite of continuing harassment) in establishing institutions of an alternative public—the extensive *samizdat* publications of books and journals and the flying university. Most important, the various movements and institutions were closely coordinated by the activities and communication networks of civil and human rights groups and also Catholic intellectuals.[38]

Another result was the economic near-collapse of the system steered by a party-state totally unwilling to undertake any reform measure that could split its ranks in the context of the threat from below. The immobilism of Polish state-economic policy was, in fact, a reflex of this threat. The massive reliance on foreign credits and imported capital goods would have in themselves required serious reform measures; without these they could only win time and eventually contribute to the proportions of the disaster.[39] Once the crisis came, as we of course know, the industrial workers were able to achieve something brand new in the history of the systems of the Soviet type: *the legalization* of an entirely independent, self-managing institution of interest representation, the independent labor union Solidarity. Beyond this, with the acceptance of the twenty-one points in the Gdansk accords, they have at least received a set of political promises that ought to have amounted to the legalization of a more or less independent cultural sphere as well as a set of economic promises that cannot be realized without large-scale economic reform. All this has occurred and is still occurring in the context of (1) a fully unreformed party-state, supported by increasing threats from the Soviet Union as well as the GDR and the CSFR; (2) a raging economic crisis; and (3) the spectacular unfolding of literally dozens of movements, and projects for self-management and self-administration under the umbrella of the independent union that now has over ten million members. It is to the possible outcomes of such a fluid and anomalous situation that we must turn.

Society and the State: The Question of Dual Power

Without Soviet intervention Poland will never be the same. But what kind of society can emerge on the basis of a structural reform from below that is to leave the institutional core of the old system, the party-state, intact? It was in 1976, I believe, and in no particular relationship to the emerging strategic pattern in Poland, that the term "dual power" (*Doppelherrschaft*) was first applied to the perspectives of radical social change in Eastern Europe by Rudolf Bahro. What he probably had in mind was a repetition of the classic pattern of February to October 1917, itself interpreted as the growing hegemony of the Bolsheviks in society (i.e., in the soviets) coexisting with a classical form of bourgeois state power, leading to the establishment of a new, one-party, *mono*-organizational state-society. For Bahro, a new League of Communists is to play the role of the Bolsheviks, split from the Communist party, but the core of a future unified power structure.[40] The irrelevance of this strategy to the contemporary East European opposition—their explicit rejection of anything like it independently of its tactical demerits—needs no further emphasis here. What is more interesting is that in 1978, in effect describing the actual forms of the new Polish strategy, Pelikán interpreted or deliberately misinterpreted Bahro's "dual power" as the emergence of "parallel structures alongside the official institutions—for example, book publishing houses and periodicals, universities, autonomous trade unions, workers' committees, petitions to official agencies, committees to defend the persecuted, etc."[41] Though very sympathetic, the description involves institutions with rather different relationships to political power, and it is in any case no longer adequate to a situation in which one institution, the independent trade union, because of its new legal status, the size and militancy of its membership, and its network of organization and communication, has become the embodiment of an unprecedented type of challenge to the party-state. Outside of Poland, there is still some inclination to refer to the new situation, the opposition of Solidarity and the party-state, as double power, which according to some can be stabilized and expanded within the existing limits[42] and to others is a contradiction in terms which is itself the logical ground for the use of force from above *or* outside.[43] While in Poland the party center takes something near this second position (with reverse evaluative signs), a significant part of the Western mass media complement this by considering Solidarity as de facto Poland's second (or perhaps third) political party. What are we to make in this context of the repeated insistence of the union leadership—in the face of some legal and journalistic provocation—that they represent something nonpolitical?[44] First, one should stress once again the significance of societal interest representation, precisely the element that is new in the Polish situation as against all experiments in pure council democracy, when it is in principle a question of rebuilding a whole monolithic societal-political order from the ground up. Solidarity considers it necessary to represent empirical worker interests against whoever holds political and especially economic power—in the latter case even against what they intend to be the organizationally separate agencies of industrial self-management. This is the essential characteristic of workers participating in the rebuilding of civil society as against the extension of their spontaneous form of organization to society as a whole on the basis of their universality, mythologized in all council communisms. Here is the significance of an independent union as the organizational form of the current struggle. Second, the leadership of Solidarity (if not always the rank and file) operates fully within the program of the new evolutionism; the existing structure of the state and the leading role of the party in the state are taken as given. But third, with all this said, the topic of dual power and with it the political nature of the union is not yet exhausted. In Poland today everything is political; the comment—addressed to Adam Michnik at a public meeting in 1980—is just. The response, conceding the point in general, but cautious in reference to Solidarity, is nevertheless revealing. The independent union is not political in the sense that "it does not seek political power in the state."[45] If this is true, then we must speak of a (political) alternative power (Kuroń) or counterpower (Bence), or even more exactly a political counterpower *in society* seeking control functions vis-à-vis party-political power *in the state.* "The social movement must today tend to limit this power [party-state power], control it, constrain it to concessions."[46]

A force capable of pushing back state power, of occupying some of the vacated space, of controlling and constraining what cannot be eliminated, re- placed, or diminished, such a force on the level of its genesis at the very least must be an enormous political force in a previously totally political society. Kuroń makes this point explicitly: The movement of industrial workers now institutionalized as Solidarity has been the political agency that has brought about a new level of independence of civil society.[47] But what role is it to play in the new situation? Is it to be (1) the alternative power that is to bring about the further legal and institutional realization of civil society; (2) one of the many alternative powers that is to do so; or (3) one of the forms of interest representa- tion under the new situation, apolitical and trade-unionist? Kuroń himself says that he has moved from alternative (3) to (2) because it is his belief that only a rapid democratization of Polish *society* can save the existing *state* structure from an uncontrollable revolutionary challenge (hence disintegration followed by So- viet intervention),[48] and that such a democratization is impossible without Soli- darity continuing to play a key political role. We should note, however, that Kuroń is quite serious about this role being at the most that of a movement *primus inter pares*; no one in Poland seeks to remythologize the workers as a universal subject. The aim of Solidarity even in this most radical interpretation is to establish not unity but autonomous heterogeneity; in other words, its political function should mean precisely the defense of the self-establishment of a whole host of associations, groupings, forms of self-management that in the foreseeable future would make the workers' union indeed one institution among equals. On the other hand, there should be certainly no question for Kuroń of depoliticizing the independent union or, for that matter, the other form of autonomous associa- tion already in existence. This overall conception can be and is attacked at two ends: (1) Is it not after all seeking to repoliticize a society deeply tired of its politization, or alternately, (2) does it not propose a form of politization from below that will produce heterogeneity without any form of coordination, or integration (state integration being of course excluded)?

The first objection is directly formulated by Wojcicki,[49] one of the Catholic intellectuals advising Solidarity (along with members of the church, and also KOR at least until January 19). He deliberately contrasts his conception of what has occurred and what is still occurring in Poland with what he sees as that of KOR. As against a *social movement* better and better organized with the independent union as its avant-garde, he speaks of the creation of independent social institutions in the "historical-juridical sense" that constitute a field of social activity recuperated from the omnipotent party apparatus. To Wojcicki this achievement is the consequence more of a *cultural* than a *political* process in Poland and it expresses "the radical need to depoliticize society." In his conception the unions should remain unions, as against elements of a pluralist system in the making, that even on the enterprise level should restrict themselves to the defense of the life conditions and rights of those employed. He attributes a position to KOR that would see the unions as the potential centers of industrial democracy and self-management. While Wojcicki's own conception is clearly inspired by the West European model of civil society in general and the conduct of the Polish church in particular, it is also implicitly clear that he charges KOR with still being Marxist, of advocating (1) the repolitization of society, (2) a vanguard role for the working class, and (3) a council democracy, in effect compromising the independence of the unions. On this level, though the disagreements seem to be less sharp than he believes, KOR is post- rather than neo-Marxist. Social movements are seen even by Kuroń as the reconstitution of civil society in the historical-juridical sense Wojcicki has in mind. If he proposes anything resembling a vanguard role for the unions, this is only in helping to build other associations of independent interest representation that would challenge and abolish this role. And he insists on the full organizational separation between the unions and the future organs of industrial self-management, both because he wants to preserve independent interest representation of workers against any management including their own, and because he does not want the unions to grow into a bureaucratic-political role in society, taking responsibility for the decisions of a state system that remains (and must remain?) alien to them.

Differences concerning the level of politization of the new civil society of course remain. What is more interesting than these is that objections of the type made by Wojcicki do drive Kuroń to restate what he sees as the fundamental disagreement in a way that transcends dual power in the direction of the power of society.[50] A clear point of agreement and identity between the two sides here is that they both seek the best strategy to avoid Soviet intervention, or for that matter a final crisis of the system that could provoke it. To Kuroń, however, this danger lies not in the radical democratization of society but in its insufficient institutionalization, which would lead to chaos given the fact that the authority of the party-state is in shambles. It is not in anyone's power without military intervention to stop the process of democratization occurring on all social levels. In this sense, the first of Wojcicki's suggestions concerning the radical depolitization of society does not in this context have to be discussed. (I will return to this question later.) But this only makes the question concerning the integration of the new heterogeneity all the more urgent. Kuroń discounts the possibility that this once again can occur *either* through the reintegration from above of the new autonomous social forms because of the new level of organization of society *or* through the democratization of the *whole* system from within because of the resistance of the apparatus itself. Yet a social system that is organized according to totally opposed principles remains extremely unstable and in a condition of permanent crisis, inviting the catastrophe of intervention. It is to solve this trilemma that Kuroń proposes something that goes not only beyond the idea of dual power but also, in spite of his intentions, beyond the limits of the new evolutionism. Given the premise that the Russians cannot be fooled in any case about what is occurring in Polish society, that is, general democratization from below, he proposes to fool them all the same. Assuming that anarchy and social-political disorganization lead to intervention, but that the democratization of Polish society may be acceptable to the Soviets "within limits," that is, the limits constituted by the continued existence of the party's monopoly in the state, he proposes a form of institutionalization that would overcome social disorganization and preserve this monopoly as well, though it is unclear how much the latter is worth in the scheme. Society, that is, the existing movements, needs to develop unified institutions, a system of society[51] capable of presenting the party-state power structure with unified demands. Economic plans accordingly can be arrived at from the coordinated discussions of unions, intellectuals, peasants, and the organs of industrial self-management. It remains ambiguous what the party-state is left to do in a Poland so organized; whether it is to develop its own alternatives that are to be proposed to "society" for confirmation or rejection or negotiation, *or* whether it is to be reduced, on the level of internal policy at least, to executive, that is, administrative and police, functions—all to be supervised and controlled from below.

The second alternative, which seems to be that of Kuroń's last available statement, seems to unite conceptions of direct democracy in the cells of society, with some kind of pluralistic (perhaps quasi-parliamentary) integration that utilizes only the professional bureaucratic dimensions of the existing party-state structure in an administrative capacity. In such a system, to use an ironic formulation of Szelényi that has already found its analogues in Poland: The only thing left for the political apparatus of the Communist party, the ruling "estate" of state socialism, is to assume ceremonial functions resembling the British House of Lords. The latter, however, had no jealous imperial masters unable to see why such a solution would be more attractive than 1968, the negative lesson around which the new evolutionism was constructed in the first place.

Whether the new evolutionism remains a plausible framework for further Polish developments depends on the successful institutionalization of some version of dual power, tendentially absent from both the conception of Woycicki (who proposes the depolitization of society) and that of Kuroń (who proposes the depolitization of the party-state). Consistent with his earlier argument, Michnik in all his essays interprets the Gdansk accords of August 31 as potentially a *new* social contract between two organized agents, state and society.[52] The form of compromise is new because it is for the first time that *both* parties are organized. Michnik does admit that the duality of powers (he does not use the term) that the agreements minimally institutionalized may contradict "the sociology of power relations"—to which others in the West (e.g., Lefort) and in Poland itself (even Kuroń) appeal—and yet he argues that the knowledge of the limits in Poland on both sides makes just such an institutional solution possible. The party knows that it can destroy the new forms of social plurality only by appealing for the foreign intervention it itself abhors. The social movement, however, is again reminded that, aside from grave threats to Poland's external alliances and to the order of its urban centers, the expropriation of the party's power in the state or even its internal democratization are beyond the limits. Thus the minimum preconditions for "partnership" between state and society are defined by the external threat. Its stability, however, depends on the party-state's becoming a credible partner. Only a new respect for legality (including acceptance of responsibility for earlier violations of the law) and for the actual plurality of public opinion can relegitimate the state.

Finally, in order to avoid the spontaneous destruction of state power from below with all its consequences, negotiation, and bargaining between state and society must be institutionalized; forms of legitimate pressure *other* than strike threat and counterthreat must be found. The general framework of this is called vaguely but significantly—I repeat—"crossing the totalitarian structure of power with a democratic mechanism of corporate representation." The overall arrangement based on these components can be, according to Michnik, the basis of a stable but plastic equilibrium—plastic presumably because each side can continually hope to realize its (different) goals through the functioning of the *same* mechanism. The goal of the party-state will accordingly remain the reintegration of the forms of social association; the goal of society, on the contrary, will be the preservation and extension of its forms of independence.

Fundamental points of Michnik's conception of the new social contract remain unclear. If Kuroń is perhaps deliberately vague about the terms of the compromise (if any) between the new society and the old state, Michnik remains highly abstract concerning what he calls the contract "that society must conclude with itself, a *second* social contract." Both recognize, of course, that the present unity of Polish society—which allows one to speak of "society" as such—is primarily a negative one; in other words, overriding agreement concerning what is opposed masks potentially important disagreements and even conflicts of interests.[53] While Kuroń in fact bypasses the vertical structure of compromise with his proposal for a pluralistic "system of society" integrating perhaps dozens of autonomous democratically organized movements, strata, groups, and so forth, Michnik's strategically more plausible proposal of compromise modeled in the August 31 accords, and even the phrase "democratic mechanism of corporate representation," leave open the questions: With whom actually is the state to negotiate? Which are the social units that are to be members of the actual processes of negotiation? How are they to relate to one another? to excluded groups or individuals, if any? to their own members? to the public spheres, official and alternative?

Society and Societies: The Question of Plurality

In the contemporary language of the bulk of the democratic opposition in Eastern Europe, totalitarianism and pluralism represent exclusive alternatives of "interest integration." With a different political evaluation of the present, but with the same limited conceptual apparatus, the dominant opinion in Western social science concerning systems of the Soviet type has been for some time in a process of transition from a totalitarian, monolithic paradigm to one that considers these systems quasi- or protopluralistic, characterized by interest-group conflicts. Both sets of positions are open to the same objection. Monolithic forms of organization and interest-group pluralism evidently do not exhaust the possible forms of interest aggregation or intermediation in complex societies.[54] Nothing proves this better than the possibilities that are thematized in highly fluid political situations, such as the Poland of 1980–81. In this context some of the concepts of the recent Western critical literature on interest intermediation seems especially useful.[55] While the application of these to state socialism has not yet been done in an altogether convincing manner, we might nonetheless derive from the discussion some relevant definitions and conclusions, which also amount to a group theoretical restatement of the system theoretical interpretation above of "liberalization" as crisis management:

1.   The classical organization of intermediate social levels under authoritarian state socialism is "monistic," involving a large set of "groups," or rather organizations, that are fixed in number, singular, in part ideologically selective, in part compulsory in membership, noncompetitive, internally hierarchical, and created or totally reformed by the party-state that controls their leadership selection, formulates their "interests," and resolves their conflicts vertically.[56]

2.   Reform undertaken from above—in other words, the crisis management of this system—involves a transition to a "state corporatist" version of interest intermediation involving the possible recognition of some new groups that have emerged as a result of social change as well as the concession of some limited independence to already existing organizations.[57] This might involve the replacement of direct state controls with indirect ones, state appointment of leadership by a veto power, vertical formulation of demands, and resolution of conflicts by some combination of vertical and horizontal procedures, both free of open conflict.

3.   A transition to a "societal corporatist" variant (similar to the latter except that here the origin of groups is more independent; conflict-free procedures are guaranteed without state repression by horizontal bargaining) involves a reconstitution of *a version* of civil society and is not compatible with the organizational principle of the system. This is especially the case because in many countries the permission of independent group constitution would very likely mean the emergence of voluntary, nonhierarchical, and conflict-oriented pluralist and syndicalist forms of organization. Nineteen sixty-eight is again, for the existing regimes, the negative model of just such a development.[58]

4.   Pluralist and syndicalist forms of interest representation and conflict resolution can be in general and in particular under conditions of authoritarian state socialism institutionalized only from below. Once this occurs (as in Poland to some extent after 1956), the task of crisis management from the point of view of the regime is the reintegration of the new forms under "state corporatist" arrangements. Under such conditions, societal corporatism, as a form of crisis management to an extent undesirable for both sides, becomes nevertheless possible.

We are now ready to examine the conditions of possibility of various forms of compromise in Poland. Evidently the situation between the summer of 1980 and at least General Jaruzelski's assumption of the premiership was characterized by a highly unstable pluralist milieu characteristic of the periods of dissolution of other dictatorships,[59] in the widest sense of pluralism involving a high degree of conflict and the coexistence of interest associations of all types—monistic (the party and its transmission belts), old corporatist (the church), modern corporatist (the army), pluralist (unions, associations of intellectuals, students, and peasants), and syndicalist (locally or production-based councils and cooperatives). The situation is characterized by several existing "projects" that attempt to institutionalize a more consistent and stable set of relationships among social groups:

1.   The project of provoking violent suppression of the movement of 1980, even if at the cost of Soviet intervention, seems to be the strategy of at least some sections of the party apparatus, though perhaps not of the leadership itself. It is a question of local, regional, middle-level party interests that would have to be sacrificed in any other solution of the crisis. The goal of such a strategy is the restoration of monist forms of organization and interest aggregation.

2.   The best the ruling party can aim for without outside intervention is a structure of compromise in which the other great institutions of society— the church, the union (if a bureaucratically reorganized one), and perhaps the military—would be allowed to participate. The exclusion or serious limitation of public discussion would allow this structure to function not only in a compulsory and conflict-free manner, but also—given the exist-

ing institutional structure—preserving the undisputed primacy of the party-state in relationship to actual policy. This solution is what we have characterized as state corporatism.

3. The argument of some Catholic intellectuals powerful in Solidarity in favor of the depolitization of society. The restriction of the independent labor union to narrower concerns and the concentration of the movement on the sphere of culture,[60] modeled on the actual role of the Catholic church in the last decade, itself represents a corporatist alternative if a societal one. It is significantly different from state corporatism because of its insistence on the independence of institutions and, in particular, a public sphere that would guarantee not only the cultural autonomy of the population but also a structure of compromise that would involve genuine controls on the activities of the state.

4. One of the two alternatives defended by KOR (in particular, Michnik) could be best characterized as "societal pluralism," or pluralism restricted to civil society. Accepting the monolithic structure of the state, this alternative would consist in the independent, horizontal negotiation and compromise of the genuinely significant institutions (however organized: pluralist, corporatist, or syndicalist) of a destatized but not depoliticized society that would be the starting point of unified negotiations with state power. The independent political activity of society distinguishes this from the model in (3), though here, too, the results of compromise would be controlled by a pluralistic and uncensored public sphere.

5. Different from the above is the second alternative of KOR (in particular, Kuroń) because—as we have shown—of its deemphasis of the state in actual policymaking, but also because of its stress on a self-democratizing society on a great plurality of levels (unions, councils, cooperatives, peasant associations, cultural associations, consumer and tenant groups), all of which would actively participate in the generation of policy ("a system for the functioning of society"). Such an arrangement, which could be called syndicalist in lieu of something better, would reduce the existing party-state to the execution of the will of society in internal affairs and to the will of the Soviet Union in external affairs (Finlandization).[61]

6. Finally, the "revolutionary" alternative of the KPN (Moczulski) is political, parliamentary pluralism that presupposes the political power of Poland's traditional parties, especially nationalist and religious groupings. Applying exclusively Western models, this solution would also have no interest in the new forms of democracy that have emerged in Poland, nor especially in a politicized version of civil society. Given the nationalist character of this alternative, added to the fact that there can be no question of any compromise with the ruling party-state, it is a functional equivalent of Soviet intervention. Yet one should not underestimate its potential support, which has been manifested in several demonstrations.

Table 8.1

	Corporatism	Pluralism
1. Number of significant groups	small, fixed	larger, unfixed
2. Structure	hierarchical	generally (but not exclusively) nonhierarchical
3. Conflict potential	noncompetitive	competitive
4. Relationship to politics	some state controls over leadership selection, demand articulation (at least in form of veto)	self-managing, no state controls whatsoever over elections and demand artic- ulation
5. Ideological affinity	nationalist, Catholic	liberal, democratic, democratic socialist
6. Organizational principle	authoritarian state socialist	dual power, which preserves authoritarian state socialism in state sphere
7. Immanent evolutionary trend	state corporatist	democratic syndicalist

Given the constant danger of Soviet intervention *and* the undoubted hegemony in Polish society of the democratic movement, it is my belief that the six
reduce to two serious alternatives: societal corporatism with elements (increasing
over time) of state corporatism, and societal pluralism with elements (increasing
over time) of syndicalism. Table 8.1 indicates some key differences.

More important than this abstract comparison is the examination of the forces
in Poland that point to each direction. The interest and the aims of the democratic
movement and the ruling party are clear enough. If we assumed that either would
prefer the solution of its Polish opponent to Russian intervention (which unfortunately we cannot in the case of the party, where one must again distinguish
between the apparatus and the leadership, not to speak of the rank-and-file,
which may prefer the more democratic alternative in any case), we could reduce
the question to an immanent Polish balance. Actually, the problem is a bit more
complex, because the existence of the corporatist alternative as a serious one is
itself backed up by threat of Soviet intervention. Since this model could reason-
ably be seen as a halfway step toward the type of state corporatism achieved by
other East European regimes from above (preserving the authoritarian state socialist organization principle), it can easily be represented as Poland's best hope
to avoid the fraternal help of its allies. Nevertheless, given the already existing
level of the democratization of Polish society, the ruling party is not able to
impose this model on the basis of its own forces alone.

The ruling party can have a corporatist solution only with the help of allies. In this respect the question of the Catholic church becomes especially crucial. As a part of the antistate movement of the society, the relationship of the Catholic church to the social order and its internal hierarchical organization may predispose it toward corporatism. While old corporatist in structure (not to a high degree functionally differentiated, in many respects still an estate, and in terms of its aspirations a privileged one), this need not represent a fundamental inability to participate in a neo-corporatist structure of compromise any more than in several other Catholic countries. Neither the past nor the present of the church gives us unambiguous clues with regard to its future. An integral part of the authoritarian republic before the war, in the postwar period it represented the only institutionally legalized element of an independent civil society. The democratic opposition is therefore right to stress the model character of the church[62] for the possibility under totalitarianism of an independent institution to exist, to exert pressure, and to enter into acceptable compromises with state power. But as an element of civil society, the church ambiguously enough represents *both* the old "civil society" of privileged orders and the modern one based on legal equality and individual rights. It battles in particular what it, and now the democratic opposition, regard as the communist established church, with its atheistic state religion, in the name of religious freedom (hence the separation of church and state), but it battles *also* in the name of at least some of its lost privileges, and as an alternative established church seeking to be again recognized on the level of public law in the sense of the Concordat of 1925.[63] Such a legal status is not sought only in and for itself. At the very least the episcopate seeks an increasing role in the educational system and in family-oriented legislation (concerning divorce, abortion, etc.).

Facing a power militantly atheistic and theocratic at the same time, this ambiguity initially amounted to little, except in relationship to the democratic left critics of the regime. As Michnik shows in his detailed book on the subject, *The Church, the Left: A Dialogue*, this relationship underwent a significant evolution for the better.[64] While more or less until 1968 the church hierarchy was regarded by "the secular left" as retrograde and reactionary, and the latter's opposition to the regime was seen by the church as a family quarrel among its enemies, the battle for human rights in the 1970s provided the necessary minimum framework of unity. In this context the fight of the church for legality, free public expression and association—hence for the restoration of civil society in some sense—fully complemented and significantly supported the democratic movement; this is not to speak of the more immediate protection provided to members of oppositional groups and activities.[65] Nevertheless conflict and support for the opposition do not exhaust the history of the relationships of the church to state power. This history is also one of a series of compromises in which there have been several constants:[66]

1.   gradual violation of the terms by the regimes of Bierut, Gomułka, and finally Gierek;
2.   the pressure of the Vatican, from the papacy of John XXIII onward, for a more flexible church policy toward the state;
3.   the pressure of collaborationist lay Catholic groups (PAX, ODISS) for a compromise on the basis of the "totalitarian" status quo; and
4.   the staunch resistance of the episcopate to all attempts to change its "anti-totalitarian" line, its defense of civil society in the broadest possible sense.

As a result, the compromises that actually functioned did so in periods of the regime's weakness and search for new legitimation (post-1956, post-1971 in particular). The significance of these compromises for Poland, for Polish Catholics, and for the Catholic Church cannot be underestimated. In the process a minimum of independent parliamentary representation (*Znak* group), a small independent if censored press, and a network of discussion clubs were permitted to emerge. It was indeed in a great measure the activities of Catholic representatives, press, and clubs that prepared the groundwork for cooperation between the secular democratic opposition and the church. It is fair to say that the whole climate of Polish Catholicism underwent significant transformation as a result. With the development of the democratic opposition no longer hostile to the church, the political role of Catholic intellectuals itself changed. From the "neopositivist" parliamentary representation of the *Znak* group, banking on the reform of the system from above, to advising the independent union Solidarity, is indeed a significant journey. One constant of this journey however: the insistence by Catholic intellectuals that the pressure from outside the ruling institutions not be a political one. While today this may reduce to merely a semantic point, the continuity of language at least expresses the continuity of something else, the position of Wyszyński and the episcopate.

The primate has consistently defined the role of the church and its affiliates as nonpolitical.[67] Here we touch upon a different meaning of nonpolitical from what so far has been explored in relation to Solidarity, although undoubtedly the church seeks to extend its meaning to the unions as well. I believe, and I think I am supported by the events between August 1980 and the present, that the church fundamentally opposes a conflict-oriented struggle even for demands that it supports. The formula "our land should be one neither of disorder nor of political prisoners" expresses this well,[68] at a time when only the strike weapon can free political prisoners. Concerned with the security of the nation, but basing himself on organic Catholic social doctrine, Cardinal Wyszyński, as is well known, gave one unfortunate sermon (August 26) apparently arguing for a return to work, which fortunately had no effect whatsoever. The primate and the episcopate clearly supported the demands of August, but were indeed ambiguous about the use of the strike weapon.[69] Since then one can certainly attribute a cautious, temporizing role to the church hierarchy in the continuing conflict. This has taken the form of some attacks on parts of the democratic opposition, in particular KOR,[70] whose influence with Solidarity is apparently contested by at least part of the hierarchy. Indeed Wałesa, upon his return from Rome (January 19, 1980), announced the termination of the advisory role of KOR, which seems not to have been carried out fully, probably due to the strong presence of KOR in the board and the rank-and-file of Solidarity. Nevertheless, on March 5 the regime declared its gratitude to the episcopate, through a mixed government-church commission, for helping to stabilize the situation in response to Premier Jaruzelski's three-month no-strike plea. Finally, just at the time of the for-the-moment temporary arrests of Kuroń and Michnik as a result of formal government proceedings against KOR, the episcopate has again declared (March 13) its opposition to "disorder," although again in the context of supporting one significant demand of the opposition—an independent union for peasants and agricultural workers.

How are we to interpret this history, which seems to produce new twists and turns each day? Here we must rely on the discussion of the democratic opposition, which in effect points to three alternatives for the church.[71] Given the present weakness of the regime, and hence its extreme willingness to deal with the church, the following possibilities are open to the episcopate:

1. Acceptance of a hitherto unprecedented level of confessional liberty as the price of political passivity, a modern version of the position represented in Poland by the thoroughly discredited group PAX, and elsewhere (e.g., Hungary) by the actual arrangements accepted by the church.

2. Search for a new authoritarian solution in which Catholicism would somehow become the basis (explicit or implicit) of a new type of ideologically monolithic but now nationally "legitimate" political order. Here the effort in the 1970s of the group ODISS to seek an alliance with the nationalist, anti-Semitic Moczar wing of the party (recently strengthened once again) is a significant factor.

3. Refusal to make a separate deal, and continuation of the battle for a pluralistic solution, which by definition would involve a continued separation of church and state, and defense of other forms of institutional autonomy in society. This is clearly the position of the Catholic intellectuals advising Solidarity—who, by the way, have ties in the West with the *Ésprit* circle—Mazowiecki, Cywiński, and Wojcicki, as well as the related clubs and journals.

Of course, the real question is the choice of the episcopate. Without a doubt the line of PAX, or any contemporary version of it, remains unacceptable to the hierarchy because of its different and even compromising stance on the issue of national sovereignty. The church, of course, sees itself as the major carrier and defender of Polish national identity. Also, for the moment the democratic Catholic intellectuals seem to be setting the tone for the church community as a whole; a pure version of what Michnik called the Iranization of Poland is not apparently in the cards. But what happens if the immediate factual outcome of a tacit adherence to the third alternative is interpreted as increasingly threatening to the *national* economy and to *national* sovereignty? This is the possible context of the relevance of a neo-corporatist solution which can be seen as a possible synthesis of alternatives (2) and (3), that is, the defense of a form of plurality where conflict is avoided on the basis of national considerations by a set of compulsory compromises in which the great (and therefore bureaucratic) organizations of society alone participate.

The internal structure of the Polish church as well as its specific relation to civil society indeed predispose it to an authoritarian solution, as long as such a solution is not antinational and of course not anti-Catholic. This point is often disregarded by the democratic opposition because of its desire to preserve its new alliance with the church at all costs. There are some crucial distinctions to be made here, distinctions that can be posed only as questions to be answered by the Polish opposition, democrats and Catholics. Is the church hierarchy today pluralist, as Kołakowski argues, or is it only a defender of some kind of plurality, as Jan Gros seemingly more rightly stresses? Is the church an "unyielding repository of traditional libertarian values" or is it a defender of primarily its own particular interests, whose internal record on civil rights is rather dismal?[72] Does it condemn social militancy from below only because of its fear of Soviet intervention, or also because of its own conception of social order? Would the church, as Gros implies, be willing in return for genuinely significant privileges (which up until now never have been seriously offered) to suspend its support for the democratic movement, leading to the latter's isolation? While it is true enough that the church is "the strongest and weakest link in the coalition of liberalizing forces, . . . the only partner able to enter into a separate peace with the regime," it is also true that the church hierarchy does not today alone represent Polish Catholicism, and the bulk of the Catholic intellectuals who are in the democratic movement stand in the way of the separate peace. This limit should not make "the secular left" forget a fundamental historical point first formulated by the critical Catholic intellectual Bohdan Cywiński: The hierarchy of the Polish church, once that of a "Constantinian church" (state church), represents today a "Julian church" (referring to the temporarily disestablished and persecuted church under emperor Julian the Apostate), in intransigent opposition to the state persecuting it, but waiting to be restored, not perhaps in its economic and political privileges but in any case as the established moral, cultural authority in the life of the nation.[73] Hence its solidarity "with society" is conditional, based on the identification of society with it and not the reverse. What can be interpreted as signs of the voluntary renunciation by the church of its Julianism (that is, solidarity with the social efforts independent of it) has until now occurred in the framework of a defensive tactic that allowed the unification of all of the opposition around a program of the restoration of minimal elements of civil society. But what holds for a defensive tactic may not hold for an offensive one in a period in which legitimate state authority is in shambles.

For the moment, the decisive terrain where the church could play with its inclinations toward a neo-corporatist form of compromise is, of course, the third potential partner for such a solution, the independent union. Combined government and church pressure to separate Solidarity from the democratic opposition seemed to have failed until now; at the moment of writing, similar pressures to accept a period of conflict-free coexistence (which was already used to crack down on KOR) seem to have succeeded. Yet today Solidarity is organizationally quite at the opposite pole from the church and the ruling party: It is a mix between syndicalist and pluralist structures and practices. It is exactly for this reason that what could be successful pressures on its leadership (and in particular its leader) run into resistance on the part of the constantly participating rank-and-file. Only a bureaucratic hierarchical restructuring, with state and/or church influence on the process of leadership selection, could in the longer run make it a viable neo-corporatist partner. It is to their credit that, along with KOR, the Catholic intellectuals advising Solidarity have stressed the fight against bureaucratization.[74] The refusal of the unions to take on management functions is part of this fight for an organization that is independent, democratic, whose leadership is not institutionally separated from its membership, and hence a model (though not a vanguard) of a different version of civil society from that represented by the church. Will the church learn to accept this model, or better still that of a fully pluralist civil society capable of accommodating different types of institutions of interest intermediation? While Solidarity is today under various pressures, so is the church, and the outcome is still unclear.

While the answer of the church to the question of social alternatives depends on the actions of several social agents of which the hierarchy is only one—agents that find themselves in a fluid pluralistic but not adequately institutionalized situation—the needs of the party-state with respect to the church can be extrapolated from the dynamics of the present system crisis. In summary: The regime, in the midst of a deep legitimation crisis, has not nor will it have the reserves of loyalty to carry out an internally based authoritarian solution. It also does not have the popular support needed to reform the economy, which would require restraining both social consumption and social conflict for a period.[75] Given the ideological uselessness of Marxism-Leninism, or of a technocratic reformist ideology that cannot promise immediate benefits or demand rationalization at the cost of unemployment, the key to any policy whatsoever (except calling on Russian military intervention, of course) is the reactivation of the third component of the eclectic ideological mix that characterizes the ideological grab-bag of all authoritarian socialist ruling parties: nationalism. The reemergence of Moczar, the appointment of the commander-in-chief as prime minister, the convergence of anti-Semitic slogans of the Moczar people and of the far right KPN opposition (vigorously repudiated by Solidarity) all point in this direction. But in Poland it is the church that holds the key to the nation. Clearly it is predisposed to give the regime a chance to restore the national economy and preserve national sovereignty: hence its important if not decisive support for the three-month strike-free period. But the regime will have to start doing something with this opportunity other than just repress dissidents; it will, in other words, have to do more than just rely on the church, which will most likely reject alliance with a force that continues to perpetuate the crisis of the national economy. Nationalist legitimation in Poland, unlike the Soviet Union,[76] may not be an alternative to economic reform, but in the present state of things, its complement or even result.

Society and Economy: The Question of a Socialist Civil Society

In spite of having had some of the foremost market socialist theoreticians (Lange, Kalecki, Brus, and Lipiński), and two periods of intense discussions concerning economic reform (after 1956 and after 1971), Polish development is not characterized by any sustained effort at decentralization when compared with Hungary in particular. While the hardening of the ruling parties against reform after 1968 was a more or less general East European phenomenon (except for a hesitant new start in Hungary in the mid-1970s), the Polish "solution" of the consequences of nonreform, the massive indebtedness to the West that led first to a dramatic upturn and then to disaster given the existing overcentralized structure, was unique.[77] Today, after the dramatic events of 1980, everyone in Poland is speaking of economic reforms,[78] although remarkably enough, up until now (March 1980) no relevant measures have been actually proposed by the state.[79] While the evaluation of the specifically economic dimensions of the proposals is beyond my competence, I also believe that in East European countries the possibility or impossibility of serious reform of the economy is as a rule never determined on primarily the economic level. The reason why these economies have not in fact been significantly decentralized is certainly not to be found in the fear of adverse economic consequences or even in the dogmatic belief of the ruling institution in its ridiculous, orthodox doctrines. Rather, up until now no foolproof method has been found for combining a largely destatized economy and preservation of the self-identity of the ruling institution. And yet, the crisis of planning rationality has been everywhere intensifying. The existing planning systems have been decreasingly able to cope with either the growth or the specific dysfunctions engendered by planning itself. In principle, therefore, economic reform remains on the East European agenda, even if for the moment alternative forms of "crisis management" or "avoidance" seem to dominate.[80]

Most generally, economic reform in Eastern Europe can be interpreted as a part of the transition of the state socialist systems, in process since the death of Stalin, from the "positive subordination" of all social spheres to the party-state (high level of penetration), to "negative subordination" (a qualitatively lower level of penetration, preserving the functional primacy of the party-state).[81] Most interpreters are nevertheless right in concentrating on the economy (where the same transition appears as that from "extensive" to "intensive" development), not because the transformation of this sphere necessarily brings about the liberalization of the whole system but because of the opposite: In principle, at least, a general economic decentralization of authoritarian state socialism is possible—as the example of Yugoslavia seems to show—leaving the principle of organization of the system intact. Only—and this is also shown by the Yugoslav example—the party-state withdrawing from the centralized management of the economy—must derive at least some degree of legitimacy from some other sources than the claims of "rational redistribution" and "substantive material justice." Second, the ruling party must be able to preserve its functional primacy in the spheres of society other than the economy: social organization, culture, as well as state administration, in order to satisfy for itself (and in Eastern Europe, for the Soviet Union as well) the necessary condition of self-identification expressed by the vague slogan of the "leading role of the party." Finally, economic reforms will not in such a situation be initiated from above unless the type of relationship the party-state has to the economy can be effectively uncoupled from the relationship it has to the rest of society. The legal preconditions of a decentralized economy alone cannot be allowed to develop into a full-fledged system of private law without endangering the real basis of the leading role of the party—its power of arbitrary intervention.

The difficulty of satisfying these three interrelated conditions is the explanation for the oscillation between partial decentralization and recentralization, in some form characteristic of all East European societies. In Poland, I believe, the first two conditions have been historically absent (the inability of the party to reconcile national identity with partial sovereignty; the existence of *another* institution powerful and influential in the cultural sphere) to an unusually high degree even in Eastern Europe. Here the reform attempts always came (or were feigned rather) in the wake of popular risings. A charitable interpretation of the economic manipulations of Gierek's government might indeed be that it hoped to achieve the necessary legitimation for reform through a prior dramatic improvement in the standard of living. If so, the timing was totally false. Today, in any case, all the conditions mentioned as necessary for economic reform from above are absent in Poland more than ever. Does this mean the impossibility of significant economic reform, given what even the bulk of the opposition assumes as given, namely "the leading role of the party"?

Today in Poland, structural reform from below has decisively altered the conditions for economic decentralization as well. In the process the leading role of the party vis-à-vis the spheres of social organization and culture has been reduced to something very small indeed. As a result, both reform and nonreform have *apparently* become impossible. After long hesitation, the party may ultimately reject economic decentralization and for the following already implied reason: The primacy of the party-state over society is today limited to the sphere of economic planning and management. Any significant withdrawal from this sphere, too, might lead to a serious identity crisis of the party, possibly a deep internal split reminiscent of 1956 and 1968, very likely followed by Soviet intervention. The leading role of the party over the state would mean little (or would be reduced to its foreign policy implications) if the state were deprived of the bulk of its functions vis-à-vis the economy. The scenario indicates no reform, and even that the opposition should not seek it.

Yet no economic reform is today *also* a road to disaster. How can an already bankrupt economic system plagued by elementary shortages (the socialist version of inflation) survive the fact that its most powerful economic agent is today an independent labor union, which cannot in the long run (despite its striking responsibility in this regard) avoid battling for the standard of living of its members, that is, their real wages? Aside from all the existing significant reasons for the decentralization of the system,[82] independent unions require independent management (including, of course, workers' self-management) simply to be able to resolve local demands according to local interests and capabilities. With the state as the ultimate manager in the shape of the central imperative planner, local management, far weaker than the associated unions, either gives way since it does not foot the bill alone *or* defers to the state, causing every economic conflict to become immediately a political one. In the context of the present centralized command economy even self-restraint by the workers would only put off the day of reckoning; their greatest efforts to increase productivity would yield little under the conditions of capital utilization characteristic of such economies.[83] The system thus cannot solve its economic crisis without significant decentralization, but if it does not, it will collapse and along with it the achievements of 1980–81.

It may be absurd for anyone outside Poland to speculate about possible ways out of this dilemma, but it is also irresponsible to paint by omission a hopeless picture, especially when one thinks it need not be. The formula seems to me to be the acceptance of economic reform as the system's crisis management.[84] The economy must indeed be significantly decentralized, with all the economic consequences of such a decentralization: the autonomy of branches and units, the gradual elimination of unproductive units, a high degree of market determination of most if not all prices, and the fundamental shift of priorities in the direction of demand, that is, consumer goods sector and agriculture, the permission of horizontal links among units, and so forth. For such a policy to be instituted effectively the unions must give it a great deal of breathing space, by restraining—as they have all along—economic demands. The lesson of 1980 shows that such self-restraint can be converted into political demands and achievements. The next foreseeable period should be continued as one of syndicalist organization building rather than pluralist interest conflict. Of the many results of such a process, one could indeed be worker self-management of industry, another the securing of institutional arrangements by which societal associations would negotiate with the state power concerning economic plans. If for no other reason than to satisfy the conditions imposed by the possible logic of the political collapse of the party-state, the economy would have to remain a planned state socialist one quite in the sense of the economic reformers of the 1960s.[85] In other words, it is not enough for the opposition to try to keep the party-state from falling apart—as I believe Kuroń ironically suggested—it must also be left with something to do. Within the context of dual power as established in Poland, it is in the economic sphere that the power and self-identity of the existing system must be preserved, and this is possible only through the continuation of macro-economic planning. Must this concession be seen as a purely tactical one? This question can be tackled through raising two others: Is a socialist civil society desirable and possible? and what is a conceivable road to it in Poland?

Following a suggestion by Ivan Szelényi,[86] I would like to go beyond the position of Kołakowski according to which the effort to establish the state–civil society duality necessarily leads to authoritarianism, and also maintain that a socialist civil society would be a more consistent realization of the goals of the democratic revolutions of the eighteenth century than contemporary bourgeois-capitalist civil society. The literature on the first point, that is, the critique of totalitarianism, is, of course, immense. On the second, unfortunately without histori-cal examples to rely on, it is necessarily sparse. Such a future literature, in my opinion, needs to explore the possibility of: (1) the nonidentity between private law and private property; (2) market without capital formation, and planning without authoritarianism; (3) plurality without corporatism, indeed syndicalist plurality of self-managing entities; (4) critical publics in a world of mass communications; (5) a structure of political compromise among particular, independent units that encom-passes the universal; (6) the reduction of political and economic bureaucracy to purely technical, administrative functions under the control of democratic assem-blies; and (7) a fruitful combination of direct and parliamentary democracy.

Some of these areas, of course, recall the concerns of early modern political theory; some are more modern. Are they hopelessly irrelevant? The thrust of this paper was to show otherwise, concerning points (3), (4), and (5). A negative answer to (7), and on the political level (6), belongs to the givens of the Polish situation. In a full sense, a socialist civil society cannot be established in today's Poland. But, barring Soviet intervention, is what is in formation a *socialist* ver-sion of civil society? The argument so far established only the possibility of the emergence of a radically democratic model of society.

The part of the opposition in Poland that describes itself as democratic social-ist (which the Western press often calls social democratic, although in a non-capitalist country the distinction is meaningless), namely KOR, along with the leadership of Solidarity repeatedly described its goals as compatible with social-ism. This, however, is generally not explained further than not wanting to restore the former owners or to abolish the system of social welfare. To this Wałesa adds only: "Socialism is a good road. But it should be a Polish road." At the moment,

KOR says little more on the subject. Even the point concerning the need to combine parliamentary democracy (that need not be incompatible with public ownership) with direct democracy is stressed only by Kuroń among the intellectuals, although the interest of the workers in autonomous self-management (independent also of the unions) is clear enough. And yet even this stress amounts "only" to radical democracy.

The restoration of capitalism always was and remains unacceptable as an explanation of any of the stages of development of East European societies, whose organizational principle, new in history, is authoritarian state socialist. The same may not be true for the institutionalization of yet another "contradictory" model of civil society in the fully hypothetical situation in which this organizational principle were abolished, or even in the hopefully not merely hypothetical case of the consolidation of dual power, in which a fully destatized economy would be composed of self-managing units horizontally related through a self-regulating market.[87] Although industrial democracy is incompatible with capitalism as we know it in the West, is it in principle incompatible with the emergence of new forms of dependence and inequality? The question becomes serious especially given the power of the world capitalist economy to which Poland even now in part belongs. In a Poland free of the threat of external intervention it would be the task of workers' parties as well as other groupings of socialists in a freely elected Sejm to represent the interest of the preservation of socialism, including projects of equalization. But this Poland is today impossible. And yet universality, which never emerges spontaneously from plurality, must somehow be represented. The state part of the ruling institution, separated out as an administrative and planning bureaucracy, could find its function here. The continual representation of the need to preserve and develop the welfare state features of the system, that is, the exclusion of some domains of life from market principles, the protection of unproductive yet culturally and socially significant enterprises, the prevention of capital accumulation by units through laws if necessary, the representation of the whole in foreign trade and indicative, macroplanning of growth, investment, etc., are functions enough for a state in which it remains significant to be the leading force. These are all redistributive functions, although hopefully in the Western sense of redressing inequalities rather than in the Eastern sense of engendering new ones.[88] The difference, of course, could not be left up to the party. The social plans worked out by experts that encompass these tasks of redistribution must be represented in negotiations in which the party would be only one of the partners, and the others too would be able to rely on experts and even present counterplans. The arrangement would preserve the party's identity as "the leading force of the building of socialism" even if now it would be the question of an entirely new and unprecedented stage of state socialist development, issuing, perhaps, in a self-managing socialist society.

All this, of course, must sound highly unrealistic, since at present the independent union has not insisted on anything resembling this type of reform of the planning system. Indeed, although insisting on participation in the ratification of plans presented by the state on the basis of proposals worked out by its own experts working with its "research institute," Solidarity has made few specific demands relating to the structural reform of the economy. While its distinct unwillingness to accept the possible unemployment and price rises that might accompany some rationalization and decentralization plans does block the union's way toward the acceptance of most readily available reform strategies, I believe that its reticence on the subject is also motivated by something even more fundamental: the interest in preserving the independence of the social sphere, which would be compromised once again if the leading social institution assumed responsibility for state proposals that, no matter what, will have to be biased against some social interests, including some of the interests of the workers. The institutions of Polish society cannot accept responsibility for the dysfunctions of the present system, or for the dysfunctions that will inevitably arise from any attempt to try to reform it.

Actually, the case I am trying to make is strengthened by the formal unwillingness of Solidarity to participate directly in governmental reform discussions (although, of course, individuals associated with the union have worked out proposals, and even attended as observers to reform discussions of various government task forces). The spheres of social organization and to a lesser extent culture having been restored to civil society, a relative primacy over the economy is left by omission to the state as the token of its continuing social function as well as the basis of the party's continuing social identity. It is to be hoped that the policy that will result will not issue in disaster.[89]

In other East European countries under Soviet rule, even the reform of the economy from above halts before the specter of civil society. In Poland, civil society having been reconstituted from below, even the reform of the economy is now possible. It is thus that the democratic movement in Poland has put the program of a socialist civil society, suspended as a result of 1968, back on the agenda of East European alternatives.

Notes

1. Z. Erard, G.M. Zygier, eds., *La Pologne: une société en dissidence* (Paris, 1978).
2. Interview in *Les Temps Modernes* quoted by A. Drawicz in Pelikán, Wilke, eds., *Opposition ohne Hoffnung?* (Hamburg, 1979).
3. "Zeit der Hoffnung," *Der Spiegel* (September 15, 1980), 38, p. 153.
4. In R. Tökés, *Opposition in Eastern Europe* (Baltimore, 1979), pp. 60ff. The same terminology is used, but for the Soviet Union without adequate justification, by Moshe Lewin, *Political Undercurrents of Soviet Economic Debates* (Princeton, 1973).
5. "Staat, Partei, Gewerkshaft: Thesen zu Polen," *Links* (November, 1980), p. 17.
6. "Bahro's Ideas on Changes in Eastern Europe," in R. Wolter, ed., *Rudolf Bahro: Critical Responses* (New York, 1980).

206   FROM NEO-MARXISM TO DEMOCRATIC THEORY

7. A. Michnik, "Die letzte Chance," *Der Spiegel* (December 23, 1980).
8. "Zeit der Hoffnung," p. 152.
9. For this concept, cf. C. Castoriadis, *L'institution imaginaire de la société.*
10. In his classic *Strukturwandel der Öffentlichkeit* (Newied, 1962), Habermas speaks of the contradictory institutionalization of the bourgeois public sphere (the logic of publicity and the logic of private property, i.e., the logic of an all-inclusive discursive process without domination, and that of a new form of exclusion-domination) that, of course, in his language is the central aspect of the state–civil society duality. Since the "contradiction" has at least three terms (corresponding to the logics of state, society, and economy), it may be better to speak of the heterogeneous institutionalization, a term that Castoriadis has coined to indicate his own distance from an earlier position when he spoke only of the institutionalization of capitalism. In a joint study with Jean Cohen, I explore the structure of this "contradictory" or "heterogeneous" institutionalization of civil society, the developmental lines inherent in it (which we do not interpret only in the sense of a *Verfallsgeschichte*), the authoritarian implication of revolts *against* civil society, and the conditions of possibility of the resurgence of civil society in contemporary social movements against either/both the state and the economy. For the present, the problem in all its generality has been explored only on the level of the history of the concept of civil society, cf. the important works of Manfred Riedel, most recently: "Bürger, Staatsbürger, Bürgertum," and "Gesellschaft, bürgerliche," in *Geschichtliche Grundbegriffe* I (1972), and II (1975) (Ernst Klett Verlag, Stuttgart).
11. On the most general level, though not yet adequately differentiated according to national contexts, Habermas's *Strukturwandel* remains the fundamental study of the fate (or one of the possible fates, or structural tendencies, rather) of civil society given its contradictory institutionalization. Nevertheless, while for some countries his economy–society polarity (constitutive also of the *political* contradictions) is somewhat one-sided, for others his lack of emphasis on the role of social movements in constituting civil society, in other words, the bourgeois public sphere, needs correction. More differentiated if far more limited are a series of available historical studies on the force field between state and society in pre-1848 Germany; cf. R. Koselleck, *Preussen zwischen Reform und Revolution* (Stuttgart, 1967) as well as his "Staat und Gesellschaft in Preussen 1815–1848," and Werner Conze, ed., *Staat und Gesellschaft im deutschen Vormärz* (Ernst Klett, Stuttgart, 1967); O. Brunner, *Neue Wege der Verfassungs- und Sozialgeschichte* (Göttingen, 1968 reissue of 1956 volume); L. Gall, "Liberalismus und bürgerliche Gesellschaft: Zu Charakter und Entwicklung der liberalen Bewegung in Deutschland," in Gall, ed., *Liberalismus* (Köln, 1980).
12. In this context an immanent critique of the works of Talcott Parsons may be indeed a worthwhile enterprise. Cf. his *System of Modern Societies* (Englewood Cliffs, 1971) in particular. Jean Cohen undertakes such a critique from the point of view of a critical stratification theory.
13. This was indeed the theoretical line taken by the leading contemporary theorist of social movements, Alain Touraine, in a 1980 James lecture at New York University. In this context, cf. his *L'après socialisme* (Paris, 1980), and in particular his *La voix et la regard* (Paris, 1978).
14. It would be certainly possible to interpret February 1917 as the last great democratic revolution in the Western tradition, as obliquely enough *even* Perry Anderson does in his *Lineages of the Absolutist State*. Given the obliteration of all traces of this in subsequent Russian history, including that of the post-1945 empire, it may be possible to put Hungary 1956 and the current Polish struggle (that also started in 1956 ultimately) in the same tradition of revolutions. As against Czechoslovakia, these two countries have participated in the history of Western civil society (not culture) only peripherally and only

for extremely short periods (Poland, for example, only 1919–26, or at most till 1930).

15. For Prussia, cf. Koselleck in the works cited above. For the general problem, cf. Habermas, op. cit., Gall, op. cit.

16. For the Russian context where the element of constitution from above was surely the most extreme, cf. Dietrich Geyer, "Gesellschaft als staatliche Veranstaltung. Sozialgeschichtliche Aspekte des russischen Behördenstaats im 18. Jahrhundert," in *Wirtschaft und Gesellschaft im vorrevolutionären Russland*, ed. D. Geyer (Köln, 1975).

17. Cf. Perry Anderson, op. cit.

18. It is another question—and here Tocqueville's thesis is fully applicable—concerning the continuity of pre- and postrevolutionary state organization.

19. Here lies a crucial difference among the various countries of today's Eastern Europe. In Russia the destruction of the old society after 1917 coincided with the enormous strengthening of a state power that was to destroy also the new society in the making in the 1930s. In Bulgaria and Romania the destruction of the old society in 1945 was not even followed by the emergence of a new, modern one. Poland and Hungary represent societies where the interwar period involved uneasy mixtures of survivals from the old regime and elements of the new society. Such a mixture already characterized pre–World War I Germany, with modern elements coming to the fore in Weimar to be destroyed by the fascist revolution against modernity. Only Czechoslovakia evolved a fully modern society in the interwar period. In all of the last four countries in the Western periphery of Eastern Europe, the social mix was fully statized after 1948 at least, with some countries enjoying a brief period of social ferment expressed in parliamentarianism and social reform till 1948.

20. See A. Arato, "Critical Sociology and Authoritarian State Socialism," Chapter 3, this volume. The concept of the prerogative state (*Massnahmenstaat*) comes from Ernst Fraenkel's *Dual State* (New York, 1941).

21. On this I am preparing a paper entitled "The Modernity and non-Modernity of Authoritarian State Socialism," which examines the place of Soviet and East European societies in various (functionalist, action theoretical, and normative) developmental frameworks.

22. Cf. F. Fehér, "Kadarism as the Model State of Khrushchevism."

23. There are some important exceptions, notably Szelényi and Konrád in their *The Intellectuals on the Road to Class Power* (New York, 1979), whose thesis presupposes the viability of technocratic reform. They have since then stressed this aspect less, and even in the original work there is room for the idea of reform from below. For some of Konrád's current views on the subject, which seem to also have been affected by the new strategy in Eastern Europe, see *Az autonomia kisértése* (Paris, 1980).

24. Most impressively by M. Rakovski, *Towards an East European Marxism* (London, 1978).

25. Bahro's *Alternative in Eastern Europe* (London, 1979), i.e., the building of a new communist party outside the existing one which is to replace and reabsorb its predecessor as a result of its social hegemony is doubly impossible from the outset: Under conditions of East European state security such a party cannot be built; and more important, nowhere does the population have an interest in yet another Leninist vanguard.

26. "Thèses sur l'espoir et le désespoir," in *La Pologne*, pp. 83, 95.

27. I am using the French translation "Une stratégie pour l'opposition polonaise" in *La Pologne. Survey* has apparently published an English version: "The New Evolutionism" (Summer–Autumn 1976).

28. "Pour une platforme unique de l'opposition," in *La Pologne*.

29. J. Kuroń, K. Modzelewski, *Monopolsozialismus* (Hamburg, 1968).

30. Kasimierz Wojcicki, "La reconstruction de la société," in *Esprit* (January 1981).

Some of the same arguments are beautifully made in Konrád's new book, op. cit.

31. Cf. Wojcicki, op. cit., as well as A. Smolar, "Afghanistan et Pologne" in the same number of *Esprit*. To mention only two sets of contrary sources here: the recent literature (Skilling, Gryffiths, Hough, et al. in political science, Rittersporn in history) on interest conflict in the Soviet Union, as well as the various political-culture schools stressing the compromises of the party–state with traditional Russian forms.

32. Hegedüs, "Democracia és szocialismus Keleten és Nyugaton" (Democracy and Socialism in East and West), *Magyar Füzetek* (Paris, 1978), I. There is an English version in Coates, Singleton, eds., *The Just Society* (Nottingham, 1977).

33. In their critical response to Hegedüs, in the same journal issue, "Megjegyzések Hegedüs András nyilt leveléhez" (Notes on the Open Letter of András Hegedüs). In more or less the same debate, M. Vajda has also stressed the possibility in Hungary of an alternative public sphere, but also implicitly warned that under conditions entirely different from Poland the mechanical imitation of the specific model of the Polish opposition would lead to a new vanguardism. Cf. *Magyar Füzetek* (Paris, 1978), II.

34. Cf. his two articles, "Der Kampf um Menschenrechte," in *Menschenrechte: Ein Jahrbuch zu Osteuropa* (Hamburg, 1977), and "Reform und Revolution die falsche Alternative," in *Opposition ohne Hoffnung? Jahrbuch zu Osteuropa 2* (Hamburg, 1979), as well as his "Bahro's Ideas."

35. Hegedüs, "Democracy," p. 85. It is another matter that he does not propose any scheme for the official state sphere being made public in any other sense than the premodern representative public sphere in Habermas's typology. He consciously rejects the historic, western model of creating a political public in parliament.

36. Cf. interview in *Menschenrechte*, p. 394.

37. Kis and Bence, op. cit, p. 111.

38. For three good summaries and analyses: cf. Rupnik, op. cit., as well as Joseph Kay, "The Polish Opposition," and Andrezej Drawicz, "Experience of the Democratic Opposition," both in *Survey* (Fall, 1979), XXIV, 4.

39. Cf. Renate Damus, "Ökonomische und politische Ursachen der Streikbewegung," *Links* (October, 1980).

40. For a critique, see Arato, From Western to Eastern Marxism: Rudolf Bahro, Chapter 4, this volume.

41. "Bahro's Ideas," p. 181.

42. Cf. Bence, "Une nouvelle formule," *L'Alternative* (January–February, 1981), p. 34; he more carefully uses the term "counter power" to indicate that there is a form of political power here that does not seek to substitute itself for the party or the state. Bence along with Kis are the spokesmen in Hungary for the "new evolutionism," and in their evaluation of the Polish situation too there is an ambiguity between a strategy that seeks to institutionalize the present achievement (based on direct democracy) and a hope that projects a moment when the one party will become one of many.

43. A conclusion that is somehow to be avoided on the level of action. Cf. Lefort, "Reculer les frontiers du possible," *Esprit* (January, 1981).

44. "Les dirigents de 'Solidarité' face au pouvoir," *L'Alternative* (January–February, 1981).

45. "Ce que nous voulons et ce que nous pouvons," in *L'Alternative* (January–February, 1981), p. 12.

46. Ibid., p. 8.

47. See the interview with him in *Der Spiegel* (December 15, 1980), p. 107.

48. Cf. ibid., pp. 105–107, and especially "Un chemin sans retour," *Esprit* (January, 1981), pp. 68–72. Indeed, between these two statements (the one in *Esprit* is the earlier one) one can indeed perceive such a shift in his position—if a slight one.

49. "La reconstruction de la société," pp. 61–62.

50. "Un chemin," pp. 68–71.

51. Ibid., 72; December 15 *Spiegel* interview, p. 106.

52. I am drawing on the already cited three statements: "Die Zeit der Hoffnung," "Der letzte Chance," "Ce que nous voulons, ce que nous pouvons."

53. Michnik, "Ce que nous voulons," p. 10; Kuroń, December 15 *Spiegel* interview, p. 106.

54. If the Western conflict paradigm of Skilling et al. too easily transposes to Soviet-type societies the pluralistic model, this is because of their not particularly democratic interpretation of this for Western societies. Even this version of the model is not easily applicable to the East. The East European oppositionals realize that the pluralist model does not describe their societies but they realize this in part because of their uncritical identification of a highly democratic version of pluralism with the existing societies of the West.

55. See especially the essay that started the discussion: Philippe Schmitter, "Still the Century of Corporatism?" Pike, Strich, eds., *The New Corporatism* (Notre Dame, 1974), as well as the special issue (April 1977) of *Comparative Political Studies*. For our context see the interesting but in many respects problematic article by Daniel Chirot, "The Corporatist Model and Socialism," *Theory and Society* (March, 1980), and the much older, but still useful article by Andrew Janos, "Group Politics in Communist Society: A Second Look at the Pluralist Model," in Huntington, Moore, eds., *Authoritarian Politics in Modern Society* (New York, 1970).

56. Cf. Schmitter, op. cit., for this concept as well as for the distinction between "state" and "societal" corporatism used below, and for redefinitions of "pluralism" and "syndicalism."

57. Cf. Chirot, op. cit. Unfortunately, Chirot overestimates the completeness of this transition (especially for his example: Romania) and underestimates the oscillation between monism and corporatism that he also mentions. Postulating that the East European societies are already corporatist, he mistakenly believes that "liberalization" (i.e., reform from above) involves a shift to a more democratic, societal form of corporatism.

58. Yugoslavia, as Chirot argues, indeed has some significant societal corporatist elements that indeed have been initiated from above. But this occurred under conditions of political, national, and revolutionary legitimacy (cf. Bodgan Denitch, *Legitimation of a Revolution*) that are not easily to be duplicated elsewhere. And even here one may ask, as does Janos, op. cit., whether or not societal corporatism (i.e., local and worker's control) represents conflict resolution primarily in areas defined as nonstrategically central by the ruling party (whose central concerns are organized according to monistic or state corporatist criteria).

59. Schmitter characterizes, e.g., the post-Franco epoch in Spain this way (op. cit., p. 127) and indeed the example of Spain has come up several times in the writings of the Polish opposition, especially Michnik.

60. Cf. Wojcicki, op. cit.

61. For the latter aspect Kuroń has used the term "Finlandization."

62. Cf. Michnik in the essays already quoted, as well as: *L'église et la gauche. Le dialogue polonais* (Paris, 1979), and "Was die Polen von dem neuen Papst erwarten," in *Opposition ohne Hoffnung*. See also Kołakowski, "Church and Democracy in Poland: Two Views," *Dissent* (Summer, 1980). But see the characteristically different stress of Kuroń who speaks of the movement of Catholics, as one among several, in "Pour une plateforme," pp. 126–27.

63. Stefan Cardinal Wyszyński, "Der Geist des Evangeliums in der Organisation des gesellschaftlich-beruflichen und des öffentlichen Lebens in Polen," in Dross, ed., *Polen.*

Freie Gewerkschaften im Kommunismus? (Hamburg, 1980), p. 114.

64. *L'Église et la gauche.*

65. Cf. Rupnik, op. cit., Drawicz, op. cit., and in particular Michnik, "Was die Polen von dem neuen Papst erwarten."

66. For this story, cf. Anna Kaminska, "The Polish Pope and the Polish Catholic Church," *Survey* (Fall, 1979).

67. Wyszyński, op. cit.

68. Quotation from a declaration of the episcopate, March 13, in *Süddeutsche Zeitung*, March 14–15, p. 5.

69. Cf. Stefan Cardinal Wyszyński, "Verantwortung, Pflichten und Rechte im Leben der Nation" and "Kommuniqué des Zentralrats des polnischen Episkopats," both of August 26, 1980, both in *Polen*, pp. 158–59 and 161–63.

70. Father Orszulik, spokesman for the episcopate, had declared that KOR "increases social tensions and angers Poland's neighbors," according to *Der Spiegel.* According to Michnik he represents only part of the episcopate (cf. "Die letzte Chance," p. 63).

71. These three are presented by Michnik in "Ce que nous voulons," which indeed reveals a more critical attitude than his book on the same subject. Between them L. Kołakowski and Jan Gros represent the three alternatives in their juxtaposed essays, "Church and Democracy in Poland: Two Views," op. cit.

72. For some of this record: Hans-Hermann Hücking and Marek Tadeusz Swiecicki, "Die laizistische Linke—ein Verbündeter für die Kirche?" in "Polen 1980," *Sozialistisches Osteuropakomitee* (Hannover, 1981), pp. 81–84.

73. Though Michnik (*L'église et la gauche*, pp. 114ff.) is my source for this point, it seems to me that even he does not always pay sufficient attention to the argument he reproduces from Cywiński's *Généalogies des insoumis*, perhaps for tactical reasons.

74. T. Mazowiecki, "Les Tâches de Solidarité," *L'Alternative*, January–February, 1981).

75. To be sure, the opposition suggests that a full democratization of society in the spirit of August 31 could yield the relevant credibility for the regime in order to attempt economic reform. "Only" this solution is the greatest threat, as I have tried to show, to the organizational principle of the system, implying "dual power" at least. Only under constraint and if the regime had no better alternatives will the suggestion be accepted.

76. Cf. Zazlavsky, "Why Afghanistan?" *Telos* (Spring 1980), Castoriadis, "Facing the War," *Telos* (Winter 1980–81), as well as Arato, op. cit.

77. Cf. Renate Damus, op. cit.

78. There seem to be at least four proposals around, of which three coming from government related agencies are close to the market socialist *cum* worker's control formula of the 1960s of Brus, e.g., while the other proposed to *Solidarność* focuses on the fundamental shift of priorities to consumption in general and agriculture in particular. There also seems to be the expected difference between the two types of proposals on the level of who is to formulate reform proposals as such: on the level of who is to formulate reform proposals as such: the government (and Sejm) or the union and its experts along with the government. Cf. "Vorschläge für eine neue Wirtschaftspolitik" in "Polen 1980," pp. 63ff. As far as I can tell the major difference of content among the proposals is timing; Solidarity seems to want the whole package including worker's control from the beginning to avoid the bitter experience of post-1956 and post-1971 reform proposals.

79. But perhaps there will be such proposals at the coming extraordinary congress of the PUWP which, however, is still being delayed, apparently because of a fear of rank-and-file demands of vast democratization of the party.

80. These involve in general various degrees of oscillation between decentralization and recentralization, and in particular the constant shifting of the negative consequences

for social consumption and productive "consumption" from industry to industry, branch to branch, region to region, stratum to stratum (the Soviet Union, whereby only the "military subsociety," as Castoriadis argued, is consistently favored), the implicit but heavy reliance on a second economy (Hungary) and various types of massive dependence of Western credit and trade advantages (Poland and the GDR).

81. Arato, op. cit.

82. Cf. Wlodzimierz Brus, *The Economics and Politics of Socialism* (London, 1973), for some of the best summaries.

83. Marc Rakovski, *Towards an East European Marxism* (London, 1978).

84. This is the thrust of Rakovski's critique of market socialism, as well as of my thesis in the already cited article. One must immediately say, however, that from a normative point of view the crisis management of the present system in Poland (one based on dual power) is a different thing altogether from that of systems unaltered by reform from below.

85. Cf. Brus, op. cit., pp. 35ff, for example.

86. "Socialist Opposition in Eastern Europe: Dilemmas and Prospects," in *Opposition in Eastern Europe*, pp. 200ff.

87. For a different formulation of the problem which stresses socialism as self-managing society (what I called radical democracy), cf. the brilliant article of Fehér, "Eastern Europe in the 80s," *Telos* (Fall, 1980), p. 17. I am in full agreement with what is said here, but I wonder if socialism, however redefined, must not also mean the protection of at least some sphere of life (nature, health, perhaps habitat) through macroplanning. This, however, is a spontaneous result of no radical democracy in the cells of society which must, rightly, represent particular sectoral interests. Hence the role of planning supervised by parliamentary compromise in achieving the universal dimensions of socialism in what could be future democratic socialist systems, hence the legitimate role of the surviving elements of the *Planstaat* under the next, more democratic stage (Konrád) of state socialism that is emerging in Poland.

88. Szelényi, "Social Inequalities in State Socialist Redistributive Economies," *International Journal of Comparative Sociology* (Spring–Summer 1978).

89. For any sensible policy to emerge, leading forces of the party must very soon realize that the provocations of some of the apparatus and the security forces are threatening national disaster. It may be that the leadership fears a potentially democratizing movement at the coming extraordinary congress of the party rank-and-file far more than its conservative elements. Paradoxically, the opposition may be best off with a fundamentally unchanged party that however fully honors the Gdansk accords. Is this a contradiction in terms?

9

Empire vs. Civil Society: Poland 1981–82

Western Critics of the Polish Opposition

Support for the Polish democratic movement should have been easy for all those supposedly opposed to the totalitarian status quo in Eastern Europe. All Marxists should have been convinced by the overwhelming working-class character of the Polish opposition (one of the rare proletarian revolutions in history). Remnants of the libertarian New Left should have seen its stress on an alternative public sphere and on direct democracy as one of the few authentic continuations of their own efforts. New Western social movements should have been very sympathetic to the rebuilding of whole domains of autonomy and the democratic utilization of counterexpertise.[1] Unfortunately, such has not been the case.

Sustained response by all these tendencies after December 13 could have made some difference in Poland—especially if it called for political and economic sanctions by Western governments as requested by every important member of Solidarity in the West (and now by Bujak, the organization's senior underground leader). How much of a difference it would have made is difficult to say because, with the exception of France and Italy, public response has been relatively negligible. Most European governments have limited themselves to anything from moral outrage (France) to a slightly veiled apology for the lesser of two supposed evils (West Germany). In particular, the peace movement that a few months earlier was able to mobilize hundreds of thousands of people in several countries, managed to respond to the Polish military *coup* with little more than confusion and equivocation.[2] The remarkable convergence of the attitude of the most extensive social movement in Western Europe with what is assumed (in part mistakenly) to be the short- and long-term interests of European banking

Reprinted with permission from *Telos* 50 (Winter 1981–82): 19–48. © Telos Press.

and industrial interests sealed the fate of a serious European response without which limited American economic sanctions cannot have much force.

Without overestimating the strength of various Left groups and social movements, the point is clear: The East European opposition can count on Left opinion only in those few European countries where, for important political and intellectual reasons, mass socialist and/or communist parties had to totally distance themselves from the Soviet model. This situation is all the more disastrous because the fate of Western Europe also hangs in the balance.

The positions of many spokesmen for a peace opinion in particular converge with the logic of the Polish repression. Accordingly, what was wrong with the Polish opposition, what provoked its suppression, and what cancels the solidarity of many Western political activists with Solidarity is supposedly the fact that, given geography and the realities of communist power (thus both the interests of the internal peace of Poland and external peace), *Solidarity went too far*. Had the organization followed "a reasonable middle course,"[3] had it been "willing to pause as recently as a month or two ago—to rest a while on its laurels and to give time for Moscow to satisfy itself that freedom in Poland did not mean the immediate collapse of the heavens—it would already have had to its credit a historic achievement. . . . But this of course was not the road that Solidarity, or part of Solidarity, took."[4]

What would *not* have been *too far*? Today's Polish regime, or rather its so-called reformers, have a simple answer: Solidarity should have remained a trade union and stayed out of politics altogether, as Western unions do.[5] Those in the West who accept this account should realize what everyone in Poland knows, that under political, legal, and cultural conditions of an unreformed Soviet-type society, this approach would have meant co-option, integration, and assimilation. Many Western Marxists have criticized the Polish opposition precisely on the basis of such a potential outcome. For them, *Solidarity did not go far enough*. To their credit, these sectarians (whose political weight is, of course, insignificant) support Solidarity in its defeat. Unfortunately, this support is always followed by an irrelevant "I told you so," which, although made plausible now by the movement's defeat, loses sight of some of Solidarity's greatest achievements. If the Polish opposition must be defended in the face of the distanced attitude of pacifists, social democrats and left liberals, their achievements must similarly be rescued from the sectarian Left's "critical support."

This "critical support" was already formulated when Solidarity was still thriving—hence the unabashed "told you so" today. Predictably, orthodox Marxists supported the movement's working class character, but found its Catholicism, nationalism, civil libertarianism, and interest in political democracy incompatible with inherited dogma. The last two sins at least, and again predictably, were blamed on the intellectuals' association with the movement—especially the KOR representatives. These intellectuals committed a great offense: They did not have the same theoretical assessment of the situation and the same model of social emancipation as the sectarian Left. Of course, the attack on intellectuals, with its not-so-hidden ouvrierist demagogy, corresponds to the regime's own attack on the same intellectuals dubbed variously as "antisocialist elements" and "Zionists," with one important difference: The Western sectarians argue that it was because of intellectuals that the movement did not go far enough.[6]

What would have been *far enough*? According to Ticktin, the Polish movement has more or less become the vehicle for the intellectual's interests whose model of a liberal, parliamentary system based on the restoration of market rationality could be established in Poland only against the resistance, and at the very least the working class's interests. While Ticktin does not do justice to the democratic opposition's programs (there were several), he shares, at least, one important feature with the regime and the Soviet leadership for opposing democratization: the fear that it might work. He is right in noting KOR's unwillingness to risk "Poland as . . . the sacrificial lamb of world socialism" (this was part of the organization's very principles). He does not share this reservation. After noting the impossibility of "socialism in one Poland" and the certainty of Russian intervention if the working class moved directly to take state power, he reminds Polish workers "that their struggle is not national, i.e., not specifically Polish, nor religious but part of an international movement of the working class in which their only real success could be in establishing workers' power for however short a time before it is crushed."[7] Here orthodox Marxism reveals itself for what it probably always was: rather than a theory *of* workers' emancipation, a program for disaster.

Under the impact of recent events, the argument has been further refined. Stressing the impossibility of structural reforms in Eastern Europe under the conditions of an intact totalitarian state rather than their undesirability, the sectarian Left today seems to argue that the December 13 tragedy could have been avoided after all by a Polish workers' attempt to take state power. Had they been as honest as Ticktin, they would also have admitted that their antidote to one disaster would have involved the probability of an even greater one.

Indeed, the two arguments that Solidarity "went too far" and that it did not "go far enough" are both right against each other, and complementary. What is not "too far" for the first interpretation is co-option or eventual repression from the viewpoint of the second. And what is "far enough" for the second interpretation is a formula for disastrous Soviet intervention from the viewpoint of the first. Together, they reinforce a fatalistic view: Despite all valiant efforts to the contrary, in Poland and in Eastern Europe no significant transformation is possible.[8] To reject both arguments is *not* to endorse uncritically Solidarity's course. What is needed is an evaluation of the hitherto unparalleled achievement of a democratic movement in Eastern Europe, along with an analysis of its defeat, hoping thereby to isolate the history of Solidarity's contribution to future struggles for emancipation in Poland and elsewhere.

The Democratic Movement's Achievement

Sixteen months of detotalization of a totalitarian system[9] by a highly disciplined and self-restrained movement affecting almost every aspect of society is a remarkable and unprecedented achievement. In the process, a path for the social transformation of East European societies was invented. Remarkably enough, it attempted to be *more compatible* with the preservation of the identity of a Soviet-type society (and therefore with the rationally understood interests of the Soviet Union) *and richer in forms of democratic experimentation* than its historical forerunners: 1956 and 1968. Were it not for economic disaster that was more one of its causes than its effect, the Polish sixteen months would have put an end to the myth that Kádár's "liberal absolutism" is the highest stage of development for East European societies today.[10]

Similarly, the achievement of the Polish democratic movement reaches beyond its East European context. While Polish society liberated itself from a form of state organization obsolete from a Western viewpoint,[11] in the process civil society began to reinvent itself in forms that point beyond the institutionalization of civil society in the West—forms extremely relevant for the democratization of Western social life.

Of course, it is hazardous to consider forms of Polish civil society as a model, for they were limited in the generation of a Western-type parliamentary state by the threat of Russian intervention. Indeed, efforts not to seek state power but only some freedom from and control over this power was largely a function of historical constraints and only partly the participants' principled and conscious choice. The Polish opposition was thus forced into a program theoretically articulated in the West by people such as Gorz and Touraine: the self-organization of society. In Poland, neither a nonexistent independent economy nor the state could generate social independence. Civil society, organized as social movements, had to undertake the task within limits that made self-organization an end in itself. Thus, the paradoxical result: A social movement seeking only to instruct itself, and avoiding all theoretical articulations of its project, managed to contribute important clues concerning a democratic and socialist civil society based on solidarity, plurality, communication free of domination, and democratic participation.

The emergence of a new type of civil society in Poland in the last year and a half was characterized by several institutional innovations. In *legality* the movement's stress was on political freedoms of assembly, association (independent union), collective action (right to strike), and freedoms of press and of speech. Individual rights and freedoms were seen as necessary presuppositions of collective rights rather than, as in the West, being tied to private property. Instead of expressing "the mute identity of interests among competing individuals" the Polish workers' and intellectuals' legal demands aimed at a civil society based on "voluntary solidarity within and among the various particularistic interest groups."[12] This is important because it points to another dimension of civil

society: *plurality.* The Polish democratic opposition abandoned the Jacobin suspicion of the organization of particular interests. While the industrial working
class alone had sufficient power to pressure the regime, no one postulated its
interests as universal or the desirability of establishing a pure working class form
of rule. These myths were left to the ruling party—though for a decade or so it
has also substituted national for Marxist legitimacy claims. Instead of claiming to
represent society, the workers' organization played a major role in helping organize
other strata such as peasants and students. There was no substitutionism: Intellectuals
could either work with Solidarity or form their own organizations.

The pluralism that emerged differed significantly from the liberal model of
voluntary associations. The major new organizations were movements organized
as democratically as possible and in fundamental solidarity with each other, in
spite of differing interests. Unlike voluntary associations, social movements do
not operate within established institutional patterns, but challenge their very
interpretation.[13] Within its own sphere, each social movement in Poland challenged the meaning of the new institutional situation resulting from the historical
achievement of the summer of 1980. Organized as social movements, pluralism
generates not only a new solidarity but also contributes to the emergence of a
new public sphere.

Even before August 31, 1980, the alternative literary *public sphere* created by
the opposition had a new structure. The world of the *samizdat,* which came to
involve the immense majority of the population, replaced commercial and propagandistic cultural goals with self-education. Market exchange and central redistribution in culture were replaced by comprehensive reciprocity.[14] While this
state of affairs could not have survived in its original form after the post–August
31 stabilization, its democratizing impetus was incorporated in the new diversity
of publics that emerged. As in all East European societies, the official public
sphere in Poland has had primarily demonstrative and substitutionist functions:
The power of the party-state is demonstrated through the open control of symbolic life and *the occupation* of all the key channels where socially significant
information about society is produced and disseminated. The strictest secrecy
and censorship surrounded all decisions and compromises—including those with
the church and with some intellectuals' and workers' groups during the Gierek
period.[15]

Point 3 of the Gdansk "21 points" squarely called for respect for constitutional freedoms of speech and of the press by guaranteed access to official media
and full toleration of unofficial publications. Eventually, there *was* a partial
liberalization of the official press and a demonstrative, if only selective and
lamely manipulative, attempt by government and party organs to publicize their
own procedures. More importantly, in Poland, the conflict between manipulative
and critical public opinion became a far more balanced one than in any other
industrial society. Above all, the opposition's principle of a democratic sphere
aiming at self-educating and based on reciprocity was applied to the very organi-

zations of the opposition: The demands for public openness were extended from state organs to all organizations carrying on significant activities vis-à-vis the state.[16] During the sixteen months there was an effective opposition not against compromises as such, but against secret ones unsupervised by public opinion. The journals and pamphlets of the *samizdat* period changed from being exclusively an alternative means of information into supervising and thereby democratizing the new social movements. Thus, in Poland the public sphere was restored not as the media for individual intercourse (the liberal model) but as the media for organized groups able to pressure both the state and their own organizations.

Democratic participation, however, was not limited to the new public sphere, or even to the internal rules and procedures of the new organizations. Polish workers learned quickly to substitute demands for democratic participation for purely economic demands that could not be satisfied under conditions of near economic collapse. Solidarity itself could emerge only as a result of such a substitution. Furthermore, all sides realized that the reconstruction of the Polish economy required a long period of austerity. From the workers' viewpoint the trade-off could only be further democratization. The whole discussion of economic reform between government and Solidarity experts reflected this situation. All seemed to agree that some version of workers' self-management and some form of democratic control-mechanism over global plans would have to be parts of the urgently needed comprehensive economic reforms. On the technical economic level, discussions concerning planning,[17] market, and self-management merely continued earlier East European discussions and experiments. But, politically, reformers on both sides assumed that the Polish solution would go beyond every hitherto completed reform of state socialist economies. Government-oriented reformers saw this in limited terms; any form of self-management would go far beyond the Hungarian model, the continuation of global planning beyond the Yugoslav one. The democratic opposition saw the gains as more dramatic because of one crucial fact: the existence of the independent, self-managed union. Thus, both workers' control and planning could take on new forms. Against the Yugoslav version of a manipulated self-management with uninformed workers facing local directors and a disorganized working class confronted with top-down party decisions, Solidarity was in a position to contribute to workers' self-determination in the factories and to mediate their participation in national planning.[18]

Solidarity, plurality, public opinion, and participation: These are the Polish movement's accomplishments. But, in defeat, the very achievements of a revolution become ambiguous; they can be regarded either as signs of what could have been or as causes of the negative outcome. The objection that under the given historical conditions Poland could yield no clues toward a new type of civil society can thus be replaced by a new one: To the extent that such clues did emerge, they could only indicate that the whole enterprise was impossible. In other words, these very achievements could only exacerbate the *steering* problems of the resulting new version of authoritarian state socialism. The objection here is inevitable: Such a dualistic arrangement in which civil society renounces creating a state adequate to it in return for social independence and some control over existing state power is inherently unstable and must lead to either society or state moving to abolish the other's institutions.[19] Thus, the Polish revolution's normative gains, that is, an independent civil society, could not be stabilized under Polish conditions.[20] Could the outcome have been avoided? Even in the affirmative case, it is unclear whether some of the movement's very achievements were not in the way of such a stabilization.

Two Conditions for Compromise

Leaving aside the hidden project of the Soviet leadership and of hard-liners in the party, state security and military bureaucracies, the duality of powers that developed after August 31, 1980, could in principle have been institutionalized. Two conditions, however, were necessary: the development of entirely new institutions mediating society's and the state's interests; and new structures of socioeconomic steering through comprehensive economic reforms. Neither of these had to involve totally unprecedented innovations. There had been recent trends in post-1968 crisis management in some countries, including Poland, toward state corporatist forms of compromise with some selected social groups and organizations.[21] In Poland, the generalization of such a solution to the Church, the unions, and perhaps key sectors of the intellectuals has, since August 1980, been the best hope of some so-called party reformers to contain the current crisis and to integrate its undesirable results without Soviet intervention. To the extent that this solution left no room for social independence and an authentic public sphere, it was always unacceptable to Solidarity, whose own projects for compromise included various forms of corporatism, pluralism, and syndicalist versions of direct democracy. Something important was at stake here: the authoritarian state socialist organization principle (even if in a posttotalitarian form) on one side,[22] and the newly conquered social independence on the other. Nevertheless, during 1981, a compromise formula on how to compromise evolved in large-scale public discussion. It involved: (1) state corporatism in the state-administrative sector, including elements of the party, the army, the Church, and Solidarity in a government of national salvation constructed similarly to the existing one; (2) Social corporatism in the sense of the two or three independent organizations of society, Church, and Solidarity (perhaps also Rural Solidarity), negotiating with the ruling party in the name of society as a whole within the context of a partially independent public sphere;[23] (3) The coexistence of a heterogeneity of the internal organization of group life; monistic (the Communist Party), old or new corporatist (the army, the Church); representative democratic or "pluralistic" (Solidarity, Rural Solidarity) and syndicalist (factory councils and cooperatives).

Such a system of social compromise represented only the basis of a possible consensus in Polish society and it was neither institutionalized nor unopposed. By not representing the real aims of either side, the whole package would have made and already made both sides dissatisfied. But it was the only basis on which the existing party-state could have attained the long-term stability of a system still continuous with the existing one, and the social movement could have preserved some of its achievements.

In the case of economic reforms, the consensus was far more impressive: what opposition *did* exist was far less open. The disastrous state of the Polish economy, unprecedented in the history of state socialist societies, was the background of an almost general expectation that this time, as against all other false starts, a radical, structural reform would have to take place.[24] The outcome of Gierek's economic strategy and crisis management had discredited, even within the ruling party, those who had resisted even hesitant past reform attempts. Solidarity remained committed to economic reforms even if for a period it rejected formal participation in developing reform proposals. In line with its early self-image as a nonpolitical trade union, the new organization did not want to be identified with programs of austerity necessitated by the regime's earlier failures. But it was always demanded that, as soon as possible, the regime had to present society with proposals for reforms. Furthermore, Solidarity experts informally participated in the work of several commissions and some Solidarity economists quickly realized that without their pressures reform would not come about.[25]

Altogether, seven different projects of economic reforms came into existence in sixteen months.[26] These programs were developed by very different groups of economists associated with various governmental commissions and some near Solidarity. Their remarkable feature was their overall compatibility. In fact, the later draft of the government's official program also reflected suggestions contained in proposals related to Solidarity. The overall trend of the proposals was not new. The main ideas went back to earlier models by Lange, Kalecki, and especially Brus. Nevertheless, all reform drafts aimed at an economic structure combining a new system of planning concerned only with long-term macroeconomic trends and using as its instruments only indirect forms of regulation (tax, credit, currency and, for a period, pricing) with a system of decentralized microeconomic management involving rational accounting based on "income" or "profit" and eventually market-oriented mechanisms of pricing and workers' control. Furthermore, all proposals involved roughly the same reorientation of investment priorities. They reflected simultaneously the interests of consumption and of greater economic returns—which in state socialist societies are nearly the same thing and both suffer at the same time.

While the various proposals involved few differences in the mechanism and growth priorities, crucial disagreements emerged in timing and political implications. The government preferred the introduction of reforms in stages that were reduced from three to two. The first of these, the so-called "little reform" (supposedly instituted January 1, 1981, but without any effect) was to confine itself to the "decentralization of difficulties" desired by central authorities and to a partial reorientation of investment priorities that were not touched in 1980, despite signs of impending collapse in the consumer goods market.[27] The existing state of the economy was the apparent justification for not introducing more radical measures, the "great reform," until later. In particular, a market determination of prices was judged unsuitable during a period characterized by dramatic shortages. Whatever the merits of this argument, the economic situation certainly deteriorated because of the failure to implement the "great reform." The argument of those who demanded immediate implementation was based not so much on this sad reality, as on the Polish experiences in the 1950s, 1960s and early 1970s with reforms that involved a similar incrementalism and allowed the mobilization of the opponents of reforms when the hesitant moves already implemented could not yet bring benefits.[28] Thus, the slightly more radical aspects were scrapped even before implementation.

The crucial political difference among the proposals involved the meaning of workers' control. Once Solidarity became actively interested in self-management,[29] the version the workers' movement sponsored was clearly in conflict with the nomenklatura system of top-down party appointments that the government drafts tried to preserve.[30] Remarkably enough, the compromise eventually worked out, while not pleasing either side,[31] would have gone a long way in giving workers control over the appointment of most directors.

Despite such a high consensus concerning economic reforms, there were weighty structural reasons inhibiting their realization. Economic reforms of authoritarian state socialist systems are in principle possible only if they do not challenge this system's organizational principle. In Poland, such a development was difficult, not only because of the raging economic crisis as a result of drastic shortages of investment funds (without which decentralization could hardly work better than the original system), but also because of three serious political problems: (1) Given the *de facto* duality of power, an institutional mechanism involving at the very least the communist party, Solidarity and Rural Solidarity was required to institute the reforms (or at least to gain through bargaining the consent of the two major social organizations) and to supervise its implementation. Although proposed by Solidarity under the heading of a national council of the economy, such an institutional mechanism was never established. (2) Given the *de facto* withdrawal of the ruling party from social organizations and, to an important extent, from culture (not including the electronic media), a large-scale withdrawal from economic management would have deprived the party of most of its remaining functions. This could exacerbate the party's already serious identity crisis and threaten the employment of large sections of its apparatus. While the middle apparatus would be against reform in any case, the reformist section of the leadership might continue to dream of reforms *à la Hongroise*: reforms in the context of having regained the lost social and cultural ground, that is, reforms without Solidarity.[32] (3) Given the unavoidable consequences of any reform of the Polish economy (inflation, austerity, unemployment as well as the possibility of new inequalities among industrial branches, regions and professions), it was more difficult to obtain the same overall consensus in Solidarity on the issue of economic reforms than on many others. While committed to reforms, for a while the organization unfortunately did not pursue them relentlessly enough (at least until the economic situation really got out of hand). After all, a trade union can sponsor unemployment and inflation only at the cost of its own identity crisis.

Yet, without reforms, the economic situation remained hopeless—all the more so, because with the existence of the independent union, a centrally managed and planned system could not function at all. If reforms were impossible, it was similarly impossible not to reform as long as society remained organized. But for reforms to become truly possible an institutional system of compromise had to be established. Everything depended on this. It was on this level that the regime's ultimate intentions regarding large-scale economic reforms became eventually clear.

The Fate of Compromise and Reform

Ultra-left critics of Solidarity as well as believers in the totalitarianism thesis generally claim that it was always unrealistic to postulate the possibility of compromises with the Polish regime. Aside from the fatalistic character of such an approach, a whole series of important compromises were actually reached. The government did enter into key agreements with organized workers, from the original August 1980 accords to compromises on the length of the work week, the creation of Rural Solidarity, and the definition of the role of workers' councils. The problem with these agreements was not that each side later sought to interpret them from its own viewpoint. This is the case with any agreement between antagonists with different interpretations of their common social framework. The real problem was the failure of all compromise over the question of institutionalizing compromise itself.

As already indicated, there was no shortage of suggestions on both sides concerning such institutions. The best known proposals were the ones for the council of the economy and a government of national salvation—both involving broad social participation, one pluralistic, the other corporatistic in structure. Until the very end, however, actual negotiations seemed to avoid the topic altogether. Their pattern became rather simple. Under extreme pressure and the threat of disaster, a few *Solidarity* leaders and a few experts in closed meetings repeatedly managed to get government negotiators' agreement (or vice versa) to compromise formulations that in all major instances managed to please neither side. Such agreements were immediately followed by charges of weakness on the part of party conservatives and undemocratic procedures by important groups in Solidarity. The second charge was technically right but missed the real problem. Under the existing extraordinary conditions, it was inevitable that Solidarity in some respects duplicated its antagonists' practices: without general legal regulation of conflict and compromise, a fully democratic participation of all levels of the organization was impossible and undesirable. Negotiating power had to be and was delegated to Wałesa and his circle. What could have been attempted and was not was to place questions of procedures, democratic or not, in the forefront of demands. More important than the democratization of the union's own practice would have been the creation of some legally sanctioned institutions in which the representatives of society and the state could have negotiated on an ongoing basis and not just in emergency situations. It may be doubtful whether the regime would have conceded any such demands. Yet, at its greatest strength, Solidarity did not push for such a solution. Only when the regime began its final push toward a repressive solution did such demands become central.

Solidarity's September congress expressed (and did not cause) a very high degree of polarization between state and society. It was in this context that various groups came forward with the idea of a government or front of national salvation whose main elements would be the Communist party, the Catholic Church, and Solidarity. Leaders of the collaborationist Catholic PAX and the official peasant party, but also of the reform communist DIP (Experience and Future) were among the sponsors. But so was the hard-line Politburo member Olszowski. Among important Solidarity leaders, Kuroń, now the key adviser to Wałesa, strongly defended this position as the last way out of the crisis. He saw the compromise over workers' control and a government or front of national salvation as complementary parts of the best institutional solution under difficult circumstances. Jaruzelski discussed such a plan with Wałesa and Archbishop Glemp on November 4, and the issue came up again during formal government-union talks November 17. But nothing came of it. Probably the opposition of the Moscow-supported party apparatus was strong and Jaruzelski, already in the process of completing preparations for the coup, most likely offered Solidarity only an unacceptable junior partnership in a coalition of five of six members—thus as part of the potential blame for actions which others would formulate. In any case, the Politburo did apparently approve *some* version of the plan on November 10, 1981. Significantly enough, however, the opposition to such a plan, in any version, was apparently strongest in Solidarity itself. Even Kuroń's proposal was seen as becoming involved in a moral swamp and as potentially discrediting Solidarity in the population's eyes.[33] According to the arguments, Solidarity could enter government only if the totalitarian structure was smashed (Rulewski) or gradually replaced by an alternative based on self-management (Modzelewski).

Such long-range projects had nothing to do with solving the current economic crisis. In this context, Solidarity chose to concentrate on one substantive issue (workers' self-management) and one institutional proposal (a pluralistic national economic council). For once, a substantive demand was linked to a key institutional innovation of far broader implications. Both aspects were linked to the discussion of economic reforms in Parliament. Without a significant self-management component, the union could not agree to the necessary sacrifices involved in the government's reforms, and without a national economic council there was absolutely no confidence that after a year of delays, major reforms would actually be instituted. After all, some government spokesmen (Szeliga) even admitted that the so-called "little reform," technically in effect since January 1981, had achieved little because of the resistance of the apparatus and of a significant part of the managerial elite. It was in this context that the last compromise between the regime and Solidarity emerged—one that followed the earlier pattern. While the agreement on workers' control and thus the whole reform package involved significant concessions to Solidarity, on the institutional question the government absolutely could not be moved. But now it was crystal clear to the union that within such a context the substantive concession itself meant nothing. Self-management without economic reforms was meaningless, and the fate of economic reforms without the institutionalization of the participation of the social forces behind it was highly uncertain. As a result, Solidarity had little to offer its rank and file already devastated by the economic crisis. "Moderates" such as Wałesa and Kuroń could not answer "radicals" who saw no alternative to polarization and confrontation. After concluding a series of compromises that, however, did not involve any compromises concerning institutions of compromise, Solidarity faced two potential disasters: the possibility of an uncontrolled uprising on the part of the population, and an attempt by the government to repress by force all independent social organizations. A very real fear of the first of these, all the more plausible because of internal tensions and possible splits in Solidarity itself, made the organization powerless in the face of the second, toward which party policy after July unfailingly aimed.

Crisis and Strategy of the Regime

Failure to institutionalize compromise and economic reforms, though not stage-managed by major social agents, had something to do with definite strategies. While Solidarity did not always pursue these objectives with sufficient determination, was lukewarm concerning a new type of government coalition, and in September even threatened to boycott economic reforms, unless they included an acceptable formula for self-management, reforms and compromise corresponded to the most fundamental interest of the organization and its members—and this was expressed in the policies of its national commission. The same cannot be said about the party-state. There is little doubt that the party membership did not represent a separate constellation of interests in Polish society. But with the exception of a short and turbulent period before the party congress, this membership that supported democratic "horizontal links" within the party counted for little. The apparatus, that is, all those who owed their position to the nomenklatura system, as well as the hierarchies of the state security organs, were resolutely for the preservation of the old system—hence against reform and compromise. These were the ones that supported reactionary forums and chauvinistic associations in the party. While there were hardly any "liberals" in the top leadership, for a period a pragmatic reformist faction amply balanced the hard-liners and the weak centrists. This overall picture, however, does not explain the outcome, and in particular the shift from the generally reformist attitude of the first few months to a strategy aiming to split, demoralize, and destroy Solidarity. Today, the party blames Solidarity's radicalism for this shift. This, however, confuses cause and effect.

The existence of an organized society in general and an independent organization of industrial workers in particular created fundamental identity problems for the party. It was not so much the destruction of its claims to represent society and the working class that was difficult, but the loss of the immense number of organizational, control, and cultural functions involved. The party could protect itself in the midst of crisis by a partial withdrawal from the various social spheres and by divesting itself of its polymorphic character (Staniszkis). But to preserve its identity it had to find a new suitable sphere of operation: new roles and functions. According to Smolar,[34] in the new framework three clear-cut possibilities were open to the ruling party: (1) to become the mass party of the rulers and managers and to be forced into opposition; (2) to become fully democratic and to incorporate social plurality as its factions and tendencies; or (3) to remain Leninist internally but accept purely ceremonial functions in society, that is, a kind of self-neutralization. None of these possibilities were acceptable to the apparatus and to the leadership—not to speak of the Soviet Union. For all three it was necessary that in some way the old identity of the party be preserved: thus, the meaning of the "leading role" formula. The party could either successfully stabilize something like its old role in a reduced but real sphere of operation, or it would have to destroy Solidarity and with it, the new situation causing its identity crisis. But both these roads could also mean the party's destruction. Evidently, the party leadership first chose the first alternative, exposing itself to the membership's democratizing spirit and to the machinations of the apparatus and security forces, and settled on the second only after its July congress.

The first strategy was already full of ambiguities. It is implausible to argue, with Staniszkis, that the party-state regime as a whole sought a new kind of legitimacy based on a "social contract." But she is right in that there was a new division of labor between party and government, with the latter pursuing the policy of dialogue and the former, in accordance with Soviet wishes, creating minor roadblocks (e.g., conflict over registration of Solidarity). In such a situation, and with the *de facto* loss of party supervision over industry as well as social life and culture, the party's role became a negative one. In this sense it is wrong to describe its unwillingness to initiate policy and its sluggishness to enter into and execute agreements, as "tactical errors."[35] Without such a course of action, the party would have lost its last possible role. Nevertheless, in the new division of labor, the government seemed to dominate—thus both lending some of the aura of renewal to the top interlocking party leadership and making the leading role formula questionable even in its last possible sphere of operation, that of the state itself. This leading role was now reduced to a veto power, and even that, apparently, could be overruled.

Such a paradoxical outcome exposed the top leadership to a double attack. On the one hand, the apparatus and the security forces were mobilized with Soviet support, against a policy of weakness and retreat. Their activities turned into reactionary, ideologically oriented propaganda (the Katowice forum), attacks against opposition groups working with Solidarity—especially KOR—an attempt to use anti-Semitic campaigns against key figures of the democratic movement and, when all this failed, open police provocation against Solidarity culminating in the Bydgoszcz crisis. On the other hand, there was an open attempt on the part of rank-and-file organizations, the "horizontal links" movement, to force a democratization of the party in general and the party congress in particular. After successfully repulsing an internal challenge in the highest levels, it could only deal with the overall situation that threatened the party with disintegration by making important concessions to each side. This was revealed by the masterful orchestration of the party congress. Kania's group showed that it could manipulate formal democracy just as skillfully as the leaders of Western mass parties. (Of course, having a dossier on all delegates certainly helped Kania, the ex-security chief.) The resulting election of a new Central Committee and political bureau strengthened Kania's group, although key conservative and reform figures were included. More important was the fact that the bulk of those elected were new in politics and easily manipulated. They gave their greatest applause to a supposed reformer (Rakowski), but barely elected him to the Central Committee, and not to the Politburo.

The real victor in the party congress was the apparatus. From then on, the leadership adopted *their* "policy" of no retreat. To be sure, the partisans of horizontal links did not disappear, and the membership was not converted to the new line. But without a congress to prepare for, rank-and-file groups had no institutional means in the party to contribute to policy. While neither the membership or Polish society were fooled by the congress' "democratic" results (if the party managed to relegitimate itself anywhere, it was in the Western press), it was not immediately clear even to the opposition that the reunification of the leadership and the apparatus (in a context when they no longer had to fear the membership) allowed the party as a whole to develop a unified strategy.[36]

This strategy, which also meant the reestablishment of the party's full hegemony over the government, was neither new nor positive. It became clear rather early that the Soviet Union's attitude toward the new situation in Poland would be one of neither war nor peace, since, unwilling to face the disastrous consequences of an invasion, the Russians preferred crisis and decomposition to the stabilization of an undesirable social model.[37] The attitude of important parts of the party apparatus toward their own society was probably similar. There was an unmistakable desire to tire and discipline the population through a crisis that is not allowed to be solved. The party congress that formulated positive tasks only for the government but not for the party as such opened the way to a consistent pursuit of this same negative strategy. From this point on, leaders like Rakowski, earlier identified with reform and dialogue, came to ominously shift their emphasis to confrontation and irresolvable conflict.[38] As a result, in the midst of an economic crisis totally out of control, a dreaded polarization occurred that deprived the population of any real hope of solving the crisis through reform and compromise.

While some already predicted that the army-state would replace the party-state after Jaruzelski became the party first secretary,[39] the military commissions' missions to the countryside were only tests of things to come. Governmental structures, in particular the Parliament, continued some of the earlier work toward reform and compromise, if in a very subordinate capacity—except for the important compromise on workers' control where it passed a version of the bill that, unlike the party's draft, could be accepted by Solidarity. It was the party, in the face of possible parliamentary resistance, that threatened a state of emergency and demanded the suspension of the right to strike. Jaruzelski himself represented the party's new line. This negative line, however, which provided functions only for the security and propaganda apparatuses, also brought a massive alienation of the membership, and exacerbated the identity crisis of the organization as a whole. It is clear that the apparatus and now the leadership's only response to this untenable situation was to press for a repressive solution for which the party itself had neither the organizational means nor even the minimum loyalty required.

Solidarity as a Social Movement

As a social movement, Solidarity developed under a double impact; its own immense success in organizing Polish society and the increasingly negative Communist Party strategy in blocking economic, legal, and political reforms. There are two suggestive ways of looking at the resulting contradictions in Solidarity. With Nuti, one can see Solidarity as alternating from the beginning among three different and even incompatible roles: an oppositional political party effective in extorting concessions; a Western-type trade-union whose demands are incompatible with the priorities of economic recovery; and a "socialist-type union demanding responsible partnership in economic management." Although it is well informed, this scheme comes dangerously close to the position of some Communist party reformers, who condemned what they took to be the first two of these roles, and defined union responsibility primarily through the need to discipline a supposedly unproductive work force. To be sure, Nuti defines responsible participation in terms of a trade-off between austerity, inflation, and workers' control, but he misses the obvious point that such a deal was possible only on the basis of immense political pressure, and that before reforms were instituted, Solidarity could not act "responsible" under institutions that were yet to be created. And while he sees the need for Solidarity under the threat of suppression and absorption, to shift and alternate among its various roles, he does not realize that there was also a trend from emphasis on the one he takes to be that of a union to the other he takes to be that of a political party.

Such a development is stressed by Staniszkis. In her more abstract and more adequate scheme, Solidarity moved from a stage of "self-limiting revolution" characterized by "too tight" a trade union formula (September 1980–March 1981) to a period of identity crisis involving the growth of its veto power over policy and the movement's partial implosion (up to July 1981) and finally to a stage of "open conspiracy" characterized by the "social movement formula" masking a contradiction between the activities of a mass movement and those of a "political party of activists." Here the difficulty is the opposite of Nuti's. The synchronic, rather than the diachronic, dimension is deemphasized. While always too tight, the trade-union formula was never entirely abandoned (in particular by Wałesa). The whole history of Solidarity was characterized by some identity crisis (a union without a legal sphere of operation, a revolutionary movement without a revolution); and the formulas of self-limitation and social movement apply and were applied to all stages of development. While those elements seeking to transform Solidarity into a party contesting political power became organizationally strong only in the last stage—the KPN (Confederation for an Independent Poland)—they were opposed by a contrary position still on the ground of the "new evolutionism" represented by Wałesa and Kuroń and were outmaneuvered by the compromise on workers' control that was the key achievement of this period. Their rhetorical victory during the last few days was a response to the coming disaster and not its real cause.

To understand Solidarity is to understand two unprecedented types of movement within Soviet-type societies: a historical movement that institutionalized a new, dual stage of this system, and a social movement (at first one among many) seeking to realize the maximum possible freedom and participation in this new stage.[40] The broadly based democratic movement of workers, peasants, intellectuals, and Catholics that paved the way for August 31, 1980, has every right to the adjective historical. Yet it was an *interrupted* historical movement to the extent that the necessary preservation of the leading role of the party formula meant that in a still unspecified state sphere, the authoritarian socialist organizing principle would be preserved. This sphere, however, always included the domains of legislation and administration of justice, allowing the regime to deprive the newly founded union of the means for legal, everyday functioning. Never claiming a vanguard role for all of Polish society, the independent union moved to relieve the pressure on its only weapon, the political strike, by helping through advice, example, and actual participation the democratic self-organization of several other social spheres. It is in this area neglected by both Nuti and Staniszkis that the most dramatic initial victories of Solidarity were won, including the registration of Rural Solidarity and of the Independent Student Association. The trade-union formula was sustained to the extent that the independent organization representing industrial workers, while preserving a movement form,

was paralleled by a multiplicity of other interest representations—other movements challenging institutional structures and policies relevant to them.

Given the increasing self-organization of society, Solidarity could follow a
trade-union tactic in yet another respect without having to fear the absorption of
all new gains: in the context of the economy's disastrous conditions, the new
prime minister Jaruzelski's call for a three-month voluntary strike pause was
accepted even before the likely registration of Rural Solidarity. It was during this
pause that the apparatus counterattacked by severely harassing KOR—then
somewhat alienated from the inner circle of union leadership—and then stage-
managing the Bydgoszcz provocation.

It was not merely because of the supposedly mistaken and certainly undemo-
cratically reached compromise following the Bydgoszcz crisis[41] that the stress on
the trade-union formula was abandoned. Solidarity now had several reasons for
seeking a new political posture and a new identity: (1) the continued nonexistence of a legal framework for everyday interest representation and negotiation
for any new social entities; (2) the nonexistence of weapons other than the
increasingly problematic strike, possessed only by Solidarity and not by other
movements; (3) the apparatus' increasingly provocative attitude supported by the
Soviet Union; (4) the simultaneous immense growth of Solidarity and the dramatic worsening of the economic crisis; (5) the internal challenge to union
leadership on the issue of democracy but in a context of increasing radicalism of
many union activists. Even under such pressures, however, Staniszkis is right:
For a period of three months or more no new identity and political profile was
crystallized. For a while, several possibilities were simultaneously put forth. This
was the only time when none apparently had primacy. The reason seems obvious. This was the period of the democratization wave in the Communist party
and of the open reemergence of conservative forums in the party. Equally important, the Soviet Union intervened on the party's highest level and a power
struggle took place within the Central Committee. Remarkably enough, the
storm was weathered out by the existing leadership, but this outcome was far
from certain at the time. While the reformist group's triumph at the party congress could have alleviated pressure on society, it could also have meant another
1968. Under those circumstances, while Solidarity could do little to influence a
favorable outcome that might not have brought the party near collapse, it also
had to await the outcome of the party congress and its ramifications in economics and politics.

That outcome as we now know only reinforced the worst confrontationist
trends within the party—even if the ideological guise was not borrowed from the
party conservatives. Preparing for its own congress, Solidarity countered with a
new self-definition: a social movement for "the defense of union interests, social
interests, national interests . . . against state power."[42] This was not a passive
defensive tactic, but the full adoption of the drive for self-management already
prepared by Solidarity's "networks" in fifty or more enterprises. The launching

of a self-management strategy meant that Solidarity could now push for economic reforms and at least hope to decentralize the political burden the organization was forced to assume. Given the Communist party's confrontation course,
Solidarity became the one movement of Polish society—its efforts to the contrary notwithstanding. The organization's new self-definition sought to concede
such a state of affairs while preparing another strategy to go beyond it.

Only in orthodox Marxist mythology is it to the advantage of workers to
represent universal social interests. In Poland, the unavoidability of such a course
was a sign of society's profound weakness. When the social movement formula
was introduced, there was already strong sentiment for the redefinition of Solidarity as a political party. Probably very few people in the organization understood Kuroń's point that the self-limitation of the revolution was not only a
necessity but also a virtue and that when a social movement becomes a party,
and that party gains state power, society loses its organization and defense. If the
formula of a political party lost in the organization, it did so because of pragmatic reasons and maybe Wałesa's personal role.

At any rate, the social movement formula was profoundly ambiguous. Did the
organization of society as *one* social movement mean the resumption of the
interrupted revolution?[43] Or did it signify an increasing struggle within a self-
limiting revolution for the maximum possible social freedom and participation?
Those who otherwise understood the necessary self-limitation of the Polish revolution and who rejected attempts to form either a revolutionary or a parliamentary party were divided on this all-important point. Even Modzelewski was
thinking ahead to the adaptation of the state, reorganized through self-management structures, to new social conditions, at a time when Kuroń saw participation in a front of national salvation as the last way out of the crisis, and to save
Solidarity. Solidarity's congress embodied the contradiction in a more extreme
form. (Here even Modzelewski was reluctantly on Kuroń's and Wałesa's side.)
The resolutions of the first session clearly expressed the majority's opinion that
the interrupted revolution must be continued. But this outcome was on a purely
rhetorical level and Polish and Soviet authorities, in spite of their propagandistic
manipulation of the results to scare all those anxious to be scared, always knew
this to be the case. The real winners at the congress, in terms of decisions on
actual strategy, were the partisans of the new evolutionism. The all-important
compromise on workers' control demonstrates this. And yet, by this time, they
were in a numerical minority not only in the congress but among the
organization's activists.[44] Among the rank and file, there was a new fundamentalism opposed to compromise (based on the rejection of any contaminating
contact with the regime)—a fundamentalism that even before the coup and its
aftermath could be recognized as in essence unpolitical and in effect less radical
than the politics of the so-called moderates. (Staniszkis, whose own earlier analyses were marked by a touch of fundamentalism, is very perceptive on this
point.)

The rise of this new fundamentalism is easily explained. All along Solidarity incorporated activists of opposition groups who sought the overthrow of the existing state. Only towards the end did they attain some political importance. If the project of a total political revolution was always impossible, now that of a self-limiting social movement was rapidly approaching the same status. For Solidarity's rank and file the fact that their movement represented the country's most powerful social organization and, unlike the party and the government, possessed overwhelming legitimacy, yet was unable to do anything about the disastrous economic situation, must have appeared intolerable. When they realized that neither the radicals' rhetorical victory nor the moderates' strategic victory would change this state of affairs, they responded with the wildcat strike movement. In Modzelewski's words, the Polish crisis became a "crisis of hope."

A self-limiting social movement is impossible without social reforms. But reformism in the party leadership (if not in some government branches) was abandoned or at least suspended after the Communist party's July congress. It is one of the lessons of the Polish events that in extraordinary situations structural reforms can even be achieved from below, that is, extorted from state power. It is unfortunately another lesson that the institutionalization of these important structural reforms further presupposes economic, political, and legal reforms from above. Some clearly understood this lesson. Hence, Kuroń's support for a national government of salvation, and Wałesa's desperate attempts to bring the wildcat movement under control. The real problem, however, was the economy. There were plans to organize a pure self-managing system from below, beginning with an alternative network of distribution disposing over the results of unpaid overtime work. As with all activities within a second economy in Eastern Europe, however, such a solution presupposed the regime's tacit cooperation. Thus, the union discovered that it did not have the material means for instituting it. An alternative economy, just like a parasitic second economy, presupposes a functioning first economy, something that only economic reforms could reestablish. Given the international context of the Polish economy, there was obviously no hope of an alternative economy replacing the official one. In this context too, Solidarity discovered that a reconciliation with the regime could not be bypassed. But while the regime remained powerless to institute its own version of economic reforms without Solidarity's consent, it was also unwilling to institute any reform with that consent. Hence, the all-important Solidarity proposal for a national economic council that could have ironed out all remaining differences was rejected precisely because it promised success.

In the context of a social movement without reforms, the successes of the union's national commission to disarm wildcat movements could only be temporary. Aside from the danger of state repression, the leadership had to face related dangers of losing its own remaining influence with its base, and the possibility of a mass explosion. They knew that this second set of dangers could only lead to disaster and they believed that the government left them no other way of dealing with it than to make continual rhetorical concessions to an increasing radicalism culminating in the Radom meeting December 3 and the resolution during the night of December 12. This way they hoped to save Solidarity's influence which they saw as the last chance for containing what could have become an uncontrollable popular outbreak. This policy of swimming with the radical tide, however, was based on one fundamental mistake: an underestimation of the sovereign power of the Polish state.[45]

Sovereignty and Legitimacy

Undoubtedly, Solidarity was unprepared for the December 13 events. Although there is some evidence that the eventual scenario was brought to the attention of relevant persons in Solidarity,[46] the problem was most likely not the lack of information so much as its overabundance.[47] Solidarity's leaders were convinced of the overwhelming hegemony of their organization in Polish society. But, they wrongly believed that this would protect them from political repression by Polish forces alone. They were right to seriously doubt the possibility of Soviet intervention, that in any case could be resisted only by all of the Polish nation and not the union as such. But they were wrong to think that between their own power in Polish society and the power of the Russians over the Polish state there existed a political vacuum, presided over by *the fiction* of sovereign Polish political power. Given the collapse of the regime's legitimacy and its inability to govern, and given the reduced sovereignty of the Polish state, it was not entirely unreasonable to discount the ability of this state to repress the mass movement of almost all of Polish society. Unfortunately, massive collapse of legitimacy did not have to mean that the regime possessed no bases whatsoever. Similarly, "impotence" to govern could be part of a deliberate strategy seeking to rebuild the state's sovereign power in the context of a stalemate unacceptable to certain key strata of the population—first and foremost, the officer corps. Finally, the Polish state's residual sovereignty could be expanded if a specific Polish version of an authoritarian state socialism could successfully tap the resources of national legitimization.

Legitimacy is equivalent neither to interest, nor to sovereign power; delegitimation need not mean the absence of social interests implicated in the survival of a form of rule, nor the automatic collapse of sovereign power. All East European state socialist systems have created social structures that privilege the existence of far wider social strata than merely party members and the state apparatus.[48] Some of these interests were at stake in a fundamental social transformation such as the one occurring in Poland in 1980–81. Large-scale economic reforms were utterly dangerous to the apparatus, but also a large part of the planning and managerial elite, and even to many industrial workers. The independence of the workers' movement may have been generally welcomed, but the same may not have been the case for the inevitable status revolution threatening to reverse the existing social evaluation of blue- and white-collar workers and intellectuals. Finally, while the general national enthusiasm was certainly shared by the members and even officers of the armed forces and perhaps the police, the weakening of all authority structures and the alleged threat to public order was probably resisted.

In the context of the self-organization of society, such a constellation of opposed (but passive and disorganized) interests could not by themselves have seriously affected the drive toward a new social order. They could become relevant, as what the authorities now evocatively call the Polish "silent majority," only if the state could generate sufficient sovereign power to act decisively and repressively. While sovereignty is not identical to legitimacy, it is nevertheless doubtful that on August 31, 1980, the Polish regime possessed any sovereign power at all. The democratic movement faced, however, the very real power of the Soviet Union, and the implication was that the tottering Polish regime could not be overthrown. Its sovereignty had to be accepted as a double fiction in relation to both Polish civil society and the Soviet imperial state. But precisely because it was double, that it, because this very limited form of sovereignty was protected against each of the real possessors of power by the other, it actually amounted to a form of residual sovereignty rebuildable under certain conditions. A pluralistic social order seeking above all to limit the power of the state and its key branches could have contributed to the strengthening of this state which continued to possess all the legal means of violence.

Neumann has discussed the problem of the relation of a "pluralism" grounded in social "contract" and the sovereign power such agreements seek to render purely residual.[49] According to him, the functioning of such a system presupposes the fundamentally unchanged existence of the contracting parties, their continued willingness to abide by the terms, and the existence of a neutral coercive instance in case they do not. Neumann, however, considered these conditions highly unlikely: They did not exist in the Weimar Republic he analyzed, nor did they in Poland after the Gdansk agreements. Of the two contracting parties, Solidarity was unavoidably on the path of organizing all of Polish society, and eventually becoming its one social movement. The party-state, too, went through a rapid transformation that decisively affected whatever willingness it might have had to abide by the terms of the agreement. And while there were neutral instances—the Church, some groups of intellectuals and even at times Parliament—they all lacked any coercive power. In such a situation, Neumann, warns, the strengthening of executive power is almost unavoidable.

Unfortunately, the argument works all too well for the Polish crisis. While the social movement was hegemonic in society, it was forced to discover that there were key tasks in the economy and in society that could be solved only by *a state*. More particularly, in the Polish situation they could be solved only on the basis of a structure of compromise that was deliberately sabotaged by the other party necessary to it. The Communist party could not force its will on society, but it could insure the emergence of a "decisionless" political order. Through economic crises, the projected result was the exhaustion of society. While the extent of this success cannot be fully evaluated, yet another aspect—perhaps unintended—was dramatically successful: the reconstitution of sovereign power itself.

Sovereign power, in the context of political stalemate and the radicalization of Solidarity's rhetoric, could now be represented as saving the country from both economic crisis and foreign intervention. While the Polish movement was blocked by the Soviet threat, this same threat worked in reverse for the violent abrogation of the Gdansk accords from above—something that the Soviet Union continually sought through the Communist party. This strategy could succeed, that is, avoid a bloody uprising leading to a highly undesirable Soviet intervention followed by a Budapest-type scenario in far worse internal and external circumstances, only if its agents were other than the Communist party and appeared in national colors. Through the whole period, Solidarity was wrong to assume that the army was unambiguously on its side. For the key officer corps that may have been true only, at best, in the context of Soviet intervention or perhaps in the case of repression initiated directly by the Communist party. As is now clear, this officer corps could act in its own name, had ample forces at its disposal, and could isolate the bulk of pro-Solidarity recruits.[50] Most importantly, this officer corps had an ideological medium to justify its actions to itself and to the Polish "silent majority": authoritarian nationalism.

The availability of nationalist ideology for authoritarian purposes must be seen as the long-term result of a process in which both government and the opposition participated. It is too simple to argue that the opposition represents all that is good in the Polish tradition, the government all that is bad. As with all Soviet-type states, the Polish regime has gravitated since the late 1960s toward replacement, or rather supplementation, of an increasingly empty official ideology by nationalistic justifications—at times (1968) a very ugly sort. The use of nationalism, however, was a double-edged weapon.[51] The opposition could easily utilize various aspects of it against a state that lacked the crucial criterion of any nationalist ideology: independence. Within the milieu of the opposition's alternative culture, the national issue had pride of place. This, of course, involved a revival of many aspects of the Polish national tradition, ranging from an extreme chauvinistic rhetoric to the linking of the issues of national independence and social justice.[52] But just as the revival of nationalist justifications could be turned against the regime, their wide dissemination and revalidation contributed to an intellectual atmosphere that could be turned against the opposition. From early 1981, the reactionaries in the party (e.g., the so-called Grunwald league) reintroduced anti-Semitic chauvinism and have made ample use of it ever since—especially after the coup.[53] And above such sordidness, but making at least negative use of it to enhance his own "milder" authority, stands General Jaruzelski, draped in the mantle of the nation's savior: Jozef Pilsudski.[54]

Poland, Russia, and the West

The coup's outcome remains far from clear. The military putschists undoubtedly had their own scenario. Dressed in national colors and hoping for at least the church's passive support, they sought to convince the nation not only of the need for their action in the face of the dangers of civil war and external intervention, but also of their intention to vigorously pursue the reform policy that was bogged down in political and social crisis. Their early treatment of Wałesa indicates that they perhaps hoped to reactivate the corporatist alternative that was periodically raised earlier, but this time only with a rump of Solidarity—and therefore with a strongly reduced component of social independence. Finally, it is possible that what some of the so-called reformers like Rakowski hoped from the coup was a kind of Polish Kadarism. If they were anything more than a campaign for internal and external deception, these hopes were based on delusions.

Kadarism in Hungary was based on a violent and bloody war against the Hungarian population that presupposed armed Soviet intervention, the destruction of the older party apparatus by the uprising, the forced collectivization of agriculture followed by relaxation and a rational division of labor between collectives and private plots, and a relatively good international context for an economy that was deformed only for a relatively short time by the most rigid form of Sovietization. None of these conditions can apply in Poland after the coup. Here economic reforms presuppose the large-scale, long-run voluntary cooperation of the Polish people. It is in this context that the military putschists turned out to be criminally ignorant. Their dreams of collaboration by a rump Solidarity and Wałesa were soon shattered, and this brought a visible hardening of the Church that seemed to be split in the early days of the coup. Most importantly, after the short period of open resistance of the population was broken, a period of passive resistance followed, the extent of which cannot yet be estimated. Without the revival of some social independence, Poland confronts a long period of stagnation. The corporatist dreams of some of the putschists cannot be revived without serious concessions to the population. The new regime, however, seems incapable or unwilling to make such concessions.

To consider alternative developments requires an understanding of the social actors involved. There is some question whether the army acted on its own or merely as a proxy for the Soviet Union and the Communist party. Most of the forces actually used belonged to the ministry of interior and the police. This, however, is not very relevant. The coup had to presuppose the officer corps' active or passive support. Similarly, the leading generals seemed to regard themselves as independent agents while the hard-liners hoped to reestablish their earlier authority. No matter who actually initiated the course of events, the army, the Soviet Union, and the Communist party are stuck with one another for the foreseeable future. The Polish and the Russian Communist parties cannot endanger the delicate balance of authority, thus risking rebellion involving the armed forces in order to reestablish a more orthodox type of communist system. Given the new importance of the Soviet military-industrial complex,[55] however, they need not reject an openly militaristic version of authoritarian state socialism. If a partially reformist experimentation, corresponding to the preferences of some Soviet interest groups, can be permitted in Hungary, why not allow similar experimentation with yet another model? After all, satellites that have developed their own version of a Soviet-type society tend to be the most stable partners in the imperial system.

Yet, the army leadership cannot move against the party hard-liners or the apparatus. The Soviet Union may not allow them to go so far in the direction of a uniquely Polish road. Furthermore, in the context of a crisis that threatens to become permanent, the generals cannot do without the reliable administrators that they do have in the apparatus, and they cannot further reduce their mass bases already shrinking as a result of the coup's bleak impact on economic life.

Army and party leaderships are stuck with one another and they limit each other's freedom. The party apparatus and hard-liners cannot be as repressive as they would want, and the army leadership and "reformers" allied to them seem constantly checked in their efforts to make even the mildest concessions necessary for minimal negotiations. The future orientation of the junta is riddled with similar contradictions. Thus, unless social pressures manage to balance out the apparatus' pressure, there can be no "reform alternative" which, under Polish conditions, presupposes some measure of social independence.

Such pressures today depend on the Church and Solidarity. While the Church could live with a corporatist solution involving the restoration of some elementary rights, it has by now lost the earlier confidence of some of its members that such a solution would be instituted from above after calm had been restored. Under conditions of martial law and internment, it will not give the regime even passive support. As Glemp's sermon in Rome shows, the Church considers the regime responsible for the threat of a violent uprising and civil war. Given this attitude, the regime's nationalist legitimation remains very shaky.

While Solidarity suffered a crushing defeat, it was by no means destroyed. Despite all its internal criticism, it was a highly democratic mass organization— and thus one in no position to prepare for the coup by establishing secret networks, an alternative leadership, etc. The arrest of its existing leaders and the destruction of its communication network completely incapacitated it during the coup's first few crucial days. On the other hand, a democratic and decentralized organization is not destroyed along with its leaders. In 1980–81, the learning experience involved hundreds of thousands directly, and millions indirectly. Whether industrial workers are capable of a major victory without the help of the communication networks of the democratic opposition remains uncertain. What is clear, however, is that they will try. A sign recently spotted by Western correspondents in the Lenin shipyards may turn out to be prophetic: "Winter is yours, Spring will be ours!"

It is in this context that the potential role of Western governments becomes relevant. It is clear that the only possible way to support the Polish democratic movement is with the stick of economic sanctions and the carrot of large-scale economic aid. To be effective, *threats and promises* must be addressed to both Polish and Soviet governments, and must be presented in stages to affect events as they unfold. The American government's motives for half-heartedly undertaking such a policy and the Western Europeans' refusal to follow are equally suspicious. What is really unclear, however, is why, with the exception of the French,[56] the European Left so wholeheartedly shared their governments' position.

Most European pacifists and socialists seem to feel that participation in sanctions would strengthen American influence in Europe and block the way toward European disarmament that presupposes the good will of the Soviet Union and the survival of *Ostpolitik* at all price. This attitude presupposes what Reagan's and Weinberger's rhetoric seems to prove, that is, that the United States is the greatest threat to the peace and independence of Western Europe. It further presupposes that those seeking a third road for Western Europe have little to fear from the Soviet Union—and this at a time when the Russians have demonstrated that they have now mastered genuinely modern, that is, indirect, forms of restoring order in their empire!

All political postures involve some assumptions. Today, Leftists tend to assume one of two positions concerning Soviet development: Either the Soviet Union is seen caught up in a hopeless crisis that will make it increasingly cautious and conservative, or it must inevitably undertake reforms implying commitment to detente and to wide-ranging, new economic relations with Europe. Both have some validity. The Soviet system *is* in deep crisis, and economic reforms remain one of its alternatives. But they are by no means the only ones. As Castoriadis has shown, the failure of the Soviet economy has not meant the failure of its military-industrial complex, just as the collapse of its Marxist-Leninist ideology has only led to its replacement by what he calls the nationalist-imperial imaginary. Castoriadis thus deduces only one possible policy alternative for the Soviet empire: military-geopolitical expansion. It is his merit to have seriously confronted the Western Left with this developmental possibility. Yet this road, too, while more plausible than the old-fashioned idea of the inevitability of reforms,[57] is only one alternative. Since Stalin's death, Soviet history has oscillated between half-hearted reforms and re-Stalinization, corresponding to a regular cycle of shifting investment priorities.[58] Yet, there has been neither a consistent implementation of reforms nor a complete reversion to Stalinism. The first seems too threatening for the system's principle of identity while the second is too dangerous to its elite's physical existence. Today, however, the system's cyclical oscillations have resulted in a dangerous economic stagnation. The most likely choice, therefore, seems to be between cautious but now irreversible reforms or re-Stalinization, but with Great Russian nationalism rather than terror as its cement.[59] Either of these forms, however, would involve the great danger of social or national conflict. Thus, the Soviet leaders who will follow Brezhnev's generation will hesitate to adopt either option without more serious revisions than have hitherto been suggested.

Any explanation of Soviet development alternatives must take into account the immense military buildup that only apologists can now see as defensive.[60] On the Left, so far this task has been taken up only by Castoriadis. His is the only way to give substance to the alternative of re-Stalinization. Only in a dynamically expanding empire could Soviet internal nationality conflicts be contained. Today, however, no power can hope to combine a land-based as well as an overseas empire. In fact, Eastern Europe by itself seems to exhaust Soviet capacities for a type of imperial synthesis based on direct military authority. Thus, Soviet foreign policy as well as its military and trade postures point to a somewhat different direction suggesting cautious and stabilizable reforms.

Evidently, Soviet foreign policy is based on *both* military buildup and expansion of many-leveled economic relations with Western Europe. The former is aimed at establishing an absolute military superiority in Europe (and not worldwide, where it would be meaningless). The latter is based on a trade-off of primarily raw materials for investment capital, high technology goods, and food. While the latter threatens to reduce the Soviet Union to a permanently dependent economy, the former establishes it as the strongest European state, involved in a balance of terror stalemate with the United States. For orthodox Marxists, this is a contradiction: Even Wallerstein's sophisticated model involves a correspondence between strong states and dominant economies. But the Soviet economy cannot match today's capitalist economies. Its political-military strength, however, means that under certain conditions it can exploit them. The danger for Western Europe is not it Sovietization, nor its Finlandization. The danger is Hong-Kongization, that is, the exploitation (the control of the terms of trade) of an economically advanced Eurasian peninsula by the militarily superior land power. The moral, political, cultural, and economic consequences of such an arrangement for Western Europe can be nothing short of disastrous in the long run.

In this sense the unfortunate Gierek, who hoped to break the investment cycle of Soviet-type societies and simultaneously increase investments and real wages by combining cautious technocratic reforms and massive indebtedness to the West, might yet turn out to be the unsung hero of the coming new Soviet developmental strategy—with one decisive difference. Unlike Gierek's clique, the Soviets will have the means to ensure that the funds will be forthcoming for a much long time—especially if the current campaign for withdrawal of the United States from Europe will be successful, and if the balance between both conventional and nuclear forces in Europe itself is not restored or preserved. Military superiority, in this sense, could be their long-term guarantee against troublesome pressures, boycotts, sanctions, and human rights policies.

The implications for a Western foreign policy that socialists and democrats should aim for is clear. On a military level, there should be an insistence on finding the lowest possible equilibrium instead of any unilateral moves including illusions of a nuclear-free Europe with Soviet missiles on the other side of the Urals. On the level of trade, its expansion should everywhere be tied to political considerations, as is already the case from the Soviet viewpoint. It is not in the interests of Western Europeans to subsidize precisely the ability of the Soviet Union to maintain its empire intact or to be irreversibly connected for economic reasons to a system that might one day have the power to exploit them. Trade should be made contingent on a development which, however slow, is, in the spirit of the Helsinki accords, away from the consolidation of an imperial system to which Western Europeans otherwise might one day have to surrender a piece of *their* sovereignty, perhaps with consequences analogous to the ones the Poles have recently experienced. In this sense, the slightly paraphrased slogan of the nineteenth-century Polish revolutionaries remains as true today as then: The democratic movement in Poland has indeed the right to demand that we act on behalf of "their freedom and ours."

Notes

1. Many things should have made this first independent working class organization in sovietized Eastern Europe an inspiring model and a potential partner: to pacifists, the remarkably disciplined, nonviolent character of Solidarity; to left liberals, its stress on civil and political rights; to Social Democrats, its insistence on reform instead of revolution in the sense of the violent overthrow of the existing state; to democratic socialists, its general openness and experimental attitude toward new forms of a self-managed socialist economy.

2. The naiveté toward the Soviet Union of all advocates of unilateral disarmament was clear even before the Polish crisis. When faced with the argument that in the East no corresponding pressure could be exerted on the state, and in particular on its military-industrial arm, people such as Kaldor, Thompson, and Eppler emphasized the possibility of independent pressure represented by Solidarity. This could not have been completely honest because the movement in Poland had clearly renounced raising any issues pertaining to the military framework to which the country belongs. At any rate, the defeat of Solidarity has not only *not* led to revisions of this argument, but, on the contrary, in many cases a strategy of at least partially blaming the victim allows several spokesmen for the peace movement to maintain faith in pressure groups in the Soviet Union and East Europe equally solicitous of the results of Yalta (not Helsinki, to be sure) and of the economic interests involved in disarmament.

3. See Rudolf Augstein's editorial in *Der Spiegel*, December 21, 1981.

4. George Kennan on the Op-Ed page of *The New York Times*, January 5, 1982. Kennan mentions membership in the Warsaw Pact and the "retention of a 'Socialist' (whatever that means) form of government" as two limits that could not be challenged. Of course, the first was never challenged, and Kennan's uncertainty regarding the meaning of the second indicates that it could not serve as a clearly defined limit. After all, from the Soviet viewpoint, an independent trade union already challenged a "socialist form of government." On the other hand, Solidarity always officially accepted "the leading role of the party." After the Gdansk agreements, however, it considered its meaning subject to further negotiations and clarifications that never took place. In any case, till the very last day, and then under extreme provocation, Solidarity made no deliberate move to over-

throw or even to hasten the decomposition of the communist party. At any rate, Kennan's two limits amount essentially to a restatement of the program of the new evolutionism that Solidarity inherited from KOR and accepted up to the very last days. See Adam Michnik, "What We Want and What We Can Do," *Telos* 47 (Spring 1981), pp. 66–77. Kennan also speaks of the disastrous decline of Poland's "economic and financial position" as a result of the "combination of a semi-paralyzed Communist government and a Solidarity well set up to obstruct this government, but in no way prepared to replace it." Presumably, this does not mean that Solidarity should have tried to resolve the social and economic paralysis by moving to replace the existing government. The Russians, about whose sensibilities he is so solicitous, would not have liked that at all. What he is saying is that Solidarity's aims, laudable in principle, could in Poland only lead to a stalemate that it was in almost everyone's interest to end. Only the state's repressive action, however, could do this.

5. In fact, the regime demanded two contradictory things from Solidarity: It did not want it to be political, yet it was urged to take responsibility for the government's policies. Brus, "Die Revolution in Polen," in Włodzimierz Brus et al., *Polen—Symptome und Ursachen der polnischen Krise* (Hamburg, 1981).

6. Unlike the sectarians, a regime that has always deliberately misrepresented this point seems to realize quite well the immense importance for industrial workers of the communications network and the expert advice provided by intellectuals. The military regime's very first measures were to neutralize all such links.

7. Cf. "The Victory and the Tragedy of the Polish Workers," in *Critique*, 1981. Aside from standard mythology, the point is supported by entirely mistaken assumptions about the internal Soviet consequences of an intervention in Poland based on sympathies for their Polish colleagues by a supposedly highly discontented Soviet working class and intelligentsia.

8. Both accounts can be combined. Such was Jadwiga Staniszkis's position in "The Evolution of Forms of Working-Class Protest in Poland: Sociological Reflections on the Gdansk-Szczecin Case,' August 1980," *Soviet Studies* 33:2 (April 1981), pp. 204–31. According to her argument, which made her reject the compromise on the leading role of the party formula, the movement should have either aimed at political power from the beginning, or accept integration into the existing union structure. However, as events wore on, Staniszkis apparently changed her mind and accepted what she called the program of the "self-limiting revolution" with all its contradictions.

9. Ferenc Fehér, "Die sozialistische Länder Osteuropas am Beginn der 80er Jahre," in *Polen—Symptome und Ursachen*, p. 221.

10. Mihály Vajda, "Polen—Ungarn," in Sozialistischer Osteuropakommittee, *Polen 81* (Hamburg, 1981). The point retains its validity even if the so-called liberals associated with the Polish Junta have made a Kadarist system the ideal goal of their efforts. With most of the presuppositions of the Hungarian solution missing, they can achieve either a semipermanent authoritarian solution that will lead to stagnation of all levels of life or will have to accept a return to the path of development that will immediately surpass the terms of Kadarism. Cf. Mihály Vajda, "Is Kadarism an Alternative?" in *Telos* 39 (Spring 1979), pp. 172–79, and Ferenc Fehér, "Kadarism as the Model State of Khrushchevism," in *Telos* 40 (Summer 1979), pp. 19–31.

11. See my "Civil Society vs. the State: Poland 1980–81," Chapter 8, this volume.

12. György Márkus, "Planning the Crisis: Remarks on the Economic System of Soviet-type Societies," *Praxis International* 3 (October 1981), p. 257.

13. See Alain Touraine, *The Voice and the Eye* (New York, 1981). I strongly disagree with Touraine concerning the possibility of only *one* movement in a given society. Concerning Poland, see Jacek Kuroń, "Pour une Platforme Unique de l'Opposition," in *La Pologne: une Société en Dissidence* (Paris, 1978).

14. The literary public sphere is thoroughly analyzed by Jeffrey Goldfarb, *On Cultural Freedom. An Exploration of Public Life in Poland and America* (Chicago, 1982).

15. Cf. Staniszkis, op. cit. pp. 204–05.

16. Of course, Habermas came up with this formulation in terms of a possible and desirable critical public sphere in the West. Cf. Jürgen Habermas, *Strukturwandel der Öffentlichkeit* (Neuweid and Berlin, 1962), pp. 274–75.

17. Cf. "Wirtschaftsreform in Polen," interview with Szeliga, economic editor of the journal *Polityka*, in *Polen–81*, op. cit. pp. 60–61.

18. Brus, op. cit., pp. 11–12; cf. also Aleksander Smolar, "L'Ancien Régime et la Révolution en Pologne," in *Ésprit* (June 1981), pp. 122–23.

19. Claude Lefort, "Reculer les Frontières du Possible," in *Ésprit* (January 1981).

20. Staniszkis has made this objection even independently of the possibility of repression from above. While she was clearly wrong in 1979, in "On Some Contradictions of Socialist Society," *Soviet Studies* (April 1979), pp. 184–86, KOR's strategy based on the rebuilding of independent forms of social life would be only functional to the state from the viewpoint of containing and ritualizing the opposition, her objections remain relevant from the viewpoint of the institutionalization of a dualistic arrangement. In particular, she stressed the interpenetration of state and society and that the unity of society itself must be considered illusory. To be sure, the unity of society in confronting the authoritarian state was maintained. Developments, however, did lead to the interpenetration of the two sides. Thus, a struggle ensued for democratization in the party and against bureaucratization in society, along with some serious divisions in society. As a result, both possible steering centers were damaged; first of all, the party-state lost its ability to act positively in all key sectors of the economy and society, but also Solidarity lost its freedom of action vis-à-vis its own mass base. On the eve of the military coup the organization was threatened by splits and resignations. In Staniszkis's various articles it is unclear how such an outcome could have been avoided.

21. Cf. Daniel Chirot, "The Corporatist Model and Socialism," *Theory and Society* (March 1980) and Staniszkis, "The Evolution," op. cit.

22. See my "Critical Sociology and Authoritarian State Socialism," in Held and Thompson, eds., *Habermas: Critical Debates* (Cambridge, Mass., 1982), chapter 3 in this volume.

23. Both aspects of this were of course themes of great contention. KOR especially initially sought to establish a pluralistic system of the aggregation of social interests. Thus, it advocated a national economic council in a sense that could be incompatible with the survival of the party-state. Similarly, Solidarity sought to extend the independence of the controlling role of the public sphere by demanding access to the electronic media.

24. Cf. Brus, op. cit., and Domenico Mario Nuti, "Poland: Economic Collapse and Socialist Renewal," *New Left Review* (November–December 1981).

25. In the first few months this pressure was unfortunately restricted to a shift in investment priorities to the benefit of agriculture and consumption. S. Kurowski, "Die Wirtschaft im Jahr 1981," in Sozialistisches Osteuropakommittee, *Polen 1980* (Hamburg, 1980).

26. See Nuti, op. cit., and J. Mujzel, "Vorstellungen über eine Wirtschaftsreform in Polen," *Polen 1980*, op. cit., pp. 66ff.

27. Kurowski, op. cit.

28. Brus, op. cit., and Mujzel, op. cit.

29. Prodded by its "networks" already organizing *de facto* self-management, the National Commission of Solidarity fully adopted the issue as a center of its political strategy in July 1981. Cf. Staniszkis, "One Year after August 1980: An Anatomy of Revolution," manuscript, pp. 15–17. Interesting in this context is the interview of the journal *Polityka*

with the leaders of Solidarity, November 1, 1980. Now in *L'Alternative* (January–February 1981).

30. Nuti, op. cit., pp. 31–32.

31. Cf. Karel Modzelewski, "Polen steckt in einer Krise der Hoffnung," interview in *Der Spiegel*, November 9, 1981.

32. Nuti is right when he claims that the regime was unable to act without Solidarity's consent. Cf. Nuti, op. cit., p. 30. He should have added, however, that it was unwilling to act *with* this consent.

33. Cf. *Der Spiegel* interview with Modzelewski and the interview with Ewa Milewicz concerning the response to Kuroń's proposal (January 18, 1982).

34. Smolar, op. cit., p. 124.

35. Nuti, op. cit. p. 28.

36. Adam Michnik, "Auch verbündete Notabeln sind sterblich," in *Der Spiegel*, 33 (1981).

37. Smolar, op. cit., p. 125; and S. Bialer, "Poland and the Soviet Imperium," in *Foreign Affairs*, February 1981, pp. 522ff.

38. See the remarkable interview with Rakowski in *Der Spiegel*, September 14, 1981, in which Augstein turns out to be just as "hard" as the vice premier himself.

39. Staniszkis, "One Year after . . .," op. cit., p. 2.

40. Touraine, *The Voice and the Eye*, op. cit., pp. 125ff., 129ff.

41. Staniszkis, "One Year after . . .," op. cit., pp. 10ff.

42. Cf. Jacek Kuroń, "Wir leben gleichsam in einer Wüste," a speech given July 25, reproduced in part in *Der Spiegel*, 34 (1981).

43. S. Blumsztajn, "Jaruzelski's Versprechungen sind Wertlos," interview in *Der Spiegel*, January 1982.

44. See report in *Le Monde*, October 1, 1981.

45. Maria Zielińska's and Jan Walc's report in *Der Spiegel*, December 14, 1981 (but written several days before the coup) documents both these aspects. While they maintain that the radical rhetoric at the famous December 3 Radom conference of the Solidarity leadership was a response to repeated threats of a state of emergency by the Communist Party's Central Committee that were vigorously resisted by the Church and Parliament, the two authors, Warsaw journalists of Solidarity, seem to endorse a drive toward state power because of their own fear of an uncontrolled popular explosion. Even at this very late date, however, they considered the threat of a state of emergency to be more or less empty. And the leadership that did believe in the threat on December 3 was also convinced that the regime did not have the power to carry it out. They seemed to believe that such an attempt would lead to Solidarity's forming a provisional government as long as the Russians could be given suitable guarantees. Such was the meaning probably of their last resolution, calling for a possible referendum, one that was apparently resisted by Wałesa. We now have the testimony of longtime KOR member Ewa Milewicz that Kuroń more or less accurately predicted on December 4 the outcome of a state of emergency. Cf. *Der Spiegel*, January 18, 1982. Neither he nor Wałesa, however, attempted to dampen the radical enthusiasm at Radom with such considerations, probably because they also feared a popular explosion above all.

46. Cf. interview with Gen. L. Dubicki, in *Der Spiegel*, December 28, 1981, p. 57.

47. The regime went a very long way to misinform Solidarity on this score. It repeatedly threatened the calling of a state of emergency through Parliament, and by December 3 convinced the Solidarity leaders of the reality of this actually discarded version of what was to happen. When it provoked the desired radical rhetoric at Radom, the state of emergency threat was abandoned, thereby convincing the Solidarity leaders of what they were in any case highly inclined to believe, i.e., that because of the expected popular

response, the whole strategy was abandoned. All this is clearly reflected in Zieliński and Walc, op. cit. Cf. also Blumsztajn in *Le Nouvel Observateur*, January 9–15, 1982.

48. For three views on this subject see Mark Rakowski, *Toward an East European Marxism* (London, 1978); Ivan Szelényi and György Konrád, *The Intellectuals on the Road to Class Power* (New York, 1979); and Rudolf Bahro, *The Alternative in Eastern Europe* (London, 1979).

49. Cf. Franz Neumann, "The Change of the Function of Law in Modern Society," *The Democratic and the Authoritarian State* (New York, 1957), pp. 47–50.

50. See the interview with Dubicki, op. cit., and M. Checiński's letter to *The New York Times*, January 6, 1982.

51. Cf. my "Understanding Bureaucratic Centralism" in *Telos* 35 (Spring 1978), pp. 73–85.

52. Adam Michnik, "Les ombres des ancétres oubliés," *Recherches* (October 1978).

53. See the report of I.S. Karol in *Le Nouvel Observateur*, December 26, 1981.

54. Even now, members of the Polish opposition hesitate to point to Jaruzelski's deliberate attempt to play Pilsudski's role. Yet, several parallels with Pilsudski's military dictatorship are inescapable, especially since Jaruzelski's regime avoids all appeals to any Marxist-Leninist or even vaguely state socialist legitimations. Cf. J. Rothschild, *Pilsudski's Coup d'État* (New York, 1966). This does not mean that the outcome will resemble Pilsudski's *sanacja*, whatever the actual intentions of some participants may be.

55. Cf. Cornelius Castoriadis, *Devant la Guerre* (Paris, 1981) and "Facing the War," in *Telos* 46 (Winter 1980–81), pp. 43–61.

56. See the special issue of *Le Nouvel Observateur* on the gas deal, February 8, 1982.

57. Cf. Moshe Lewin, *Political Undercurrents of Soviet Economic Debates* (Princeton, 1974).

58. Cf. Márkus, op. cit., p. 241.

59. Cf. Paul Piccone and Victor Zaslavsky, "The Socio-Economic Roots of Re-armament," in *Telos* 50 (Winter 1981–82).

60. The most recent such effort on the independent Left is by the Medvedev brothers. Cf. their "Russia, USA, Western Europe," *New Left Review*, 130 (November–December 1981), pp. 5–22.

10

The Democratic Theory of the Polish Opposition: Normative Intentions and Strategic Ambiguities

This presentation is based on a much larger manuscript provisionally entitled "New Democratic Theory as Critical Social Theory: The Program of the Polish Opposition 1976–82," a manuscript that stands at the crossroads of two projects, one dealing with the fifty-year confrontation of varieties of critical social theory with societies of the Soviet type and the other with some historical and systematic problems of the theory of democratic civil society. The theory of the Polish democratic opposition and above all that of KOR (the Workers' Defense Committee), the most sophisticated and influential of its parts, belongs to both of these projects, that is, to the history of Marxian ideas in East Europe and to the history of democratic theory. Aside from its intrinsic theoretical interest, the theory of (in particular) two members of KOR, Adam Michnik and Jacek Kuroń, both anticipated important aspects of the movement of 1980–81 and helped to articulate on an intellectual level two of the ascending stages of the sixteen months of Solidarity, which could indeed be called, after Michnik and Kuroń respectively, "new evolutionism" and "self-limiting revolution." It will be my first thesis that KOR and in particular Kuroń worked out a normative project of significant interest toward what I would call "the plurality of democracies" that was to express rather well the developing political philosophy of the Solidarity movement. My second thesis, however, will argue that the strategic dimensions of this project remained ambiguous before, during, and after Solidarity's sixteen months. And finally, I will present a third thesis according to which some of the strategic ambiguities can be traced back to theoretical failures, and more specifically to the unfortunate inflation of a normatively based democratic theory of

---

Working paper of the Kellogg Institute, Notre Dame University, 1984.

action to the whole of social theory in a renewed totalitarian thesis.

The development of the political theory of KOR, in particular of Kołakowski (at home and in exile), Kuroń, and Michnik, toward post-Marxian positions reveals much about the crisis of Marxian theory in Eastern Europe and the difficulties of working even with neo-Marxian paradigms in context of the existing movements. I would first like to stress rather what constitutes the importance of KOR in the context of the history of democratic theory. In my opinion, two major antinomies of this history were successfully addressed: one between statism and pluralism, and the other between political and socioeconomic meanings of democracy. Both of these were explored as early as Tocqueville, who pointed to the deep potential tension between the centralistic organization of the modern state, however formally democratic, and the democratic life of small-scale associations of all kinds as well as that between democracy in the sense of democratic self-government and democracy in the sense of "equality of conditions." While it is obviously true that Tocqueville's sympathies were with small-scale associations and self-government, and his fears were of the authoritarian consequences of centralism and leveling, he knew, of course, that without the general laws provided by a central political instance plurality could degenerate into local or sectional oppression and hierarchy and that without a form of social equality *more* than a merely formal equality of opportunity genuinely equal political participation is not possible. Neither Tocqueville nor anyone after was really successful at confronting these antinomies, which represent the embarrassment of democratic theory in face of the modern state and the modern capitalist economy respectively. Amazingly enough, however, Eastern Europe in the years after 1945, and around 1956 and from 1968 to the present, has been an important laboratory for experimentation with new solutions that represent the resumption of the program of the democratic revolutions in new, noncapitalist contexts.

As the Hungarian political philosopher Istvan Bibó has repeatedly and eloquently argued, the struggle for political democracy where the road to capitalist private property was closed (among other things by the very social character of those in struggle) had a good chance of developing a *third road* combining high measures of political democracy and social equality. The implication is, of course, democratic socialism, as long as under socialism we understand, as did Bibó, not statist controls but the free economic self-management of all manner of councils, cooperatives, and associations. Bibó, furthermore, squarely in the Tocquevillean tradition, understood political democracy itself as the combination of central and local forms of self-government. One may add to his analysis a crucial reason why East European democratic struggles always seem to favor such a combination. In the double context of imperial oppression *and* suffocating centralism these struggles are simultaneously for the *restoration* of national sovereignty and the *devolution* of the authority of the state, a double result that can be achieved only in the combination of different types of democracy.

In different East European movements the two problems of democratic theory I have just mentioned have received rather different weights. In Hungary in 1956 the stress was on the combination of parliamentary and council forms of democracy; the issues of constructing an economy compatible with both political freedom and social equality were hardly raised. In 1968, in Czechoslovakia the stress was reversed and in this period a formula emerged for combining market, workers' councils, and state planning and redistributive mechanisms, which has since dominated most discussions of economic reform among critical intellectuals in Poland and Hungary as well.

The theory of the Polish democratic opposition, not only of KOR but also of the discussion group DiP (Experience and the Future), the Catholic intellectual clubs, and most importantly the economic program of Solidarity worked out by its "networks" of self-management all presuppose some version of such a tripartite economic structure. The real contribution of the theory of KOR, however, involved another reversal, that is, a renewed stress on the problem of sovereignty and plurality. The difficulties with the conception too are related to this context.

While it is sometimes contested that East European movements experiment with *new* forms of democracy with respect to the West, the historical record that has already inspired people such as Arendt, Castoriadis, and Lefort among others should by now speak for itself. Although it is indisputable that milieux of critical intellectuals tended in 1956 and 1968 to simply reinvent parliamentary democracy, the movements in which they have participated have always aimed at more. And some theorists such as Bibó in Hungary and now Kuroń in Poland have produced principled arguments anticipating and reexpressing the very real tendencies of their movements to creatively combine different forms of democracy. Kuroń, a longtime advocate of council democracy, continued to operate from this position as his starting point even as he turned in a post-Marxian theoretical direction in the 1970s. But from this time on he refused to totalize his direct democratic position, which he still saw as the best way of representing the interests of workers as producers. His "vision," as he once called it, now became far more general and he was one of the first in Eastern Europe to formulate under the heading of "radical pluralism," a position that I would rather call the "plurality of democracies." To be sure, the combination of parliamentary and council democracy is not entirely unprecedented in political theory—we find it in the works of the Austro-Marxists Karl Renner and Otto Bauer and the British socialist Harold Laski. But while in their cases the issue was how to enrich parliamentary democracy, in Kuroń's it became rather how to initiate a general program of democratization in which the monolithic implications of any version of democracy would be avoided. Only the Hungarian workers of 1956 anticipated him here, but Kuroń actually went further. Without parliamentary democracy, he argued, direct democracy is at the mercy of the state. Of course, this is necessarily true if the party-state structure remains intact as in Yugoslavia—but to speak of Utopias, would the argument apply even to a pure council democracy? The answer is yes, as long as such a system is constituted as a *modern state*. Kuroń *only implies* this point, but consciously takes up another—the potentially authoritarian implications of pure council democracy in a truly *modern* society. Assuming a type of society that in fact was the goal of so much oppositional activity in Poland since about 1976, one organized in the pattern of a multiplicity of associations with different interests, values, and ideologies, the integration of all these forms of plurality on the basis of an organization typical for one of them—the industrial workers—would be necessarily authoritarian, creating new patterns of selection and exclusion. Whatever parliamentary structures of representation have become elsewhere, only these, according to Kuroń, would be able to integrate through a necessary system of compromise a social plurality of a heterogeneous set of associations while giving some voice (unlike council democracy) even to those who are not themselves organized.

Let us make no mistake about it, Kuroń never—unlike some other East European intellectuals—mythologized Western liberal democracy. He is conscious of the fact that it too has its own exclusion rules, its own selectivity, its own monolithic potential. While he only implicitly assumes that without the corrective of direct democracy parliamentary democracy involves a structural differentiation of rulers and ruled and becomes merely formal, he states clearly enough that a democratic *paideia*, a democratic political culture, can only emerge on the basis of actual and significant small-scale participation. Furthermore, in a manner again reminiscent of Laski, he argues that since parliamentary democracy favors the interests of consumers, direct democracy is needed to represent producers' interests. In fact, this argument implies that he is committed not only to the combination of central and local forms of participation, but also to that of territorial and functional principles of representation. The implications of this latter position were developed only in the heat of the struggles of 1980–81, during what turned out to be an unsuccessful search for formulas of compromise between social movement and regime. In this context the old idea of Laski and Renner of a second chamber of parliament, a chamber based on a pyramidal structure of direct democratic organizations was revived, as a potential formula for institutionalizing in the state structure some democratic elements and creating a parliamentary framework of compromise while reluctantly preserving the monolithic structure of a part of power. But the idea was, in Kuroń's case at least, also rooted in principle. A democracy of producers can be a corrective to a democracy of consumers only if both are nationally organized. It was, of course, the peculiarity of the Polish situation that the direct democratic corrective seemed already attainable when the thing to be corrected, parliamentary democracy, was only a distant vision.

It may seem strange to Westerners accustomed to representative, rather than direct, democracy, that in Eastern Europe the institutionalization of direct forms seems more feasible than of parliamentary forms. In fact, all the major reform attempts since 1956 testify that this is the case. One may locate the reason, as does Hegedüs in the different political cultures of East and West, or as do Trotskyists in the supposedly deformed worker-state character of the regimes. I would, however, argue rather differently. The organizational principle of authoritarian state socialism, its principle of desperately protected self-identity, I believe, excludes power-sharing on the central level but not to the same extent, as the Yugoslav example shows, at the peripheries. In fact, historically and in Poland after 1956 in particular, industrial council forms, powerless against regime cooptation, have been used to disarm working-class protest. For this reason demands for industrial self-management did not emerge during the first phase of the 1980 movement. Even such old defenders of council communism as Kuroń were originally evasive on the subject. The creation of a classwide, territorially organized institution of interest representation, such as a labor union, seemed to be a far greater priority because it was less open to regime manipulation. Interestingly enough, in Hungary in 1956 workers initially organized in the forms of workers' councils also demanded independent unions to defend the workers as employees against themselves as employers. In Poland the reverse was to happen, with the same theoretical result. The existence of the unions now became the political guarantee that organs of self-management could remain truly autonomous. Kuroń and some members of the Solidarity national commission close to KOR as well as several rank-and-file movements realized early that the economic reforms that were generally recognized as necessary even if involving drastic austerity measures could become justifiable to workers only if there was a trade-off in terms of industrial democracy. As the possibilities of large-scale political compromise were blocked, the ongoing plans of economic reform gave an opportunity to the movement both in theory and in actual industrial experimentation to channel its democratizing energies in the direction of programs of self-management. But it is crucial that the organizational separation between Solidarity, territorially and nationally organized, and the agencies of self-management, locally and in part functionally organized, was always strictly preserved, and possibilities of conflict between the two were recognized and considered beneficial. Such a project, while not fully anticipated by any theorists of the democratic opposition, represented in fact a practical filling out of ideas originally formulated in the abstract by Kuroń as early as 1976.

When we turn from visions of the plurality of democracies to strategies of democratization, the picture darkens. This is unfortunate, because some of the best creative energies of people like Kuroń and Michnik, and more practically, the experts and leaders of Solidarity including Wałesa, were expressed on this strategic level. The key to all the best strategic conceptions of the democratic movement is the idea of self-limitation. We must be careful though: The idea of self-limitation also involved normative principle. This can be first of all articulated by the movement's project of the reconstruction of civil society, which I have discussed elsewhere and have no time to review now. In face of the authoritarian state the Polish democratic opposition has articulated a program of the defense of all independent societal forms and the expansion of those already in existence by the social movement in formation in the direction of institutional- ized forms of free association such as Solidarity itself as well as alternative forms of public life. However, it has become axiomatic for many theorists of the opposition and especially Kuroń (who in this respect anticipated Touraine and Gorz in the West), that the democratic movement should not aim at becoming a new form of state power, which would mean that society would lose its new- found forms of self-defense and self-representation. Only when society is thor- oughly organized should some of its organizations, but only some, directly participate in the reorganization of state power—other conditions permitting. The Polish opposition, in other words, understood the state-strengthening logic of modern revolutions and sought to avoid it. Secondly, for a long time the workers' movement was seen both in theoretical conceptions and in actuality by its own militants as only one movement among many or within one larger, looser one for the liberation of society. This too involved self-limitation, which took the form of helping to organize the movements of others one could be potentially in conflict with it, for example, Rural Solidarity, the organization of peasants. Fi- nally, both the workers' movement and the theorists of the democratic opposition conceived of economic reform as the liberation of properly economic principles from statist politization without seeking the "reembedding" of economic activity in social institutions, including the workers' collectives. This meant the emanci- pation of economic actors not only from state controls, but in part from their own direct control as well—workers' self-management was conceived as a kind of representative democracy with elected managers who would maintain a definite degree of autonomy.

All in all, these self-limitations in principle do not subtract much in the context of a Soviet-type society from the democratizing impact of a political philosophy such as Kuroń's, which was more or less equivalent to the ultimate goals of the program adopted by Solidarity and its September–October 1981 Congress. One might indeed ask how anyone could after the disastrous outcome of the Hungarian revolution and the Czech reform hope to realize such a pro- gram, which was evidently more radical then its predecessors? The strategic self-limitations worked out in the Polish opposition's various programs in fact involved some serious reflection on these previous experiences. According to the reasoning of the main theorists of KOR, Kuroń, and Michnik, the Hungarian and Czech attempts failed because through their different methods they hoped to transform *the whole* of their social systems. The concept of the reconstruction of civil society, which appeared in Poland under many guises, allowed one to in effect argue that it is possible to democratize whole sectors of society while leaving the system's principle of identity intact in the all-crucial state sphere. This, of course, meant that democratization would have to be conceived as a complicated and perhaps long process in which the full democratization of the state could only be a last step. This difficulty was in part turned into a theoretical advantage as already argued, because it allowed one to focus on societal democ-ratization—something rather unusual in the history of democracy. But much would depend on (1) whether the boundaries between state and society could be convincingly drawn, (2) whether some kind of balance between these spheres with two organizational principles could be established, and (3) whether the system's identity could be maintained if restricted to the state sphere alone.

While many different strategic suggestions emerged in relation to these prob-lems, for the theory of the democratic opposition and for the development of Solidarity two turned out to be most significant: Michnik's "new evolutionism" and Kuroń's "self-limiting revolution." What the two strategies had in common was the focus of all their efforts on the emancipation of societal institutions and the concessions of the hegemony of the ruling party in the state as well as that of the Soviet Union over Poland's foreign and military affairs. But while to my knowledge these two leading figures of KOR did not (until perhaps very re-cently, from prison) ever explicitly indicate disagreements between them, their conceptions almost always were and are significantly different, to be sure within a common family. The reconstruction of society in Michnik's "new evolution-ism" has implied above all the creation of some important organized centers both anticipating a future democratization and capable of putting pressure on the state. The historical model for this was at least in part that of the church in Poland. According to Michnik the immediate aim of democratization should be the legal-ization of already existing forms of social organization and alternative forms of publicity; the method was seen as that of a compromise between society and state that was to be ultimately beneficial to both sides. While Michnik addressed his proposal to what he called independent public opinion, his solution pre-supposed a rational calculation of the pragmatic interests of a ruling party that will always manage to checkmate its own efforts at economic reform until com-pelled from below to carry them out. Michnik appealed, furthermore, to the common interest of all Poles and the Soviet leadership as well to avoid a bloody Polish-Soviet military confrontation. Kuroń's self-organized civil society on the other hand was one to be thoroughly organized by all forms of movements constituted by and through associations, cooperatives, unions, organs of self-management, free forms of intellectual life, and so forth. It was not so much the anticipation as the actual realization in the present of a vast part of what has been called here the plurality of democracies. Instead of putting pressure on the re-gime, this proposal involved bypassing it and presenting it with an enormous number of accomplished facts. Kuroń seemed to put, at least until the summer of 1981, far less emphasis than Michnik on legalization and compromise. His ap-peal to the rational interests of his opponents was to those of the Soviet Union—that presumably would benefit greatly from Poland's economic recovery, which could no longer be managed by a Soviet-type regime. Again the point was made that Soviet interests would be irreparably damaged by a Polish-Russian war, the result of intervention. While Kuroń too conceded that the ruling party could not be overthrown, the conception of the self-limiting revolution had, in fact, no function for it. For the steering of social processes Kuroń postulated the need to create what he called a "system of society" and even foreign and military affairs were conceded to the party only in its capacity as agent of the Soviet Union. Thus while Michnik's position seemed to have postulated only the emergence of a new, more socially emancipated version of authoritarian state socialism, Kuroń's tended toward what he himself called "Finlandization," that is, an evident rupture with the existing social formation with the exception of its overall imperial structure,.

Kuroń in fact had one powerful argument against all positions more gradualist than his, implicitly including Michnik's. According to him, the danger was not only repression from above, but also being swept away from below. Kuroń was in fact about the only Polish intellectual to anticipate the magnitude of the movement of 1980–81. If the organized movements stopped too soon in the context of the impending social and economic collapse, uncontrolled spontaneous outbreaks would everywhere emerge and a bloody confrontation with Soviet power would be unavoidable. What he sought, therefore, was a program that went *both far enough and not too far*. It is, however, a question whether he actually managed to answer both of these criteria. The model of society he projected in fact needed, according to his own overall conception, a parliamentary mediation, and he was forced covertly to sneak in such a conception under the heading of a "system of society." This, however, transgressed the idea of self-limitation, especially since it was always unthinkable that the Soviet Union entrust the representation of its interests in Poland either to an agency that is socially powerless or to a constellation of forces open to constant popular pressure. I believe the proof of this criticism is provided by Kuroń's own development. During the first phase of Solidarity some version of the "new evolutionism" also supported by DiP and the Catholic intellectuals predominated, and Kuroń in this context rightly anticipated great popular pressures for further democratization. After the Bydgoszcz provocation by the apparatus a radicalization of the movement occurred and now with Kuroń becoming perhaps the key adviser of Solidarity's leadership a version of the self-limiting revolution with its stress on social movements was adopted. When, however, given the regime's new strategy of disorganizing society by passively allowing the economic crisis to simply unfold with devastating results, many in Solidarity wanted to give up all self-limitation, Kuroń instead became the defender of a program that resembled more and more the new evolutionism and which involved a tireless search for formulas of compromise between movement and regime. It was in this context that he fought for the idea of a second parliamentary chamber, seeking to institutionalize a part of the political power of the movement in a way that would help the government regain its freedom of action and create a new institution for social compromise. He further defended, alone among the leading figures of the democratic opposition, the participation of Solidarity and church as junior partners in a governmental coalition with clearly corporatist overtones in order to help relegitimate the regime and to prepare the ground for a stabilization that would allow the movement to preserve some of its gains.

We, of course, now have to assume that the really significant elements of the regime leadership and the party apparatus as well as the Soviet Union were not interested in any form of compromise. But what is crucial is that the framework of ideas of the social movement, notwithstanding all talk of self-limitation, also did not on balance favor such an outcome. Kuroń's development was, as I have implied, unique. A good deal of articulate opinion within the milieu of Solidarity tended to give up by the fall of 1981 on the very possibility of compromise with communist power and more and more voices (mostly from the milieu of the right-wing group KPN to be sure) called for an impossible *unlimited* revolution. In the present context I am interested only in the role of the theory of the democratic opposition in such an outcome as well as in the inability of the movement to anticipate the prerequisites of martial law. The last is all the more important since the democratic theorists' relative success in predicting Soviet inaction was fully matched by their failure to prepare for the possibility of internal Polish repression.

In one of his essays written in Bialoleka prison, Adam Michnik maintained (without much explanation) that the failure of the democratic movement was also that of theory. I believe that he is right and that many of the opinions of the strategic conceptions just outlined can be traced to the theory that the post-Marxist democratic opposition, including Michnik, continues to hold to this day: the theory of totalitarianism. The adoption of this theory to Polish society begun, I believe, by Kołakowski in the 1970s was always in contradiction with both the famous models of the 1950s and Polish realities. Kołakowski himself originally tended to speak only of a totalitarian tendency of the party-state that could be opposed by countertendencies based on the reconstruction and defense of independent social life. In his own estimation the regime was becoming less ideological, and more dependent on an eclectic intellectual mix for legitimation—points at variance with the totalitarianism thesis of Friedrich, Brzezinski, Arendt et al. More importantly, a whole series of Polish writers following the investigations of S. Nowak demonstrated in the 1970s the existence in Polish society of wide circles of small-scale social life neither atomized nor penetrated by the values, rules, and motivations proposed and required by the ruling institutions. I would argue, therefore, that in Poland the reasons for adopting the totalitarianism thesis were practical rather than theoretical, and were dependent on a construction of social reality quite characteristic for not only the Poland of the 1970s but for Polish history since the partitions. In no country, to make the point short, does the idea of society against the state have such a historical resonance; the preservation of Polish culture by a culturally unified society against three occupying states in the period of the partition and the defense of Poland by an underground society during German occupation both speak for this imagery. In the 1970s

Polish writers of widely different political persuasions found it meaningful to renew this language under the opposition not only of society against the state, but also nation *against* state, social order *against* political system, "pays réel" *against* "pays légal" or "pays officiel," public life *against* the state, private life *against* public life, and so on. While it is extremely important to note the immense significance of such imagery for popular mobilization, it should also be clear by now that speaking analytically this way of conceiving Polish social reality was also seriously misleading. Standing on the ground of an empirical-analytical systems theory rather than a normatively based action theory of society, Jadwiga Staniszkis—one of the few neo-Marxists in Poland—has pointed to the impossibility of assuming the unity of either state or society or for that matter their entirely sharp separation. In fact, the very reemergence in the 1970s of new and heterogeneous forms of association, protest, and public expression itself speaks against the postulated unity of society. To be sure, the legalization and institutionalization of this plurality and its protection from state penetration remained tasks for the future: In this sense the reconstruction of *civil* society retained its normative importance. But the achievement of this reconstruction seemed to require the full unity of society *which would be decreasingly given as the program actually progressed.* The totalitarianism thesis was, I believe, for many the practical resolution of this difficulty: Against a totalitarian state, of course, all social forces would have to be fully united whatever their potential differences in ideas and interests. While for social mobilization this intellectual turn surely had its importance, in the process a theory was smuggled into the program of the democratic opposition that was incompatible both with the strategy of self-limitation (especially its more dependable, new evolutionist version) and with an adequate theoretical assessment of the political situations facing the democratic movement. Let me list some of the major theoretical difficulties in an unavoidably schematic manner:

1. A modern society, and in particular the one projected by the Polish opposition, requires the outputs of a state (legality, interest intermediation, socioeconomic steering, sovereignty, etc.). A totalitarian state in Eastern Europe could not, either by definition or in context of historical experience, produce most of these. But since the Polish state could not be overthrown, the opposition in effect postulated a self-contradictory strategy of social reorganization.

2. The theory of totalitarianism is incompatible with the idea that Soviet-type systems can actually develop and can have distinctly different stages. Thus it implies an all-or-nothing relation to the existing system—ultimately its revolutionary overthrow. Little thought could be given in such theoretical context to changing essential aspects of the system and yet allowing it to preserve its principle of identity even though such was the implication of the new evolutionism. Thus the existence of the independent union legally

recognized had to seem just as anomalous (at least secretly) to the opposition as to the regime.

3. The theory of totalitarianism allows for only two modes of interest intermediation: monolithic from above and pluralistic from below. In fact, plurality can take many others, including various corporatist forms, and important sectors of Polish society, in particular the church and perhaps even parts of the regime, in fact had various types of corporatist projects of compromise and stabilization. Such a solution could have been less incompatible with the principle of identity of the system than the pluralistic ideals of the opposition and could have constituted an important half-way house toward further democratization.

4. The theory of totalitarianism presupposes, as I have argued, the necessity of complete coordination of all social forces versus the state. This assumption turned out to be especially misleading in the case of the episcopate of the church, which quite evidently has not for a long time treated the system as totalitarian. Thus while the democratic opposition operated with a theory that made compromises with the regime or its parts very difficult, its presumed partner in the struggle for democratization could make its own compromises totally justified from its own point of view, as we have seen after martial law but in fact should have known since 1956. The church must, of course, struggle for *some* societal independence to operate where it is not a state church, but its definition of civil society is quite different from that of the democratic opposition, and the amount of societal independence it needs is also considerably more limited.

5. The ideology of society against the state reinforced by the totalitarianism thesis papered over deep differences in the social movement and in particular Solidarity itself. This made it more difficult both to deal with legitimate conflicts having to do with the internal democracy of the movement, and to defend the organization against the destructive tendencies of political fundamentalism and at times aggressive nationalism.

6. The theory of totalitarianism made the regime and the ruling party appear as more monolithic than they had to be. Thus the opposition found it difficult to exploit internal tensions and conflicts; above all no support was given to democratizing forces during the party congress of June 1981. Even Michnik characterized (I believe wrongly) the language of the "horizontal links" rank-and-file movement in the party as Marxist-Leninist "newspeak." Such an attitude of course weakened precisely those in the ruling structure ready for some kind of compromise—though their position was rather weak to begin with.

7. Paradoxically, the same theory made the party-state regime appear also weaker than it actually was. The experience of Hungary in 1956 in fact spoke for the extremely rapid collapse of an apparently all-powerful structure of power under pressure. Such a thing did not happen in Poland in

1980–81, as Krysztof Pomian has forcefully argued. No longer caught up with a totalitarian identity the structure did not collapse when its penetration of Polish society was drastically reduced. The identity crisis of the membership did not immediately lead to leadership splits—the overall institution was no longer cut from a single organization or even ideological cloth. The politically disruptive congress of the party was masterfully stage-managed through a good dose of formal democracy and the result was a coherent strategy.

8. It was a related and a complementary mistake to assume that the regime had no social bases whatsoever, another implication of the classical totalitarianism thesis. In fact, while it could count on little active support, its passive support among some managerial and white-collar strata, the officer corps, some workers and unorganized strata, especially in the case of a social stalemate, seems significant, even if it is still too early to systematically assess its extent and importance.

9. Even more important was the consequence of the synthesis of the totalitarianism thesis with the, in itself, not invalid conception of the Soviet system of states as an empire. The result was invariably the assumption that, the Soviet Union being the totalitarian center of the whole complex, the Polish state had no independent sovereign power. To be sure, the partial sovereignty of the Polish state in comparison to the Ukraine or Lithuania has been repeatedly noted by people such as Kołakowski and Michnik, as well as the DiP reports. In context of the emergence of Solidarity and the massive loss by the regime of even negative legitimation, it was assumed that this residual sovereign power has disappeared. In fact, the decisionless stalemate promoted by the apparatus and played into by the fundamentalist tendencies and rhetoric of some of Solidarity, led to a dramatic reconstitution of sovereign power.

10. Finally, the *society against the state* conception was identified with the symbolism of *nation against the state*, as I already said. This meant that in spite of Kołakowski's pointing out as early as 1971 that nationalism and raison d'état have become key legitimating principles of the regime, it was assumed that the national issue belonged entirely to the opposition. This was, however, not the case either for aggressive, anti-Semitic forms of nationalism promoted by sectors of the regime that may have had some appeal to groups in the parts of the movement mobilized by right-wing groups such as KPN (Congress for an Independent Poland), or for the much more important defensive, organic forms of nationalism, which in the hands of the church became an argument against any possible action that carried the slightest risk for the nation. While the regime's use of nationalist legitimation eventually favored the opposition's utilization of national symbols against the regime, the converse was also true to a lesser extent. While the party apparatus in particular had little success in clothing

its actions in national symbolism, the situation was rather different for Jaruzelski and the officer corps. One should recall even Wałesa's repeated expressions of sympathy for the military before martial law. Several surveys before December 13 show that this attitude was very general indeed. In this context the defense of the early parts of Pilsudski's career even by people like Michnik seems to have been unfortunate in retrospect.

Let me conclude: The normative intentions and strategic ambiguities of the Polish democratic opposition are not a matter only of yesterday. Today the vision of the plurality of democracies—under the name of the "self-governing republic"—the strategy of the new evolutionism, and the theory of totalitarianism remain basic components of the program of Solidarity underground as well as of the world view of a large number of Polish workers and intellectuals. Nevertheless, it is today more of a mistake than ever to describe the regime as totalitarian—indeed the opposition might be facing the future self-differentiation of a specifically Polish road of Authoritarian State Socialism. As János Kis put it, the present regime is hard, yet full of inconsistencies and discontinuities. Its reliance on the army and the church is both a source of strength and a source of weakness. It is certainly in no position to violently reverse the immense development of the general political culture in a democratic direction. It seems powerless to produce, unlike the Kádár regime in the 1960s, a workable solution of the economic crisis. This situation favors a strategy of the "long march" proposed by the two leaders of the underground, Bujak and Kulerski, and seconded by Michnik from his jail cell, even if the idea of building a parallel, alternative society remains as problematic as ever. It does not seem to favor Kuroń's call from prison for a centralized organization working toward the rapid and perhaps violent overthrow of the regime. But all plausible strategies presuppose, as I tried to show, a better theoretical assessment of the situation than currently available to the opposition: In this sense even a self-limiting anti-Leninist revolution will continue to presuppose a critical social theory. In spite of its weak force for social mobilization, a reconstructed neo-Marxism, such as that of Jadwiga Staniszkis, may still have the best chance of providing aspects of such a theory that are screened out perhaps necessarily by post-Marxian democratic theory.

11

Some Perspectives of Democratization in East Central Europe

East Central Europe and Democracy: neither term is self-explanatory. East Central Europe as a term of *political geography* refers to the four countries at the western periphery of the Soviet imperial system: Poland, Czechoslovakia, the German Democratic Republic (GDR), and Hungary. There are weighty reasons not to accept Milan Kundera's provocative division of Europe and the East, or even Perry Anderson's somewhat different and more traditional two-part categorization of Western and Eastern Europe. As a brilliant article by the Hungarian historian Jenö Szücs argues, Central Europe has represented at least since 1000 A.D. a third autonomous, if intermediate, lineage of historical development.[1] The expression Central Europe is needed to delimit that part of this area under Soviet occupation, excluding the western and southern portions which are part of Western Europe and Yugoslavia respectively. What is important here is that the political situation and perspectives of East or Sovietized Central Europe be treated as a unique cluster.[2]

Democracy or democratization as expressions of *political philosophy* also call for some explication especially because in current political discourse the meanings are generally taken for granted and are identified with the macroinstitutions of representative democracy in the West. As the Greeks knew, democracy—or rather citizenship—in a true *politeia* involves both some significant relativization of the distinction between the ruler and the ruled, and some relevant participation of the ruled in the ruling process. All historical democracies have had exclusionary rules (e.g., toward slaves, women, children, foreigners, non-property-owners, etc.); by definition a democracy is democratic only vis-à-vis its own citizens. Modernity has affected the meaning of democracy in three significant ways: (1)

Reprinted with permission from *Journal of International Affairs*, vol. 38, no. 2, pp. 320–35. © Trustees of Columbia University in the City of New York.

The meaning of citizenship has been greatly extended; modern democracy and democratic ideals are universal in principle; (2) The modern (vs. the estate) representative principle has decisively altered the meaning of participation, and has involved along with the advantages of large territorial size and large-scale participation, the cost of the emergence of new extralegal exclusionary principles; (3) The modern differentiation of society has potentially pluralized the meaning of democracy: In principle democracy now is relevant not only to political but also to social, economic and even cultural institutions.

Any version of modern democracy implies universalism, representation, and pluralism. However, democratization remains everywhere an open task. The exclusionary principles or representative democracy can imply its routinization and thereby the depolitization of its citizenry. The restriction of democracy to the political sphere can easily mean that some truly significant power relations remain exempt from democratic control. The "Democratization of democracy" as a utopia implies the coexistence of representative and direct forms of political, social and economic democracy. This utopian conception will be called here the plurality of democracies.

As a regulative principle the plurality of democracies is especially relevant to East Central Europe. Experiments in this direction proliferated from Hungary in 1956, which saw the revival of party pluralism and the creation of workers' councils; to Czechoslovakia in 1968, where pluralism, emerging *within* the Communist party and other official organizations, was eventually complemented with workers' councils; and to Poland, where a free alternative public sphere[3] helped to consolidate a struggle for independent interest representation that rapidly developed into a multitude of free associations, forms of worker self-management and even a grass roots campaign to democratize the Communist party itself.

To be sure, all these struggles also aimed, in the short or long run, at parliamentary democracy. But as a series of important theorists from Istvan Bibó to Jacek Kuroń have recognized, their goal consisted of both *more* and *less*.[4] The conception of the plurality of democracies allows this apparent paradox, because while as a *utopia* it means more than merely parliamentary or even political democracy, as a program, the logical implication is that of a process of *democratization* that can begin in any of the relevant societal spheres. Thus the achievement of confessional freedom or a free trade union, of a workers' council or an independent peace group, represents democratization even where parliamentary democracy cannot yet be put on the agenda. Given the macrostructure of Soviet-type societies based on the monopoly of public life by a single *party* and their historically polemical attitude to Western types of democracy, parliamentary pluralism can be achieved only by a total break with the existing regime. Correspondingly, all programs of "self-limiting revolution" or radical reform from Bibó to Kuroń required some degree of self-denial precisely with respect to parliamentary democracy.

With regard to the eventual attainment of full-blown institutional democracy, including but not limited to free elections and political parties, the present self-limitation of East Central European struggles need not be seen only in terms of pathetic efforts to achieve some minimal gains relevant only because of Soviet domination. From Aristotle to Machiavelli, to Montesquieu and Tocqueville, the major theorists of political republicanism have recognized that without civic virtue and education, self-government is impossible. Tocqueville explicitly warned against mechanically transferring the institutions of a democratic republic (in particular those of the United States) to another society with very different traditions. Genuine democratic self-government in his conception was possible only on the basis of a political culture born of actual political participation, preferably on a small scale. We should note the obvious: with the exception of Czechoslovakia, prewar East Central European society had little experience with such a political culture. Nazi Germany, Pilsudski's Poland, and Horthy's Hungary were poor schools of democracy. Furthermore, forty years of Communist authoritarianism would have had ample chance to eclipse the democratic traditions which did survive from the various labor movements, from the institutions of Masaryk's republic in Czechoslovakia, from Weimar Germany, from the early Polish republic and from the Hungary of 1945, had it not been for the countermoves of Communist revisionism and popular uprisings. The defeated struggles always involved significant learning experiences and included small-scale forms of participation. The role of this small-scale organization is especially clear in the case of Poland where the production of underground literature, the organization of study and discussion groups, the creation of the cells of possible future interest representation, and the participation in independent cultural and religious activities, all helped to determine the scope and the character of the movement in formation. Thus, in East Central Europe, democracy must be seen as a process operating on several possible levels, or rather as processes of democratization, whose common denominator is always the implicit struggle to achieve the democratization of the political culture itself.

Three Models of Democratization

Without a doubt democratization of the political culture will only be stable if at least some democratic institutions are created and preserved. In East Central Europe three models of such institutionalization have emerged. Hungary's *popular revolution* in 1956 simply overthrew the institutions of authoritarian state socialism and was in the process of replacing them with those of parliamentary and industrial democracy when the Soviet invasion ended this development. The Czech *reform from above*, steered to the end by the new leadership of the Communist party, sought to democratize the ruling institutions from within, but this process also became more generalized in that it managed to release the popular energies of intellectuals and workers continuing even after another Soviet intervention. The program of the Polish democratic opposition, first formulated in 1976, incorporated what it had learned from its two predecessors. Having noted the impossibility of radical popular revolution, the Polish *revolution* would be *self-limiting*. Given the loss of Soviet confidence in a self-reforming Communist party, the Polish *reform* would have to come *from below*. "Self-limiting revolution" or "radical structural reform"; by either name the democratic movement, culminating in a workers' movement for the liberation of society,[5] aimed at partial but significant democratization of the overall social structure.

The goal of the movement, whose first and greatest triumphs were the accords of August 1980, was to exert popular pressure for political compromise and thereby achieve a series of democratic reforms that would still leave the identity of the existing systems intact. This formula would have to be self-contradictory to the extent that the identity of the existing system was defined as totalitarian. Such a definition, however, can be qualified in at least two ways: (1) the ruling center need not actually penetrate all spheres of life but needs only the prerogative of being able to do so, and (2) there is some historical evidence that even this prerogative may be abandoned in some carefully limited spheres of social life, the best example being the cultural sphere in important part abandoned to the Polish Catholic church. Accordingly one might reason that the system's totalitarian identity can be kept intact as long as the prerogative power of the ruling party survives in some significant social spheres. To be sure, the institutions of Soviet-type societies are generally not sufficiently differentiated to make such a conception fully plausible. The response of the Polish movement (or that of its best theorists) to this dilemma, was an audacious reformulation of its aims and its limits in terms of the classical state-society duality. In a *society* on the path toward self-organization the ruling party would be deprived of its power but it could still preserve its power in the *state* apparatus. That is, even as the mass media were made open, the economy decentralized and self-managing, and social organizations autonomous, the legislative, judicial, bureaucratic, and military bodies of the state would remain under party control.

While this fundamental conception was realized only tendentially in 1980–81, it is nevertheless possible to speak of a dualism of power in this period. I have analyzed its breakdown elsewhere[6] and would like here to stress only the double difficulty inherent in the original project. First, in the sphere of the state which the model allotted to the party, several key institutions, in particular the economic, cultural, and organizational bureaucracies, would necessarily lose their original function and power. Thus the identity of the party-state, even in its own sphere, would be highly threatened[7]—an imploding authority would lose all freedom of action even where it was desired by society, for example, in processes of bargaining, economic reform, and steering, etc. Second, both the economic and the social life of Soviet-type societies are fully tied up with the command and steering functions of the party-state institutions.[8] In the context of a truly independent society these would have to be replaced by an alternative system or state. By conceding the state to the ruling party, by banishing the party from society, and by necessarily denying Polish society the possibility of creating alternative state institutions, the movement tendentially deprived this society of a state which could assume the roles necessary under modern conditions.[9] While the raging economic crisis was a product of both an almost ten-year-old policy and the palpable desire of the Soviet and Polish leaderships to discipline society through economic hardship, in fact the highly unintended consequence of the opposition program was to dislodge the party-state from its command position from where it might have managed the crisis and reformed the economy, while no social agency, not even Solidarity, could assume such a role. The crisis helped of course to devastate much of the remainder of the party-state's own authority, leaving it, in the end, with only the capacity to strike at society.

To be sure, this remaining capacity was nourished above all by the Soviet threat. But certainly many sectors of Polish society, whatever their emotional solidarity, tacitly, if passively, accepted the *Putsch* not solely as the only way to head off Soviet intervention, but also as a distasteful but unavoidable means for reestablishing some working order. The dramatic reconstitution of sovereign power in a decisionless political apparatus presupposes the majority of the population acting as subjects rather than citizens.

With the defeat of Solidarity and the dualistic program of the democratic opposition, the obvious question is whether or not the three East European experiments exhaust all rational strategies of democratization. Revolution from below, reform from above, and radical reform from below do seem to constitute an exhaustive list. But we should not confuse our logical categories with fluid realities. The model the Polish opposition constructed has already shown that reform and revolution did not exhaust the possibilities of change. Under new and different circumstances, internal and external, suitably reworked versions of any of the three strategies could again become relevant. New strategies could be invented, or features of the existing models could be combined as many sympathetic observers and participants like J. Pelikán[10] have suggested. The circumstances will always be new and different, not only because trivially everything changes, but because the movements themselves, in spite of their failures, decisively altered their environments in three possible ways: (1) Lessons learned by both regime and society from their conflict could shape the bases of novel forms of restabilization, as in the case of the Kádár regime in Hungary. (2) Lessons of societies from the struggles of their predecessors could be the bases for new projects of change, as in 1968 in Czechoslovakia, and 1976–81 in Poland. (3) Where confrontations with the population sufficiently threaten the survival of the Communist party itself, as in Hungary in 1956 and Poland in 1980–81, both local rulers and Soviet leadership receive sufficient incentive, even after a restoration, to allow a model of development more tailored to national needs, whether on an economic level (Hungary) or an ideological one (Poland).

The Crisis of Soviet-Type Regimes

The regimes of East Central Europe must fear not only popular opposition, but also their self-induced crisis tendencies. The current "political-economic" difficulties of the majority of Soviet-type societies are evident to all serious observers. Declining growth rates approaching stagnation in most countries, including the Soviet Union, are only the most ominous signs of structural underdevelopment, the cycle of shortage and waste, and industrial disequilibria.[11] The official economy ("first economy") is everywhere moribund, with the exception of the Soviet defense-related sector[12] and perhaps the East German economy—the latter's secret not being the much vaunted technocratic reform,[13] but a special relationship to West Germany (FRG) and thereby the European Economic Community (EEC). Poland is not the only country that has experienced the bankruptcy of a strategy of heavy borrowing in investment funds in the context of basically unchanged institutional structures; Romania and Hungary are deeply affected, and only the almost unlimited raw material reserves of the USSR and the generosity of the FRG vis-à-vis the GDR help to avoid similar outcomes. Czechoslovakia's nearly total stagnation of the industrial level shows the alternative to borrowing from more dynamic economies. Finally, the relative success of the Hungarian "second economy" is apparently no longer a guarantee of the gradual expansion of a consumer society in an overall economic context that is only very partially reformed.[14]

I. Szelényi and R. Manchin[15] summarize the theories of economic crisis in Soviet-type societies as (1) cyclical, (2) a product of the transition from extensive to intensive growth, and (3) a failed modernization leading to total stagnation. The first of these, based on the work of T. Bauer, stresses the oscillation between periods of heavy investment focused on the first sector of the economy, leading to widespread overtaxing of resources and resultant shortages, and periods of redirected investment in the second sector and agriculture for principally political reasons. The second theorem, often associated with F. Janossy, stresses the need for, and the difficulties of, a transition from an economy of extensive growth based on constant increase of the size of the labor force, low levels of consumption and monolithic steering institutions, to one of intensive development based on increases of productivity and consumption along with mixed economic steering structures. The third theorem disparages the success of Soviet-type industrialization and modernization for producing only "quasi-growth" and an overall structure that cannot be the basis of a transition to a modern, intensive growth economy.

The three arguments, each with a good deal of empirical-descriptive plausibility, can be combined. First, cyclical oscillation seems to become especially relevant to East European economies when the downward turn of the cycle comes in a period when the labor reserves for extensive growth are no longer available. In such a context the turn to a policy of greater stress on consumption must fail unless productivity can be dramatically increased. Second, the transition to intensive development and a final blockage of modernization should be seen as alternative outcomes which are dependent on political choices. Intensive development may not be possible within the present structure, but it remains an open question whether and to what extent that structure can be changed within a system which continues to maintain the same identity. I will return to this last issue.

Interestingly enough Szelényi indicates that the transition to an intensive stage could itself take the form of strategies oriented to peaceful consumption and military consumption. We need not consider the Soviet Union a complete "stratocracy" (stratos: army), as does Castoriadis, to recognize the profound truth of his theory, namely that for the imperial center, only the military alternative avoids the centrifugal tendencies that all serious economic reform would imply, tendencies that can be contained on the imperial peripheries only because the center is militarily intact. No society of the Soviet type, however, has according to Szelényi carried out the transition to an intensive economy in either form, because of the power of the classical forces arrayed against such a transition.[16]

Economic crisis in Soviet-type societies is different from that of capitalist economies. The absence of an economy fully differentiated from the state, requires us to speak above all of a crisis of administrative rationality[17] rather than a strictly economic crisis. It also implies certain advantages and disadvantages for the affected regimes. Social life in such a crisis is disorganized on a continuum, with uncertain thresholds of tolerance. The agencies of crisis management are able to disperse the most dangerous effects toward the relatively weak strata, regions, and institutions. However, such crises are neither self-adjusting nor self-regulating. At least in theory, politically generated reforms offer the only way out of such a crisis.

The experience of all East European regimes in 1968, possibly based on a false generalization from the single and rather unique Czech case, was that fundamental economic reforms threatened the identity of authoritarian state socialist systems. The identity of this prerogative state[18] is based on its primacy over all social spheres, meaning, as I have already said, not necessarily constant penetration but the ability to penetrate at will and to be able to reverse at least in principle all spontaneous social change.[19] No genuinely modern economy can function in the context of a prerogative of this type, which means that the only hope of reform from above would have to be based on the ability of a regime to differentiate economic life from the rest of society, and to establish forms of economic autonomy which do not spill over into the rest of society. Only in Hungary are there experiments and even proposals in this direction. On the whole, however, the Polish experience of 1976 to the present remains binding for Eastern Europe in general: No genuine reform of Soviet-type societies will occur without fundamental pressure from below.[20] Paradoxically, it is only autonomous social activity, inconsistent with the identity of the East European regimes, that can usher in a second structural stage of development *within* this identity.

The possibilities of muddling through an extended period of stagnation, of undertaking reform either in the sense of militarization or "economization," as well as the chances of social forces to influence developments, are all dependent on the reserves of legitimacy of the regimes. One might say that economic value, administrative force, and cultural meaning are three key aspects in the social integration of Soviet-type regimes, that can, to an extent, compensate for one another. But since the excess of administrative and police force that characterized the early stages of the regimes most likely cannot be reestablished[21] everything depends on the reserves of cultural meaning. In an epoch in which versions of Marxism or even other modernizing ideologies have been more-or-less tacitly abandoned, variations of national or nationalist legitimation and appeals to national traditions seem to represent the regimes' only real options.[22] From the implicit pursuit of Great Russian mythologies to the historicist tone of the late Kádár era, from the Dacian myth of Ceauşescu's clique to the Luther and Prussian revivals of the GDR, national legitimations, positive or negative, have almost everywhere come to the forefront. Even in Poland the Jaruzelski regime has since coming to power on December 13, 1981, assiduously cultivated the national colors. But national legitimation requires a minimum of national independence or, at the very least, the plausible negative argument (much used in Hungary and Poland) that even under the given conditions of restricted sovereignty a national optimum of some kind is somehow being achieved. Such a legitimation also requires tolerably good relations with culture-carrying forces, for example, the Catholic church in Poland, the FRG in the case of the GDR, and the populist intellectuals in Hungary. Finally, if used by the regimes, national legitimation is most effective when it comes from below: Solidarity in Poland, the small peace movement in the GDR, and the small opposition in Hungary all operate with and within the national identity—though in these cases these groups are largely free of nationalist particularism. As in the case of economic reform as a form of crisis management, national legitimation potentially increases the freedom of action not only of the regimes themselves but also of their opposition. whereas economic reform tends to reveal the identity of interests within and among strata, the national issue establishes a language through which these can begin to be articulated. The regimes themselves vary in the normative content they give to the national problematic: Hungary and East Germany represent a possibility that is not particularly aggressive and chauvinistic, Whereas the Romanian regime and some elements of the Polish regime represent the most authoritarian aspects in their own traditions, including oppression of minorities and anti-Semitism. But the various oppositions can also choose between a universalistic national language and a particularistic and aggressive one. One of the primary tasks of an intellectual opposition is not only to recapture the national issue from its regime, but to give it a democratic content. Today more than ever chauvinistic nationalism can only play into the integration of the imperial system.[23]

Strategies of the Opposition

The emergence and survival of a viable democratic opposition depends on acts of self-constituted organization and is never merely the spontaneous result of structural trends. This organization, in turn, depends on important prerequisites such as existing forms of social solidarity, of informal association and the capacities of action acquired through historical learning processes. Poland remains, even after Jaruzelski's *Putsch*, a country where all these prerequisites exist to a very high degree. The experience of Solidarity's sixteen magnificent months can never be forgotten. It is primarily the underground and at least some of the institutions of the movement—the extensive samizdat press, the informal lectures and get-togethers, the forms of self-help and mutual assistance—that keep alive that memory. The effect of this underground on possible institutional development and change within the regime is uncertain. However, the character of the martial law regime and of its "self-limiting repression" is an unmistakably important, if unintended, consequence of the social movement before and after December 13, 1981. For the regime, the necessity of appearing in national colors was imposed by the fact that Solidarity and the democratic opposition had recaptured the national issue from the regime and, to an extent, even from the Church. The continued central role of the military is connected both to the needs of legitimation and to the functional collapse of the party apparatus. Even if party-state and army and state are still fused at the top, the continued dominance of a military-based faction rather than orthodox hardliners demonstrates the need of the regime to placate both its own "society" and that of the Soviet Union. Hard-line orthodoxy could not play such a role in the Polish regime. Potential or actual social pressure remains a key facet of the Polish situation.

The role of the episcopate of the Catholic church, its great influence and especially its ability to bargain, also have been revitalized by the existence of popular pressure. One may indeed consider it a betrayal of the underground when the episcopate agreed to the terms of the pope's second visit on the eve of a potentially extensive strike in November 1982. However, the pope's visit was something the Polish people desperately wanted, and it presented a definite risk for the authorities. Only the threat of continuing popular actions could exact such a concession. To be sure, the episcopate has been rather weak in exercising what is objectively a strong bargaining position. This in part flows from a less than fully conscious rivalry with Solidarity during its sixteen months, in part from the different interests of the Church and the democratic opposition that imply a more limited set of civil freedoms, in part from a cultural-religious rather than political definition of emancipation with a preference for slow, "organic" rather than conflict-oriented political activity. But even assuming all this, the leadership of the episcopate, and especially Archbishop J. Glemp, had no real reason to call for the end of the actors' boycott, to purge dissident priests at the regime's request, or to defame (as Glemp did in Latin America)[24] Solidarity and the democratic opposition. The state had no cards on the table (given the impossibility of using force under present circumstances) which could make the episcopate do any of this, as the incident over the crosses eventually showed—an incident that involved, to be sure, concessions by the regime only on a purely religious issue. In fact the acts in question by the episcopate came at a time of its hitherto unprecedented power, influence and even access to the regime itself.

The tactical weakness of the Church has been clearly demonstrated by the amnesty issue. When the episcopate cooperated in recommending a series of more-or-less humiliating bargains to the KOR (Workers' Defense Committee) and Solidarity defendants facing trial, the latter's courageous and unanimous refusal forced the regime eventually to capitulate on almost all serious points. Evidently the Church does not recognize the strength of the society for which it is the only negotiating partner recognized by the regime.

It is a constantly repeated claim of the Jaruzelski group that it established martial law in the hope of instituting both a Hungarian-type economic reform and a something like state-corporatist bargaining arrangement with the Church and perhaps a rump of Solidarity. However, neither the national nor the international context would allow for a Kádárist economic policy in Poland and the peasantry might be the only beneficiary of such attempt even if sufficient foreign capital for agricultural investment could be generated. State corporatism, on the other hand, requires strong partners in civil society, which the Church turned out not to be, and which could be supplied only by the social movement which the regime refused to deal with. The result is a stalemate. Though the opposition has no means of influencing policy the regime still cannot break what remains of the movement. Alternatively, without negotiating partners within society, the regime cannot consolidate its power or legitimize its rule.

A strategic debate that occurred within the underground in early 1982 is quite significant in this context. Within an overall agreement on theoretical assumptions involving, among other things, a rigid juxtaposition of society and state as well as some kind of adherence to the idea of self-limitation, maximalist and minimalist positions were advocated respectively by J. Kuroń (then in jail) and Z. Bujak and W. Kulerski (leaders of the underground). Jacek Kuroń , fearing the possibility of a total collapse, and hoping for a revival of a movement on the scale of the summer of 1980, proposed unprecedented radical political actions culminating in a "controlled" uprising. In addition he recommended, for the first time, a centralized directorate to lead a unified opposition strategy. Both ideas represented significant breaks with his moderate, anti-Leninist positions during Solidarity's sixteen months. By contrast, Bujak and Kulerski proposed instead a "long march" of a parallel society, the task of which would be the rebuilding and preservation of social bonds. Adam Michnik, in supporting the ideas of Bujak and Kulerski, added the task of developing a democratic political culture. "The resistance movement must be school for freedom and democracy." It is not clear however under what conditions the new or renewed social solidarities and political culture could again be politically significant. Kulerski and Bujak, at least in 1982, seemed to presuppose the gradual internal decomposition of the structure of power.

To assume however that over a long period of time a regime would have no options, especially given the (reluctant) acceptance by the Soviet Union of polymorphic development in East Central Europe, is not entirely convincing. Even the collapse of the Gierek regime was the result of seriously mistaken choices, not historical necessity. If continued stagnation might led to eventual political decomposition, the roads of at least partial economic reform and/or of corporatist compromise under national-religious colors are not yet closed to the regime. The opposition must be ready for all these eventualities, lest they be exploited by other forces. At the very least such preparedness would have to involve serious participation in discussions on the institutional and legal aspects of economic reform, and the continuing development of a concept of national identity that would distinguish the democratic opposition from both the authoritarian concepts of the defenders of the regime and the defensive organic conceptions of the Church. The tasks of the present can rightly be seen as educational; the tasks of the future appear, for the moment, to exist on the level of theory. A theoretical orientation will be needed to exploit the opportunities which arise from the choices available to the regime and from the potential interaction of the regime with other social forces, in particular the Church.

While the small Hungarian opposition lacks connections to a popular movement, its level of theoretical reflection and self-reflection is very advanced indeed. Hungarian writers both within the self-declared opposition and in the regime's reluctantly permissive *theoretical* public sphere (forced into competition with the culture of the *samizdat*) have been particularly conscious of the growing crisis of all Soviet-type societies and (unexpectedly to many Westerners) of the Hungarian economy itself.[25] Conclusions offered within legally published journals emphasize the need for a second reform, presumably to be instituted from above, while the most radical statements also stress forms of social independence, especially industrial self-management. It is to the credit of the samizdat journal *Beszélő* and especially János Kis, one of its editors, to have posed the question of what the opposition (and other social forces) must do in an epoch in which the Hungarian regime, whose ideological self-understanding remains reformist, has lost the internal impulse and resources for reform. Highly influenced by the Polish writers of KOR, the bulk of the Hungarian opposition is radical reformist and has for a long time advocated a program of some kind of dualistic reconstruction of the system within its original identity.[26] Interestingly, after Polish martial law this dualism has been reformulated in unusually minimalist terms by the journal *Beszélő* some of whose editors were originally quite critical of all such efforts to fundamentally restrict the drive toward democratization.

The fundamental starting point of János Kis's debate-opening article was, to be sure, "Polish."[27] In a period of economic decline in East Central Europe which, in Hungary, is manifesting itself in the form of a squeeze on real incomes, a new round of reforms is desperately needed. But since the regime's leadership is deeply fearful of mobilizing public support for such a policy—needed in order to break the resistance of the apparatus—only the self-generation of pressure for reform *from below* could usher in a "second reform," without which both the leadership and the populace face highly undesirable political outcomes. The role of the second public sphere of the opposition is precisely to help enlighten the potential sources of such pressure, to inform relevant groups of the population about the dangers of the situation, and to give shape to potential demands. The editors of *Beszélö* including Kis do not doubt that there is still a serious if abstract desire for reform within the leadership: To this extent the situation is unlike the one in Poland in the 1970s and 1980s. But in Hungary too the opposition believes that only public pressure could move reform beyond abstract discussion which is otherwise drowned in internal bureaucratic bargaining.[28] The proposals of *Beszélö* are striking in their moderation. The nature of their radical reformism implies finding the minimum institutional change that could make a difference, and to pursue this minimum in a radical and uncompromising manner. Kis and his colleagues attempt thereby to conceive of a form of division of labor between the regime and other social forces that would meaningfully maintain the prerogatives of the ruling structure and still give society an independent voice and an independent role in political initiatives. "There are important political goals that can be approached without attacking the fundamental institutions of the system." The slogans of publicity, defense of interests, "rule of law," (the German *Rechtsstaatlichkeit* would be a better, more limited term and a more accurate translation of the Hungarian *jogàllamisàg*) are of course radical enough: but *Beszélö*'s interpretations of these primarily involve extensions of existing Hungarian trends, not the creation of new institutions and organizations. There is, however, one issue of fundamental principle which is raised, in particular, by the discussion of rule of law (*Rechtsstaatlichkeit*). In Kis's later restatement[29] this issue occupies a central place: He proposes the clear legal definition and codification of all the relevant changes (economic, cultural, and personal rights) that have occurred in Hungary in the epoch of Kádárism, and a clarification of what is permitted or administratively restricted regarding the rights of various social agents. This proposal does not require the regime to do anything new, only to give a codified and guaranteed legal form to what it already does: for example, the toleration of forms of private enterprise, of serious intellectual work within the official public sphere, and the right to travel. In other words, the proposal concentrates on the revitalization of the judicial sphere which makes sense only in the context of a thorough reform, not only of the legal code, but also of the system of the administration of justice. The implementation of these reforms requires no new institutions, but only that the existing ones be granted greater independence from the prerogative power of the state.

The model of emancipation thus implied by Kis's proposal is that of the

nineteenth-century constitutional state (or rather *Rechtsstaat*), important historically in the three East European imperial systems. Is this a plausible historical
model for any Soviet-type society? As I have repeatedly argued, the essence of
the identity of authoritarian state socialist systems is to maintain the primacy of
the prerogative state, which implies not that nothing can be changed but only that
all changes are to be always revocable, and that there can be no rights as such
vis-à-vis the regime.[30] Under such conditions, strictly speaking, only a modified
Rechtsstaat is imaginable, one that restricts legal guarantees to a well-defined
sphere such as the economy. Some Hungarian writers like G. Konrád and I.
Szelényi believe that such a step would be sufficient to guarantee the further
development of the "bourgeoisie" (i.e., actors within the second economy) as a
class, who, according to I. Szelényi,[31] could then eventually become "citoyens,"
in a course of development that might be like the supposedly standard Western
European path. The model to which Szelényi refers, however, is in fact the
German path of development—economic rights without political liberties—
while the Polish model of the constitution of a modern civil society before
economic reform is in fact closer to the French revolutionary democratic and
English constitutionalist precedents. The Marxian assumption that the citizen is a
product of the formation of a bourgeois class is generally false. The German
path, as it has been often argued, has produced only a deformed version of civil
society and citizenship. Similarly, the Hungarian reform has not tended to produce citizens. The existence of the opposition itself, which speaks against this
thesis, is sociologically speaking a very limited phenomenon. M. Vajda and J.
Kis argue convincingly that next to the "many good things" brought by
Kádárism, the increased dependence on semilegal and illegal economic activities
has tended to loosen social solidarities connected to legal, rule-governed conduct, has brought on an extreme privatization of action, and has produced a
morality of adaptation to all political realities. As a result, the greatest task ahead
is precisely the building of the elements of a democratic political culture which
must involve important collective learning processes. For Vajda the preservation
and further development of an alternative public sphere as an end in itself is the
most important contribution a primarily intellectual opposition can make to such
a political culture. According to Kis, however, this opposition must try to initiate
explicitly political projects relevant to others outside itself in order to contribute
to collective learning on the level of actual conflicts. Whether or not his proposal
concerning the gradual introduction of elements of a genuine *Rechtsstaat* is
acceptable to the regime, two conclusions follow from his argument: (1) new
economic reform is unthinkable without new forms of legal guarantees for independent economic activity, and (2) struggle for legality is a struggle against the
degeneration of *social integration* itself.

We should not assume that the Hungarian opposition is no longer interested in
issues like workers' self-management, free unions, or free legislative elections.
The new minimalism that *Beszélö* seeks to formulate is meant to address a very

difficult immediate situation, which could help refurbish the regime's own reformism and at the same time encourage the development of the political culture
in a more positive direction. The opposition's attitude toward the national question takes, to an extent, the same form.The regime's increasing reliance on
national meanings and traditions[32] along with its potential use of nationalist
rhetoric as a replacement for diminishing economic goods is recognized by the
opposition.[33] At the same time the national issue cannot disappear for a population that continues to experience a diminished national sovereignty and the
highly unsatisfactory condition of Hungarian minorities in Czechoslovakia and
Romania. Again, the opposition's formula seems to be to try to push the regime's
unavoidable concern for the national issue in a more positive direction and to
initiate a positive learning experience for the population. This double intention is
made clear by G.M. Tamás in an article published abroad[34] after a series of
refusals in Hungary. According to him, even given the geopolitical restrictions
imposed by the Soviet Union, the Hungarian regime could do much more (on the
level of bilateral negotiations) to improve the conditions of Hungarian minorities
abroad. In crisis situations (e.g., during the attempted trial of the Hungarian
dissident Duray by the Slovak authorities) one of the tasks of the opposition is to
stimulate the regime to make the right moves by publicizing the issue and by
mobilizing popular support. While, for reasons of legitimation, the regime cannot
disregard the fate of Hungarian minorities abroad, neither the regime nor the
population is particularly sympathetic to the problems of national minorities
living in Hungary. It is only the opposition, along with like-minded persons who
have sufficient access to the official public sphere, that can link the two issues
together—the fates of Hungarian minorities abroad and of national minorities in
Hungary—and thus contribute to the emergence of a democratic form of national
identity, which at present is not the standard form in the Hungarian political culture.

Thus, the open tasks of the Hungarian opposition are to help bring a *will from
below* into the reform discussion and to help give any future reform a desirable
direction within the form of *Rechtsstaatlichkeit*; and to contribute to the development of the political culture, and increasingly the forms of national legitimation,
in a democratic direction. The Polish opposition, even after its great defeat, has
incomparably more power and influence to bring to bear on issues such as this.
In Hungary, however, the internal tendencies of the regime itself offer distinctly
better chances for the desired developments. What is common in Poland and in
Hungary is that a democratization of the existing system can be achieved only in
the context of popular pressure whose central medium for the moment remains
the alternative public sphere of the opposition.

East Central Europe and the West

Can we do anything to promote the difficult democratization of East Central
Europe? A brief response here must suffice. Western governments should begin

by avoiding two lines of policy that endanger democratization. The first is the military and political posture of the Reagan administration vis-à-vis the Soviet Union since 1981. Whether the development of a Soviet stratocracy (stratos: army) is only a very real tendency (Szelényi) or an already completed process (Castoriadis), or the Soviet Union is indefinitely caught up in the rule of a conservative gerontocracy (Heller), all aggressive posturing and intensification of the arms race can only strengthen the national-imperial legitimations consolidating the system. From the Soviet point of view, in the context of such legitimation even the most moderate economic luxury, and all East Central European manifestations of independence are under constant threat.

The second incorrect strategy is détente in the sense that the German Social Democrats mean it. Such a policy offers good economic relations without any quid pro quo concerning human rights within the Soviet empire. It is striking, for example, to compare the political backwardness of the whole East German scene with the Hungarian one in spite of the massive economic involvement of the FRG with the GDR. Pressure from abroad does play a role: The Hungarian government, for example, can never be as sure of automatic Western good will as apparently the GDR can be with respect to the support of the FRG, regardless of who controls the latter's government. As far as the Soviet Union is concerned either a conservative oligarchy or a new stratocracy could utilize a détente with no strings attached to avoid all internal reforms in the center and the peripheries of the empire. Though not relevant for this discussion, it is also worth pointing out that peace and security for the West can also not be attained through this type of Western policy.[35]

"Détente with strings" was, of course, the policy of the Carter administration. It had some significance with respect to East Central Europe. It is my conviction that the period of the preparation of *Solidarity* in the Gierek era and the continuing spirit of reformism in Hungary owes much to this policy. The dangers of such a policy, however, have become apparent to the Soviets, whose invasion of Afghanistan was in part a loud "no" to this kind of détente. And yet, in the context of the Polish martial law, a selective application of the principle of "détente with strings," in the form of American sanctions, has helped to bring about the most dramatic amnesty in the history of repression in Soviet-type societies. This has been amply demonstrated in the rhetorical linking of the sanctions with the amnesty by several Polish leaders. But the policy cannot work in the long run while a very different one exists vis-à-vis the Soviet Union. The recent attack on Honecker's détente indicates that the Soviet leadership will not easily permit such important private deals for its satellites. At a time when the East Central European oppositions are learning not to link their fate to economic disaster, the American government too should expect little positive to come from such economic difficulties, inevitably the product of an intensified arms race. Even in Poland it was the Gierek era that helped to nourish the seeds of Solidarity while the insoluble economic crisis was one of the real foundations of its defeat.

Under what conditions should Western governments opt for a policy of "détente with strings"? Only if their self-interest requires it: They too must be pushed from below. This, rather than any unilateral disarmament, would be the program of a movement for peace and democracy in the West concerned not only with the dangers of the arms race but also with the fate of East Central Europe.

Notes

1. J. Szücs, "Vázlat Europa három régiójárol" [An Outline Concerning the Three Regions of Europe], *Bibó Emlékkönyv* (Budapest, samizdat publication, 1981).
2. M. Vajda, "Kelet-Középeurópai perspektivák" [East-Central European Perspectives] (ms., Budapest, 1984).
3. J. Goldfaru, *On Cultural Freedom. An Exploration of Public Life in Poland and America* (Chicago: University of Chicago Press, 1982).
4. A. Arato, "The Democratic Theory of the Polish Opposition: Normative Intentions and Strategic Ambiguities," Chapter 10, this volume.
5. A. Touraine et al., *Solidarity. The Analysis of a Social Movement: Poland 1980–81* (New York: Cambridge University Press, 1983).
6. A. Arato, "Empire vs. Civil Society," Chapter 9, this volume.
7. J. Staniszkis, *Pologne: la révolution autolimitée* (Paris: P.U.F., 1982).
8. F. Fehér, A. Heller, G. Márkus, *The Dictatorship over Needs* (New York: St. Martin's Press, 1983), part 1.
9. A. Arato, J. Cohen, "Social Movements and State Sovereignty," forthcoming in *Praxis International.*
10. J. Pelikán, "Der Kampf um Menschenrechte. Osteuropa vor grossen Veränderungen," in J. Pelikán, M. Wilke, eds., *Menschenrechte* (Hamburg: Rowohlt, 1977).
11. G. Márkus, "Planning the Crisis," *Praxis International* 1, no. 3 (Oxford), October 1981.
12. C. Castoriadis, *Devant la Guerre* (Paris, 1982).
13. A. Nove, "The Politics of Economic Reform," in *Political Economy and Soviet Socialism* (London: George Allen and Unwin, 1979). Also see R. Manchin and I. Szelényi, "Eastern Europe in the 'Crisis of Transition,' " in B. Misztal, ed., *Polish Solidarity and Beyond* (Boulder, CO: Westview Press, 1984).
14. J. Kis, "Quelques idées pour l'opposition hongroise," *Ésprit* (Paris, February 1983), originally in *Beszélö* no. 3 (Budapest, 1982) and T. Bauer, "A második gazdasági reform es a tulajdonviszonyok" [The Second Economic Reform and Relations of Property] in *Mozgó Világ* no. 11 (Budapest, 1982).
15. Manchin, Szelényi, op. cit.
16. For a good summary see Nove, op. cit.
17. J. Habermas, *Legitimation Crisis* (Boston: Beacon Press, 1975).
18. E. Fraenkel, *The Dual State* (New York: Oxford University Press, 1941).
19. A. Arato, "Critical Sociology and Authoritarian State Socialism," Chapter 3, this volume.
20. Manchin, Szelényi, op. cit.; also see A. Arato, "Civil Soviety vs. the State," Chapter 8, this volume.
21. Fehér, Heller, Márkus, op. cit., part 3.
22. A. Arato, "Understanding Bureaucratic Centralism," *Telos* no. 35 (Spring 1978);

M. Vajda, "Existing Socialism in Light of the Traditions," in *The State and Socialism* (London: Allison and Busby, 1981), as well as ms. cited in note 2. G. Schöpflin's "Problems of National Identity in Hungary," to my knowledge still unpublished, is also extremely relevant.

23. L. Kołakowski, "Thèses sur l'espoir et désespoir," in *La Pologne: une société en dissidence* (Paris: Maspero, 1978).

24. See the report in the *New York Times*, March 3, 1984.

25. See Bauer, op. cit.; Kis, op. cit.; and J. Kis, "Másfél év után ugyanarról" [A Year and a Half Later on the Same Topic] in *Beszèlö* (Budapest, 1984).

26. See the debate in *Magyar Füzetek* no. 1 (Paris, 1978) between A. Hegedüs and G. Bence and J. Kis.

27. Kis, "Quelques idées," 49ff.

28. See the editorial of *Beszèlö* no. 5–6 (Budapest, December 1982).

29. Kis, "A Year and a Half Later," 86ff.

30. Heller, Fehér, Márkus, op. cit., part 2.

31. Szelényi, Manchin, op. cit, 29.

32. Vajda, "East-Central European Perspectives," *passim*.

33. Kis, "A Year and a Half Later," 84.

34. G.M. Tamás, "A magyar kérdés" [The Hungarian Question] in *Magyar Füzetek* no. 11 (Paris, 1982).

35. See the articles dealing with the peace movements by A. Gorz, P. Thibaud, A. Heller and F. Fehér, and A. Arato and J. Cohen in *Telos* nos. 51, 53, 58, 59.

12

Social Theory, Civil Society, and the Transformation of Authoritarian Socialism

I

Consider the following depiction. Under an autocratic state, in what is juridically the private sphere, a new form of public life is constituted. No legal authority, no political power is claimed here, only the power of conscience, the authority of morals. In effect a new social realm is carved out from the state, or in other words, the social world is reduplicated as civil society *and* state. Initially the institutional spaces for the new "society" are provided by private homes, clubs, cafés and educational institutions. Soon its activity finds a true medium in some legal, illegal, and emigré publications. Society is unable to directly challenge the state, yet its very process of self-institution as well as its monopoly of moral legitimacy delegitimizes a state based exclusively on *raison d'état*, while the weapons of public criticism begin to erode a sovereignty based on secrecy. Public enlightenment thus helps to constitute a social movement whose apolitical claims appear entirely hypocritical to the established powers. The repressive activity of the state can reprivatize society, or drive it underground and even force it to turn (against its own principle) to secrecy. Nevertheless, the parallel society survives on the basis of its intellectual authority and especially the moral solidarity of its members. The apparently purely spiritual operation of a republic of letters using the medium of critical public opinion continues to exercise political influence and achieve political results. From the polemical point of view of the state, the ongoing challenge to *raison d'état* threatens to institutionalize not civil society, but civil war. Thus Reinhart Koselleck (writing in 1959), to be sure in my free adaptation, depicts in *Kritik und Krise* the political crisis of the French Enlightenment. All of us are indeed familiar with similar depictions, as well as

---

Reprinted with permission from *Crisis and Reform* (New Brunswick, NJ: Transaction Press, 1990).

juxtapositions such as society or civil society *against* state, nation *against* state, social order *against* political system, *pays réel* against *pays légal* or *officiel*, public life *against* public power, etc. While the analogies between a depiction of the eighteenth-century struggle against absolutism, and the self-understanding of the contemporary actors are striking, from the point of view of the social theorist they are necessarily disquieting. Can self-interpretations remain politically relevant when they reproduce the orientation of a very different social and political epoch? It may be that the twentieth-century historian is engaging in unacceptable backward projection, but also that the metaphor of the actors is a hopeless projection of something already past into the present and future. Of course, there cannot be much doubt about the great mobilizing power of these dichotomies, shown especially by recent Polish experience. Nevertheless, the general theoretical validity of the constructs and thus their usefulness for orientation cannot be thereby automatically assumed.

To my knowledge, the most challenging critique of the society against the state metaphor has been presented by Jadwiga Staniszkis in several of her writings. Let me outline and expand her general line of attack:

1.   The polarization of society versus the state is connected to the Polish political tradition, based on contexts in which three foreign imperial governments represented the state.
2.   Polish culture could survive the age of partitions by preserving its own traditions, mentalities, practices, system of education, and religion in isolation from the state(s).
3.   The strategy was, however, always a purely defensive one, and is not suited for real social change.
4.   The posttotalitarian state is more subtle and penetrating, more invisible and corrupting than the openly repressive foreign-ruled states of the past. Thus the isolation of state and society is in principle not possible.
5.   The unity of society is illusory on the empirical level, and normatively speaking a populist and solidarist uniformity imposed on society (as according to her in the sixteen months of Solidarity) is in any case undesirable.
6.   The unity of the party-state is also illusory, and from the strategic point of view hardly desirable. The *society against the state* metaphor has made it impossible to exploit internal cleavages and tensions in state and party. Reformist attempts from above and within the ruling structure had to be pronounced as *a priori* illusory and compromise could be understood only as strategic compromise, that is, in principle unstable. Party oppositions were continually driven back into the party.
7.   Popular mobilization and conflict under the aegis of the dualistic conception can only amount to merely ritualized forms of channeling opposition, and has not been and will not be able to produce any significant change in the existing system.[1]

One could, of course, criticize in turn several of these points, and in any case, the last one has been proven dramatically wrong by the events of 1980–81. Contrary to Staniszkis's original expectation, the society *versus* the state metaphor has not lost its power to mobilize (a point she later admitted),[2] and only juxtaposition with some schematic idea of total transformation could allow us (or her) to denounce the results as involving no significant change. Nevertheless, there remain essential differences between the ideological needs of highly mobilized situations and those of more normal, everyday contexts of conflict and interaction as well as between interpretation taking the point of view of participants and social theory needed to understand the constraints faced but rarely understood by those very participants, the collective actors. If Staniszkis's criticisms are to be answered, it is thus insufficient to point to the thirteen-year continuous and productive history of the strategy associated with the name KOR, and we must undertake a theoretical reconstruction, one that will hopefully escape her strictures and save what is best in the model of the rediscovery of civil society.

Within the framework of this presentation I would like to sum up the theoretical arguments against the concept of civil society in two points. The first puts a question mark next to the model of differentiation on the basis of a fusion argument. The second questions the unity of those plural and heterogeneous elements that are supposed to constitute "society." The first looks back to the Western tradition of criticism going back to Carl Schmitt. The second resembles the position of Niklas Luhmann and his followers. In the context of Western societies I would try to refute the first on the basis of a reconstructed theory of differentiation derived from Luhmann himself, while the second would have to be countered on the basis of the Habermasian theory of the lifeworld.[3] Without going into detail now, I would try to prove by these conceptual strategies that: (1) The increasing complexity of the network of relations among social spheres need not mean dedifferentiation. (2) Even in the context of fusion of some spheres (a) the normative validity of differentiation should not automatically be given up and (b) new contexts of differentiation may open up empirically. (3) The internal heterogeneity of institutions need not mean that subsystems do not reproduce themselves on the basis of a differentiated logic. (4) The end of organized, collectivistic political society (*societas civilis*), one built on traditional norms, as a collective actor does not mean the disappearance or the nonmodernity of a sociocultural lifeworld, or of its institutions of reproduction. Thus Habermas's concept of the lifeworld, or rather its institutional forms (family, face-to-face relations, forms of association and publicity) implies the reconstruction, in a version compatible with modernity, of Durkheim's social sphere—that is, the very concept that Luhmann takes to be a reproduction of traditional political society.

This whole theoretical line is, of course, not easily utilizable for Soviet-type societies, in the context of which Staniszkis made her stand against the theory of civil society. I believe, nonetheless, that while it is true that under state socialism one must generally speak of a lower level of differentiation than under capitalism, the post-Stalinist forms nonetheless everywhere did involve some important processes of differentiation. This process meant less frequently the differentiation of political and economic logics than the partial emancipation of spheres of the lifeworld whose independent contents were never entirely eliminated even by "totalitarian" regimes (private sphere, aspects of cultural and religious life, some associational forms—always in this order and to very different degrees). My point, therefore, is simply (but important for what follows) that (1) it would be absurd to treat (as does Staniszkis) the post-Stalinist system as more subsumed from the point of the lifeworld, more penetrated and controlled, than its predecessor (which also did not fully destroy the lifeworld's independence), and (2) it makes sense to speak of a sphere of social life that at least in principle could be the foundation of the constitution or reconstitution of an independent civil society. However, all this does not mean at all that we could actually describe any state socialist society in terms of the dualistic terminology of society against the state, or that it is sensible and meaningful to aim at such rigid bipolar differentiation in practice.

To this extent we must accept part of Staniszkis's critique. I would incorporate her general thesis in terms of the following points: All modern societies and in particular state socialist ones presuppose the outputs of a state on four levels— legality (even if this is in the form of a *dual state* where prerogative power remains primary), interest aggregation (even if in the form of "plan bargaining"), economic steering (even if in the form of the state socialist command system), and sovereignty (even if seriously reduced sovereignty). We cannot interpret the program of society against the state simultaneously as leaving the existing state in its place (i.e., not replacing it) and as entirely bypassing it through some kind of unexplained system of society as Jacek Kuroń, one of the architects of KOR's program, once thought.[4]

To be sure, neither the notion of differentiation, nor even that of the sociocultural lifeworld does in itself reconstruct that of civil society. When we say, for example, that the social or the lifeworld resists totalitarian power and at the same time that the aim of this resistance could become the restoration (or creation) of civil society we evidently cannot mean that the social, or society, or the lifeworld, is already civil society, or is the same as civil society. I would like to suggest that the stabilization of a modern sociocultural lifeworld against the great potential threat of historically unprecedented forms of state power is possible only in the forms of rights that imply a juridical "self-limitation" of that power, potentially enforced by societal actors from the legal profession and social movements, who draw on the resources of a political culture in which rights have acquired a place of dignity. Accordingly, the well-known rights of the private sphere, of social associations and of the public sphere first constitute the social as civil society in the modern sense of this term, on the institutional level.

This definition of civil society has the advantage of being distinguishable from differentiated forms of social life, and even from forms of social resistance and solidarity in the face of state and economic power. Whereas "totalitarian" power failed in spite of its great threat to subsume the sociocultural lifeworld, it has certainly eliminated civil society. To be sure, to deal with the threat especially in the long run under modern conditions of repression, surveillance, control, and manipulation, social institutions must be stabilized in the form of civil society. It is at this point that a defensive strategy becomes and actually became in Poland at least offensive, implying the constitution of a social movement for the restoration of civil society. Civil society, if institutionalized, is in turn the ideal terrain for a plurality of independent networks, initiatives, and indeed movements. Thus it is necessary to make a further distinction, namely between a passive and an active sense of the concept of civil society, the former referring to the institutions (in general linked to fundamental rights like association, assembly, and speech) that differentiate and stabilize it, and the latter to the forms of collective action, small and large scale, required to defend, reproduce, and expand its potentials.[5]

Thus, a unified social movement for the restoration of civil society is not yet identical to its actual institutionalization. If the project were successful, however, the outcome would inevitably pluralize society, and its forms of collective action, or allow the public emergence of its implicit plurality. The end of a unified movement at the same time need not mean the inevitable disappearance of a consensual base thereby. To my mind there has been in Poland at least for a long time rather impressive consensus about the validity of an independent civil society as a social order even if there are deep disagreements about the type of civil society (e.g., liberal or solidaristic, democratic or corporate) valorized and fought for. Civil society, as a normative framework, allows, however, disagreement about desirable forms of life; it presupposes only the existence of normatively grounded procedures for arguing and negotiating and even fighting over these differences.

In the form that the Solidarity promoted, for example, civil society further presupposed the possibility of *solidarity* among potentially conflicting interests, ideas, and even forms of life. Thus the name of the movement was extremely well chosen from the sociological point of view. On this level, even the creation of a pluralistic civil society need not have destroyed the solidarity needed to bring it into being. Indeed as the analysis of Touraine and his coworkers has shown, the weakening of an underlying consensus and solidarity was not the result of the partial restoration of civil society and unfolding of plurality but was a phenomenon of decomposition of the movement in the face of insoluble strategic difficulties and impending failure. To be sure, this failure *was* in many respects traceable to a theory and practice relying on a schematic version of the dualistic conception that Staniszkis has rightly criticized. I have also attempted several critiques on this line, hoping, however, to reconstruct the original conception of new evolutionism and self-limiting revolution.[6] Here I will touch only on the broader implications of the "model" I adopted, as the foundation of a series of remarks on the problems of the reconstitution of civil society in a comparative context of East European attempts at radical reform.

Let me briefly explore, first on the level of the philosophy of history, and then on the level of politics, one possible line that could make fruitful the translation of the political-philosophical category of civil society into the language of critical social theory. In Western European history the typical forms in which modern state and civil society relations have been structured, starting with (1) the absolutist state-society of orders duality are (2) the monarchical, bureaucratic *Rechtsstaat*, (3) the liberal, (4) the liberal-democratic, and (5) the liberal-democratic welfare state. Leaving aside some well-known reversions to authoritarianism and the emergence of one version of the total state, the types listed all can be linked to civil societies understood as ambiguous from the point of view of their impact on the sociocultural lifeworld. Putting the issue schematically, the first three forms (linked to classic capitalist economy) instituted rights of the private sphere, public sphere, and in the third case, also political participation, at the historical cost of the strengthening of the socially destructive trends of the self-regulating market economy at the expense of the cultural, social, psychological, and even biological resources of the lifeworld (Polanyi). The structure of rights helped to modernize the lifeworld; the linkage of rights to the primacy of the economy threatened its reification or colonization in the sense of commodification. The fourth formation linked to the advanced capitalist mixed economy to an important extent has done the reverse. While the creation of rights of labor, of the old and the young, and of marginals did much to at least reduce the destructive side effects of the market economy, the cost has been an extensive administrative, bureaucratic and even therapeutic penetration of the framework of the reproduction of the lifeworld (Foucault).[7] Thus, struggling against the forms of absolutist-bureaucratic power, liberalism as a social movement inadvertently strengthened the economic "reification" and "commodification" of the lifeworld; struggling against forms of the capitalist market economy, the movement of the industrial working class strengthened the administrative penetration of the lifeworld.

Though the issue does not belong to the present paper, let me simply mention what in my opinion the political response to these historical givens could be today.[8] Today, in the Western representative or capitalist democracies, neither an *étatist* nor a market-oriented strategy can serve the interests of human emancipation. While neither the achievements of the market economy, nor of the welfare state should be abandoned, social movements *today* can defend the sociocultural lifeworld only if they are willing to bring both modern state and modern market economy under some measure of control. A societally or civil society oriented program—aptly called the reflexive continuation of the welfare state (Habermas)—must focus on two dimensions: (1) the reorganization and expansion of societal autonomy in terms of new institutions and associations, and (2) bringing political and economic subsystems under some form of social influence. The medium of influence whose primary terrain is the public sphere, however, cannot function (unlike power and money) if there is no minimum normative continuity between influencer and influenced (subject and object of influence). Thus a democratizing of the economy and redemocratization and even renormatization of state (to be sure not in terms of fundamentalist notions of participation) remain important items on our Western political agenda. How does any of this relate to the countries of authoritarian state socialism?

First of all, where should one put the authoritarian state socialist formation in our historical typology? Certainly there is no question here of a transitional society between capitalism and socialism, whatever the latter is to mean. Should we understand authoritarian state socialism as an alternative path of moderniza- tion parallel to the rise of the liberal state in the context of classical capitalism except here establishing the primacy of the political system rather than the eco- nomic? Or should we make it parallel to the welfare statist response to the self-regulating market, that is, one of the several twentieth-century *étatisms*, bringing the economic under control at the cost of political-administrative pene- tration of the lifeworld? Obviously we must say yes to both these alternatives and (leaving aside the historical samples that are as different from one another as Bohemia and Romania) speak of a kind of telescoping of the two types of processes in the institutional structures that were imposed in a wide variety of contexts. What is, however, paradoxical from the point of view of any modern- ization theory, is that such a telescoping occurred without any of the normative protections with respect to either economy or state that characterized the respec- tive western stages of development. A modern civil society was neither estab- lished nor transformed; a framework of rights protecting the lifeworld was in fact abolished wherever and in whatever form those existed. The penetration of the lifeworld, in other words, was not in terms of the vehicles provided by civil law, that is, juridification with its demonstrably two-sided consequences.[9] Rather, as Habermas puts it, coercive formal organization decked out with the emblems of democracy (actually bureaucratic forms in a less than modern sense) were to be the vehicles of subsumption. We now know, however, that those vehicles were only temporarily more effective in penetrating the lifeworld than legal instru- ments, and that when their eventual failure in this respect became clear, the empirical evidence points to the survival of more or less the forms of social integration and cultural reproduction characteristic of the given political culture before the imposition of authoritarian socialist institutions.[10]

The lifeworld was neither subsumed, *nor* really modernized, and the poten- tials of resistance of traditional or least inherited forms of life turned out to be astonishing. If anything the official political cultures, and even more the official institutions, had to be in part adapted to what political scientists came to call the dominant political culture. Of course, ever since the existence of alternative cultures or public spheres in some countries the situation has been changing for all those affected. The forms of opposition and in Poland its social movement are evidently fully modern, in my opinion often surpassing in self-reflection all their Western counterparts. In particular the notion of self-limiting radicalism that has been articulated and practiced here corresponds to that reflexive continuation of the welfare state which has been only theoretically formulated in the West. Nevertheless, and this is a question I would address to Touraine and his colleagues, can one generalize from the experience of public participation to private mentality? A follow-up study by M. Wieworka seems to indicate that we cannot.[11] The modernization of the lifeworld through the public sphere apparently cannot fully compensate for the absence of juridification.

It is my thesis, therefore, that the authoritarian socialist formation is a contemporary of the West only at two opposing poles profiled, to be sure, by different countries: (1) military political-diplomatic competition (the center); (2) circulation of cultural imagery and worldviews (especially the East Central European periphery). However the formation is in a sense contemporary with classical capitalism as well because of the still existing positive primacy of one subsystem, in this case that of the system identity-forming political one over the rest (or most) of the social spheres. Thirdly, the survival of traditional forms of life in the private sphere and the ideologies based on this represent a temporality that can only be linked to the precapitalist epoch, even if such survivals to a much lesser degree can be found in the West as well. However in the East, these are in a symbiotic relation with neo-absolutist or neo-autocratic state structures that tend to try to suppress modern forms of independent social life while they are powerless with respect to the traditional forms, and indeed produce forms of neo-traditionalism even where there are few survivals to be built on.[12] Thus the relevance of the uncanny *déjà vu* I reproduced in the beginning of my paper.

To be sure, a political model linked to the West's *past* cannot be complete. Of course, I should also say very clearly, to avoid any unnecessary objections, that I do not have in mind any political model that would imply a hoped-for convergence with the West's *present*. Indeed, given the heterogeneity of temporalities, it is not surprising that the defense of the lifeworld and bringing the subsystem of steering under control in the societies of authoritarian socialism requires a heterogeneity of political options with a highly uncertain overall political telos. Almost all political options (easily condemned or attacked in themselves) must be and indeed are advanced in terms of antinomies. The restoration of economic rationality is clearly on the agenda (as all reform hopes from above and below indicate) but so is the protection of the human, ecological, and cultural substance of society from a restructured market economy. As several Hungarian writers (e.g., Vajda, Kis) noticed with regard to the second economy, the destruction of normative structures of solidarity is once again a consequence of market rationality. Above all, the Solidarity movement continues to embody just this contradiction, which can be dealt with only if we recognize the legitimacy not only of the differentiation of a genuine economic sphere from the state, but also of the need to protect civil society from its potential economic colonization. Indeed, with the end of étatization the issue of societal influence over the economy, the classical problem of socialism, will have to be posed anew.[13]

There are further paradoxes on the present-day East European political agendas. The struggle for greater national sovereignty is obviously a key issue, but we have seen the possible consequences in a country like Romania when this is not accompanied by a real devolution of sovereign power. Indeed, even in Poland the need to strengthen the sovereignty of the state against outside forces, has had the unintended consequence of strengthening internal sovereignty based on the doctrine of raison d'état. Similarly, while it is important to initiate a transformation of parliament, and wherever possible the formation of parties, civil society as the primary terrain of democratization should not thereby be neglected or forgotten. Equally important: What already exists in the form of privilege must be recast in the form of *Rechtsstaatlichkeit*, that is in the form of rights even if to begin with somewhat restrictive in content. And yet the possibility of extra-institutional forms of protest from civil disobedience to movement pressure must also be "institutionalized" outside the legal system (i.e., in the political culture). Finally it remains crucial to seek a solution by compromise but at the same time the erosion of already made gains in autonomy must not be jeopardized. Thus all compromise must be compatible with fundamental principles; reform can be workable and justifiable only as radical reform. Revolution on the other hand should remain a self-limiting one, both because of the "geopolitical" strategic context and because only such a "revolution" is compatible with the creation and democratization of civil society.

II

The projects of radical reform and the reconstitution of civil society came into being together in the Poland of the mid 1970s. At that time a crucial argument behind both was provided by the supposed end of all Communist reformism from above, and the continued impossibility of radical revolution replacing the existing system altogether. Today we are witnessing, above all in the Soviet Union, the reappearance of reform from above and at the same time mobilizations in a diverse set of contexts (Poland, Hungary, the Baltic, Slovenia) apparently aiming to abolish so many features of the system that any continuity with the existing principle of organization might become implausible. Yet the idea of the reconstitution of civil society has not disappeared, and indeed its current reformulations throw some light on the present processes of change.

Interestingly enough, today reformers "from above," even in the Soviet Union, have taken over the concept of radical reform. According to Abel Aganbegyan, attempted economic changes in the Soviet Union had failed in the past because (1) they targeted only the economy, (2) they did not go far enough even in relation to the economy, and (3) their only agent was the ruling institution above, excluding all forces from below.[14] All these points belong together. Assuming that Aganbegyan's interest is first and foremost an economic reform that would go "far enough" to actually work, he was telling us that this is possible only if other areas of life were transformed and if other actors than the party-state participated in the overall project. He was, I believe, claiming in effect that civil society is part of the environment needed for a new type of economic coordination and that this environment could not be created without a movement or movements for the constitution of civil society.

This thesis can be best demonstrated by the arguments of Hungarian reform economists, in the period of the crisis of Kádárist economic consolidation. According to a near consensus among them[15] the reform of 1968 indeed abolished the old command or short-term mandatory planning system, but established only a structure of informal controls and vertical bargaining that left only very partial room for genuinely economic mechanisms linked to market demand and hard budgetary constraints. Described as "dual dependence" or "neither plan nor market," the post-1968 system established no viable new mechanism of coordination, and, according to Kornai at least, was successful only as long as the informal, nonstate, secondary economic sector, itself deformed by the overall political and legal context, could be rapidly expanded. The primary, state-owned sector, only very partially improved in its functioning, could not in particular adapt itself to the negative changes in its two international environments in the 1980s. The result was heavy borrowing and indebtedness, austerity without foreseeable end, and decline of the standard of living.

According to Hungarian economists the overall outcome of the "first" reform was the function of its bureaucratic recuperation, from the very outset. Here some writers like T. Bauer stress (on the level of action) the cyclical nature of bureaucratic intervention, namely the ability of conservative groupings in the apparatus and leadership to consciously impose in the beginning as well as during the "roll-back" (*visszarendeződés*) of the 1970s compromises that preserved important elements of the earlier command system, for example, rigid price controls, the naming of managers through the *nomenklatura* system, the inviolability of large unprofitable, monopolistic firms, etc. Another line of interpretation, in particular that of Kornai, stresses the systemic effects of an unchanged, overall bureaucratically structured environment on a reform package that was unambiguous only concerning what it sought to eliminate. The 1968 reform, by abolishing the command economy, created only a vacuum of coordination that in the given institutional setting could not be taken up by comprehensive coordination by the market, despite the naive expectations of the reformers and the fears of conservatives. Instead, in the state sector the institutions were present that allowed the spontaneous replacement of one type of bureaucratic control by another, this time informal and indirect. If indirect controls meant any shift of economic power, this was only to the benefit of the managers of the largest, and usually the least profitable enterprises themselves part of the political apparatus, who gained in the new structure of bargaining over investments, subsidies and prices that replaced the earlier "plan bargaining structures." This result, however, only preserved the debilitating system of paternalistic, soft budgetary constraints.

The first explanation points to the need of other agents than the authorities themselves to mobilize on behalf of a reform that cannot be introduced in a consistent manner in the context of internal bureaucratic compromise. The second indicates a necessary change in the political and social environment to avoid a deformation of reform through the "spontaneous" emergence of informal regulation and control by the monopolistic holders of political power. Both explanations point to civil society as the context of radical or second reform, the first on the level of agency, the second on the level of institutions. These two levels are moreover linked, as the reform discussion in Hungary reveals, because in the context of the inevitable sacrifices that any rational policy linked to reform will have to ask for, independent mobilization on behalf of reform will require the important "trade-offs" for the population in terms of new institutions of negative rights as well as new forms of participation and will formation.

Kornai's and Bauer's different yet complementary remarks on rebureaucratization can be developed in a direction unexplored by them. If rebureaucratization remains the potential threat to economic reforms both on the level of action and that of system, this has much to do with peculiar nature of administration in Soviet-type societies, combining aspects of expertise and politocracy. It is the second feature, deeply rooted in forms of selection, appointment, promotion, criteria of success, and organizations of authority that leads to forms of intervention in economy and society incompatible with differentiation. The official, unlike the expert administrator, is rewarded for the expansion of bureaucratic influence and control over various administrative areas, and not for the success of these areas in their own terms. The paradox all reformers face is that while no reform can succeed without administrative execution and application, the only administration available has a logic and interests incompatible with the reforms. This administration cannot be simply dismissed, and it has a well-known ability to absorb all structural changes and new, even expertly trained personnel. The only answer is to change, along with personnel changes, its environment as well. Such a change cannot be restricted to a formal one that merely posits new rules and regulations that can be evaded, as we have seen by the invention of informal devices. Here too the creation of a vacuum by the abolition of one system of coordination opens up only opportunities for its reinvention in new forms. What is essential rather is the creation of institutions, in particular legally defended forms of association capable of battling all arbitrary bureaucratic intervention. Here legalization involving the freeing of the courts from the apparatus is all important for the protection of managers and associations against an otherwise overwhelming administrative power. As Max Weber knew, only the fusion of legal proceduralism and bureaucracy is capable of producing a modern expert administration, which as he should have but did not notice is possible only with an active civil society as its environment.

The concrete proposals of the radical economic reformers in Hungary reflect a new sensitivity for the complementary political conditions of economic reform. To be sure, they have not yet solved a dilemma formulated by Kornai, one leading only to the alternative of resignation or revolution, namely that political reforms that will be possible will be insufficient, while those that would be sufficient are impossible. Here one line of interpretation seeks to show the sufficiency of the possible. Bauer in particular argued (in 1985) that "spectacular reform of the political system is not a precondition of the development forward of economic reform."[16] Unlike the economic sphere, in the political sphere a slow, step-by-step transformation may be sufficient according to him, if it is tangible and not illusory. In his writings from roughly the same period he limited such incremental reforms to constitutionalism in the economic sphere, that is, the creation of genuine economic rights of firms against the state enforceable through independent courts, and to public discussion and control over what remains of the economic direction of the state. The second of these points, however, could easily be interpreted as a rather spectacular change, especially in terms of Bauer's earlier argument that links the development of a prepolitical public sphere to the creation of some elements at least of genuine parliamentarianism. Here the rest of his argument was much more cautious, and significantly seemed to presuppose that while the functions of the party apparatuses would no longer include informal control over the enterprises, the status of the party in society would be unchanged. In this context, however, the argument can easily be criticized for being too minimalist, in the sense of allowing the continued existence of a point of entry through which all significant changes could be reversed.

Bauer's proposal corresponded to a new minimalist interpretation of radical reform prevalent in the period immediately following Jaruzelski's coup among those who first imported the dualistic Polish conception into Hungary, in particular the group around the samizdat journal *Beszélö*. Among the economists Bauer's position was first contested among the authors of "Fordulat és Reform," who tended to oscillate between a reform communist conception in which the party retained much of the reform initiative, and a conception more or less implying the replacement of the whole existing political system by liberal democracy. In my own view the 1987 program of *Beszélö*, "Social Contract," represented a more promising linking of radicalism and compromise by focusing on the establishment of a genuine civil society, based on civil rights, free associations and an open public sphere. For the political system proper this proposal suggested "only" the creation of semiparliamentary *Rechtsstaat* in which the role of the communist party would be constitutionally regulated and circumscribed. It is easy to link in this conception the new institutions of civil society, whose justification is hardly only economic, to the idea of an environment necessary for the functioning of a decentralized market economy. Laws and rights would accordingly provide predictability for rational economic actors, the freedom of association would mean the possibility of the representation of group and collective interests in particular in face of bureaucratic pressures seeking to reduce new laws to mere formalities, while the freedom of public communication would make the actual trend of institutional changes *and* global policy making open to discussion and criticism. Thus while the rule of law and economic rights are the most indispensable conditions of economic functioning, the freedom of association and publicity are required to give a system of rights its necessary sociological supports.[17]

Similarly, according to the "Social Contract," a relevant model of civil society could not be stabilized under the conditions and given the history of state socialism without a complementary, if less radical reform of the political system. Here was a crucial difference with earlier, primarily Polish versions of radical reform. In one respect, at least, the program of *Beszélö* remained "Polish" by postulating that groups and associations outside the official institutions must have the primary role in pushing through such a political reform.

Today the program of "Social Contract" has become paradoxical in Hungary, since the ever-mushrooming network of independent associations and forms of public expression, the *de facto* and soon very possibly *de jure* recognition of civil rights, the erosion of censorship, and the various plans for parliamentary, legal, and constitutional reform, seem to indicate to many (probably wrongly) that the reforms proposed in 1987 remain compatible with the debilitating monopolistic and extralegal political powers of the ruling party. Thus the mobilized parts of the population, almost exclusively intellectuals who in effect constitute the early elements of a new political society, now seem to be guided by ideas that go beyond any version of radical reformism,[18] while reformist sectors of the leadership seem to have verbally at least accepted a program close to that of *Beszélö* in 1987.[19] Nevertheless, the entirely novel situation of an increasingly pluralized political society drawing on mostly a counterelite of intellectuals as the spearhead of reform does hide some dangers, especially given the absence of any large-scale popular mobilization, and the continued control of the means of violence by the established regime. First, the possibility of a clash between the regime and the independent political associations cannot be excluded, either now or more likely in a later stage when and if the contemporary political ferment has not led to economic solutions. Nor can we simply dismiss the less likely possibility of vertical or horizontal agreements with some groups and even parties that provide for some kind of supposed parliamentary solution at the cost of institutionalizing the long-term depolitization of the population—a deal between state and a part of political society at the expense of civil society.[20] Such an outcome is made possible by the liberal turn of most of the intellectual opposition that is theoretically quite understandable, but which may, nonetheless, leave many important social interests, those of industrial workers in particular, unrepresented.

Thus parts of the regime may be able to appeal to some of the interests and solidarities that are in Poland focused around Solidarity, even if not without some contradictions. Such an appeal could even produce some surprises in competitive elections. To avoid such outcomes, it is evident that a longer term learning experience of the still very young opposition is needed, one involving ideological pluralization, and for this a principled compromise between some official reformers and mobilized intellectuals would represent a better context, perhaps, than some kind of falling into a parliamentary democracy, paper-thin because it is not rooted in a reconstructed civil society. For such a compromise, in my opinion, the dualistic model of *Social Contract* remains extremely relevant, though obviously there would be nothing wrong with a political reform more democratic with respect to the sphere of public law than that of this proposal, as long as the trade-off is not a greater restriction of democracy vis-à-vis the forms of self-organization of civil society, measurable by rights, legality, associational freedom, and publicity. Within such a perspective the program of radical democratization within a framework of self-limitation has not lost its raison d'être.

The point is all the more valid in context of Soviet developments, which in turn will influence both the possible radicalism and the need for self-limitation in other countries. While any direct comparison with Polish and Hungarian models remains hazardous, the analysis of the political constraints of economic reforms by Hungarian economists fits the Soviet situation rather well, as indicated by Aganbegyan's conception of radical reform. Indeed the existence of a far more intact, and historically continuous apparatus in the Soviet Union, unlike in China and Hungary, has repeatedly led to the early sabotage of serious reform proposals successfully avoiding the overcoming of the initial threshold constituted by the system of detailed, mandatory planning. To be sure, radical economic reform, or the so-called *perestroika*, is supposed to represent the heart of Gorbachev's modernization program. While the first ("East German") phase of this reform (until about June 1987) seemed to have represented an effort at recentralization, rationalization, and above all the reintroduction of discipline, the second phase seems to have initiated a reform of the "Hungarian" type, though in several key respects more restrictive. The goals of abolishing compulsory plan targets and affirming new forms of enterprise autonomy were, however, presented in less consistent and radical versions than in the Hungarian New Economic Mechanism of 1968. Nevertheless, the illusions of the latter concerning the shift from administrative to economic criteria are shared. In particular, much of output was still to be related to governmental rather than genuinely commercial "orders." Furthermore, the enterprise like its Hungarian counterpart not only did not gain control over investment, but unlike the latter it also did not get any real choice concerning its material suppliers. Without such a choice, as A. Nove has pointed out, the directive planning system survives, since administrators will be issuing binding orders regarding material inputs. Finally, the price reform envisaged was a good deal less radical than the also incomplete measures introduced in Hungary in 1968. Only in one area, in the establishment of the right-of-work collectives to elect managers, did the Soviet law of the firms surpass its Hungarian counterpart, at least until the organizational changes inaugurated by the latter in 1984. And yet even here there is little to indicate (in either country) that anything but an informal version of the nomenklatura system has been established. Thus on balance it remains difficult to figure out how the 1987 Soviet proposals are supposed to establish full commercial principles, real financial responsibility, and a hard budget constraint, some of its stated objectives.[21]

According to Seweryn Bialer's optimistic scenario, the reforms that will not work in themselves are to establish "the organizational and psychological preconditions for reform that will come later."[22] We should note, however, that in the only case (itself debatable and still undecided) of such possible acceleration of reform in relationship to industrial production, in the Hungarian case the essential precondition for this consisted in a step that is not yet implied by the Soviet reform proposals, not to speak of the actual practice. In Hungary the initial threshold constituted by the system of compulsory plan orders was transcended right in the beginning of the reform. Moreover, even here the initial "acceleration" was to occur in the direction of reaction.

To be sure, acceleration of reform could occur by shifting to an area other than the most intractable one of state-owned industry. And indeed the only reforms of Soviet-type systems that could be seen as involving the introduction of new mechanisms of coordination, the Hungarian and the Chinese, gained their energy and whatever successes, as Kornai recently argued,[23] from concurrent privatization, of the "second economy" in the first case and of agriculture in the second case. As a magisterial article by A. Nove on agrarian policy has argued,[24] while agricultural reform is on the agenda in the Soviet Union, it is nevertheless going to be difficult to match the radicalism and the results of the Chinese dismantling of the system of collectives. This point is all the more important to keep in mind as after a period of very hesitant, and much resisted, introduction of the possibility of individual and contractual arrangements, in part vitiated within the state and collective farm structure, there is a recent and dramatic plan of the Gorbachev group, approved by the Central Committee on March 16, 1989 in spite of strong opposition, to introduce a genuine system of mixed property in the countryside, involving long-term ("fifty years or more"), inheritable contractual arrangements, some competitive form of investment banking, a gradually decontrolled system of prices, and a dismantling of all unproductive state and collective farms. It is not yet clear from the proposals to what extent the replacement for the latter is to be by entirely voluntary cooperatives who would be legal owners of their property. It seems, however, that surviving state and collective farms (that are to remain the mainstay of agrarian production!) are to be restructured in a still unspecified form of control by "amalgamations" of lease-holders, which this time is not supposed to be a mere "ruse" for bureaucratic controls.[25]

Superficially then, we might speak of the beginning of a "Chinese phase" of the Soviet reform, but once again (as in the "Hungarian phase") there are reasons to think that the radicalism of the original is diminished from the outset. First, there are apparently already bad compromises on the level of the formulation of the general project. The decontrol of farm prices is to be very gradual, hence economically irrelevant, even if it is also true that free agricultural prices as in China would have many negative side effects. The system of large-scale governmental procurements, "orders" is to be kept, but this time for unexplained reasons it is somehow not supposed to turn into one of centralized commands. It seems, furthermore, to be up to the collective and state farms to sell or not to sell leases to individuals or groups, making the chances of the emergence of a private sphere competitive with the *kolkhozy* and *sovkhozy* all the weaker. Second, it remains entirely unclear how many new concessions will be given to existing local and regional hierarchies when it comes to the difficult process of turning the general project into a system of microregulations. Third, in the absence of comprehensive legal reform, we have little idea what kind of legal system in the countryside is supposed to be the foundation for the confidence of a peasantry now extremely suspicious, and reluctant to enter into new, and easily reversible arrangements. Unlike in China, here a much larger and more pervasive local political and economic bureaucracy is largely intact while spontaneous and traditional support systems among peasants are notoriously weak, and it is hard to see how and by whom the transformation of the new proposed system into one of informal and indirect bureaucratic controls is to be avoided. At issue are once again the elements of a civil society, this time a rural one, as the environment of decentralization and as the foundation of autonomous pressures supporting change. One is forced to hazard the guess, that outside the republics where there is a large-scale national mobilization often coupled with reformist leadership and even organized opposition, the agrarian reform can work only if supported by (1) a comprehensive reform of the legal system and (2) the organization of peasant society in ways still difficult to anticipate.

As far as activities of the second economy type are concerned two tendencies must be discerned. On the one side there is a limited legalization of individual private and cooperative enterprise, whose quantitative results are small but whose effects on the quality of life in a few areas have already become significant. In this context only long-term toleration and support, and above all legal guarantees that go beyond a few statutes, could lead to any significant expansion. The atmosphere is, however, made more difficult in context of the second and increasing trend consisting of attempts to uproot the illegal private economy along with corruption, an economy certainly far more extensive than the legal private one. While these attempts are sure to fail, the plans to legalize private economic activities will be compromised as long as they are linked to a campaign against the actually existing forms of these activities. This is all the more so in context of renewed attempts to restrict, tax, and control various forms of cooperative and private enterprise. Legalization thus becomes associated with suppression, or at least with obvious economic disadvantages. To be taxed, controlled, and possibly dissolved is hardly an incentive to take the step from illegality or semilegality into the open. A strategy that is to rely on the stabilizing functions of a second economy cannot be based on forced legalization in a state in which the rule of law as such does not exist.

Whatever their success, the new agrarian proposals demonstrate that in the overall context the blockage of economic reform, both on the level of promulgation and that of implementation and execution, remains coupled with the leadership's continued interest in *perestroika*. Thus it is extremely important to stress the need for a new social environment for economic functioning, such as represented by the institutions of some version of civil society. The most important new fact about the Gorbachev team is their own realization that neither the creation of this environment, nor even the passing of the threshold for a genuine change in the system of economic coordination, can occur without the mobilization of independent actors. In this context there are at least four big questions. (1) Do such actors exist already? (2) If they do not exist, can they be created from above? (3) Is the need on the part of the regime to rely on new actors greater than the deep seated desire to control them? (4) If a genuine reformist movement for the constitution of civil society were to emerge, could it stay within any limits acceptable to the reformers?

First and foremost we must reject an interpretation according to which civil society already exists in the Soviet Union of the 1970s and 1980s, and that the reformism of Gorbachev's group from the beginning expressed the pressure of independent actors rooted in an independent society.[26] This interpretation is rooted in a general sociological conception that, contrary to the various totalitarianism theses, maintains that the ruling party-state has been able neither to eliminate nor especially block the formation of functionally differentiated social processes, independent cultural forms, different strata rooted in the division of labor and urbanization. According to this version of the modernization thesis it is increasingly difficult to rule a more and more complex society, from a single, undifferentiated control center uniting political, economic, and cultural controls. And indeed, it is hard to argue against the thesis so far. But as I have argued in this article, a differentiated, and in a residual sense independent, society and civil society are not the same; at most the former is a condition of the possibility of the latter. In particular, society or social differentiation as a function of complexity is a feature of social systems that does not tell us anything about social actors. If the Soviet system could not (tautologically) abolish complexity in context of its own modernizing drive, it could indeed abolish a system of rights, plurality of associations, and free forms of public expression, thus civil society and along with it the institutionalized possibility of independent actors.

To be sure, M. Lewin and F. Starr are right to point to the emergence of new types of networks, informal groups, and unofficial forms of public expression. These forms and activities, by no means spontaneous products of any systems differentiation, do represent the possible seeds for larger scale mobilization and association.

On their own, however, they are able to exercise no relevant pressure on the regime. The origins of the Gorbachev reform drive must be explained on the basis of a combination of an external challenge and internal economic decline along with cultural demoralization.[27] Even more important, the difficulties of this attempt will be inevitably underemphasized in an overall evolutionary perspective if we assume that the agents required to push it through have been organically and spontaneously produced by modernization itself.

Gorbachev's team does not share the world-historical optimism of some Western scholars. The attempt to constitute civil society from above, and thus the possibility of the mobilization of independent actors on behalf of reform has been openly declared and attempted. Thus Bialer is probably right to argue that "Gorbachev's program for Russia's future seems to envisage the creation and cultivation of selected elements of 'civil society' never before known in Soviet or even much of Russian history."[28] Civil society here refers to the autonomy of organized social units in the face of state power, and in the present context Bialer identifies both cultural freedom and low-level participation as its, to be sure, "selected" elements. And yet Castoriadis seems also right when he claims, though recognizing the successful appeal to an intellectual constituency, that this does not yet represent the making of a "social historical movement" for reform, "ready to fight for reform and invent on the innumerable spots of life whatever is necessary for its successful implementation." To him the attempt to create a self-active political-civil society from above *and* within powerful, but never strictly defined, limits is deeply antinomic and self-defeating. If it were successful, movements within such a civil society could not remain within any limits acceptable to the reformers above.

We must make a few distinctions. While the positive work of constituting a movement for the creation of civil society can only be its own, important if negative steps are obviously possible from above, capable of facilitating the project of self-constitution. In particular the elimination of fear, the ultimate cement of integration in a society without much genuine legitimacy, represents an important step in creating such negative preconditions. In this context the work of the Gorbachev group has been important especially where the organs of international public opinion extend. The genuine flowering of clubs, associations, *samizdat* publications, as well as the new-found desire of many to openly participate in politics, would be unthinkable without the lowering of threshold of fear, as concretely symbolized by the release of prisoners. Indeed, as Kis has argued, a kind of simulated *Rechtsstaat* has been created that seems to keep open the spaces for independent political activity. To be sure, the permission for the formation of an independent bar association points even further, by allowing the potential emergence of one indispensable element of a genuine *Rechtsstaat*, the independent legal counsel. However, other measures point in a different direction. The continuation of a conception of fundamental rights as forms of protection of the state rather than of individuals points away from any kind of constitutionalism.[29] The new laws restricting free assembly, personal security, and samizdat publishing ventures are more ambiguous; one could rightly argue that if the new code, unlike its predecessors, will be taken seriously this must mean a certain hardening of restrictions. However, in the context of the continued delay of a promised comprehensive legal reform nothing positive can be achieved by new repressive statutes. Indeed these measures do raise the question whether or not the regime already wants to restrict and depoliticize independent initiatives, before they have had a chance to contribute to structural change. Their inclinations in this respect are all wrong as one repeatedly is forced to notice. And yet by now it is an open question how easily and at what cost the processes of forming associations and openly assembling and speaking out could be reversed, or even coopted.

The issue of legal reform, along with all the elements of the rule of law, is all important not only because it is a precondition of both the expansion of wider public mobilization, and of an environment in which economic decentralization and market rationality can take hold. Indeed, as we have seen in Armenia and the Baltic under the banner of national self-determination, large-scale mobilization can occur even in the context of a simulated *Rechtsstaat* given a significant decline of fear. Just such mobilization holds out the possibility of open clashes, especially if the regime is not able to live up to the expectations of both continued reformism and of improvements in the standard of living. In the short run there may be furthermore strong disappointment with the rather limited reform of the political system as a whole, in particular the electoral system and the new form of national representation, coupled with the increased involvement of wider circles in independent activities.[30] Such a constellation full of dangers could be stabilized only if both sides were to learn self-limitation. For this the rule of law has been historically a generally indispensable instrument.[31] Thus, legal reform is not only a precondition for the acceleration of the reformism associated with Gorbachev, but represents a precondition for stabilizing the present situation, at least buying time for future reforms. From the point of view of movements and independent initiatives, legalization in terms of a "law of associations" would represent a great gain, even if the trade-off were between open-ended but unprotected activity, and somewhat restricted but legally guaranteed forms of action. But as we have emphasized, juridification can protect only if the system of legal protections (including independent courts, independent counsel, a publicly available and rational legal code, and ultimately constitutionalism itself) is itself legalized. For the time being, this prospect is still remote in the Soviet Union, in this respect unlike Hungary and Poland. Nevertheless, it should be stressed that there are two ways of saving the Gorbachev reform process: either by initiating a new cycle of economic reforms that are capable of producing results, or by producing some kind of modus vivendi stabilizing the increasingly conflictual present situation,[32] based on mutual self-limitation between regime and the mobilized sectors of society. In my opinion, at least, comprehensive legal reform aiming at some version of the rule of law is indispensable for both of these options.

That a self-limiting popular movement is not impossible has been proven by the whole Polish experience since 1976, when such a project was first declared. Even more remarkable is the fact that in Poland normalization has failed in the 1980s, for the very first time in East European history after the defeat of a movement of emancipation. Undoubtedly the fact that it was now the turn of the state to practice (reluctant) self-limitation reinvigorated the idea that an independent society could be somehow defended even in the context of demoralizing defeat. "Independent civil society" was not according to Michnik annihilated. "Instead of resembling a Communist system after victorious pacification, this situation resembles a democracy after a military *coup d'état.*"[33] In spite of the reappearance of some martial metaphors like "a dramatic wrestling match between the totalitarian power and a society searching for a way to attain autonomy" and "the stationary war between an organized civil society and the power apparatus," the new situation actually indicated the coming into its own of the cultural model of an independent society. The major independent activities, at least until 1986–87, were publishing, lecturing, discussing, and teaching, and the key hope seemed to have been the building of the moral basis of democratic structures and practices, that is, a democratic political culture. While the army-state was powerless against these trends, it was rather successful in the marginalization of its major political opponent: underground Solidarity (which, however, always continued to play a role). In this context, the democratic opposition moving within the paradigm of civil society had to face the open question of how and when the survival, and even dramatic expansion, of an independent culture could become the foundation for the reemergence of new above-ground political organizations, now more pluralistic and differentiated than ever before, capable of making effective demands.

The regime's continued failure to enact a workable economic reform and to gain some acceptance for an austerity program, as symbolized by the failure of the referendum of 1987, put an end to the defensive phase of the history of the Polish democratic movement. The new strike waves of spring and summer of 1988 have also demonstrated, however, that it is now misdirected to dream of the rebirth of the one great movement, and counterproductive not to promote and utilize reforms from above that are compatible with the institutionalization of a genuine civil society. New potential fissures have now emerged, exploitable by the regime: on the one hand between those stressing a neoliberal reform program and those most concerned about the welfare of working-class constituencies, and, on the other, between moderates willing to compromise with the regime and fundamentalists seeking an ultimate confrontation. These divisions were not new, but took on new meaning with the regime dreaming of "Thacherite" reforms without any genuine devolution of power. Such a policy, if consistently pursued, could easily have led to the decomposition and fragmentation of the democratic opposition.

In this context, it is rather amazing that the Solidarity leadership has been not only able to confront the regime in an extensive process of bargaining, but also to recover a good deal of popular support, at least for the time being. Fortunately, this leadership seeks to avoid a role that seems to be continually thrust upon it, namely that of reconstituting the one big movement, in the long run impossible, and certainly undesirable, representing all the economic as well as political aspirations of an increasingly pluralized society. The original intentions of the regime were clear: the formal institutionalization of a powerless parliamentary opposition under the name of Solidarity. This device, not actually new in Poland, was meant to provide legitimation for austerity measures of the regime's own choosing, and certainly would imply a delegitimation of Solidarity. The initial counterdemand for a new law of associations along with the union's own legalization, as well as genuine electoral competition for at least a portion of parliamentary seats represented the continuation of its original dualistic program: the liberation of civil society, but now coupled with political reform. If the actual solution in the end really embodies the two-chamber solution, one popularly elected in a contested election, the other proportioned in the old single-slate manner between regime and the opposition, such an arrangement could for the first time both produce an ongoing structure of compromise and stabilize dualism in the classical Hegelian manner, by reproducing it within the structure of the state itself. This model, actually quite close to the spirit if not the precise letter of the "social contract" of the Hungarian opposition, having the Senate as a mediating institution between state and society, should provide the beginnings of a new political society more capable of expressing the actual ideological plurality of society as a whole than the model of the one big movement of civil society facing state power in an unmediated manner. The emergence of presidential power in the compromise formula hides new dangers, to be sure, but can also serve as the vehicle of minimum continuity with the old regime in the spirit of Kuroń's ideas in the 1970s concerning the inevitable need for self-limitation in order to protect Soviet interests, in a scheme misleadingly labeled as "Finlandization." If the overall model, whose details are insufficiently known at least here, is actually instituted this year, and if Solidarity can generate the necessary support for it, Poland might very well have passed an even more important threshold in the reconstitution of civil society, now in the context of complementary political democratization, than was represented by the Gdansk agreements of August 31, 1980.

Notes

1. Staniszkis 1979; 184–186; 1984: 144–145, 36–67. An analogous criticism has been developed by Alfred Stepan in relation to Latin American uses of the metaphor of civil society.

2. Staniszkis, op. cit, 1984, p. 145.

3. A. Arato and J. Cohen, "Civil Society and Social Theory," in *Thesis Eleven* (Sidney, 1989).

4. J. Kuroń, "Un chemin sans retour," *Ésprit* (Paris), January 1981), pp. 68–72; see also A. Arato, "Civil Society vs. the State: Poland 1980–81," Chapter 8, this volume.

5. The political science literature on the processes of democratization in Southern Europe and Latin America tends to restrict the concept of civil society to this second, active sense that focuses on group or collective actors. See, e.g., the essays in the four-volume *Transitions from Authoritarian Rule*, edited by G. O'Donnell and P. Schmitter (Baltimore: Johns Hopkins University Press, 1986). Some puzzles, for example, the role of civil society in overcoming the cycle of democracy and dictatorship, are impossible to solve within such a narrow perspective. For a critique, and for a broader conception of civil society, see J. Cohen and Andrew Arato, *Civil Society and Political Theory* (Cambridge: MIT Press, 1992), in particular chapter I and our chapters on social theory, and social movements.

6. "The Democratic Theory of the Polish Democratic Opposition: Normative Assumptions and Strategic Ambiguities," Chapter 10, this volume.

7. Habermas, 1981, II, chapter 8.

8. See Jean Cohen and Andrew Arato, "Civil Society and Social Theory," as well as "Politics and the Reconstruction of Civil Society," forthcoming in a Habermas festschrift edited by A. Honneth, T. McCarthy, et al.

9. Habermas, *Theory of Communicative Action* (Cambridge: MIT Press, 1987), II, chapter 8.

10. I developed this conception after an exchange with Habermas in *Habermas, Critical Debates* (Oxford: Blackwell, 1982). See A. Arato, "Autoritärer Sozialismus und die Frankfurter Schule," in *Die Frankfurter Schule und die Folgen* (Berlin: deGruyter, 1986).

11. See Touraine et al., *Solidarity* (Cambridge: The University Press, 1982), and M. Wieworka.

12. See A. Walder, *Communist Neo-traditionalism*, for an argument stressing the creation of new traditionalist practices as against a model stressing survival of traditions, e.g., M. Vajda's in *The State and Socialism*.

13. I believe that to deal with the problem of the liberation of the economy, and the need to protect civil society from independent economic structures, is best handled in a Gramscian-Parsonian-Habermasian three-part framework that distinguishes civil society from both state and modern economy. See my "Reply to John Keane," in *Praxis International*, vol. 9, nos. 1/2 (April–July 1989).

14. Lecture at the Graduate Facility, New School for Social Research, February 22, 1988, reported on by the *New York Times*, February 28, 1988. Also see A. Nove in "What's Happening in Moscow," *National Interest* (Summer 1987), p. 14.

15. I am relying on the writings of J. Kornai, T. Bauer, and the authors of the semi-official report "Fordulat és Reform" (1986).

16. Monor, (samizdat pub.) 1985, p. 56.

17. To be sure functional equivalents are imaginable and possible. In China, for example, agrarian transformation has been possible apparently because of the surviving strength of village and extended family. One would on this basis at least tend to predict that the same type of decollectivization is not possible in the Soviet Union unless new structures of rural civil society emerge to give new formal regulations some social support against surviving apparatuses seeking to informally evade, bypass, or even replace these.

18. See "Hongrie: pluralisme en deux manifestations," *Libération* (Paris), March 16, 1989.

19. See the interview with M. Haraszti in *Uncaptive Minds* (New York), vol. 2, no. 1 (January-February 1989).

20. The experience of the southern dictatorships points to such a possibility. See especially G. O'Donnell and P. Schmitter, *Transitions from Authoritarian Rule* IV (in particular the chapter on the resurgence of civil society).

21. See Nove in "What's Happening in Moscow," p. 16.

22. In F. Fehér and A. Arato, eds., *Gorbachev: The Debate* (Oxford: Polity Press, 1989).

23. Lecture at the Graduate Faculty, New School for Social Research, December 4, 1987.

24. See *Gorbachev: The Debate*.

25. See the excellent articles by Bill Keller in the *New York Times*, March 15, 16 and 17, 1989.

26. See in particular Moshe Lewin, *The Gorbachev Phenomenon* (Berkeley: University of California Press, 1989), pp. 80–81, 146–147; as well as S. Frederick Starr, "Soviet Union: a Civil Society," *Foreign Policy* (Spring 1988). Lewin deserves the credit for first raising the issue of civil society in context of the Soviet Union in *Political Undercurrents in Soviet Economic Debates* (Princeton: Princeton University Press, 1974).

27. Cf. the interpretations of Lewin and Starr.

28. See "Gorbachev's Move" in *Gorbachev: The Debate*.

29. I. F. Stone, "The Rights of Gorbachev," *New York Review of Books*, February 16, 1989.

30. The 1989 elections illustrate the paradox by producing both a manipulated and controlled process of choosing the new Supreme Soviet, and important forms of independent mobilization on behalf (or against) some candidates.

31. In Poland the atmosphere of the Catholic church has been in this respect a functional equivalent, which, however, has no counterpart in any other East European country.

32. "Le chaos créateur," as Bernard Guetta called it in *Le Monde*, March 17, 1989, forgetting to indicate beyond the absence of any political alternative to Gorbachev on the part of the conservatives, the minimum conditions for stabilizing such an explosive constellation.

33. See *Letters from Prison and other Essays* (Berkeley: University of California Press, 1985).

13

Revolution, Civil Society, and Democracy

Can social critics in the West learn anything from the dramatic events in the East? Is there anything radical democrats in the East can learn from at least those in the West who have learned from them?

The discourse of civil society, reinvented in Poland in the 1970s, brought us together in a way that Western Marxism, unable to understand Soviet-type societies, never could. Within this discourse one could thematize the struggles to radically reform Soviet-style state socialism, the transitions from bureaucratic authoritarianisms in the South, and the efforts of new types of movements to democratize the really existing democracies of the West. And it was a sterling cast of characters that did the work: Kołakowski, Michnik, Kuroń, Havel, Vajda, Kis and Bence in the case of the East; Cardoso, Weffort, O'Donnell, Stepan, Schmitter for the South; Lefort, Touraine, Habermas, Offe, and Bobbio in the West.

To be sure, from various conservative points of view the project of reconstructing civil society under the aegis of self-limitation could be accused of hypocrisy: What was declared to be self-limitation in principle could be thus unmasked as self-limitation due to weakness; interest in civil rights, free associations, and alternative publics, and social movements could be denounced as temporary replacement for the real motivation, namely taking state power; a principled postrevolutionary stance could be declared to be only prerevolutionary mystification. This charge was difficult to answer unless one made a virtue of weakness, postulating a rigidly dualistic reorganization of civil society and state, of realm of freedom and realm of necessity, a long-term solution that was hardly ever imagined to be workable except by some in the West.[1] But given the existence of representative democracy in the West, rooted in wide ranging social consensus, the idea of the democratization of civil society linked to the opening

Reprinted with permission from *Praxis International* 10, 1/2, April and July 1990.

of new structures of public discussion and political influence in the context of a continuous parliamentarianism did represent a highly plausible replacement of the illusory revolutions of the New Left. Thus here a civil society–oriented perspective had definitely broken not only with étatism but with the aura of revolution as well.

It had to be otherwise under the dictatorships. In the East and South few could believably deny that only a parliamentary democracy—one incompatible with the identity of the existing regimes—could integrate a modern civil society, and indeed as a long-term goal such a regime was affirmed by those who rediscovered the topos of civil society.[2] And yet the geopolitical constraints that involved the suspension of this goal could be turned into an advantage. The rebuilding of civil society, in its various cultural and political forms, was to involve long-term learning experiences that were not to be bypassed if the parliamentary regimes of the future were to be different—more pluralistic, more open and more stable— than those of the past. (In the West we secretly thought: different and more democratic than ours as well).

The year 1989 in Eastern Europe puts the whole train of thought linked to civil society and self-limiting radical democracy into question. On the one side, the figure of "revolution" has reappeared in several countries. Such revolution seemed to presuppose only very quick extra-institutional mobilization, the overthrow of crumbling old regimes, and the establishment of entirely new ones. The reconstruction of civil society, for which there was no time, was not needed as the basis of revolutionary mobilization, and the new political parties and governments had other things to worry about than such reconstruction in the future. Thus, on the other side two projects increasingly characterized the transitions of 1989: the establishment of elite-pluralistic systems of party competition, and that of liberal market economies. The first of these actually tends to the demobilization of civil society either directly, or indirectly by reducing its influence to the narrowest possible channels. The second, quite compatibly, tends to reduce civil society to economic society.

Given these two projects, "elite pluralism" and "bourgeois society," the context and the participants of a possible common discourse seem to decisively change. If any learning is now to take place it seems to be destined to be entirely one-sided; the new intellectual and political elites of the East are already invited to learn the relevant strategies of success from the established political and economic organizations and institutional actors of the West, who never imagined and do not imagine now that they ever had anything to learn from their oppressed and impoverished neighbors.[3]

More exactly, those coming from the earlier democratic oppositions of East European politics are now seeking to learn from the European past if they are economic liberals, and the European present if they are social democrats. And indeed, deeply tired of all future oriented experimentation, what could they use among the perspectives of those who are critics of both this past and this present, of economic liberalism and welfare state? But if this were true they could teach us nothing else than to simply appreciate what we already have,[4] wish for what we have left behind, or, at most in some cases, desire what the Swedes have, exercises that for some of us remain rather unattractive.

But does the increasing allergy in the East concerning Western forms of radical criticism actually extend to the version of radical democracy whose major inspiration came from the rediscovery of civil society? Up till now at least this has not been the case. And if not, there is a good chance to continue the really productive dialogue began roughly in 1976 with Adam Michnik's visit to Paris, to help commemorate and, surprisingly also to "transcend" the Hungarian and Polish revolutions of 1956.[5] Working together, even talking together, pre-supposes however that we in the West understand deeply enough the Eastern desire to choose the "second best," namely *our* existing societal model. But it also involves that our friends in the East do not forget, or try to remember, that the second best in all its varieties is by definition a society in need of radical criticism.

It is my normatively motivated hypothesis that the theory of civil society not only helps to describe at least some of the transitions from Soviet-type systems, but provides a perspective from which an *immanent critique* of all these pro-cesses can be and should be undertaken.[6] The aim of such a critique is to point to the choices available in the creation and development of new, democratic, and liberal institutions. In particular I would like to counterpose the options of (1) radical self-limitation (or: "self-limiting revolution") as against (radical) revolu-tion, and (2) the democratization of civil society as against elite democracy (the latter in the contemporary setting having strong links to economic liberalism.)

1. It is perhaps hard to remember that the original ingenious constructs of the "new evolutionism" and "self-limiting revolution" involved normative principle as well as strategic considerations. There is no need to detail here the geopoliti-cal-military constraints and the negative learning experiences associated with 1956 and 1968, that led Michnik and Kuroń to postulate important strategic reasons why the societies of East Central Europe could be radically transformed only within determinate limits. Beyond these reasons, however, the democratic oppositions in the East had even better reasons to reject the *via revolutionaria* than did their contemporaries in the South.[7] It was implicitly recognized that all the great revolutions from the French to the Russian and the Chinese not only demobilized the social forces on which they originally depended, but also estab-lished dictatorial conditions that were meant to block the reemergence of such forces at their very root for as long as possible. The project of "self-limiting revolution" had, of course, the opposite goal: namely the construction from below and the long-term defense of a highly articulated, organized, autonomous, and mobilizable civil society. This project had to and did involve the renuncia-tion of the utopia of revolution, in the sense of the dream of a single, imposed model of the good society that breaks completely with the present, that is beyond conflict and division.

While the full range of meanings in the concept of self-limitation was never really articulated, with hindsight it is possible to reconstruct the core of the conception in a way that goes beyond the original formulations, hopefully in their spirit. To link the notion of emancipation to that of self-limitation meant not only the need to avoid the transformation of the movement of society into a new form of unified state power, but also that one will not attempt to impose the logic of democratic coordination on all spheres by suppressing bureaucracy, and economic rationality. Movements rooted in civil society have learned from the revolutionary tradition the Tocquevillean lesson that such fundamentalist projects lead to the breakdown of societal steering, productivity, and integration, all of which are then reconstituted by the new-old forces of order by dramatically authoritarian means. It is this outcome that leads to the collapse of the forms of self-organization that in many cases were the major carriers of the revolutionary process: revolutionary societies, associations, clubs, councils, movements. These forms of a nascent civil society in turn are powerless against a form of revolutionary state power with which they fully identify. Paradoxically then the self-limitation of the actors of a self-organizing society allows the continuation of their social role and influence beyond the moment of the foundation of a new form of power.

Since 1988, and most obviously after the electoral triumph of Solidarity in 1989 and the specific resolution of the crisis of government formation, the reasons for geopolitical self-limitation have more or less disappeared. The democratic opposition first in Poland and then in Hungary kept pushing against these limits, extending them, until suddenly under the impact of the perestroika of Soviet foreign policy they were hardly there at all, as the beneficiaries in East Germany and Czechoslovakia were to find out.[8] Until this point hardly anyone spoke of revolution; afterwards, especially in context of the transitions beginning late in 1989, the term is everywhere. To be sure the adjectives "peaceful," "gentle," or "velvet" are generally added except in Romania; the East European revolutions are said to be "without civil war," "negotiated," "legal," and even "constitutional." All the same the implication is that what is occurring in the five relevant countries, as well as some republics of the Soviet Union and Yugoslavia, accomplishes all that revolutions accomplish but without using the supposedly contingent means of violence, which unfortunately had to be used in Romania. But how can the revolutionary founding of something new, ungovernable in principle by old *or* new rules that no longer *or* not yet apply be anything but violent?[9]

The implication however that we are simply dealing with revolutions that smoothly fit into the history of revolutions is rather misleading. To determine whether or not a revolution has occurred or is occurring we would do well to focus on three dimensions, which could be stylized here as structural, phenomenological, and hermeneutical.[10] These dimensions imply three questions: (a) Are analysts justified in speaking of the transformation of the fundamental structures of a society? (b) Do the participants perceive and thematize their experience and action as revolutionary? (c) Can they make sense of these perceptions in terms of the revolutionary tradition? (or are they forced to continually react against this tradition in order to understand themselves?)

The answer to the first question in Poland, Hungary, Czechoslovakia and in its unique way East Germany is obviously yes. The essential institutional patterns of these regimes, which I define by the primacy of prerogative power linked to paternalistic shortage economies, bureaucratic bargaining and clientelism, and cultural heteronomy, have already been shaken beyond any possibility of reconstruction. Equally important, the outlines of the new, consisting of parliamentary, multiparty rule of law states, interest group pluralism, market economies and emancipated publics, have been already laid down. Thus the Hungarian Alliance of Free Democrats, who have given us one of the clearest statements of such proposed changes, are entirely right to call their program that of "change of systems."[11] In this context we can no longer speak of reform, even radical reform, which would imply changing some or more institutional patterns in order to preserve the identity of others deemed more essential.[12] Moreover, the experience of Hungary and Poland especially tells us that programs of radical reform will not succeed in those Soviet-type societies where they are still being tried (especially the Soviet Union); at most, valuable time can be gained under the aegis of such programs. At the same time, for the postreformist countries the term "political" revolution seems also inadequate in view of the transformations of the social and economic system already in motion. And yet, can one speak of "social" revolution, indeed any kind of "revolution" where the systemic changes have begun fifteen (Poland) or twenty (Hungary) years ago, and where they may take as long as a decade still, without reducing the term revolution to a loose metaphor?

Criticizing Tocqueville's model of institutional continuity linked to state-building, and, even more, fighting against the Marxian topos of the *bourgeois* revolution, F. Furet reminds us that the point of view of the analytical observer will yield both continuity and change, and cannot in itself locate that break in temporality within a process of change that we could define as revolutionary. In order to do this we must interrogate the participants. And though I have not attempted to do this in any way systematically, it is my belief that there are three distinct patterns of self-understanding in today's Eastern Europe that we should note. In the countries where the process of transformation has been the longest, involving a reliance on civil society–based strategies, initially without the hope of total system change—in Poland, Hungary, and the Soviet Union—the term "revolution" is used rather rarely still. In Hungary to be sure, under the impact of the events of late 1989, intellectuals have been increasingly using the term, but with qualifications like "negotiated," "legal" and "constitutional" which represent serious hidden reservations concerning the usage itself. Both in Poland especially and occasionally even in Hungary there are moreover critics of the negotiated transitions who attack these precisely for not being revolutionary. In the Soviet Union the term "Gorbachev revolution" is a loose metaphor, or worse, stands for the standard, and, in the present context misleading Russian figure of "revolution from above" which will easily become the justification only of a "reform dictatorship" that is bound to fail. As we know Afanasyev's call for a "second February revolution" led only to some preelectoral mobilization.

In Czechoslovakia and East Germany, on the other hand, the term "revolution" is used constantly, and not only by intellectuals. To be sure, even here almost always there are qualifications like "peaceful" or "gentle" or "velvet," terms that do not involve a self-contradiction as do "negotiated," "legal" and "constitutional." Finally, in Romania no qualifications are used for obvious reasons, except for the recent use of the term "stolen," which, however, is not actually a qualification but a part of the standard repertoire of revolutionary discourse.

To be sure, the differences among national usages may seem irrelevant in light of a process that is transnational, indeed seemingly worldwide.[13] It is striking therefore that the global process of transition from Communist regimes as a whole is increasingly depicted as a "revolution."[14] It is as if the truth of the present phase were best definable in terms of the consciousness of the actors in East Germany, Czechoslovakia, and Romania, just as an earlier phase was depicted through the themes of the Polish opposition primarily. The implication is that the most rapid transformations of 1989 best represent, in a compact form, what has occurred elsewhere during an extended period, one with defeats as well as victories.

But the actors could themselves be wrong.[15] Such a possibility is indicated by the ability, during 1989, of the Polish and Hungarian oppositions to force through many more elements of systemic change than their Czech or German counterparts. Indeed the Romanian example seems to show that the closer a transition to the classical revolutionary model, the more difficult it seems to be to carry out systemic change in a Soviet-type society.[16] The Czech and German actors indeed seem conscious of this; the adjectives "peaceful" and "gentle" indicate "more" rather than "less." They also indicate more obviously reservations with respect to the revolutionary tradition.[17]

In Eastern Europe, one might of course claim, that there are two revolutionary traditions, one of struggles for national independence and another of social revolution in the path of the French, and Russian revolutions.[18] The former is considered almost universally positive, the latter only within the terms of Leftist discourse. As the example of 1956, however, shows it is not always easy to disentangle the two dimensions: in this case the struggle against Soviet occupation was combined with elements of an internal civil war; attempts to restore the parliamentary system of 1945–48 were combined, as in many of the great social revolutions, with direct democratic projects of especially industrial ownership and control. There was, moreover, every chance that the beneficiaries of the short-lived Stalinist old regime would be radically removed from all relevant positions of power and influence.

For many reasons, however, the "revolutions" of 1989 cannot be compared to the mixed model of 1956. They are not, first and foremost, for obvious reasons, against foreign occupiers; there were in comparison to 1956 very few anti-Soviet manifestations and demands in the popular movements. But more importantly, they do not fit into the tradition of social revolution, and the actors are conscious of this. Analyzing the transformation of the GDR before the drive toward unification, the constitutional lawyer Ulrich Preuss finds that two fundamental and related components of social revolutions are absent: the radical rupture involved in the displacement of one sovereign power by another, and the elimination of an enemy through mechanisms which in their extreme form imply civil war.[19] While the democratic movement has had a well-developed notion of its enemy to which it owed its unity, remarkably enough this enemy, the former state-party was exposed neither to radical expropriation nor organizational elimination. Its conversion from *enemy* to *opponent* has been in all respects facilitated. Indeed only in Romania did the issue of a legal ban on the Communist party ever come up. And while the properties of these parties are exposed to potential (but not absolute) redistribution, this occurs everywhere according to preexisting legal titles that benefit the state (Hungary) or other organizations (GDR). As a token of constitutional continuity, moreover, criminal cases against members of the old regime are initiated under the preexisting legal structures. Most importantly, perhaps, the public law structures of the existing regimes, especially parliaments, are allowed to play a crucial role in the elaboration of new constitutional forms, to be sure in part subordinated to new instances, mainly roundtable negotiations.

All these examples supplied by Preuss demonstrate that we have by no means left behind the epoch of "self-limiting revolutions," rooted in civil society as an end in itself rather than as a claimant of sovereign power. This civil society uses its own means, especially public discussion and existing legal institutions against the former possessors of sovereign power, instead of the utilization of the necessarily violent and extralegal instruments of a new state sovereignty that would endanger societal autonomy itself.[20] This analysis can be sustained with reference to procedures and discussions in the other countries. I am thinking of the debate concerning the expropriation of the PUWP in Poland, and the argument, hypocritical in the case of members of this party and principled in the case of a conservative revolutionary like A. Hall, that the expropriations of 1945 should not now be repeated under different colors. In Hungary too, G. M. Tamás comes close to articulating a consensus when he warns against social revolutionary expropriation, even if his views provide for a more than a commonly accepted latitude for converting earlier political-economic power positions to market-oriented economic advantages.[21] In Hungary there is today an almost universal rejection of the so-called B-lists of evil repute, that would once again involve a wholesale removal of office holders for political reasons. It is well accepted that one must oppose the results of earlier counterselection by the principle of merit, and not a new political process of selection.

Generally speaking, then, if one is to speak of any revolution in the East perhaps it should be a "conservative" one, in the spirit of Hannah Arendt's analysis of the American revolution where organized society (the state legislatures) came to represent the *pouvoir constituant*, rather than atomized individuals in a juridical state of nature, as in the views of Sieyes anticipating French reality. And yet the idea of "conservative revolution" does not seem to fully grasp what is stake. Arendt herself never succeeded to link up what was in effect a notion of conservative revolution derived from America with a figure derived from the tradition of radical revolutions, namely direct democracy.[22] Thus she could not solve her greatest problem even in principle, namely how to preserve in the *pouvoir constitué* something of that of the *constituant*; how to save something of the spirit of revolutionary public freedom in settled constitutions. She could not among other things do so because she sought a revolutionary answer to this question.

The issue is all the more serious where the constituent power is composed not of legitimate provincial legislatures but illegitimate communist parliaments and entirely self-appointed roundtables. Not only the democratic structure conducive to public freedom but also the legitimacy of future constitutions is thus at stake. In Hungary the second problem was fortunately and successfully addressed by the petition campaign and referendum on the structure of the presidency, one that revised an arrangement that to the outside looked suspiciously like a bargain of some old and some new elites.[23] The coming elections, given that the tasks of the next parliament themselves will be foundational and constituent, will hopefully further contribute both to societal mobilization and political legitimacy. But the preservation of the spirit of the democratic movement would require more: the establishment on the level of the constitutional structure and political culture an active role for initiatives (petitions, citizen initiatives, self-organized referenda) from civil society concerning constitutional revision itself. Such provisions could range from a strong conception of constitutional rights that by definition leave room for learning through civil disobedience,[24] as well as a multichanneled process of legislative and constitutional initiation, confirmation and revision that would recognize and institutionalize the right of an organized society to participate in the determination of its own fundamental rules. While the politics of radical self-limitation everywhere in East Europe has avoided outcomes in which the organization and development of civil society would be jeopardized, only the production of constitutions incorporating elements of radical democracy can provide contexts in which civil society could remain a viable component of the developing political process. If this were possible, the self-limiting revolution would be distinguishable from the radical revolutionary model also in the survival of its spirit beyond the institutionalization of a new sovereignty. Today such an outcome would have to mean the self-limitation of political as well as of civil actors, in other words the avoidance of the temptation to use the elements of civil society, so important in the dissolution of the Polish and to a lesser extent the Hungarian (and hopefully also the Soviet) old regimes, as merely stepping stones for a new elite democracy.

2. Analysts from A. Stepan to J. Kis are right to insist that a civil society–based strategy with its dualistic assumptions about change should not be absolutized, and that the transition to democracy presupposes the activity of a political society with its competitive, strategically oriented, party political organizations.[25] The pathologies of a purely civil society–oriented strategy as we know from recent Polish history are the overunification of society and a form of political polarization without ways of resolving it. In the context of democratic transition the consequences of this strategy inhibit the emergence of a genuinely competitive party pluralism. While the unification of society contributes to the legitimacy of governments trying to negotiate a difficult transition, this same unity is incompatible with the differentiation of democratic institutions.

It should be noted, however, that the turn to political society too has its pathology, namely elite democracy in its classical Schumpeterian or modified pluralist descriptions. In Eastern Europe those who first initiate this turn, the most sophisticated and calculating elements of Communist leaderships, indeed seek to recreate political society because of its very pathologies: the demobilization of a civil society which is increasingly active against them and in which they could never be included. For all their recent talk about civil society they prefer the atmosphere of political society where their bargaining skills pay off, and where they can hope to convert themselves and their organizations into competitive parties, at best *Koalitionsfähig* and at worst capable of preserving a niche for themselves in an oppositional role.[26] The instruments of this strategy are the legalization of parties, the arrangement of roundtable negotiations, and competitive elections not under the pressure of an organized civil society, but preemptively to forestall such a self-organization.

Several analysts of Latin American transitions ask the semirhetorical question why ruling elites agree to elections that are likely to abolish their rule? The answer most often given is that these elites expect to channel politics "away from the ebullience of civil society" and perhaps to even win the elections by dividing the opposition and by being rewarded by the electorate.[27] When elections are only gradually decontrolled as in Brazil, the hope is to slow down the rate of change and to gain, nevertheless, procedural legitimacy.[28] To be sure, the hopes of victory and legitimacy are generally frustrated, but not those of demobilization, and, where pertinent, gradualism. The move to electoral parties with their less intense, more inclusive, more abstract form of political identification as well as lower degree of direct participation tends to devalue and replace movements and associations with their more particular, but also more intense and participatory forms of organization. Depending on the electoral rules to be sure, the tendency of modern elections is to indeed reduce the number of political parties capable of effectively participating in elections. In turn, and especially in periods of uneasy transition, the potentially successful parties will do much to restrain the movements of civil society that might jeopardize either the outcome or even the possibility of elections. Thus, it can be said not only for the processes leading to unrestricted electoral contests that end dictatorships, but also for the elections themselves that they are implicit negotiations between regimes and oppositional parties providing space and time to "redefine their respective roles." And while the weak legitimacy and the plebescitary possibilities of partially restricted elections can indeed lead to societal mobilization, and learning processes outside the official framework, the liberal democratic legitimacy of open contestation provides much less of a chance for such an outcome. While it is possible that where civil society is underdeveloped and passive, or is in a process of contraction, elections might draw otherwise uninvolved strata into organized politics, in context of a highly mobilized or even gradually self-mobilizing civil society the reverse may very well occur, with parties turning out to be "not only, or not so much, agents of mobilization as instruments of social and political control."[29]

Hungarian developments of the last few years support the application of this analysis to Eastern Europe. While much slower than in Poland here too civil society was beginning to organize itself. Around the hard core of the alternative public sphere of the democratic opposition that existed since the late 1970s as well as other centers of "para-opposition," movements, initiatives, associations of intellectuals, youths, ecologists, and dissident unionists have dramatically expanded their operation through 1987, and especially after the fall of Kádár in May of 1988.[30] The regime's controlled public sphere was seriously affected in its style and substance. And though relatively small, through their increasing dominance of public discussion the initiatives of civil society were in effect powerful. The government's response has been in many cases an indication of this. I am thinking not only of the victory of the ecologists on the issue of the Bös-Nagymaros dam, but also of the astonishing series of conflicts over the law of association and assembly, and strike law, where the government tried to push through coopting and repressive forms of these legal provisions, and was forced to repeatedly back down and accept versions preferred by the relevant organizations of civil society.[31] Undoubtedly the ruling party's internal weakness and splits played a role. But what strengthened the hand of the reformers was probably a dual projection involving previsions of economic collapse and of a growing, self-mobilizing civil society, in short a Polish scenario but without Moscow's threatening-protective cover.

As we know from the events connected to the conference at Lakitelek, reformist party leaders like Mr. Pozsgay feared above all the part of the opposition following the civil society–oriented path of the Polish opposition. To counter them he and those around him were willing to promote the politicization of another and more constructive opposition, hopefully splitting in advance the possible democratic agent of an "us" versus "them" scenario. The same logic was involved in the offer of early 1989 of bilateral negotiations with various groups of the opposition. Even roundtable negotiations, if they could be suitably organized, and if there was a possibility of striking an appropriate bargain with a part of the opposition, were preferred as it turned out to the losing strategy of parliamentary reform in the face of pressure in the public sphere.[32] It was moves such as these that made the shift of the terrain to political society inevitable; the most a civil society oriented democratic opposition could do was to try to reorient this shift to a form of negotiation (Oppositional Roundtable, National Roundtable) where a relative unity of oppositional groups in face of the ruling party could be maintained. It was this unity that the agreements of the National Roundtable successfully shattered, leaving the democratic opposition no other route than to rediscover its links to civil society in the petition campaign. But these links are difficult to maintain with the development of party and electoral politics, all the more because the political movements rooted in civil society have entered into an extremely unproductive conflict.

I would hope not to be misunderstood in this context. It is my view that for a whole series of reasons the democratic oppositions cannot avoid the challenge to enter and help construct a political society (Hungary, Poland) or even take the initiative in this construction (Soviet Union, Czechoslovakia). They cannot or should not avoid doing so not only because of the value of parliamentary and multiparty democracy that they rightly hold but also because (a) a transition to democracy cannot be carried out in any other way, (b) political polarization leads only to a stalemate and loss of power by both sides, (c) the economic reforms and policies for which the regime needs partners must be addressed as soon as possible, and (d) insistence on a nonpolitical movement identity as in the case of the Neues Forum means marginalization between a determined communist effort to convert old powers into new ones and the emergence of new parties willing and able to play by the party political rules of the game (e.g., the East German SPD as well as the partners of the West German CDU).

And yet an all too ready acceptance of the role of a manipulative elite party that justifies itself only by de facto Western practices (e.g., vague catchall programs against clear articulation of options and intentions, conversion of ideology into a sales effort, destruction of the political public sphere through party discipline, etc.) leads to success only at a great price: the weakening of public political motivation and legitimacy. The most extreme case of this has been the resentment and hostility felt by the activists of East German civic movements, as the political field was invaded and colonized by the Western parties, an outcome only partially caused by the mistakes of these movements themselves.

It is not easy not to notice that next to communist and ex-communist parties, their former block parties, and the revivals of traditional (nostalgic) parliamentary parties it is in reality a fourth type of party, born of self-liberating civil societies that is the most characteristic of contemporary East European politics. I am thinking above all of Solidarity's *Civic Committee*, of *Civic Forum* and

Public against Violence, of the *Alliance of Free Democrats*, the *Hungarian Democratic Forum* and the *Alliance of Young Democrats*, as well as of the already mentioned *Neues Forum* and *Demokratie Jetzt*. Even the names are revealing in themselves: They mostly refer to civil society and the public sphere, and none of them are called parties. Of these organizations all except the last two have executed a timely turn to political society, if in different ways and to different extents. Evidently the Civic Forum and the Citizens' Committee still maintain within political society something of the looseness, openness and interest in collective identity that characterizes great movements of civil society. Beyond this, especially if compared to more typical electoral parties in Western Europe, something of their origin generally still attaches to all of the organizations mentioned; their activities are characterized by relatively high level of openness, internal democracy and solidarity, interest in grass roots organizing, as well as the maintenance of ongoing relations with social movements (workers, students, ecologists) with whom formal organizational links are becoming more tenuous. While the exigencies of electoral competition imposed by communist and noncommunist rivals militates against the preservation of such a structure and identity, the requirements of building stable democracies whose initial policies will require much sacrifice speaks for their maintenance. Indeed even in a competitive setting, parties that can somehow maintain their double identity of strategic actors and organizations that expand and defend civil society can even have a comparative advantage, as the unbelievable success of the petition/referendum campaign in Hungary and the subsequent takeoff of the Free Democrats demonstrates. Such a double rather than merely an elite role for at least some political parties is the best hope on the level of organizational life for the emergence of actors capable of both sensitizing civil society of the needs of strategic action, and at the same time helping to counteract the tendencies of elite democracy to make social solidarity, public discussion, and civic initiatives irrelevant from the point of view of the political system.

To be sure, the needs of economic transformation seem to speak against the stabilization of postelitist democratic parties. After the failure of all attempts at reform dictatorship,[33] projects of thoroughgoing economic liberalization seem to have an elective affinity above all with elite democracy. It is often believed, that societies with active and mobilized civil societies cannot restrain their economic demands in a way compatible with the requirements of austerity that are unavoidable in the transition from Soviet-type economies.[34] Logically then one should seek the demobilization of society where it is mobilized, and the restriction of its activity to the narrowest institutional channel possible where it is not. To be sure the Polish case so far speaks against this simple assumption, that does not take into account the tremendous reserves of legitimacy accumulated by the Solidarity movement in the last ten years. All the same, an organized, active, and influential civil society cannot in the long run accept, beyond in effect the necessary negative phase of dismantling the existing paternalistic-bureaucratic forms, an economic scenario that would among other things have the effect of disintegrating social solidarity, commercializing the public sphere, and bureaucratizing or eliminating much of associational life. Thus the goals of elite democracy and economic liberalism do converge, and their common opponent turns out to be organized civil society. If liberalism is to be the long-term economic model, then an elite theoretical transformation of the political terrain, and thus the demobilization and normalization of civil society indeed seem unavoidable. But if the preservation of civil society, indeed its democratization are themselves valued, is there an alternative economic strategy that could be developed, if we want to fully dismantle and replace a Soviet-type economy?

Let us first examine the argument for economic liberalization. I find it entirely convincing that one cannot dismantle a Soviet-type shortage economy based most fundamentally on soft budgetary constraints by moving directly to a new system of social protection, of employment and living standards. The bargaining power, the paternalistic subsidies and investment policy, the price-setting power of the existing monopolies must be abolished as rapidly as possible, and any attempt to introduce a West European type of welfare state and interventionism at this stage can only reinforce and shield the existing forms of paternalism based on informal regulation and clientelistic networks. Moreover, any full employment policy in the present context can only contribute to the unjustifiable survival of obsolete and unproductive industries that supply the material basis as it were for the conservation of the existing structure. Can this insight however justify the conclusion of J. Kornai that even if we desired Europe's present we must go through a long period resembling above all Europe's past, namely early, unregulated free market capitalism?[35] Let us leave to the side for the moment the meaning of this recipe for a society far more atomized and disorganized, for a lifeworld far more vulnerable and deprived of resources than the society of the early nineteenth century, namely the all important question of the likely cultural, and analogously ecological, consequences of the self-regulating market for a society emerging from the destructive past of a Soviet-type regime. What Kornai and many others propose, to a society deeply tired of all experimentation, is a most counterintuitive and dogmatic experiment, namely the establishment of a market society in the context of the dramatic expansion of democratic participation, even if this were channeled into the space of competitive party politics. It is not difficult to foresee new disasters issuing from this constellation, for example destructive cycles of populism and authoritarianism. No wonder then that Kornai himself counterbalances his truly revolutionary suggestion, by a very conservative one leaving the state-owned sector mostly intact (though starved of funds!), and conceding that for the next one or two decades as for the last two Hungary will basically remain a two-sectoral dual economy.[36]

That the population's preference lies elsewhere, in the direction of a West European welfare state, is well known.[37] But with the highly debatable exception of Germany, we know that even after the dismantling of the existing system of paternalistic supports and controls there will be no possibility, this time for economic rather than political reasons, to follow any such a road. But is this option in all respects desirable? What seems to be currently missing in the whole East European context is a critical discussion not only of the consequences of unregulated liberal markets but also of welfare-state interventionism, mainly because the criticisms are left only to determined opponents of each option. There has been little learning so far from a Western discussion, coming from the left, of the reasons for the crisis of the welfare state and of the possibilities of its reflexive (i.e. self-limiting) continuation involving a restructuring of employment, decentralization of the administration of benefits, and a postregulatory form of regulation ("reflexive law") beyond interventionism and deregulation. All these options involve a relocation of the focus of societal self-regulation from the administrative state not only to the market economy, but even more to a civil society that should be distinguished from both.[38] To the answer that a welfare state must be created before it can be reflexively continued, an answer based on a dogmatic acceptance of Europe's present, my answer is similar as to economic liberals who fetishize Europe's past. The effort would involve experimentation with devices we already know from many dependent capitalist countries (e.g., Latin America) involving the redistribution of what has not been and in the given context will not be produced. In my view such a road may represent only another point of entry into a destructive cycle of populism and authoritarianism.

It may be absurd to claim that the most abstract, most programmatic, least tried option is the most feasible. But I am not actually proposing an option, but only the "methodological" presuppositions of one. All I am arguing is (a) that only an organized civil society as in Poland can provide the legitimating framework for the sacrifices involved in dismantling state socialist economies in the context of democratization; (b) that the long-term establishment of a market society will be however unacceptable to the very same organized society; (c) that in any case neither economic liberalism (neoconservatism) nor social democratic orthodoxy offer today viable alternatives of socioeconomic reconstruction; (d) that if there are to be such alternatives these would have to worked out on the basis of contemporary challenges faced also in the West, rather than through mechanical imitation of the West's past or present; and (e) that the framework for common discussion is beginning to be constructed among those who have sought to develop postwelfare statist–left strategies in the West, counterposing models based on societal autonomy to both state interventionism and unregulated markets.

It may sound highly paradoxical to come to the East and recommend a civil society–based strategy as a Western one. But stranger things than this have been said in the last amazing year. In my view it may be time to return to the East the gift that we have received from the East: the idea of an autonomous and self-democratizing civil society.

Notes

1. See A. Gorz, *Farewell to the Proletariat* [1980] (Boston: South End Press, 1982).

2. See the debate of György Bence and Janos Kis with András Hegedüs in *Magyar Füzetek* (Paris), 1978, No. 1.

3. The situation in Germany where the activists who made the "peaceful revolution" in the East are increasingly marginalized, and where the Western parties have more or less taken over the political terrain, is only the most extreme version of the new situation. To be sure, organizations like Solidarity and the Civic Forum stand in the way of such an outcome that was facilitated by the fear of politics prevalent in groups like Neues Forum and Demokratie Jetzt.

4. Which seems to be the way Timothy Garton Ash in one of his essays in the *New York Review of Books* answers his own question, concerning what we in the West could learn from the East. I am not convinced that he is convinced that this is the right answer (*NYRB*, February 1990, p. 22).

5. And who knows, it may be that from now on we will be developing critical political and social theories in far greater proximity to one another. After all, we will be living, amazingly enough, in societies that will be structurally of the same general type.

6. By immanent critique I, of cours', mean using the transitions' own normative standards to criticize them, a method only possible on the basis of deep intellectual and political sympathy. And to avoid misunderstanding, let me state from the outset that I consider the present transitional regimes of all the East European countries as well as all the short-term probable outcomes to represent fundamental emancipation with respect to the regimes that came before. To take the most extreme case, even the establishment of a normalized Soviet-type regime with important elements of liberalization as in the Romania of the immediate present represents the cause of freedom with respect to the delirious dynastic communism of the Ceausescu clan. I can say this all the more, since I do not believe that any kind of Soviet-type regime will actually be stabilized in the region: hence the extreme dynamism of the Romanian situation.

7. On the latter, see G. O'Donnell and P. Schmitter, *Transitions from Authoritarian Rule* (Baltimore: Johns Hopkins University Press, 1986), vol. 4, p. 14, and especially R. Barros, "The Left and Democracy: Recent Debates in Latin America," *Telos* (New York), no. 68 (Summer 1986).

8. Undoubtedly it was the part of the party leaderships in Poland and Hungary that decided to engage in serious negotiations that was first to notice, or to be told, that they (or their conservative opponents) cannot count on Soviet pressure, not to speak of intervention, to help contain the expanding crisis.

9. This is indeed the gist of a question of former First Secretary Grosz, one that still has a vague threat attached to it. See interview in *Magyar Nemzet*, March 3, 1990.

10. I derive the first two from Furet's great essays in which they are confronted in the context of interpretations of the French Revolution. See: *Interpreting the French Revolution* (Cambridge: Cambridge University Press, 1981). Furet shows that neither, in itself, can legitimately describe the specific revolutionary phenomenon. For all revolutions subsequent to the French, one has to also ask questions concerning their relation to this original, whose tradition cannot be simply bypassed by interpreters. This insight I owe to Hannah Arendt's *On Revolution* (New York: Viking Press, 1963), even if she hoped to escape it by postulating another history of revolution, outside its tradition.

11. All the same they do not call it a "revolutionary" program despite the views of some of their members, like Gaspar Miklos Tamas. See SzDSz, *A rendszerváltás programja* (Budapest, 1989), and Tamas's speech to a public meeting of the Free Democrats in *Szabad Demokratak* (Budapest), 1989, no. 4–5, pp. 38–39. To be sure, he speaks of a

"bloodless" and "legal" revolution, and denies the term reform to any process whose agent is below. This expansion of one concept (revolution) and restriction of the other (reform) disguises his own link to the tradition of the new evolutionism. Elsewhere he breaks with this tradition by trying to define the current process in Hungary as a struggle for "political freedom" as against a "social" revolution. See Tamás, "Tajkép a csata elött," in Elet és Irodalom, August 4, 1989. He is not clear, however, whether or not we should use the term "political revolution." Actually, as I will show, neither "political" nor "social" revolution adequately describes what is occurring even in Czechoslovakia and East Germany.

12. See A. Arato, "Introduction" to Arato and Fehér, eds., Gorbachev: The Debate (Oxford: Polity Press, 1989).

13. Though I doubt that anyone will ever describe the victory of UNO and Violetta Chamorro in Nicaragua as a "revolution."

14. See, for example, A. Michnik's "Notes on the Revolution," New York Times Magazine, March 11, 1990. Michnik does not seem to use the term for Poland.

15. Many of us can still remember many members (but not all!) of the New Left of the late 1960s and early 1970s constantly speaking of revolution in the advanced capitalist countries.

16. The Romanian transition fully satisfies the criterion of Heller and Fehér of what constitutes a revolution: change in the structure of sovereignty. Moreover it only satisfies this criterion and not (for example) the Arendtian one of the foundation or constitution of a new political order. With respect to the other countries, even the least revolutionary one of Poland (where there are indeed important continuities in the structure of sovereignty located in the presidency and the military) this same standard of change is entirely insufficient to describe what is in effect a transition from one system to another.

17. As Arendt realized there is only one modern revolutionary tradition, that of the French revolution that in her view was not a successful revolution. The one successful revolution, the American, has to her chagrin no tradition. The ever recurring council democratic experiments in this context represented for her only breaks in the continuum of the time of modernity, each erupting without reference or even consciousness of the previous ones.

18. Indeed, Hannah Arendt herself could be criticized for not seeing the difference between the American and French Revolutions also in this important respect.

19. "The Influence of Carl Schmitt on the Legal Discourse of the Federal Republic of Germany" (January 1990) (unpublished manuscript). Preuss derives these criteria from Carl Schmitt's notions of politics, sovereignty and emergency. In my opinion he rightly considers Schmitt's theory to be based on the experience of modern social revolutions, to be sure translating the social (class) question into the national question.

20. Again Romania represents the only exception.

21. Tamás, "Tajkèp a csata elött."

22. Her illusory link between the two is the figure of Jefferson, whose proposal for a "ward system" and desire of a new revolution in each generation make him, in these respects at least, a French revolutionary. It should not have been surprising that the constituted bodies that were to produce delegates to the constitutional convention and who had to ratify the results (which implied a veritable coup d'état vis-à-vis the Continental Congress, or better still a "conservative Revolution") were truly afraid of such ideas.

23. To be sure a referendum in itself would be an act of atomized society especially if manipulated by holders of state power; coupled with a petition campaign and public discussion, the actual referendum campaign of the Free Democrats and the Young Democrats gave voice to a civil society in the process of being demobilized by the emerging party system. An organized civil society to be sure should have channels of influence

open to it that would make plebescitary solutions superfluous and dangerous. There was however no other choice in the Hungarian context of last fall.

24. See for example Dworkin, *Taking Rights Seriously* (Cambridge: Harvard University Press, 1978), chapter 8.

25. A. Stepan, *Rethinking Military Politics: Brazil and the Southern Cone* (Princeton: Princeton University Press, 1988).

26. Initially, to be sure, the motivation involves that of a search for partners to enact unpopular economic measures, but soon the relevant elites and leaders may no longer insist on even remaining junior partners. The minimum they want and succeed in getting is time for institutional self-conversion. There is nothing wrong with that, except the potential price of social demobilization and normalization.

27. G. O'Donnell and P. Schmitter, *Transitions from Authoritarian Rule*, vol. 4, pp. 57–58.

28. B. Lamounier in Stepan, *Democratizing Brazil*, p. 55. This analogy best applies to the process taking place in the Soviet Union.

29. O'Donnell and Schmitter, *Transitions From Authoritarian Rule*, p. 58.

30. See especially M. Haraszti, "Salami Tactics in Reverse," as well as an interview in *Uncaptive Minds* (January 1989); and F. Miszlivetz, "Toward First Person Singular," *Across Frontiers* (Winter-Spring 1989).

31. Bruszt, "On the Road to a Constitutional State," May 1989 (unpublished manuscript).

32. The East German and Czechoslovak events of 1989 seem to demonstrate the foresight of the Hungarian reformist leaders. But of course their own actions were to greatly contribute to the relevant outcomes in these two countries.

33. See L. Lengyel, "Reformdiktatura vagy bürokratikus autoritarianizmus," *Valóság* (Budapest), 1989, no. 5.

34. J. Elster, "When Communism Dissolves," *London Review of Books* (January 1990) vol. 12, no. 2.

35. *Indulatos röpirat a gazdasàgi àtmenet ügyében* (Budapest, 1989), p. 24ff.

36. *Indulatos röpirat*, p. 49.

37. See the joint survey undertaken by *Libération*; *Frankfurter Rundschau*; *Gazeta Wyborcza*; *Moscow News*; and *Beszélö* on February 19, 1990.

38. One important exception in this context is B. Pokol's *Posztkeynesianus szociologia* (Budapest, 1986), which involves an important reception of the relevant works of Luhmann, Habermas, Teubner, Willke, and Offe. I am not sure, however, whether Pokol has applied his interesting reconstruction to the problem of economic policy alternatives facing the former state socialist societies. For my own views of the problems connected to the reflexive continuation of the welfare state see chapter 9 of J. Cohen, A. Arato, *Civil Society and Political Theory* (Cambridge: MIT Press, 1992).

14

Social Movements and Civil Society in the Soviet Union

The analysis of social movements and independent social initiatives is an indispensable part of our study of Soviet society in the midst of its great transformation. It is in this context above all that the best contemporary social science, free of the common bias for the leaderships and central elites characteristic of both older scholarship and present-day journalism, can make its most important contribution. The chapters of the present volume, taken as a whole, represent the first comprehensive assessment of the world of social movements and collective action in the Soviet Union, and the information they provide in itself expands our knowledge and potentially our comprehension of the dramatic processes now taking place.

To be sure, focusing on areas which are inevitably partial the authors for the most part cannot evaluate the general significance of the movements studied, and even less the whole world of movements and initiatives, for the transformation of Soviet society. What any reader, outside the taxonomic student of movements and collective action perhaps, will justly question after reading the essays is the difference movements and citizen initiatives make in terms of the alternative possible outcomes of what has been put in motion under the catchwords of *glasnost'* and *perestroika.*

It is my belief, confirmed by the preceding chapters, that the exact place of independent collective action in Soviet society is best understood in terms that link the concept of social movements to that of *civil society*. In turn, the complex reality of social movements in the Soviet Union can be best studied by a theory capable of distinguishing between movements dedicated to the establishment of new social systems and movements seeking to construct identities and defend interests within alternative social systems, the present one and the one that is

Reprinted with permission from *Perestroika from Below: Social Movements in the Soviet Union* (Boulder, CO: Westview, 1991). Internal references are to other essays in the collection.

313

emerging or is at least anticipated by many actors. Finally, the role of the movements of civil society in the transformation of Soviet society can be most
fruitfully evaluated at the present state of our knowledge in comparison with
other Soviet-type societies whose "transitions" from the established state socialist regimes are on the whole more advanced.

Civil Society in the Soviet Union

I understand civil society as a sphere of social interaction between economy and
state, composed above all of associations and publics. Modern civil society is
created through forms of self-constitution and self-mobilization and is institutionalized through laws, especially subjective rights that stabilize social differentiation. However, it would be misleading to identify civil society with all of
social life outside the administrative state and economic processes in the narrow
sense. First, it is necessary and meaningful to distinguish civil society from a
political society of parties, political organizations, and political publics, in particular parliaments. The latter, to be sure, generally arise from civil society and
share with it both forms of organization and communication. But directly involved with state power, which they seek to control and in part obtain, the
structures of political society cannot afford to subordinate strategic criteria to the
patterns of normative integration and open-ended communication characteristic
of civil society. Even the public sphere of political society, rooted in parliaments,
involves important formal and temporal constraints in processes of communication. The political role of civil society in turn is not directly related to the control
or conquest of power but to the generation of influence, through the life of
democratic associations and unconstrained discussion in the cultural public
sphere. Such a political role is inevitably diffuse and inefficient. Thus the mediating role of political society between civil society and state is indispensable, but
so is the rootedness of political society in civil society.[1]

Second, the differentiation of civil society from the economy on the one hand
and political society/state on the other seems to suggest that the category somehow should include and refer to all phenomena of society, outside of the state,
the economy, and political society in the narrow sense. But this is the case only
to the extent that we focus on relations of association, of self-organization, and
organized communication. Civil society, in fact, represents only a dimension of the
sociological world of norms, roles, practices, competences, and forms of dependence, or a very particular angle of looking at this world from the point of view of
conscious association building and associational life.[2]

The importance of the concept of civil society for the study of the Soviet
Union has not gone unnoticed. Whereas the earlier "totalitarian" paradigms have
generally identified the Soviet regime with the obliteration of civil society and
the total atomization of society, a whole series of scholars now contests this
judgment. Most strikingly, Moshe Lewin, who first introduced the notion of civil

society to the study of social change in the Soviet Union, considers a slowly developing and expanding civil society in the midst of modernization to be responsible for the Gorbachev phenomenon.[3] I think it is necessary to navigate between these extremes (and the conceptual framework introduced here allows us to do so). Lewin is quite right in maintaining against the metaphor of "totalitarianism" that the Soviet party-state has been able to penetrate and regulate all spheres of life at best only during the highly mobilizing and openly terroristic phase of the regime, namely high Stalinism. Subsequent developments, in particular decreasing levels of forced mobilization, economic development and related processes of stratification, growing consumption, and finally the deliberate if partial depoliticization of the private sphere—in a word, growing societal complexity—have made the central control of all societal relations and processes less and less plausible. Indeed, the surviving dimensions of a totalitarian project contributed not to greater central control but to the undermining of both the mechanisms of control as well as the integration of the society to be controlled.

Nevertheless, the train of argument implies the self-regeneration of civil society only if we identify all of society outside the state with civil society, and the building of a modern civil society with modernization *tout court*, in other words, with growing social complexity. The definition suggested here implies that we should not do so: The existence of social processes and relations independently of the state is only a necessary, but not a sufficient condition of a modern civil society. Thus the assumption of the earlier totalitarianism thesis should be in part supported; high Stalinism indeed destroyed an independent civil society, and the modernization pattern of the post-Stalinist period has reconstituted only some of its preconditions. The phenomena of growing societal complexity to which Lewin first pointed to, and even the increasing destatization of the microsphere of face-to-face interaction he seems to stress more recently are necessary, but not sufficient for the constitution of even an embryonic civil society.[4] Since independent movements and initiatives and especially legal institutionalization did not emerge in the pre-Gorbachev period, we cannot for that time period speak of a "slowly recovering" civil society.

More is at stake than simply a definition. If processes of modernization in the Soviet Union in the seventies and early eighties had in fact produced most of the elements of a modern civil society, then we might assume that the changes required today can be restricted to the political and economic realm. Such an assumption would, in my view lead to a dramatic underestimation of what is to be done; indeed to a neglect of many of the key social preconditions (legal, organizational, cultural etc.) of a successful economic and political transformation. It is time furthermore to recognize that the whole Soviet pattern of modernization is a failed and even pathological one, endangering for some time to come the building of a genuinely modern political culture. As we have seen especially but not exclusively in Romania, a democratic civil society even today is not the only possible outcome of the passing of the Communist regime. If modernization were identical to the emergence of civil society the outlook for democratization would be better than the present situation in several countries around the globe seems to indicate. And though such prospects are not at all hopeless in Eastern Europe and the Soviet Union, we should avoid a use of concepts that would lead to a false optimism.

Second, the confusion of the processes of modernization, industrialization, social stratification, urbanization, education, and increasingly modern technologies of communication with the institutional network of a civil society implies that "the Gorbachev phenomenon" can be attributed to the pressure and activity of an organized society from below which has long preexisted the actual reforms.[5] Such a view would be empirically spurious as we see from all of the studies in this volume which point to a very low level of independent social organization even in the early Gorbachev period. More seriously, the idea has deterministic consequences to the extent that political processes are reduced to functions of long-term, massive and presumably irreducible changes in the whole social structure, underestimating the instability and the risks of the processes which we currently experience, and the decisive importance of the role of social and political actors that face a variety of alternative courses of action even today. The argument substitutes abstract criteria of general sociology for categories of collective action, and tends therefore to deemphasize the role of independent initiatives and movements without which the older cycle of partial reform and retrenchment cannot be broken.[6]

The State and Social Movements

The current volume helps us to decisively break with any deterministic sociological analysis of the processes of change in the Soviet Union. The several authors bring to attention two types of collective actors, those of an independent civil society (in formation) and to a lesser extent the state. For reasons already discussed state actors cannot be left out of this volume on social movements: in the Soviet Union civil society is initially so underdeveloped (in contradistinction to Poland for example) that a series of measures from above was required to provide the "opportunity structure" for the beginning of self-organization. The reasons for launching such a risky project, the fears and expectation of the regime or some of its elites are not discussed by the authors of the more specialized studies. But it seems clear enough from the analyses of James Butterfield and Marcia Weigle, and Russell Bova in particular, that having decided on radical reform the Gorbachev group came to learn that such a policy cannot be carried out in the face of entrenched and conservative organizational interests without pressure from below, or to change the spatial metaphor, outside the organizational logic of the established institutions. The difficult project of perestroika as it was first conceived follows from this lesson: In order to have a reform radical enough to work, the regime needed independent initiatives and pressure, but in order to keep change within any possible meaning of reform (i.e., in a framework still consistent with the central principles of the system as key elites of the regime conceived them) these movements had to be kept within some definite limits. Somehow, genuine independence was supposed to be limited, planned, and controlled, almost a contradiction in terms. The dialectic of perestroika flows from this initial dilemma. As I have argued elsewhere, if movements and initiatives promoted from above are to be independent enough to really make a difference, they may be too independent to be controlled. If, however, they can be controlled, their ability to achieve their intended effects may be severely limited.[7]

The analyses of the book allow us to make this paradox more precise in terms of five possible scenarios:

1. The attempt to control and properly "dose" independence may succeed, but the groups in question fail to effect conservative resistance to change. This is the case of the creation of factory or enterprise councils by the enterprise law of June 1987, described by Bova.
2. Groups and initiatives do manage to seriously challenge and roll back conservative resistance, but the center loses control over them. This is the case of the ecological initiatives and movements presented by Ziegler and Marples; and indeed Butterfield and Weigler tend to see the complex world of independent group life taken as a whole largely in these terms. Assuming as I do that they are right, the question becomes whether the regime is capable of institutionalizing through the requisite laws and rights (rights of association, speech, press, assembly, and strike law) the functioning of such groups. Butterfield and Weigle show that so far this institutionalization has not occurred, and Bova's analysis of the strike law in my view at least supports them.
3. The state succeeds in stimulating and in the end effectively controlling a movement that retains an important role in promoting the government's policy. Bova believes that even if the miners' strike movement initially belonged to the type of independent action growing beyond all state control, the settling of the strikes and even more the strike law of October 1989 provides a framework within which strike committees will remain both effective against conservative resistance and under the control of Gorbachev's group.[8]
4. Given the fact that the state apparatus could not maintain its political unity in the face of the ongoing reformism, the success of either independent or semi-independent initiatives motivates other state actors, opposed to Gorbachev's group, to come into the game of promoting independent or semi-independent initiatives. Bova and Judith Sedaitis document such an attempted role of conservative groupings in the apparatus and the official unions to influence unofficial worker initiatives, the united or workers' fronts. These attempts have one great liability, the unpopularity of the

conservative apparatus and its ideology, and one great advantage, the largely negative effects of half-hearted or even paper economic reforms that destabilized old steering structures without producing viable new ones. But the dialectic of control and independence applies to conservative as well as reformist state actors; they may be preparing the ground for a future radical and egalitarian populism rather than for a successful conservative backlash.

5.   To Butterfield and Weigle, the various cultural and ecological movements of the most radical republics, both linked to nationalism, seem to belong to the category of movements promoted by state actors opposed to the center. It seems to me, however, that even if their judgment is relevant to early stages of development when republican administrative structures were (segmentally) differentiated parts of the imperial state, today we must analyze such contexts differently. I am not denying the splintered, multileveled, or multi-agency structure of the state, equally relevant to say Belorussia and Latvia. Rather, I am suggesting the possibility that some republican administrative organizations had been captured by their national movements, that as a result they are now detached from the central state organization without however fully attaining the status of independent states. In such contexts then, independent movements through genuine parliaments or extraparliamentary pressure now control or decisively influence fragments of former administrative structures instead of being controlled by them, in the face of an imploding imperial center which, however, retains for the moment the monopoly of the important means of violence. This scenario implies a process of politization of social and cultural movements, all the more effective because of the resources in the hands of republican governments, and because nationalist ideology helps to overcome potential fissures and conflicts among different movements and initiatives. To be sure there is a continued possibility of conflict among different nationalist movements, and in Russia itself between democratic and nationalist movements as well.

From the point of view of the state obviously only the third alternative is fully acceptable. Butterfield and Weigle present five strategies by which movements and initiatives are to be somehow channeled into a path desired by the regime: open cooperation, cooptation, preemption, mere toleration, and open antagonism. As their examples show, however, the first and fourth merely strengthens movements without any guarantee of control, the second and third tend to make them useless from the point of view of the regime's aims, and the fifth, open antagonism, cannot limit their expansion and proliferation without a turn to outright if selective repression. While this last course has not been entirely absent, any great reliance on it would endanger even the reform project of the centrists around Gorbachev. Yet as we have seen in the case of Lithuania the possibility cannot be altogether excluded and even one of the most powerful independent collective actors in the Soviet Union, the Sajudis government, had to be ready to practice the art of self-limitation. On the other side, given the proliferation of the number and type of independent challenges to the regime, the avenue of selective repression will now accomplish little. There seems to be no way today for the present crumbling one-party regime to keep independent social initiatives within desired limits.

Social Movements Old and New

The apparent inability of the regime to control "the Frankenstein" (Bova) it helped to create, namely the independent movements and collective actors, does not automatically mean that these themselves are able to resolve the crisis of Soviet society by relying on their own institutions and resources. Too heterogeneous and potentially in conflict, they would need either some fundamental framework of consensus or institutions of interest aggregation and the formation of compromise to produce anything resembling a common project. Such institutions today (or at the time of the writing of most of the essays) are still under the (to be sure tottering) control of the established regime. Too weak to simply overthrow the central authorities, but more importantly, not being revolutionary movements, unwilling to risk total rupture and the resulting chaos, the movements and initiatives would need new institutions of political mediations through which the influence of a more and more active public could be turned into power. Today we are witnessing the emergence of not only countless new parties and political movements, but even more important, on the republican level, independent and freely elected parliamentary assemblies. Given the present political structure of the whole and especially the turn toward presidentialism in the center, these new structures only raise the problem of missing mediations and polarization to the most explosive level, that between the republics and the central power. This most spectacular contradiction to some extent disguises the fact that there is no guarantee, that once fully developed, parties and independent assemblies will maintain their now close relation to independent social mobilization. Here the paradox is that the movements of civil society cannot achieve their aim without a turn to political society; the bargaining processes of a political society especially on the eve of radical economic reform may be incompatible with a full and open institutionalization of a democratic civil society.[9]

What kind of theory of movements can help us to analyze the difficult situation in which movements in the Soviet Union inevitably find themselves? For two reasons I doubt that the most recent American paradigms which some of the authors seem to rely on even if only implicitly will be of much help beyond pointing to the rather obvious resources movements must acquire in order to be successful. First, these paradigms generally do not recognize the important dimension of movements building new identities, transforming political cultures, and engaging in symbolic forms of self-expression. In the Soviet Union, given the crisis of existing form of social integration this dimension, however, is far more important than under conditions of cultural stability where a general consensus concerning symbols and values can be presupposed and hence methodologically bracketed. In this context, the earlier American symbolic interactionist paradigm used by Carol Nechemias shows more promise, though unfortunately she is forced to apply it in part counterfactually to what is at best only a protomovement, namely feminism. A method of this type stressing both identity and organization seems however indispensable to the study of all movements, and especially nationalist movements.[10]

Second, contemporary resource mobilization and political conflict paradigms on the whole do not distinguish between movements seeking to establish a new social formation and movements acting within the existing one, or for that matter between movement scenarios characteristic for different formations.[11] But in the Soviet Union, as a result of a form of "mixed temporality" due to a failed form of modernization the analysis inevitably encounters movement types that belong to different fundamental "temporal modalities" or historical contexts of action. Clearly some movements are dedicated to the establishment of a society entirely different than today's Soviet Union. The possibilities here range between the imagined Russia of the past and the Western societies of the present. Others seek to represent their interests and preserve their identities within the framework of the established society that on the whole they seek to protect. Still others seek to raise problems and represent concerns characteristic of a society yet to be established, liberal democratic society. These projects in turn divide into ones parallel to the earlier history of the existing liberal democratic societies, while others are continuous with the great issues of the day that have emerged as the results of more successful paths of modernization. Sometimes, to make matters worse, several of these levels are to be found within a single movement. At issue is not only the different intentions of these movements, but the different logic of their action with respect to the issues of the day: economic reform, political democratization and the type of civil society that is emerging, modern or semitraditional, democratic or semi-authoritarian.

What can unify such conflictual field of action, and how can its relationship to politics be institutionalized?[12] The authors of the volume help us raise if not fully answer both of these questions, first and foremost by describing the heterogeneous field of collective action. Several movements are directly studied in the volume; others like the more explicitly political nationalist and democratic movements enter only in relation to other movements. But the reality that is reproduced for us is complex enough. The working-class movements and initiatives studied by Bova and Sedaitis involve first of all groups and organizations that are directly linked to political attempts to establish a new pluralist democratic society, to institutionalize a modern civil society. These groups are allied with various popular fronts, and in Russia democratic platforms and fledgling social democratic parties. There are other organizations, the official unions (VTsSPS) and the United Workers Fronts that have the explicit political aim of preserving the established society not only against their democratic competitors, but also against the "centrist" Gorbachev reformers. To make their conservative project more acceptable, both these organizations seek to protect still existing working-class benefits or supposed benefits that are characteristics of the established paternalistic system (full employment, relative wage equality, lax work discipline, subsidized prices). Finally, there is a variety of initiatives, which as Sedaitis shows, have turned away from politics, and seek to represent worker's interest in a setting implicitly assumed to be one of an unfolding market economy. Here different patterns have emerged, if I understand her correctly, corresponding to early European radical syndicalism, industrial unionism of the American type, as well as modern unionism of contemporary West European type.

There are obviously conflicts among all these tendencies. But to make a situation more complex, single organizations may unite several of them in perhaps uneasy constellations, much like Polish Solidarity of 1980–81 which was both a movement for the liberation of civil society and a social movement combining syndicalist, nationalist, and democratic dimensions.[13] With the exception of the nationalist dimension the miner's strike committees seem to involve just such combination, whose stability in the context of radical market-oriented reform might very well undergo a difficult test. Though I do not agree with Sedaitis that workers stand only to lose from radical economic reforms that are "anti-labor in essence" (p.3), without doubt the attempt to preserve working-class living standards will undoubtedly imply further conflicts between worker organizations and the economic reformers such as the one she describes in the case of the Leningrad Popular Front, and several reformist deputies with the miners.[14]

No other movements described here involve a similar complexity. To start with perhaps the least complex trend sociologically, the unions and associations of cooperatives in Darrell Slider's presentation constitute both a movement for the establishment of a pluralist society, i.e., civil society, and the first set of genuine pluralist pressure groups acting as if they were already located in such a society. Unlike in the case of the workers' groups, the relation of the cooperative movement to radical economic reform is unambiguously positive, and relationship to the established society equally negative. The same is true with respect to the established society in the case of ecological movement, though the relationship to market-oriented reform is more ambiguous. The attitude to the established society follows from the well-documented state of affairs that the "resource constrained" economic model of authoritarian socialism has been everywhere far more destructive of the environment than any other version of modern society.[15] It is for this reason, as Charles Ziegler rightly points out, that the Soviet Union has ecological movements without any explicit emergence of postmaterialist values, and in the midst of deprivation rather than economic success as against the West. Undoubtedly, a convergence with national resistance to a system perceived as colonialist has helped the formation of ecological movements in many of the republics, even though the disastrous forms of the exploitation of nature, are in reality equally characteristic of center and periphery, and are functions of the economic model and not of the imperial structure. Nevertheless, Ziegler also rightly stresses that ecological movements will enter into conflicts with market-oriented reform as well as schemes of privatization, and attracting foreign capital. This is so because uncontrolled markets, even if in themselves less destructive of the environment than Soviet-type economies, cannot correct and would more likely exacerbate the harm done by the latter. Accordingly, the complexity of the ecological movements in the Soviet Union lies in the fact, that they combine the project of transition from state socialism, which inevitably must involve the creation of market economies, with premodern nostalgia for a civilization before industrialization on the one side, and a very modern critical attitude to the destructive side-effects of modernization in all of its existing models.

The beginnings of women's groups and networks as presented by Nechemias and Mamonova, representing the least ambiguous trend internally, nevertheless bring additional complexity and conflict potential to the whole context. Implying opposition to a system that has pushed women almost to the biological limit of survival as indicated by many demographic criteria, feminism in the Soviet Union represents an entirely modern tendency, even if this is not consciously reflected on by the few participants. Like other initiatives of course, the first feminist initiatives respond critically to a pathological model of modernization, that has combined the entry of women in the work force with the survival of traditional forms of inequality in the family, in politics, and in the sociological order of status. As a result a disproportionate part of the burdens of the economy of shortage falls on the back of women. But since women are burdened both by the version of modernization, and by surviving traditional attitudes, there is no possibility of nostalgia for the past in the case of feminist groups who find themselves, as Nechemias shows, in outright opposition to all trends preferring earlier arrangements to Soviet modernity. Such trends promote the removal of women from the world of work, and the refurbishing of traditional gender inequality.

The situation is to be sure complicated by the fact that as Mamonova points out furthermore, there is also a potential conflict with an economic reform that, in alliance with neotraditionalist mentality, might very well seek to shift the burden of unavoidable unemployment to women. But here too the target of opposition is as much the neotraditionalist mentality as the economic reform itself. It may be the case of course that given their present place in the employment structure women can only be hurt by the first stages of a genuine economic reform. But unlike some of the ecologists who may have dreams of a preindustrial national utopia, and some workers who may still prefer the paternalism of the old state-socialist regime, women must place their hopes in a new and different future that cannot come without radical economic change toward markets. It is another question, not fully answered by the chapters above, how conscious this insight has become among the earliest feminist initiatives.

National, cultural, and religious movements would further complicate this overall picture. But even on the basis of movements represented in the volume, it is difficult to escape the impression that the world of collective action that has become uncontrollable from the point of view of the reformers whose actions contributed to its emergence can now only produce chaos as well as insurmountable difficulties for any rational policy, above all transition to a genuine market economy. This impression is wrong, as are the corresponding warnings of proponents of an unworkable "reform dictatorship," in light of both East European experience as well as evidence presented here. The fact that Solidarity in Poland was not only a social movement motivated by its own identity and interests, but also a movement for the liberation of civil society implied its support and assistance for the organization of other associations, groups, and interest-representations which were potential competitors on the terrain of a new society. Furthermore, its being a postrevolutionary workers' movement implied self-limitation with respect to the organization of differentiated spheres of life, especially the requirements of genuine economic self-regulation. This attitude has continued to this day, and represents the crucial support for the institution of a market economy by a legitimate, democratic government rather than a reform dictatorship.

As different as Soviet history may be, the papers of this volume indicate many similar trends. To be sure there is little chance here of one movement for a time carrying the aspirations of a whole society, though such is the case in some individual republics.[16] All the movements described however, with the exception of the ones sponsored by conservative officialdom, contain the dimension of groups within a self-forming civil society struggling for its legal institutionalization. It is for this reason that we encounter not only instances of conflict, but repeatedly phenomena of mutual support as in the case of the cooperatives and miners, cooperatives and greens, miners and democratic initiatives, ecologists and nationalists, etc. Leaving the two main instances of conservative workers' groupings and aggressive and intolerant trends among nationalists to the side, there is a general convergence around a program that would establish a general legal framework for the normal functioning of collective action and initiative, namely an institutionalization of civil society. All the great conflicts of the day, including electoral competition, indicate the overwhelming strength of this tendency. And while the articles do not explore the relationship of the movements studied to revolutionary ideology or other forms of fundamentalism, there is little evidence that any important trends today outside of the conservatives and some nationalists seek to impose a totalized vision on the whole of society. The syndicalist movements described by Sedaitis do not seem to defend anarchist dreams or council communist utopias, but seem to fight for specific forms of solidarity, autonomy, and protection in the face of a coming market economy. As such they should in the end contribute to necessary correctives to market rationality rather than to a general resistance to it. Ultimately the same should be true of ecological and feminist initiatives as well, which need a market economy for the decomposition of the socioeconomic model that they reject, even if they will not be able to accept in the end the establishment of a nineteenth-century liberal, uncontrolled version of this economy.

Social Movements and Political Society

The argument that movements can converge in the formation of a pluralistic civil society, and that they will not inhibit the transition to a market economy does not yet provide an adequate picture of the role of independent initiatives from below in the transformation of the Soviet Union. Indeed this model takes us only, in terms of the Polish parallel used above, to a form of hopeless polarization between independent movements and state authority. In the Soviet Union two factors interfered with such outcome: the continuation of genuine reformism from above which unlike in Poland did not allow the emergence of a consistent we–they, friend-enemy scenario and a turn to political society roughly at the same time, though in a more constrained form than in Poland. Given the differences among movements, and the republican fragmentation even of the same type of movement, in particular nationalist mobilization, the elementary consensus around the desirability of a pluralist civil society remains brittle and unstable. In such a context it is difficult to develop *society versus the state* scenarios, except in individual republics whose unified movements, however, add to the disunity of the whole. Only a mobilization against a unified enemy unambiguously in the way of both the institutionalization of civil society and the autonomy of nationalities could stabilize an overarching consensus. The reformist party-state has not so far served as such a target, unlike the Polish regime but very much like the Hungarian one of the eighties.[17] Worse, on selective issues regime reformers have been closer to various strands in the opposition than some of these are to each other. As the Hungarian example from 1987 on shows, once regime reformers become conscious of this state of affairs, they can substitute a strategy of dividing different segments of independent opinion and initiative for the increasingly unrealistic strategy of controlling these. In particular, the fault line between democratic and nationalist groups has a potential for such manipulation, as the example of Russia and in different ways those of Azerbaijan and Armenia already show.

Similar fissures have opened up between nationalist and democratic movements in Hungary in 1987 and after; while in Poland such conflict, now ready to burst open, had to wait until the full demise of the original enemy. The Hungarian example thus shows that the divisions of civil society can be exacerbated by strategies of regime reformers. But this country's example also shows that it is possible to create a strategic alliance of the main antiregime groups on the level of *political* society, in the form of roundtables that assume the strictly limited task of working out electoral rules of the game. Thus, as against the chaotic states of affairs in Bulgaria and Romania with their entirely unresolved nationality conflicts, a successful turn to political society, to a system of institutionalized strategic party competition represents a potential way of dealing with the divisions of civil society in nonexplosive ways. Elections do not mend the ruptures in civil society; they may even exacerbate them for a time (given especially the importation of Western type negative campaigning). Nevertheless, parliamentary mechanisms, with their built-in socializing potential for the participants provide the possibility (not the certainty) of dealing with these by negotiation and compromise.[18]

From the point of view of independent initiatives, the turn to political society has other advantages as well, which were probably more clearly understood by the actors themselves or by movement intellectuals than the potential of dealing with fissures in civil society. First, electoral mobilizations in part compensate for the failure of developing one inclusive movement of society, for the inability of achieving a high level of ongoing mobilization against the state authority. People who are afraid of participating in independent movements whose legality is never quite clear especially in the Soviet Union, and those who may wish to "free ride" may be mobilized for the first time in obviously legal but also "low-cost" electoral activity. After such experience with its dimensions of politicization and solidarity formation their readiness to act may be in general enhanced. Second, participation in parliaments and the conditions of alliance formation and bargaining allows the pursuit of radical agendas with the help of inner regime forces that would only fear and would oppose any extra-institutional struggle even for strictly limited goals that they could support if carefully isolated from other issues. Thus, the strategy further disunites the forces of the established regime, which is important given the oppositional movements' own potential disunity. Third, presupposing substantial representation of forces of an independent society, parliaments provide potential contexts for negotiating a transition, for avoiding a destructive breakdown of the existing authority with all the unpredictable and dangerous consequences of such collapse in the case of an imperial superpower. Fourth, and perhaps most importantly, even partially controlled elections provide an opportunity for many movements to demonstrate large-scale support for their candidates, and the absence of such support for candidates tied up with the regime even when they claim independent nationalist or working-class credentials. Finally, given the inevitably self-chosen character of independent initiatives, in the absence of one overarching movement of society independent movements, however legitimate to their own constituency, suffer from a deficit of general democratic legitimacy. Having been directly or indirectly tested in elections can partially remedy this deficit, at least for a time.

From the point of view of independent movements these advantages outweigh the main disadvantages, namely that partially controlled elections can both relegitimate the regime and preserve conservative majorities. This destructive combination is worth the risk, because the surviving controls over electoral slates and procedures themselves provide focal points for democratic mobilizations. As we have seen in Hungary, Poland as well as Brazil the logic of such a development is toward more and more open elections, and the differences between the March 1989 and spring 1990 elections in the Soviet Union support this claim.

Our authors amply document the turn to political society in the case of most independent social initiatives and groups. Such a turn can involve three forms: becoming a political party (or generating one); various forms of electoral support for candidates; and establishing ongoing mechanisms of pressure and influence on deputies, and parliamentary groupings.

The problem of becoming a political party or forming political parties has surfaced in almost all the movements studied in the volume. The debates in *Zelenyi Svit* remind us of similar conflicts in Western and now East European Green movements involving the fundamental question whether or not the need for a radical shift in civilization implied by ecological criticism can be represented by electoral and parliamentary parties inevitably involved in strategic alliance and compromise. Of course, defenders of a party-type organization do point out that without engaging in the institutionalized game of politics no components of green programs can be presently actualized, with further devastating consequences to the environment. In the Soviet Union, as Marples implies, this point was countered with the similarly strategic argument that ecologically relevant concessions could be gained by avoiding an unnecessary challenge of the ruling party. A similar position seemed to have been articulated in the cooperative movement, in response to attempts to generate a political party. In the unofficial, radical working-class movements which apparently produced some small political parties, the major groups seem to justify their turn from explicit political involvement by the need to protect worker interests in face of all existing political trends. The end result of these debates about politics and antipolitics seems to have been the development of Green parties that, in the West European style hope to maintain ongoing relations with independent movements, while neither the cooperatives or worker groups produced viable political parties. To be sure, relevant to the later case, intellectual groupings do hope to establish or reestablish social democratic and socialist parties which may in the end successfully recruit the members of radical worker organizations, especially the adherents of strike committees and independent unions. But in any case it should be noted that so far parties of this type have been effective only as members of inclusive popular fronts or parliamentary platforms. The same is true of the most important ecological grouping, the Ukrainian Green party, which is an important member of Rukh.

Up until now electoral activity on behalf of independent candidates, or inclusive fronts and platforms, and, equally important, against official candidates, has been the most important political role of independent movements. As Sedaitis shows, whatever advantages conservative workers' organizations possess in grassroots organizing, in the electoral game worker groups supporting pluralist groups and candidates have been far more successful.[19] Though it is difficult to assess the actual degree of success, in relation to other organizations and groups the involvement of pluralist worker organizations in electoral demonstrations, campaigning, and voter information has been massive and candidates so supported did almost uniformly well, especially in large cities and mining regions. The same can be said for the electoral involvement of the cooperatives, which were also in position to offer financial support to friendly candidates. It should be noted that electoral participation has already been a major context for alliance building among groups with otherwise diverging social interests and visions: the cooperative movements' alliance with the Vorkuta miners is one example of this.

Perhaps the least developed form of political participation so far is lobbying activity on behalf of an organized constituency. So far only Green groups and the cooperatives have played such a role, the former perhaps as an extension of the bargaining processes of the state socialist regime providing a very minor role for ecological experts. The pressure politics of the cooperative movement, on the other hand, are entirely in line with similar forms in pluralist polities, as Slider maintains. Nevertheless, the rather unusual success in this regard of the cooperative movement seems due not only to its own vigorous activity and leadership, but also to an elective affinity between the interests of these groups and the project of radical market-oriented reform for which the cooperatives represent a spearhead. Attacks against them in turn are only slightly disguised attempts to undermine and discredit economic reform itself, and its most important advocates. Under these conditions it is not surprising that radical deputies appear as a kind of "cooperative lobby," which is more an appearance than a reality. Nevertheless the kind of lobbying activity pioneered by the cooperative movement is likely to be imitated by others, if the organizational and legal preconditions, today largely absent, will be guaranteed for pressure groups more generally.

From the point of view of social movements, the turn to political society is not without its ambiguities and negative features. Some danger signs have been noted by our authors. Sedaitis points to the fact that the electoral activity of social groups increasingly tends to be controlled and even monopolized by professional organizers, I would assume promoting passivity and demobilization at the grass-roots level. We have seen furthermore how political officials originally sympathetic to independent movements, helped to enact a repressive strike law, not in order to shore up an unloved regime, but to protect economic reform from a potential excess of economic demands. There is still a strong temptation to accomplish this goal not in negotiation and partnership with independent movements, but by legislative, and lately even presidential fiat.

The road of elite democracy and parliamentary or presidential authoritarianism are the functional equivalents of a reform dictatorship, more dangerous because of the element of democratic legitimacy they possess. Ecological, feminist as well as workers' movements, given the condition of the Soviet economy today, have good reason to fear this road. It can be blocked only if the move-ments and friendly intellectuals demonstrate that the interests they defend can be made compatible with the project of economic reform. It would be a disaster if in the end the interest of economic reform were tied up with parliamentary actors, while independent movements or what remained of them were identified with a defensive attitude toward some features of the old regime. But the new move-ments of the Soviet Union will be able to propose relevant alternatives to such a defensive posture only from a position of strength. This would in turn presup-pose that they do not exhaust their activity on the level of political society, that they continue the project of building horizontal networks and organizations, and that they continue to fight not only for a parliamentary democracy and an econ-omy consistent with their interests, but above all for a legally and constitution-ally anchored, open, democratic, and pluralistic civil society. The time for such a project, as we now know from East European experience, is by no means over with the end of a Communist regime. Some especially difficult tasks for indepen-dent movements in the Soviet Union are still ahead.

Notes

1. Both of these points were, of course, understood and stressed by Hegel (*The Philos-ophy of Right*) whose original framework is, however, modified here, in particular by distinguishing civil society and the modern economy. For some of the reasons see A. Arato, "Civil Society, History and Socialism: Reply to John Keane," in *Praxis Interna-tional*, vol. 9, nos. 1/2 (April and July 1989).

2. See Andrew Arato and Jean Cohen, *Civil Society and Political Theory* (Cambridge: MIT Press, 1992) for a full development of this conception of civil society. I am inclined to think that one needs a notion of economic society as well, as a form of mediation parallel to political society.

3. See *Political Undercurrents of Soviet Economic Debates* (Princeton: Princeton Uni-versity Press, 1974) and *The Gorbachev Phenomenon* (Berkeley: The University of Cali-fornia Press, 1988).

4. Compare *Political Undercurrents*, pp. 249ff., and *The Gorbachev Phenomenon*, pp. 63ff., 80–81, and 146–147. The two arguments are similar in their sociological determin-ism, stressing inevitability (*Political Undercurrents*, p. 262) and irreversibility (*Gorbachev Phenomenon*, p. 147). To the extent the first linked its case for a "subterra-nean political reality" to a model of action, its stress was on the (badly analyzed) reality of pressure groups and internal elite bargaining. The more recent position defines civil society (evidently in its Soviet version) as "the aggregate of networks or institutions that either exist or act independently of the state or are official organizations" capable of becoming independent and exerting pressure. While this rather loose linking of entities on very different levels of social reality and action does point to components of independent initiatives in the Gorbachev era, it is extremely misleading to point to it as the growing civil society responsible for the beginning of reform in the first place.

5. This is the mistake I sense in S. Frederick Starr's fine essay "Soviet Union: A Civil Society," in *Foreign Policy*, no. 70 (Spring 1988). Starr to be sure does not confuse civil society with differentiated society as such. Nevertheless, he seems to imply that a nonin-stitutionalized but independent society has not only emerged in the Brezhnev era, but also

that by the early eighties all social initiative has passed "from the state to society," and above all to an independent public opinion. For Starr the state only has to follow these initiatives for a genuine civil society to come to being. While the implicit idea, that legal codification of the results of independent social initiatives institutionalizes civil society is the right one, between modernization and institutionalization Starr misses the key dimension of the self-constitution of civil society in independent movements and initiatives that is by no means the inevitable result of any modernization.

6. Of the analysts stressing the link between modernization and civil society, the views of Gail W. Lapidus seem the most balanced and convincing. See: "State and Society: Toward the Emergence of Civil Society in the Soviet Union" in Bialer, ed., *Inside Gorbachev's Russia* (London: Westview Press, 1989). Like Lewin and Starr, Lapidus stresses the various dimensions of growing societal complexity. In her analysis however, in the context of an intact Soviet political and economic regime, these phenomena lead above all to the decomposition of social integration, to societal pathologies like corruption, alcoholism, low motivation and productivity, alienation and anomie, and the decline of important demographic indicators. For her the social pressure of the pre-Gorbachev era manifests itself in the form of "exit" rather than "voice." Rightly, this analysis, points to the Gorbachev leadership itself, motivated by both the external and internal consequences of social crisis, as the actor behind the beginning of the reform process, an actor seeking to adopt itself to a new and more complex society. The constitution of at least a version of civil society, one only partially independent, is a key part of this reform strategy of adaptation, one that resulted in a dramatic proliferation of independent groups. Lapidus does not yet fully recognize that such a strategy may lead to a dilemma of either too little or too much societal independence. See the contributions of Castoriadis and Arato to Fehér and Arato eds. *Gorbachev: The Debate* (Oxford: Polity Press, 1989).

7. Again see my essay as well as the one by Castoriadis in *Gorbachev: The Debate.*

8. I remain skeptical about the stability of this option, which can easily decompose into one of the other four. The recent attempts by some miner organizations to establish a new, independent trade union confirm my doubts.

9. See A. Arato, "Revolution, Civil Society and Democracy" in *Working Papers on Transitions from State Socialism*, no. 90.5; *Cornell Project on Comparative Institutional Analysis* (Ithaca, NY, 1990) (Chapter 13, this volume).

10. For a general comparison of American (interest-based) and European (identity-oriented) methods of social movements research, as well as a proposed synthesis, see Jean Cohen, "Strategy and Identity: Contemporary Theoretical Paradigms and the New Social Movements," in *Social Research*, vol. 52, no. 4. For an application of a primarily identity-oriented method to Soviet-type societies see the fine paper by Andrzej Tymowski, "East European Social Movements in the Transition to Democracy," paper delivered at the 1990 annual meeting of the American Political Science Association in San Francisco.

11. See J. Cohen, op. cit., for the development of this criticism. To be sure as Cohen shows C. Tilly distinguishes among alternative scenarios, up to the beginning of the modern capitalist epoch. But he rejects the possibility of the emergence of new scenarios since the early nineteenth-century form generated above all by the classical working-class movement.

12. In my view, a framework such as Alain Touraine's helps us to discover such a complex reality far more than the works of his American competitors. See: *The Voice and Eye: An Analysis of Social Movements* (Cambridge: Cambridge University Press, 1981); *Solidarity: Poland 1980–1981* (Cambridge: Cambridge University Press, 1983). It is another issue that his conception does not easily allow for either the bringing together of movement types based on different temporalities or a transition to the dimension of

politics. In the resource mobilization perspective these issues cannot even appear as problems.

13. See Touraine, *Solidarity*.

14. I do not agree with Sedaitis among other things because the guaranteed welfare structure she refers to was already in shambles before the Gorbachev period, as was the ability of the regime to guarantee slowly increasing living standards. More importantly, I believe the structure of interests of industrial workers links them not only to job guarantees and the subsidization of a very low standard of living, but also to the availability of goods of consumption especially apartments, to an economy of time that allows the individual some free time with his or her friends and family, to the availability of information and forms of public expression, to rights of autonomous organization, etc. I am willing to recognize, however, that all individuals under state socialism have a mixed interest structure both linking them to and dividing them from the existing regime. More importantly in the present period, most individuals have both something to gain and something to lose in a market-oriented transformation. It is probably minorities, however, and not whole classes, that will exclusively lose *or* gain from the transformation. Industrial workers will for example gain the rights to organize, assemble, and strike freely. How can such a policy be described as "anti-labor in essence"?

15. Janos Kornai, *Contradictions and Dilemmas* (Cambridge: MIT Press, 1986).

16. The unusual presuppositions for this in Poland, involving collective memories (even if partially mythological) of a single, unified society struggling for its sovereignty and a rather homogeneous national community are well documented by A. Tymowski in "East European Social Movements."

17. To be sure the combination of Gorbachev's assumption of presidential decree powers, and the subsequent rejection of the Shatalin Plan of radical economic transition that is supported by several of the republics for the first time may come to imply such a we–they, friend–enemy scenario. Given the control of many of the republics by the "we" component, this scenario tends to imply one of three alternatives: (1) civil war; (2) crackdown and repression from the center or (3) the collapse of the center and at least temporary chaos. In such a context the discussion of the so-called "Treaty of the Union" would be little more than a joke.

18. The Hungarian case so far speaks both for and against such possibility. The campaign in the national election was polarizing; the one in local elections was not. The rejection of a great coalition by the victorious MDF (Hungarian Democratic Forum) exacerbated the divisions of the first campaign: The early agreement between this party and the opposing SzDSz (Alliance of Free Democrats) on constitutional revisions and the presidency produced, however, for a time the possible beginning of a national consensus. From this whole experience three desiderata seem to emerge: (1) pluralistic electoral competition; (2) a governmental coalition transcending the main symbolic faultlines of conflict providing for the minimum national consensus necessary for the difficult policies of transition; and (3) the creation of a new constitution providing for the beginning of a genuinely common identity.

19. Unlike Sedaitis I would not pay much attention to the decline of the number of "workers" in the legislature, their earlier presence being formal and ritualistic also in her own presentation. Furthermore, I wonder whether the unwillingness of electors (also industrial workers given the numbers involved?) to vote for worker candidates expresses an "antiworker bias" or only a hostility to conservative organizations that present their candidates in these terms.

Index

Andrew Arato is a professor of sociology and a member of the Program on East Central Europe of the Graduate Faculty, New School for Social Research, in New York City. He is co-author of the recently published book *Civil Society and Political Theory* (Cambridge, Mass.: MIT Press, 1992) and is completing a book on *Civil Society and Revolution in the Transition in Eastern Europe* (M.E. Sharpe, forthcoming). He received his Ph.D. from the University of Chicago in 1975.